Transitional Justice and Reconciliation

Scholars and practitioners alike agree that somehow the past needs to be addressed in order to enable individuals and collectives to rebuild trust and relationships. However, they also continue to struggle with critical questions. When is the right moment to address the legacies of the past after violent conflict? How can societies address the past without deepening the pain that arises from memories related to the violence and crimes committed in war? How can cultures of remembrance be established that would include and acknowledges the victims of all sides involved in violent conflict? How can various actors deal constructively with different interpretations of facts and history?

Two decades after the wars, societies in Bosnia, Serbia and Croatia – albeit to different degrees – are still facing the legacies of the wars of the 1990s on a daily basis. Reconciliation between and within these societies remains a formidable challenge, given that all three countries are still facing unresolved disputes either at a cross-border level or amongst parallel societies that persist at a local community level.

This book engages scholars and practitioners from the regions of former Yugoslavia, as well as international experts, to reflect on the achievements and obstacles that characterise efforts to deal with the past. Drawing variously on empirical studies, theoretical discussions and practical experience, their contributions offer invaluable insights into the complex relationship between transitional justice and conflict transformation.

Martina Fischer is Programme Director at the Berghof Foundation, Berlin.

Olivera Simić is a Senior Lecturer in Law at Griffith University, Brisbane.

Transitional Justice
Series Editor: Kieran McEvoy
Queen's University Belfast

The study of justice in transition has emerged as one of the most diverse and intellectually exciting developments in the social sciences. From its origins in human rights activism and comparative political science, the field is increasingly characterised by its geographic and disciplinary breadth. This series aims to publish the most innovative scholarship from a range of disciplines working on transitional justice related topics, including law, sociology, criminology, psychology, anthropology, political science, development studies and international relations.

Titles in this series:

Transitional Justice, Judicial Accountability and the Rule of Law
Hakeem O. Yusuf (2010)

The Era of Transitional Justice
The Aftermath of the Truth and Reconciliation Commission in South Africa and Beyond
Paul Gready (2010)

The Dynamics of Transitional Justice
International Models and Local Realities in East Timor
Lia Kent (2012)

Gender Politics in Transitional Justice
Catherine O'Rourke (2013)

Identity, Reconciliation and Transitional Justice
Overcoming Intractability in Divided Societies
Nevin T. Aiken (2013)

Corporate Accountability in the Context of Transitional Justice
Sabine Michalowski (2013)

Families of the Missing
A Test for Contemporary Approaches to Transitional Justice
Simon Robins (2013)

Transitional Justice Theories
Edited by Susanne Buckley Zistel, Teresa Koloma Beck, Christian Braun, Friederike Mieth (2014)

Truth, Denial and Transition
The Contested Past in Northern Ireland
Cheryl Lawther (2014)

Transitional Justice and the Arab Spring
Edited by Kirsten Fisher and Robert Stewart (2014)

The Art of Post-Dictatorship
Ethics and Aesthetics in Transitional Argentina
Vikki Bell (2014)

International Trials and Reconciliation
Assessing the Impact of the International Criminal Tribunal for the Former Yugoslavia
Janine Clark (2014)

The Concept of the Civilian
Legal Recognition, Adjudication and the Trials of International Criminal Justice
Claire Garbett (2014)

After Violence
Transitional Justice, Peace and Democracy
Elin Skaar, Camila Gianella and Trine Eide (2015)

Transitional Justice and Reconciliation
Lessons from the Balkans
Edited by Martina Fischer and Olivera Simić (2016)

Forthcoming titles in the series:

The Judiciary and the Politics of Transition
Police Brutality Cases in Chile, Northern Ireland and South Africa
Marny Requa

The Trouble with Truth
Dealing with the Past in Northern Ireland
Kieran McEvoy

Reconceptualizing Transitional Justice
The Latin American Experience
Elin Skaar, Jemima Garcia-Godos and Cath Collins

Violence, Law and the Impossibility of Transitional Justice
Catherine Turner

Transitional Justice and Reconciliation

Lessons from the Balkans

Edited by Martina Fischer
and Olivera Simić

Routledge
Taylor & Francis Group
LONDON AND NEW YORK

First published 2016 by Routledge

2 Park Square, Milton Park, Abingdon, Oxon OX14 4RN
711 Third Avenue, New York, NY 10017, USA

Routledge is an imprint of the Taylor & Francis Group, an informa business

First issued in paperback 2017

British Library Cataloguing in Publication Data
A catalogue record for this book is available from the British Library

Library of Congress Cataloging-in-Publication Data
A catalog record for this book has been requested.

ISBN: 978-1-138-85169-6 (hbk)
ISBN: 978-1-138-08438-4 (pbk)

Typeset in Baskerville
by Keystroke, Station Road, Codsall, Wolverhampton

Contents

Notes on contributors

Dean Ajduković, Ph.D., is Professor of Social Psychology at the Department of Psychology, University of Zagreb, Croatia. He has extensive experience in working with refugees, post-conflict social reconstruction of communities and community-based mental health interventions. He directed several major international research projects and authored over 150 papers in peer reviewed journals and books in Croatian, English, Macedonian, Russian and Albanian. He was a Fulbright Scholar at the UC Berkeley and a visiting professor at University of Denver. He served as a consultant on trauma and violence, psychosocial program development and evaluation, and combating gender based violence in a number of countries affected by upheaval. Dr. Ajduković is the past president of the European Society for Traumatic Stress Studies (ESTSS) and president of the Croatian Society for Traumatic Stress.

Tamara Banjeglav holds a PhD degree in Diversity Management and Governance from the University of Graz, Austria. Her doctoral dissertation deals with the relation between official (public) and personal (private) memories and narratives of the 1990s war in Croatia. Her research interests fall in the field of memory studies, transitional justice and dealing with the past in post-conflict societies. She is currently engaged as a researcher on the project "Framing the Nation and Collective Identity in Croatia: Political Rituals and the Cultural Memory of Twentieth Century Traumas" at the University of Rijeka, Croatia. *Publications: RE:VIZIJA PROŠLOSTI. Politike sjećanja u Bosni i Hercegovni, Hrvatskoj i Srbiji od 1990. Godine [RE:VISION OF THE PAST. Politics of Remembrance in Bosnia and Herzegovina, Croatia and Serbia since 1990]*, Sarajevo: Friedrich Ebert Stiftung & ACIPS, 2012); 'Dealing with the Past in Post-War Croatia: Perceptions, Problems and Perspectives', in O. Simić & Z. Volčič (eds.) *Transitional Justice and Civil Society in the Balkans,* New York, Heidelberg, Dordrecht, London: Springer, 2013; 'Conflicting Memories, Competing Narratives and Contested Histories in Croatia's Post-War Commemorative Practices', *Political Thought,* Vol. 49, No. 5, 2013.

William Bartlett is Senior Research Fellow in the Political Economy of South East Europe at the London School of Economics and Political Science.

He has a BA in Economics from the University of Cambridge, an MSc in Development Economics from the University of London and a PhD from the University of Liverpool. He has previously been Research Fellow at the European University Institute in Florence and Professor of Social Economics at the University of Bristol. His research interests lie in the field of economic and social development in South East Europe. He has published two monographs: *Croatia Between Europe and the Balkans*, Routledge, 2006 and *Europe's Troubled Region: Economic Development, Institutional Reform and Social Welfare in the Western Balkans*, Routledge, 2008, as well as numerous articles in refereed journals and book chapters.

Sanja Ćopić is a research associate at the Institute for Criminological and Sociological Research in Belgrade (Serbia) and a researcher and president of the Executive Board of the Victimology Society of Serbia. Dr Ćopić has participated in research and action-oriented projects on victims of crime, domestic violence, human trafficking, truth recovery and reconciliation. A main focus of her recent work has been the use of restorative justice in criminal matters and victims' positions in restorative justice programs. In the past years she was also engaged with research conducted by the Victimology Society of Serbia and other European research institutions within the FP7 project 'Developing alternative understandings of security and justice through restorative justice approaches in intercultural settings within democratic societies – ALTERNATIVE'.

Dinka Čorkalo Biruški, Professor of Social Psychology at the Department of Psychology, University of Zagreb, Croatia. She has been involved in numerous research and training projects dealing with psychosocial consequences of war and post-war recovery. Her research interests are in the area of inter-group relations, with emphasis on divided communities, development of minority/majority identity, minority rights and minority education, and post-war social reconstruction. Čorkalo Biruški was a visiting scholar at the Kroc Institute for International Peace Studies, University of Notre Dame, a Fulbright fellow at the University of Massachusetts at Amherst, and a fellow at the Solomon Asch Center for Study of Interethnic Conflict, University of Pennsylvania. She edited or co-edited three books and (co)authored over 50 scientific and professional papers and presented her work at numerous international conferences. Dr. Čorkalo Biruški is a head of the Doctoral Program in Psychology at the Department of Psychology, University of Zagreb.

Martina Fischer is a peace researcher and political scientist, and Program Director at the Berghof Foundation (BF) in Berlin, Germany. She has worked as a senior researcher, as deputy and acting director of the Foundation's research unit (the former Berghof Research Center for Constructive Conflict Management) 1998–2011. Dr Fischer has published extensively on peace building in post-war societies and on the role of civil society in conflict transformation. She is now responsible for the BF's South East Europe Program and is a co-editor of the *Berghof Handbook for Conflict Transformation*. Furthermore she is a member of the board of the German Protestant Kirchentag, the scientific council for the German Foundation for Peace Research, the advisory council for the Centre for International Peace Operations, and for various scientific journals (Die Friedens-Warte; Wissenschaft & Frieden; Zeitschrift für Friedens- und Konfliktforschung). She has published and (co)edited 12 books and more than 200 articles; recent titles are: (with Ljubinka Petrović-Ziemer) (eds.): *Dealing with the Past and Peacebuilding in the Western Balkans*, Berghof Report 18, Berlin: Berghof Foundation, 2013; (with Beatrix Austin and Hans J. Giessmann) (eds.): *Advancing Conflict Transformation. The Berghof Handbook II.* Opladen, Farmington Hills: Barbara Budrich Publishers, 2011; Martina Fischer (ed.): *Ten Years after Dayton. Peacebuilding and Civil Society in Bosnia-Herzegovina.* 2nd edn, Berlin, Münster, London: Lit-Verlag, 2007.

Klaus Hoffmann is a Prosecutor from Germany. As a junior lawyer, he worked with the Office of the Prosecution (OTP) of the ICTY in 2000/2001. Having served as a judge and prosecutor in Germany for a few years, he returned to the ICTY in 2005 and worked as an advisor for the Office of the Prosecution. He dealt with several major cases such as Milošević, Šešelj, and most importantly the case against Stanišić and Simatović (Serbian State Security). In 2010 he returned to Freiburg, Germany, where he works as a prosecutor, dealing with cases related to drug trafficking and organised crime, cybercrime and issues of international legal cooperation.

Briony Jones is a Senior Researcher for the Dealing with the Past Program at swisspeace, an associate research institute of the University of Basel. She is currently leading a Swiss National Science Foundation project on 'Resistance to Transitional Justice? Alternative Visions of Peace and Justice'. In addition, she coordinates a project on the archives of truth commissions, and is a co-Investigator with the University of Oxford for the ESRC-funded project 'Ways of Knowing after Atrocity: A Knowledge Exchange on Methods used to Formulate, Implement and Assess Transitional Justice Processes'. Her research interests include reconciliation, citizenship, the politics of transitional justice and qualitative research methods. She has field experience in Sri Lanka, Uganda and Bosnia-Herzegovina and Cote d' Ivoire.

Vesna Nikolić-Ristanović is a full professor at the Faculty for Special Education and Rehabilitation, University of Belgrade (Serbia), where she teaches criminology, victimology, juvenile delinquency and violence against children. She is director of the Victimology Society of Serbia and former president of the European Society of Criminology. Professor dr Nikolić-Ristanović has long term experience in activism and research, particularly in the field of action research related to violence against women, war victimization, women's crime, and truth and reconciliation. In the past years she was also engaged with research conducted by the Victimology Society of Serbia and other European research institutions within the FP7 project 'Developing alternative understandings of security and justice through restorative justice approaches in intercultural settings within democratic societies – ALTERNATIVE'.

Olivera Simić is a senior lecturer with the Griffith University Law School, Queensland, Australia. Originally from the former Yugoslavia, Olivera has lived and studied in Eastern and Western Europe, the USA and South America. Her research engages with transitional justice, international law, peacekeeping, gender and crime from an interdisciplinary perspective. Dr Simić has published in journals such as *International Peacekeeping, Law Text Culture, Women' Studies International Forum, Journal of International Women Studies*, as well as in books and book chapters. Olivera is co-editor of *Peace Psychology in the Balkans* (Springer, 2012), *Transitional Justice and Civil Society in the Balkans* (Springer, 2013) *and The Arts of Transitional Justice: Culture, Activism, and Memory after Atrocity* (Springer, 2013). Her book *Regulation of Sexual Conduct in UN Peacekeeping Operations* was published by Springer in June 2012.

Jelena Subotić is Associate Professor of Political Science at Georgia State University in Atlanta. She is the author of the book *Hijacked Justice: Dealing with the Past in the Balkans*, Ithaka, New York: Cornell University Press, 2009. She has published numerous journal articles on transitional justice, identity politics and European enlargement in the Western Balkans. She was formerly a human rights coordinator for the Open Society Institute and a contributor at Radio B-92 in Belgrade, Serbia. Jelena Subotić has published extensively on transitional justice in the region of former Yugoslavia.

Miodrag Živanović is Philosopher and Professor at the Faculty of Philosophy at the University of Banja Luka (Bosnia-Herzegovina). He has been Director and Editor in Chief of the Media Centre 'Prelom' Banja Luka since 1996 and Director and Editor in chief for various other political, cultural and philosophical magazines and publishing houses (Novi Prelom; Glas; Polemos; Mala knjiga; Egzoticos; Danteon; Putevi; Helios). He has published more than 200 scientific analyses in local and international periodical magazines and has compiled documents from local and international scientific meetings. Some have been translated in English, German, French, Slovenian and Macedonian. *Published Books: End of Marxism* (1989), *Metaphor and Philosophy* (1990), *The Eye of Glass* (1997), *Lectures in Blue* (1999), *Acta Politica Serbica* (2000), *Blue and Ultraviolet* (2000), *A Letter on Nostalgia* (2002), *Creators of Miracles* (2003), *Empedocles, Fragments of Mysticism* – translation, Term: *Neprebol* (2004), *Philosophic Triptych* – amended edition (2005), *Friedrich Schiller, Ode to Joy and Other Poems* – translation (2005), *Fishes Don't Cry* (2008), *Eine kleine Nachtmusik* (2009), *Enigma poetica* (2011).

Table of Cases

International Criminal Tribunal for the Former Yugoslavia (ICTY)

International Criminal Tribunal for Rwanda (ICTR)

European Court of Human Rights

International Court of Justice

County court of Zagreb

Introduction

Struggling with the legacy of war – Croatia, Serbia and Bosnia-Herzegovina, 1995–2015[1]

Martina Fischer

The 1990s brought about fundamental changes in politics and societies within Europe. With the end of the Cold War, most of the Eastern European countries entered a period of political and economic transformation, often marked by social conflicts, which in most cases were settled in a peaceful manner. However, Southeast Europe experienced great turbulence during this decade. While Macedonia and Slovenia managed to secede more or less peacefully from Yugoslavia, the other constituent republics embarked on a series of civil wars caused by various social, political and economic factors,[2] including a strong wish for political independence (Gromes, 2007; 2009; Bliesemann de Guevara, 2009). In the course of the dissolution of the former Yugoslavia, new nation states formed around ethnopolitical identities, which led to discriminatory policies and tensions in areas with multi-ethnic populations and traditions. The conflicts escalated into brutal violence between different "ethnic" constituencies and took on a regional dimension. In particular, Bosnia-Herzegovina (BiH), Croatia and Serbia were involved in a common conflict scenario, with warfare in both Croatia and BiH.[3]

When Croatia declared its independence in 1991, hostilities erupted between Croatian forces and the Yugoslav People's Army, culminating in a so-called "homeland war," which lasted until 1995. War broke out on the territory of BiH in April 1992. Following a referendum, a sovereign state named "Bosnia and Herzegovina" was proclaimed in January 1992, with Bosniaks forming the

1 My thanks for comments on previous drafts of this chapter go to Olivera Simić and Hillary Crowe. Some of the information given in the first sections is based on research conducted in the project "Dealing with the Past and Peacebuilding in the Western Balkans" at the Berghof Foundation, funded by the German Foundation for Peace Research, previously published in a more extended version (see Fischer & Petrović-Ziemer, 2013).

2 For an overview of the discussion, see Calic, 1995; Woodward, 1995; Allcock, 2000; Ramet, 2006; Melčić, 2007b.

3 Serbia was also involved in later violence in Kosovo, followed by NATO intervention. Between January 1991 and the end of 2001, at least 130,000 people lost their lives in the wars in the former Yugoslavia. The fates of 13,000 people have not yet been uncovered, according to the Initiative for RECOM; see www.zarekom.org (accessed 29 August 2014).

dominant constituency. A majority of the Bosniak population and the Croat community in BiH supported secession from Yugoslavia, whereas a majority of the Bosnian Serb population wished to remain within the Federal Republic of Yugoslavia (FRY).[4] Meanwhile, many Bosnian Serb politicians were pursuing a policy of partition, proclaiming a Serb Republic and aiming to unite all BiH territories under their control with Serbia and Serb-controlled areas in Croatia. Croats in BiH at first favoured an undivided Republic of BiH but later fought for the country's partition. As close relations existed between the Bosnian Croat community and Croatia and between Bosnian Serbs and the FRY, both these countries were involved in the Bosnian war; Croat combatants in BiH were supported by the armed forces of Croatia, while the Bosnian Serb forces relied on supplies of weapons and paramilitary support from the FRY. The Bosnian army mainly consisted of Bosniak conscripts, but was also supported by Mujaheddin and other fighters from Islamic countries (Grigorova Mincheva & Gurr, 2013). The total number of war related deaths from the wars in the region of former Yugoslavia is estimated around 130,000. BiH endured the most destructive forms of warfare, with around 100,000 war-related deaths and half of the population displaced.[5] Croatia's decision to undertake a military operation in the Krajina in 1995, a region that had been occupied by the Yugoslav forces, resulted in a mass exodus of the Serb population from that region. Around 250,000 former Croatian Serbs were expelled or fled Croatia in August 1995. All the operations mentioned above were accompanied by war crimes and crimes against humanity. Ethnic persecution and rape became a crucial element of warfare[6] and a systematic strategy of ethnic annihilation.[7] These crimes were committed by members of various regular army units and paramilitary groups on all sides involved in the war. As Grigorova Mincheva & Gurr (2013, 70) have outlined (with special reference to the war in BiH), "'ethnic cleansing' was practiced by all sides. Many of the estimated 55,000 civilians killed during the war were victims either of sieges or of Serb, Croat, or Muslim massacres in mixed areas where locally dominating forces sought to expel civilians of different ethnicity."

The Dayton Peace Accords (DPA), facilitated by international negotiators, ended the war in 1995. By signing the DPA, the governments of BiH, Croatia and

4 The Federal Republic of Yugoslavia (FRY) was formed by the Republics of Serbia and Montenegro from the former Socialist Federal Republic of Yugoslavia (SFRY) after the secession of the other republics in 1992. In 2003, it was reconstituted as a State Union of Serbia and Montenegro, which existed until 2006 when Montenegro separated from Serbia after a referendum.

5 66% of war-related deaths were Bosniaks, 26% Bosnian Serbs and 8% Bosnian Croats; more than 40% were civilians, according to the Research and Documentation Centre in Sarajevo; www.idc.org.ba. (accessed June 20, 2012).

6 For an analysis of rape as an expression of ethnopolitical warfare in BiH, see Allen, 1996; Đurić-Kuzmanović, 2008; Hromadžić, 2004; Skjelsbaek, 2012.

7 According to the United Nations Commission of Experts (1994), most of the sexual violence was inflicted in camps. Members of militias and armies on all sides committed such crimes, albeit to different degrees. It was reported that Bosnian Serb troops fighting for an "ethnically cleansed" Serb Republic applied sexual violence systematically as a weapon of war with the aim of ethnic annihilation.

the FRY committed to mutual recognition and the peaceful settlement of disputes. They also agreed to adhere to the provisions on dealing with the consequences of the war, notably the return of refugees and the prosecution of war crimes (Articles VI and IX). In particular, the agreement obliged the governments to cooperate with the International Criminal Tribunal for the former Yugoslavia (ICTY), established in The Hague by the United Nations in 1993. According to UN Resolution 1534, the Tribunal was set up to render justice and to contribute to "lasting peace and security and national reconciliation" in the region. International actors have put a great deal of emphasis on legal accountability, in particular the investigation and prosecution of war crimes, and finding missing persons. They also assisted the governments of Croatia, BiH and Serbia to establish the national war crimes chambers and transitional justice strategies, which are expected to serve both accountability and fact-finding.

The cooperation with the ICTY was one of the criteria set by the European Union (EU) for accession negotiations with the governments in the region (Blatt & Obradović Wochnik, 2009; Rangelov, 2005). Other relevant criteria established within the framework of conditionality for the Western Balkans countries related to the rule of law and fighting corruption. According to the EU monitoring reports, many of these criteria have been met in the past few years although deficits were constantly mentioned. The prospect of EU membership has helped to initiate reforms and provided a framework for improving regional cooperation among political and economic institutions (Calic, 2005, 13). Still, due to the special circumstances prevailing in these countries, progress is still uneven. Croatia joined the EU in July 2013 and Serbia has been accepted as an official candidate for accession (along with Montenegro and Macedonia), whereas BiH is still far from taking such a step, though the Stabilisation and Association Agreement was put into operation by the EU in June 2015. In order to assess the situation today, 20 years after Dayton, and to discuss the common challenges that the three countries face in dealing with the legacies of the past, it is useful to look more closely at their development since 1995.

1. Developments in national politics and the regional context since 1995

1.1 Bosnia-Herzegovina: unfinished statebuilding, political deadlock and "no future"

Twenty years after the signing of the DPA, BiH still remains under international supervision and suffers from political deadlock due to constant power struggles between the political leaders of the various constituencies (see the contribution by Miodrag Živanović in this volume). The political system established by the DPA in 1995 is based on two entities, the Federation of Bosnia-Herzegovina (FBiH) and the Republika Srpska (RS), and Brčko District, along with institutions at the municipal, entity and state level. The FBiH is primarily inhabited by

Bosniaks and Bosnian Croats, while Bosnian Serbs form the majority population in the RS. The state institutions include a State Presidency, consisting of three representatives from the Bosniak, Croat and Serb communities,[8] a Parliament and a Council of Ministers. BiH was set up as a semi-protectorate in 1995, with a High Representative who coordinates the implementation of all civilian aspects of the DPA in cooperation with an international body known as the Peace Implementation Council (PIC).[9]

As a consequence of the Dayton constitution, state institutions remained weak, and entity institutions are invested with more power than state institutions.[10] This imbalance and the very complex administrative structures of the new federal system contributed to a situation where agreements on reforms (i.e. in the educational system or security sector) were constantly obstructed.[11] The peace implementation process initiated by the international community questioned the positions of political groups who had an interest in maintaining the conflict, and their resistance, in turn, "pushed intervention to increase intensity. As the international community intervened more assertively, its actions triggered fears among Bosnian Croats and Bosnian Serbs that the peace implementation process would ultimately strengthen the capacity of the Bosniaks to impose their will on the rest of the country. These fears led nationalist forces within both communities to challenge the foundations of Bosnia's fragile state." (Leroux-Martin, 2015, 150)

The representatives of the three constituent groups in BiH continue to express opposing views on the future state structure. The Serb representatives advocate for a confederation and a very high degree of autonomy for the entities, while Bosniak representatives would prefer a federal state with more powers for the overarching institutions. The Bosnian Croat representatives, on the other hand, would like a new BiH constitution with stronger autonomy and administrative structures for the Croat constituency. In recent years, political confrontation has increased. The Serb politicians argue that inhabitants of the RS should have the right to hold a referendum to decide whether they want to be citizens of BiH, referring in this context to Montenegro's and Kosovo's move to self-proclaimed independence. Influential Bosniak representatives have insisted on the empowerment of state institutions, and some call for the abolition of the entity structure, which has fuelled further polarization. The Croat parties called for the establishment of a

8 Bosniaks, Croats and Serbs are recognised as "constituent peoples" in the constitution of BiH. However, the legal framework requires that the Serb representative in the Presidency be elected in the RS, while the Croat and Bosniak representatives are elected in the FBiH.

9 The Office of the High Representative (OHR) oversees the implementation of civilian aspects of the Dayton Peace Agreement which ended the war in 1995, and regularly reports to the PIC. The PIC includes delegations from the US, EU Presidency and European Commission, Russia, Germany, UK, France, Italy, Japan, Canada and Turkey.

10 For in-depth analyses of BiH's development since 1995, see, for example, Bliesemann de Guevara, 2009; Bieber, 2006; Chandler, 2008; Fischer, 2007; Gromes, 2007; 2012; International Crisis Group, 2010; 2011a, b; 2014; Solioz, 2010 a, b.

11 For an overview of the multiple forms of obstructions and dynamics of international reactions see Leroux-Martin, 2015.

"third entity." These tensions escalated into a crisis after the elections in 2010, which resulted in a substantial swing towards the Social Democratic Party (SDP). Since then, the country has experienced a massive dual crisis, both on the FBiH entity level and inter-entity level,[12] accompanied by repeated announcements by the President of the RS (Milorad Dodik) that a referendum will be held on laws imposed by the High Representative regarding the State Court of BiH and State Prosecutor's Office. The legitimacy of this court, which is in charge of the investigation of war crimes and economic crimes such as corruption, was challenged by Bosnian Serb leaders. International institutions, including the Office of the High Representative (OHR), have dramatically lost authority in the past years, and the International Crisis Group concludes that "there is no broadly respected authority in the country, only regional or partisan champions" (2011, 9). The elections in 2014 were unable to change this situation (see the chapter by Miodrag Živanović in this volume). The results showed once again that the different constituencies continue to regard each other with suspicion and primarily vote for political parties that pursue an ethnopolitical agenda. Moreover, in July 2015 the RS Assembly decided to hold a referendum on the legitimacy of the institutions mentioned above.

Two decades after Dayton, state building remains incomplete in BiH and some aspects of the DPA still have to be clarified.[13] In particular, constitutional reforms are regarded by international actors as a prerequisite for EU accession. An ongoing problem is that the Dayton constitution is not compatible with EU standards, as it discriminates against those who do not assign themselves (or are assigned) to the three constituent nations but belong to minorities.[14] International initiatives aimed

12 For an analysis of the factors and dynamics of the recent crisis, see Đihić, 2010; Gromes, 2010; 2012; International Crisis Group, 2010; 2011a, b.

13 In 2008, the PIC Steering Board established the criteria that must be met by the BiH authorities prior to the closure of the OHR. It was agreed that the signing of the Stabilization and Association Agreement with the EU would depend on full compliance with the DPA. The PIC Board has regularly reviewed progress since 2008. In 2012, it stated: "While progress has been made in some areas, chronic disagreement among the main political parties has produced gridlock that has prevented the full implementation of the agenda" (www.ohr.int/print/?content_id=46773; accessed 28 March 2015). A PIC Communique (PIC SB | 22/5/2014) issued in May 2014 also outlined deficits and stated that the entrenchment of the rule of law stands out as a priority area: "Corruption (. . .) must be investigated and prosecuted, war criminals brought to justice, and court decisions at all levels must be implemented without delay." The report also expressed "particular concern about ongoing attempts to undermine the authority of the state-level-judicial institutions." See www.ohr.int/print/?content_id=48554 (accessed 28 March 2015). Nevertheless, on 1 June 2015, the Stabilisation and Association Agreement was finally put into operation by the EU.

14 This became obvious in January 2007, when the representative of the Jewish community in BiH, Jacob Finci, and the representative of the Roma community, Dervo Sejdić, complained that they were prevented by the BiH constitution from standing for election to the Presidency solely on the grounds of their ethnic origin. In June 2009, the European Court of Human Rights concluded that the applicants' ineligibility to stand for election to the House of Peoples lacked a reasonable justification and had therefore breached Article 14, taken in conjunction with Article 3 of Protocol No. 1, and that the constitutional provisions with regard to the Presidency had also to be considered discriminatory and a violation of Article 1 of Protocol No. 12 (see www.coe.org.rs/eng/news_sr_eng/?conid=1545; accessed 28 March 2015).

at mediation on these sensitive topics between the conflicting constituencies have been repeatedly disrupted. The international representatives face a dilemma, as Serb parties increasingly oppose their involvement, while Bosniak parties call for more powerful intervention and Croats hope for support for their proposed reforms of federal structures. International pressure for constitutional change is seen as an attempt to revise the outcomes of the war and restructure a state that was constituted as a confederation into a unitary state in which the Bosniaks, as the largest ethnic group, would form the titular nation (Despot et al., 2012, 4–5). No consensus has been reached so far. Citizen's protests evolved in February in Tuzla against privatisation practices and corruption, and lateron spread to other places such as Zenica, Mostar, Brcko and Sarajevo, with clashes between protesters and police. These protests led to the establishment of democratic forums in which citizens could voice concerns (see Briony Jones' chapter in this volume). However, so far these events did not develop into a broader power to change on the political situation. There is a danger that the long-lasting political deadlock and many citizens' lack of trust in the state institutions, might increase the "no future" feeling that is widespread, especially among the young generation in BiH, as a result of the desperate economic situation and high level of unemployment (see the chapters by Will Bartlett and Miodrag Živanović in this volume).

1.2 Croatia: A new EU member state struggling with legacies from the "homeland war"

Croatia has been a NATO member since 2009 and joined the EU in December 2013. In recent years, its government was eager to fulfil international expectations and meet the EU's criteria for institutional and legal reforms.[15] This was backed by a consensus among all relevant political parties, although some populist voices tried to raise anti-European rhetoric as a consequence of the ICTY's first instance verdict against the former military commanders Ante Gotovina and Mladen Markać. The verdict caused an outcry and was considered deeply offensive to all those who had defended Croatia in the "homeland war" (Despot et al., 2012, 4).

Since the 2011 elections, the political influence of the ethno-nationalists has decreased, but they remain forces to be reckoned with in state administrations and retain their potential for populist mobilization. Like other countries in the region, Croatia was strongly affected by the international financial crisis. It has also experienced several corruption scandals in the past few years. As political parties and administrations were involved in these crimes, citizens' faith in democracy has suffered. Due to Croatia's poor economic situation, there is some potential for social conflicts. Economists voice concern about the major welfare gap between urban and rural areas. The war-affected areas of Eastern Slavonia and Krajina in particular suffer from massive poverty.

15 For an analysis of political developments in Croatia after 1995, see Ramet & Matić, 2007; Ramet et al., 2007; Gagnon, 2006; Tanner, 2010.

Ethnopolitical conflicts play less of a role in daily life in Croatia than in BiH. Croats form a majority of the population in Croatia as a consequence of the war in the early 1990s: the war between pro-independence forces and the Yugoslav army left about one-third of the country in ruins and resulted in the flight of more than 250,000 Serb citizens. During and after Operation Storm, hundreds of civilians were killed and thousands of houses burnt down, and crimes from this period need particular investigation. As of December 2011, 132,608 Serb minority returnees were registered by the UN Refugee Agency.[16] However, it is estimated that approximately 50% of those who resettled only occasionally visit their former homes.[17] Today the Serb minority has decreased to an estimated 5% of the population. Nonetheless, some municipalities are still marked by distrust and inter-ethnic tensions (e.g. Vukovar, where nationalist political groups and war veterans associations have recently protested against regulations that allow the use of the Cyrillic alphabet by the Serb minority).[18] This shows that the country is still burdened by its recent past. The relationship with Serbia is still difficult. Ivo Josipović, the former President of Croatia, has tried to address this in a positive manner. In April 2010, he expressed his regret for crimes committed by Ustasha fighters during the Second World War. He has also visited places where war crimes were committed in the 1990s paying his respects to the victims (see Martina Fischer's contribution, Chapter 1 in this volume).

1.3 Serbia: A multi-cultural state burdened with the past and facing ongoing conflicts

Despite many political struggles between pro-European and pro-Russian forces,[19] Serbia's governments have openly supported EU accession. The pro-EU course also had a staunch advocate in President Boris Tadić, who sought to advance good neighborly relations with Croatia (see Chapter 2 in this volume). At the same time, international expectations were not entirely met as government politicians from different parties had clearly stated that a unilateral declaration of independence

16 See www.unhcr.hr/eng/images/stories/news/stats2012/unhcr_statistical_report_december_2011.pdf (accessed 28 March 2015).

17 See UNHCR, 2011, 81–86; for an analysis of the ambivalence of Croatia's past and the policy of the Tuđman regime in the 1990s, see Tanner, 2010.

18 Croatia's law on minority rights states that a minority has the right to the official use of its script and language in areas where it makes up more than one-third of the population. However, in February 2013, veterans' unions organized public protests against the government's decision to introduce Serbian (Cyrillic) script alongside Croatian after a census that showed that nearly 35% of the inhabitants of Vukovar are Serbs. Veterans' unions challenged the minority rights law in the Constitutional Court, and 20,000 of their members participated in a rally, chanting slogans such as: "Cyrillic never in Vukovar!"; "We died for Vukovar, Politicians Have Betrayed Us"; "Victory in War, Defeat in Peace"; and "Prime Minister, don't provoke the defenders of Vukovar". See http://inavukic.com/2013/02/03/croatia-no-cyrillic-in-vukovar-thank-you/ (accessed 28 March 2015).

19 For an analysis of the political developments in Serbia, see Clark, 2008; International Crisis Group, 2008; 2011c; 2012; Becker & Engelberg, 2008; Petritsch et al., 2009; Uvalić, 2010.

from Kosovo was unacceptable to them, making reference to the constitution, which defines Serbia's territorial integrity. However, although the government in Serbia has declared that it wants to settle the tension between Serbs and Albanians and find a solution acceptable to both sides, violent incidents at the border between Serbia and Kosovo have frequently been reported, apparently fuelled by actors involved in organized crime. However, after concessions on Kosovo[20] and several symbolic gestures by the former President (Boris Tadić) aimed at improving relations with Croatia, Serbia was granted accession candidate status in March 2012.

Socio-economic and political problems pose a serious challenge for the present government and society in Serbia. Around 9% of the population lives in poverty.[21] Poverty particularly affects jobless people, children, single mothers, refugees and internally displaced persons (IDPs) as well as ethnic minorities such as Roma, who continue to suffer discrimination. At the same time, economic structures are prone to corruption due to a lack of regulatory authorities and independent media. Reforms of education, healthcare and social insurance, the judiciary and the military are still incomplete. Another challenge is managing the peaceful coexistence of minorities and majority populations in different areas of the multicultural state. Relations between Serb and Albanian constituencies in South Serbia and relations between Serbs and Bosniaks in Sandžak are tense. In Vojvodina, there is continued antagonism between supporters and opponents of autonomy.

1.4 Conclusions

Although BiH, Serbia and Croatia are characterized by different political dynamics, they face several common problems. In all three countries, the transition from a centrally planned to a market economy has been burdened by massive corruption scandals (Kregar et al., 2010; Despot and Reljić, 2011; Donais, 2002) which has damaged trust in political institutions, and there are continuing overlaps between legal and shadow economies in some sectors, as well as links to organized crime (Ehrke, 2003; International Crisis Group, 2012, 7). All of these countries were severely affected by recent economic crises which developed on a global and European level (see Will Bartlett's contribution in this volume). In all three countries, the enforcement of laws—as a precondition for a functioning "rule of law"—is still deficient, and serious deficits remain in all of the countries—including Croatia—with regard to implementing human rights standards and

20 The government of Serbia agreed to accept symbols and signs for "Kosovo" at its borders and to accept representatives of the government of Kosovo in regional organizations.

21 Statistics for 2013, according to www.cia.gov/library/publications/the-world-factbook/geos/ri.html (accessed 28 March 2015). Around 50% of young people (between 14–30 years) are thought to be unemployed.

establishing the rule of law, border control, political and economic accountability and transparency.[22]

The international missions that monitored the implementation of the DPA, including the disarmament and demobilization of former combatants, and addressed the reconstruction of war-affected areas have helped to establish a degree of stability in the Western Balkans, and some normalization can be observed in terms of people crossing the borders and building relationships in a pragmatic sense. At the same time, all three countries still face unresolved disputes at cross-border level and tensions at local community level, often fuelled by diverging interpretations of the past. Dealing with the past remains a difficult and contentious issue in all three countries. BiH, Serbia and Croatia still face several common challenges to overcome the legacies of the violent past. Although some progress has been made in the field of transitional justice, much more engagement is needed to pave the way for reconciliation both within and between these countries.

2. Common challenges to transitional justice and reconciliation processes

The concept of transitional justice was introduced by the international human rights movement in reference to the prosecution of human rights violations committed by repressive regimes in the course of democratic transition. Later, the term also came to be used for dealing with crimes and massive human rights violations committed in armed conflicts (Kritz, 1995; Minow, 1998; 2002; Teitel, 2000; 2014). The concept has also been used by peacebuilders, international organizations and donors and extended its meaning, now also encompassing the establishment of tribunals, truth commissions, lustration of state administrations, reparations, and political and societal initiatives aimed at fact-finding, reconciliation and establishing cultures of remembrance.[23] Holistic interpretations point to the need for accountability, truth recovery and institution building and call for a combination of retributive approaches (aimed at punishing the perpetrators) and restorative approaches (symbolic reparation and material compensation that acknowledge the suffering of the victims of war crimes and refugees, and initiatives for trust- and relationship-building as a precondition for long-term reconciliation).

22 See several documents released by the European Commission in recent years on (1) Croatia, (2) Serbia, and (3) Bosnia:

(1) http://europa.eu/rapid/press-release_IP-13-283_en.htm.
(2) http://ec.europa.eu/enlargement/pdf/key_documents/2014/20140108-serbia-progress-report_en.pdf;
(3) http://ec.europa.eu/enlargement/pdf/key_documents/2014/20141008-bosnia-and-herzegovina-progress-report_en.pdf;
(All of these links were accessed on 28 March 2015).

23 For a review of the literature, see van der Merwe et al., 2009; Thoms et al., 2008.

The concepts of transitional justice and reconciliation thus show a great deal of overlap, although they are not identical.[24]

The societies in the Western Balkans—albeit to different degrees—are still dealing with the legacies of the wars of the 1990s on a daily basis and in that regard deploy different transitional justice strategies. In all three countries, there is an ongoing need to search for missing persons, with more than 10,000 persons still missing from the 1990s wars, according to the International Commission on Missing Persons (ICMP).[25] However, BiH, Croatia and Serbia have made substantial progress in the search for the missing and have established institutions that have started to cooperate, also on a regional level.

Progress is also reported with the return and reintegration of refugees and IDPs, but some challenges still have to be addressed.[26] In BiH, the process of refugee return has come to an end but the government still works in close partnership with international actors to find solutions for the remaining IDPs and minority returnees. In Serbia, Serbs and others who fled from Croatia, BiH and Kosovo have been waiting for decades for viable solutions that will secure long-term housing and other basic human rights.[27] However, this will depend on cross-border cooperation and the political will of local and national authorities to deal with a number of sensitive issues (e.g. property restitution and reparations, and political representation in local communities that reflects ethnic affiliations).

In all three countries, institutions for the investigation and prosecution of war crimes have been created. They have taken over numerous cases from the ICTY and need to open investigations and initiate prosecutions in further cases. However, the work of the war crimes chambers is not always fully supported by the governments and societies in the region, and continues to face many prejudices. To date, only a small number of the crimes committed by members of militias and regular armies on all sides have been systematically investigated by the ICTY (see Klaus Hoffmann's chapter in this volume). In all three countries, several thousand war crimes cases have to be dealt with and concluded by domestic courts. Many suspects have left their former place of residence and are at large in their own or other countries. As all three countries decided not to extradite fugitives, progress in this area will largely depend on the political will for cooperation among the governments in the region, as well as on monitoring by international actors and civil society organizations (CSOs). The courts and prosecutor's offices established

24 For an overview of the scholarly debate on reconciliation, see Bloomfield et al., 2003; Bloomfield 2006; and Fischer, 2011.

25 See www.ic-mp.org/icmp-worldwide/southeast-europe/bosnia-and-herzegovina (accessed 28 March 2015). Around 10,000 persons are still missing from the war in Bosnia, 2,000 from the war in Croatia, and 900 from the Kosovo war.

26 BiH still has a small number of collective accommodation facilities for IDPs (mostly vulnerable people). In Serbia, many Serbs who fled Croatia during Operation Storm in 1995, as well as refugees from Kosovo, continue to live in collective accommodation.

27 According to UNHCR information shared in an interview in Sarajevo on 12 May 2011. The Commissioner for Human Rights of the Council of Europe counts a total of 438,000 refugees and displaced persons in the entire region of former Yugoslavia who are still waiting for durable solutions to their claims. See https://wcd.coe.int/ViewDoc.jsp?id=1904893 (accessed 28 March 2015).

in the region have made some progress in the past decade on providing fair and proper trials and now operate much more effectively than in the post-war period. Although their performance has improved, they are still struggling with an ambivalent reputation (Fischer 2013, 74–76).

Another common problem is that all three countries rely on retributive justice as the main instrument for dealing with the past. Transitional justice strategies do not go beyond the issue of detecting and investigating the facts and establishing individual guilt for the crimes committed during the wars. Criminal prosecution is a high priority, not only for the governments but also for victims (and victims' associations), albeit for different reasons (see Chapter 1 by Martina Fischer and Chapter 6 by Vesna Nikolić-Ristanović and Sanja Ćopić in this volume). To date, none of the countries has adopted a comprehensive approach to the concepts of justice and truth which would encompass restorative elements aimed at healing painful memories and rebuilding relationships, in addition to the task of punishing the perpetrators.

Unfortunately, in all three countries, interethnic tensions persist either at a local or cross-border level, often fuelled by diverging interpretations of history, selective forms of remembrance and diverse notions of victimhood (see the contribution by Jelena Subotić in this volume). Tensions are also reflected in the increasing numbers of hate crimes in divided communities, which particularly target returnees and members of minorities.[28] Attacks are also reported against vulnerable groups such as Roma, and homosexuals, trans- and bisexual persons and their organizations in all three countries. In BiH and Serbia in particular, violent incidents against these minorities have repeatedly occurred in recent years, initiated by religious and radical groups. Further antagonisms have developed or deepened in a post-war context between refugees, IDPs or returnees and resident populations, between war profiteers and those who lost their property, winners and losers of the economic transformation, urban and rural populations, and victims and perpetrators of war crimes who find themselves living side by side in local communities. Tensions are often fuelled by propaganda based on relativization of war crimes, competition over victim numbers, and selective remembrance.[29]

Twenty years after the end of the war operations in BiH and Croatia, the legacies of past violence are still very much alive. Many civilians and ex-combatants have to cope with painful memories and are physically and/or psychically scarred by war. Various challenges must still be addressed with regard to the return and reintegration of refugees and IDPs, restitution of property,[30] and compensation for military and civilian war victims. Many of those who lost

28 In order to combat such crimes, the mission of the Organisation for Security and Cooperation in Europe (OSCE) to BiH issued a handbook (OSCE Mission to BiH/OHDIHR 2010) and held round tables with representatives of local authorities. See www.osce.org/bih/74693 (accessed 28 March 2015).

29 See Pupavac, 1997; Obradović, 2012; Ramet, 2007.

30 According to the Commissioner for Human Rights of the Council of Europe, a total of 438,000 refugees and displaced persons were still waiting for durable solutions to their claims in the region of the former Yugoslavia by the end of 2012; see https://wcd.coe.int/ViewDoc.jsp?id=1904893 (accessed 31 August 2012).

members of their families, their health or homes during the wars are still waiting for an acknowledgment of their experiences and redress for the harm they have suffered. The acknowledgment has to come from the government and should take the form of material compensation and symbolic acts of reparation.

Reconciliation between and within the societies of the Western Balkans very much depends on how governments, parliaments and societies cope with the legacies of their violent past. Scholars and practitioners have argued that in societies emerging from war, the past needs to be addressed to enable individuals and communities to rebuild trust and relationships. However, they continue to grapple with critical questions. When is the right moment to address the legacies of the past after violent conflict? How can societies address the past without opening old wounds related to the violence and crimes committed in war? Is opening old wounds detrimental to building a future? How can cultures of remembrance be established that would include and acknowledge the victims on all sides involved in violent conflict? How can various actors deal constructively with different interpretations of facts and history? Is reconciliation possible without addressing the past? The challenge remains as to how to address the legacies of the past without reinforcing the sense of helplessness (which is particularly widespread among refugees and victims of war-related crimes and those who experienced the loss of relatives and property) or fostering notions of victimhood (which dominate the public discourse), and how to address the past in a way which promotes cultures of remembrance that acknowledge injustice and crimes and the suffering of the victims of all sides involved in the war(s).

Reconciliation between and within the societies in the Western Balkans remains a formidable challenge, given that so many unresolved disputes persist and are constantly fuelled by divergent interpretations of history, not only regarding the 1990s wars but also related to the First and Second World Wars. Transitional justice and reconciliation initiatives have to take into account that many different narratives and collective memories from these former periods continue to exist; such memories have been revitalized in the violent dynamics of the 1990s and were conducive in framing the foundation myths and unification strategies of the nation-states established in the 1990s (Melčić, 2007b; Ramet, 2007; Vlaijsavljević, 2002).

This book is intended to encourage scholars and practitioners from the former Yugoslavia and international experts to reflect on some of these complex questions and to analyse the achievements and obstacles that characterize current efforts to deal with the past. Drawing on empirical studies, theoretical discussions and practical experience, the contributions offer invaluable insights into the complex relationship between transitional justice and conflict transformation.

3. The structure of the book

The twentieth anniversary of the Dayton Accords, which ended the war in BiH in 1995, offers an opportunity to look more closely at how the societies in the region deal with their violent past. This volume presents a selection of assessments by scholars from the region of the former Yugoslavia and international researchers. We asked them to evaluate the transitional justice policies pursued in the period following the signing of the DPA and to discuss the prospects of reconciliation. We also asked for their critical reflection on the achievements and shortcomings of the strategies applied in the three countries belonging to the "Dayton triangle." The contributions, which were written especially for this book, assess the policies pursued by various actors, including state institutions, the courts and civil society, and give a rich scholarly analysis of the complexities and interconnectedness of "dealing with the past" processes in the region. The book consists of two parts.

Part 1 discusses the potential, achievements and limits of legal instruments and outlines the need for restorative approaches to justice and truth. The chapters mostly address cross-cutting issues with reference to all three countries.

Chapter 1, entitled "Dealing with the past from the top down and bottom up," shows how dealing with the past requires efforts by state and non-state actors alike, and looks at the different fields of action, policies and initiatives undertaken by state institutions, governments, parliaments and civil society actors (CSOs) in order to address the challenges mentioned above. Martina Fischer discusses to what extent political leaders supported legal approaches to war crimes prosecution and fact-finding, and considers some of the initiatives taken to launch symbolic reparations (e.g. apologies). The chapter also looks at the efforts being made by CSOs at the regional and local level. One of the most prominent initiatives is the campaign for a regional truth commission (RECOM), which was launched by CSOs in Serbia, Croatia and Bosnia and gained support from other successor countries to the former Yugoslavia. One of the chapter's main conclusions is that CSOs are needed at all levels (regional, national and local community) to monitor the efforts of state institutions in establishing accountability and the rule of law and to encourage political leaders to initiate inclusive policies of remembrance.

Chapter 2 ("The ICTY after 20 years of experience") by Klaus Hoffmann balances both the merits and problematic aspects of the work of the International Criminal Tribunal for the former Yugoslavia. He outlines the Tribunal's achievements in the field of justice and fact-finding and identifies some of the problems stemming from its legal practice. Much has been written by scholars from around the world on the ICTY's contribution to international law, and its shortcomings have also been discussed.[31] This chapter is written from an insider's perspective as the author is a former lawyer at the ICTY (in 2001) and legal officer in the Prosecutor's Office (from 2005 onwards). The author presents a very honest, balanced and (self-)critical assessment, outlining the achievements and problems affecting legal procedures, witness protection, and outreach to the societies in the region, including the problematic effects of self-representation of the accused and witness proofing. The lessons learned and recommendations resulting from

31 See, for example, Allcock, 2009; Schabas, 2013; Orentlicher, 2010; Subotić, 2009.

experience with the ICTY may be helpful in improving the system and should be considered in future transitional justice processes.

Although academic work on the ICTY in recent decades fills bookshelves and libraries, most of the analysis has focused on legal practice and its contributions to international law. Its impact on the societies concerned has received less attention. Chapter 3, by Tamara Banjeglav ("The micro legacy of the ICTY in Croatia"), helps to fill this research gap and shows that the ICTY's decisions have had considerable repercussions on the societies in the region. Research conducted in Vukovar (Croatia) highlights both the complexity of these repercussions and the challenges of dealing with the legacies of the violent past in a divided community. The chapter contributes empirical findings on the acceptance and legitimacy of the ICTY and its impact on interethnic relations between people who struggle with diverging memories and war experiences. It investigates the impact of decisions in war crimes cases concerning Vukovar and concludes that the facts established by the International Tribunal in these cases were not always accepted by local communities.

Olivera Simić's contribution (Chapter 4) deals with the challenges and tension created by "Rape, silence and denial", outlining how hierarchies of victimization in a post-conflict society can contribute to new injustice and discrimination. Her chapter is based on experiences from Bosnia-Herzegovina. Simić outlines that although sexual violence in war is now accepted as a gross violation of human rights under international law, the recognition of these crimes is very much predicated on an "ideal" victim subject. Feminist scholars and activists in the region of the former Yugoslavia and international experts have extensively contributed to investigations of rape and sexual violence and shown that this was used as a systematic strategy in ethnopolitical warfare in the Western Balkans by the armies and militia on all sides. The denial of these crimes and the social taboo surrounding these crimes created additional burdens for those who were affected and had to live with the consequences. The chapter examines the excluded or silenced experiences of women who suffered wartime sexual violence and who belong to a community that is seen as a "perpetrator." It focuses on the silence and denial of Bosnian Serb women's experiences of wartime sexual violence and argues that the current discourse on wartime sexual violence results in the construction of a problematic "victim hierarchy."

Chapter 5, by Jelena Subotić, deals with "Political memory as an obstacle to justice in Serbia, Croatia, and Bosnia-Herzegovina." It shows how, two decades after the end of the Yugoslav wars, the official narratives about the violence of the 1990s in the successor states are still mutually exclusive, contradictory and irreconcilable. Subotić concludes that the ways in which post-Yugoslav states remember and interpret legacies of past violence "provide continuing obstacles in the search for truth and justice" as the political establishment in all three countries tends to use these narratives in their power struggles. Subotić highlights that there is a mutually reinforcing relationship between justice and remembrance of the past, as initiatives in the area of education and memorialization are used to obstruct efforts rather than support transitional justice mechanisms. She also presents alternative ideas on mechanisms of political memory that would be more conducive to paving the way for a concept of justice that is based on trust, respect and dignity.

Part 2 of this book presents contributions that deal with ongoing challenges and prospects for reconciliation in the three countries. Most of the chapters include results from case studies conducted in the three countries.

Chapter 6, by Vesna Nikolić-Ristanović and Sanja Ćopić is dedicated to "Dealing with the past in Serbia – achievements in the past 20 years." It shows that state policies in this country have been rather contradictory with regard to dealing with the past and reconciliation in Serbia itself and in the wider region. After a short analysis of the socio-historical context of the conflicts in the former Yugoslavia, the authors present an assessment of achievements and deficits in dealing with the past by the state institutions in Serbia during the past 20 years, based on empirical research conducted by the authors within the FP7 project "Developing alternative understandings of security and justice through restorative justice approaches in intercultural settings within democratic societies—ALTERNATIVE." The ambivalent role and approaches of civil society in Serbia to dealing with the past are also addressed in this chapter. The authors highlight several dilemmas and challenges (e.g. the limitations of CSO activities that are not supported by broader society; the role of criminal justice as an important element of transitional justice but also its potential to deepen interethnic conflict) and discuss possible further steps to deal with them constructively.

Chapter 7 by Dinka Čorkalo Biruški and Dean Ajduković ("Young adults' perspective of social reconstruction in three post-war communities in Croatia and Bosnia-Herzegovina") looks at the long-term consequences of the violent conflicts at the individual, interpersonal, communal and societal level and analyzes prospects for social recovery. The authors critically assess the assumption that both victimized and perpetrator groups need to go through various motivational, cognitive, behavioral and identity changes in order to restore trust and accomplish inter-group reconciliation. Following Tajfel's notion of an interpersonal vs. inter-group behavioral continuum, the chapter contends that processes of reconciliation are based to a far greater extent on intra- and inter-personal than on inter-group qualities. The authors argue that "social reconstruction" (rapprochement among groups that were at war with each other) encompasses a process that aims to renew the social fabric of the war-affected community and helps to normalize interpersonal and group relations. They investigate the impact of war trauma, ethnic identification and attitudes towards social reconstruction on the basis of interviews with young Croats and Serbs who experienced the 1991–1995 wars in Banja Luka (Bosnia-Herzegovina), Knin and Vukovar (Croatia). The empirical material shows that ethnic identifications are strong and there is only a modest readiness for social reconstruction.

Education in contemporary Bosnia-Herzegovina is a particularly difficult issue, given that the state structures are contested and some political leaders and communities do not identify with the BiH nation state. People disagree on ethno national identity and cultural heritage, the legitimacy and mandates of state institutions, constitutional and legal systems, and policies of remembrance. As a consequence, education policies, methods and experiences are influenced by multiple and diverging positions, with conflicting decisions over education policy, segregated schools and divergent curricula in this strongly divided country. Initial hopes among international actors (e.g. the Organization for Security and Co-operation in Europe) that the system of "two schools under one roof"[32] in divided communities such as Mostar would pave the way for rapprochement have proved unrealistic. However, in the Brčko District, an integrated multi-ethnic school system was established and has often been cited as a positive role model for the rest of the country. Chapter 8, Briony Jones's contribution ("Educating citizens in Bosnia-Herzegovina – experiences and contradictions in post-war education reform") discusses this case and investigates the intersection between education, citizenship and transition. The author analyzes the contradictions in initiatives for education reform in Bosnia-Herzegovina and looks at the efforts undertaken in the Brčko District. The chapter argues that reforms in the field of education must be placed in their broader context and protagonists of educational reforms need to actively engage with ongoing debates on what it means to be "Bosnian" in Bosnia-Herzegovina.

Chapter 9 by Miodrag Živanović ("Discrimination: from construction to deconstruction") also focuses on the prospects of reconciliation in Bosnia-Herzegovina, looking at the construction of discrimination as the main obstacle to progress in this field. In his view, Bosnia-Herzegovina has developed as a state and society based on discrimination in the past 20 years. The author looks at the various dimensions of this phenomenon, analyzing its political, normative and socio-psychological connotations. His main argument is that due to the ethnic matrix that shapes the state and society and characterizes the inhabitants of BiH not as people or citizens but as representatives of their ethnicity, a tribal structure of society has emerged. As a consequence, human rights exist predominantly as collective rights, and the individual is merely an insignificant part of one of the three ethnic constituencies. Policy- and decision-making responds to this logic; this is largely reflected in the legislative framework and affects all sections of life – vertically from local communities to the state, and horizontally from the economy to education, science and culture. The author explains that there is a deep social divide. He argues that due to two decades of daily practice, ethnically based distances are now greater than in the war years. He sees a "political autism" at work, with the space of social freedom becoming narrower. In his view, society in Bosnia suffers from an inversion of the value system, resignation and despair, contributing to a general absence of the criticism and social opposition that are needed to change the current situation and pave the way for reconciliation.

32 Schools where pupils from different constituencies use the same building but are educated separately in different classrooms or shifts.

Unfortunately, the elections held in October 2014 did not result in positive change. According to Živanović, there is a risk that the economic problems will make matters worse. More effort is needed to overcome this situation, the first step being to deconstruct the ethnopolitical logic and practice.

In Chapter 10, Will Bartlett assesses the "Economic development and perspectives for reconciliation" and discusses the connection between economic conditions and the processes of reconciliation in and between Bosnia-Herzegovina, Serbia and Croatia. This chapter shows how the international financial crisis and the eurozone crisis have had a dramatic effect on the economies in the region. The economic crisis led to a reduction in international trade, foreign investment and remittance flows, and a fall in credit for businesses and households. As a consequence, these countries have experienced a "double dip" recession, which has driven up unemployment (youth unemployment in BiH is higher even than in Greece) and lowered living standards. Declining economic performance is detrimental to social cohesion and reconciliation between the former warring parties in the region. The author argues that the combination of economic crisis and the ruling elites' resistance to pro-market reforms has created an environment in which the seeds of reconciliation have fallen on stony ground. In his conclusion, the author looks at the prospect of EU membership. Bartlett is convinced that the EU in particular has the potential to support the process of reconciliation by providing a more attractive outlook, namely future integration. He argues that the process should be accelerated, and although the challenge of admitting new member states seems difficult, there is much the EU can do to encourage pro-reform forces in BiH and Serbia. It is particularly important to encourage a progressive perspective among young people by stepping up support for their intra-European mobility and improving job opportunities through more inclusive and better-resourced vocational education and study programmes. Bartlett concludes that the EU "should take its foot off the brake and demonstrate that reconciliation is not simply a Balkan issue but should tie European countries together in a time of profound uncertainty and change."

Chapter 11, the final chapter by Martina Fischer ("Dealing with the past violence as a long-term challenge – lessons from the Balkans") draws conclusions from the various and contradictory experiences of dealing with the past in the region of the former Yugoslavia. It argues that although it is not possible to offer universal solutions and transfer experience from one country or cultural context to another, some general lessons can be learned regarding the potential and limits of dealing with the past. These lessons should also inform scholars and practitioners engaged in framing or evaluating transitional justice policies in other regions.

References

Allcock, J. B. (2009). 'The International Criminal Tribunal for the Former Yugoslavia'. In C. Ingrao & T. A. Emmert (Eds.), *Confronting the Yugoslav Controversies. A Scholars' Initiative* (pp. 347–389). West Lafayette, IN: Purdue University Press.

Allcock, J. B. (2000). *Explaining Yugoslavia*. New York: Columbia University Press.
Allen, B. (1996). *Rape Warfare. The Hidden Genocide in Bosnia-Herzegovina and Croatia*. Minneapolis: University of Minnesota Press.
Becker, J. & Engelberg, A. (2008). *Serbien nach den Kriegen*. Frankfurt: Ed. Suhrkamp.
Bieber, F. (2006). *Post-War Bosnia: Ethnicity, Inequality and Public Sector Governance*. London: Palgrave MacMillan.
Blatt, J. & Obradović-Wochnik, J. (Eds.) (2009). *War Crimes, Conditionality and EU Integration in the Western Balkans*. Chaillot Paper, June 2009. Brussels: Institute for Security Studies, EU.
Bliesemann de Guevara, B. (2009). *Staatlichkeit in Zeiten des Statebuilding. Intervention und Herrschaft in Bosnien und Herzegowina*. Frankfurt a. M.
Bloomfield, D. (2006). *On Good Terms. Clarifying Reconciliation*. Berghof Report No. 14. Berlin: Berghof Research Center.
Bloomfield, D. et al. (2003). *Reconciliation after Violent Conflict. A Handbook*. Stockholm: IDEA.
Calic, M. J. (2005). *The Western Balkans on the Road towards European Integration*. Beitrag für Internationale Politikanalyse, Frieden und Sicherheit 12/2005. Berlin: Friedrich Ebert Stiftung.
Calic, M. J. (1995). *Der Krieg in Bosnien-Herzegowina. Ursachen, Konfliktstrukturen, Internationale Lösungsversuche*. Frankfurt a. M.: Suhrkamp.
Chandler, D. (2008). 'Post-Conflict Statebuilding: Governance without Government'. In M. Pugh et al. (Eds.), *Whose Peace? Critical Perspectives on the Political Economy of Peacebuilding* (pp. 337–355). Basingstoke: Palgrave.
Clark, J. (2008). *Serbia in the Shadow of Milošević. The Legacy of Conflict in the Balkans*. London: I. B. Tauris.
Despot, A. et al. (2012). *Zehn Jahre Einsamkeit*. SWP-aktuell, 23, Berlin: Stiftung Wissenschaft und Politik.
Donais, T. (2002). 'The Politics of Privatization in Post-Dayton Bosnia'. *Southeast European Politics*, Vol. III, No. 1, 3–19.
Đurić-Kuzmanović, T. et al. (2008). 'Gendered War, Gendered Peace. Violent Conflicts in the Balkans and their Consequences'. In D. Pankhurst (Ed.), *Gendered Peace. Women's Struggles for Post-War Justice and Reconciliation* (pp. 265–291). New York, London: Routledge.
Džihić, V. (2010). *Ethnopolitik in Bosnien-Herzegovina: Staat und Gesellschaft in der Krise*. Baden-Baden: Nomos.
Ehrke, M. (2003). 'Von der Raubökonomie zur Rentenökonomie. Mafia, Bürokratie und internationales Mandat in Bosnien'. *Internationale Politik und Gesellschaft*, 2, 2003, 123–154.
Fischer, M. (2013). 'Analysis of Interviews with International Actors'. In M. Fischer & Lj. Petrović-Ziemer (Eds.), *Dealing with the Past in the Western Balkans*, Berghof Report No. 18 (pp. 71–87). Berlin: Berghof Foundation.
Fischer, M. (2011). 'Transitional Justice and Reconciliation – Theory and Practice'. In B. Austin, M. Fischer & H. J. Giessmann (Eds.), *Advancing Conflict Transformation. The Berghof Handbook II* (pp. 405–430). Opladen & Farmington Hills: Barbara Budrich.
Fischer, M. (Ed.) (2007). 'Bosnia's Challenge: Economic Reform, Political Transformation and War-to-Peace Transition'. In M. Fischer (Ed.), *Peacebuilding and Civil Society in Bosnia-Herzegovina. Ten Years After Dayton* (pp. 441–470). 2nd edn, Münster: Lit-Verlag.
Gagnon, V. P. (2006). *The Myth of Ethnic War: Serbia and Croatia in the 1990s*. Ithaka: Cornell University Press.
Gromes, T. (2012). *Ohne Staat und Nation ist keine Demokratie zu machen: Bosnien und Herzegowina, Kosovo und Makedonien nach den Bürgerkriegen*. Baden-Baden: Nomos.

Gromes, T. (2008). *Gemeinsame Demokratie, geteilte Gesellschaft. Die Unmöglichkeit einer Friedensstrategie in Bosnien und Herzegowina.* HSFK-Report, 9/2008, Frankfurt a. M.: Hessische Stiftung für Friedens- und Konfliktforschung.

Gromes, T. (2007). *Demokratisierung nach Bürgerkriegen. Das Beispiel Bosnien und Herzegowina.* Studien der HSFK. Frankfurt am Main: Campus.

Grigorova Mincheva, Lj. & Gurr, T. R. (2013). *Crime-Terror Alliances and the State: Ethnonationalist and Islamist Challenges to Regional Security.* London: Routledge.

Hromadžić, A. (2004). 'Kriegsvergewaltigungen in Bosnien. Alte und neue Erklärungsansätze'. In R. Seifert (Ed.), *Gender, Identität und kriegerischer Konflikt. Das Beispiel des ehemaligen Jugoslawien* (pp. 112–130). Soziologie, Forschung und Wissenschaft 9, Münster: Lit-Verlag.

International Crisis Group (2014). *Bosnia's Future.* ICG Europe Report No. 232, 10 July, Brussels.

International Crisis Group (2012). *Kosovo and Serbia: A Little Goodwill Could Go a Long Way.* ICG Europe Report No. 215. Pristina, Belgrade, Brussels, 2 February.

International Crisis Group (2011a). *Bosnia: State Institutions under Attack.* ICG Europe Briefing, No. 62, Sarajevo, Istanbul, Brussels, 6 May.

International Crisis Group (2011b). *Bosnia: What Does Republica Srpska Want?* ICG Europe Report No. 214, Sarajevo, Istanbul, Brussels, 6 October.

International Crisis Group (2010). *Federation of Bosnia and Herzegovina—A Parallel Crisis.* ICG Europe Report No. 209, Sarajevo, Istanbul, Brussels, 28 September.

International Crisis Group (2009a). *Bosnia's Incomplete Transition. Between Dayton and Europe.* ICG Europe Report No. 198, Sarajevo, Brussels, 9 March.

International Crisis Group (2009b). *Bosnia's Dual Crisis.* ICG Europe Briefing No. 57, Sarajevo, Brussels, 12 November.

International Crisis Group (2008). *Will the Real Serbia Please Stand Up?* ICG Europe Briefing No. 49, Belgrade, Pristina, Brussels, 23 April.

Kregar, J. et al. (Eds.), (2010). *Corruption and Trust,* Zagreb: Center for Democracy and Law Miko Tripalo. Zagreb: University of Zagreb.

Kritz, N. J. (Ed.) (1995). *Transitional Justice. How Emerging Democracies Reckon with Former Regimes.* 3 Volumes. Washington DC: USIP.

Leroux-Martin, P. (2015). *Diplomatic Counterinsurgency. Lessons from Bosnia and Herzegovina.* Cambridge, UK: Cambridge University Press.

Melčić, D. (2007a). 'Croatia's Discourse about the Past and Some Problems of Croatian-Bosnian Understanding'. In S. Ramet et al. (Eds.), *Croatia since Independence: War, Politics, Society, Foreign Relations* (pp. 107–139). Munich: Oldenbourg Verlag.

Melčić, D. (Ed.) (2007b). *Der Jugoslawien-Krieg: Handbuch zur Vorgeschichte, Verlauf und Konsequenzen* (pp. 377–400). Wiesbaden: VS Verlag für Sozialwissenschaften.

Minow, M. (Ed.) (2002). *Breaking the Cycles of Hatred. Memory, Law and Repair.* Princeton, NY: Princeton University Press.

Minow, M. (1998). *Between Vengeance and Forgiveness. Facing History after Genocide and Mass Violence.* Boston: Beacon Press.

Obradović, J. (2012). *Ethnic Conflict and War Crimes in the Balkans. The Narratives of Denial on Post-Conflict Serbia.* London: I.B. Tauris.

Orentlicher, D. (2010). *That Someone Guilty Be Punished: The Impact of the ICTY in Bosnia.* New York: Open Society Institute.

Organisation for Security and Cooperation in Europe Mission to Bosnia and Herzegovina & OHDIHR (2010). *Understanding Hate Crimes. A Handbook for Bosnia and Herzegovina.* Sarajevo: OSCE.

Petritsch, W. et al. (Eds.) (2009). *Serbia Matters: Domestic Reforms and European Integration (Southeast European Integration Perspectives.* Baden-Baden: Nomos.
Popov, N. & Gojković, D. (2000). *The Road to War in Serbia. Trauma and Catharsis*. Budapest: Central European University Press.
Puhalo, S. (2009). *Ethnische Distanz und (Auto-)Stereotypen der Bürger Bosniens und Herzegowinas.* Sarajevo: Friedrich Ebert Stiftung.
Ramet, S. P. (2007). 'The Denial Syndrome and its Consequences. Serbian Political Culture since 2000'. *Communist and Post-Communist Studies*, 40, 1, 41–58.
Ramet, S. P. (2006). *Thinking about Yugoslavia. Scholarly Debates about the Yugoslav Breakup and the Wars in Bosnia and Kosovo.* New York: Cambridge University Press.
Ramet, S. P. et al. (Eds.) (2007). *Croatia since Independence: War, Politics, Society, Foreign Relations.* München: Oldenbourg.
Ramet, S. P. & Matić, D. (2007). *Democratic Transition in Croatia: Value Transformation, Education, and Media.* E. and H.M. Stewart 26 Series on Eastern Europe, Texas: AM University Press.
Rangelov, I. (2005). *EU Accession Conditionality and Transitional Justice in the Former Yugoslavia.* Paper presented at the European Foreign Policy Conference, 1–2 July, London.
Schabas, W. (2013). *Kein Frieden ohne Gerechtigkeit? Die Rolle der internationalen Strafjustiz.* Hamburg: Hamburger Edition.
Skjelsbaek, I. (2012). *The Political Psychology of War Rape: Studies from Bosnia and Herzegovina.* London: Routledge.
Solioz, C. (2010a). '(In)Terminable Intervention in Bosnia and Herzegovina'. *South East Europe Review*, 13, 2, 285–291.
Solioz, C. (2010b). 'The Long and Winding Road'. *South East Europe Review*, 13, 3, 299–311.
Subotić, J. (2009). *Hijacked Justice. Dealing with the Past in the Balkans.* Ithaca and London: Cornell University Press.
Tanner, M. (2010). *Croatia: A Nation Forged in War.* 3rd rev. edn. Newhaven: Yale University Press.
Teitel, R. G. (2014). *Globalising Transitional Justice. Essays for the New Millenium.* New York: Oxford University Press.
Teitel, R. G. (2000). *Transitional Justice.* New York: Oxford University Press.
Thoms, O., Ron, J. & Paris, R. (2008). *The Effects of Transitional Justice Mechanisms. A Summary of Empirical Research Findings and Implications for Analysts and Practitioners.* Working Paper. Ottawa: Centre for International Policy Studies, University of Ottawa.
United Nations Refugee Agency (UNHCR) (Ed.) (2011). *Minority Return to Croatia. Study of an Open Process.* Zagreb: United Nations High Commissioner for Human Rights.
United Nations Security Council (1994). *Final Report of the Commission of Experts Established Pursuant to Security Council Resolution 780 (1992)*, S/1994/674 – 27 May 1994, New York.
Uvalić, M. (2010). *Serbia's Transition: Towards a Better Future.* Houndmills, Basingstoke and Hampshire: Palgrave Macmillan.
Van der Merwe, H. et al. (Eds.) (2009). *Assessing the Impact of Transitional Justice. Challenges for Empirical Research.* Washington DC: USIP.
Vlaisavljević, U. (2002). 'The South Slav Identity and the Ultimate War-Reality'. In D. Bjelić & O. Savić (Eds.), *Balkan as Metaphor. Between Globalization and Fragmentation* (pp. 191–207). Cambridge, Mass.: MIT Press.
Woodward, S. (1995). *Balkan Tragedy. Chaos and Dissolution after the Cold War.* Washington DC: The Brookings Institution.

Part 1

Legal Justice and the Need for Restorative Approaches

Chapter 1

Dealing with the past from the top down and bottom up – challenges for state and non-state actors

Martina Fischer[1]

1. Introduction

Scholarly debates and practitioners' discussions largely build on the assumption that coming to terms with the past is a necessary precondition for establishing sustainable peace between nations and social groups that have been at war with each other. The concepts of *transitional justice* and *reconciliation* show a great deal of overlap (Fischer, 2011b). In political science and peace studies, it has been increasingly emphasised that holistic approaches to transitional justice (Boraine, 2006) are needed, covering legal mechanisms (retributive approaches) to establish accountability on crimes committed in war, along with institutional reforms and restorative approaches to truth recovery and justice, including material compensation or symbolic forms of reparation to address victims' needs. It is pointed out that divided societies need truth-seeking and truth-telling mechanisms, and that efforts to prevent the instrumentalisation of facts and history are needed, given that most of the contemporary wars are fuelled by nationalist myth-making based on historical distortion. After violent conflicts between ethnic and religious groups, where extremists are eager to tie responsibility for past crimes to their adversaries, truth commissions can counteract such tendencies by engaging all of society in a national dialogue. A precondition is a clear political will by state institutions and political leaders to support such processes, and a strong civil society is also crucial (Kritz, 2009, p. 18).

Many authors who promote the concept of reconciliation consider legal approaches as necessary preconditions for reconciliation. At the same time, they point out that prosecution alone is no guarantee of achieving stable peace. They strongly emphasise that initiatives for restoring trust and relationship building are crucial in advancing conflict transformation and reconciliation in war-torn societies. The need for reconciliation is emphasised in particular for societies that have experienced ethnopolitical conflict, as these societies are marked by a loss

1 I would like to thank Dr Olivera Simić and Barbara Unger for their helpful comments and Hillary Crowe for corrections to a previous draft of this chapter.

of trust, inter-generational transmission of trauma and grievances, negative interdependence (as the assertion of each group's identity is seen as requiring the negation of the other group's identity) and polarisation. Given that antagonists live in close proximity, not addressing these legacies means risking that they will become the causes of new spirals of violence and create a desire for revenge. It has been argued that reconciliation needs both top-down and bottom-up processes (Bar-On, 2007, p. 81), and although the process may begin either with the leaders or at the grassroots, to be effective it must always proceed in both dimensions simultaneously (Bar-Tal & Bennink, 2004, p. 27). It has been emphasised that civil society actors have a special role to play in this regard (Assefa, 2005; Kritz, 2009; Kriesberg, 2007; Kriesberg, 2004). Structural and political (top-down) and cultural (bottom-up) forms of reconciliation have to be seen as complementary and mutually supportive (Bloomfield, 2006; Bloomfield, 2008). There is a widespread understanding that once a top-down political settlement has been achieved in a war-torn society, a bottom-up process should follow, in which unresolved conflict issues are addressed.

In the debates about transitional justice and reconciliation, it has been pointed out that for a society to come to terms with its past, initiatives from both the political top level and at the grassroots level are needed. The ongoing question, however, is whether and where bottom-up and top-down approaches converge, and how initiatives at the top level undertaken by governments, state institutions or parliaments relate to those undertaken at the grassroots level by civil society actors.

This chapter gives an overview of relevant developments in transitional justice policies by state institutions and political leaders in Bosnia-Herzegovina (BiH), Serbia and Croatia, and looks at activities developed by civil society actors. In part, it builds on insights from the research project 'Dealing with the Past and Peacebuilding in the Western Balkans', which was conducted at the Berghof Foundation and funded by the German Foundation for Peace Research.[2] The second section discusses how far the governments, parliaments and political leaders in the region supported legal approaches for war crimes prosecution, which contributions they made to establish facts, and which initiatives were taken in terms of symbolic reparations (apologies). The third section looks at civil society engagement in the field of transitional justice and reconciliation. Civil society actors have undertaken a variety of efforts both at the regional (cross-border) and

2 The project 'Dealing with the Past and Peacebuilding in the Western Balkans' was conducted by Martina Fischer (project director) and Ljubinka Petrović-Ziemer (researcher) with support from Srđan Dvornik (Zagreb), Ismet Sejfija (Sarajevo) and Katarina Milićević (Belgrade). We are also grateful to Vesna Nikolić-Ristanović and her team for support during our field research and to Josefina Bajer for her assistance. The project analysed the activities undertaken by international and local actors, legal institutions, civil society organisations and political parties. Specific emphasis was placed on the interaction between these different actors. The project followed an empirical approach, building on a total of 150 interviews conducted in 28 municipalities in Bosnia, Serbia and Croatia in the period 2010–2012. For a detailed presentation of the results, see Fischer & Petrović-Ziemer, 2013. This chapter partly builds on this previous publication.

local level. Among the most prominent is the campaign for a regional truth commission (RECOM), which was started by civil society organisations (CSOs) in Serbia, Croatia and BiH but later gained remarkable support from activists and organisations from other successor countries to the former Yugoslavia. The fourth and final section presents conclusions and identifies some challenges in progressing policies in the field of dealing with the past. One of the chapter's main conclusions is that civil society initiatives are continuously needed at all levels (regional, national and local community) to monitor the efforts of state institutions in establishing accountability and the rule of law, and to motivate political leaders to initiate inclusive policies of remembrance.

2. Official policies for transitional justice – incentives for reconciliation?

2.1 Support for war crimes prosecution and legal approaches

By signing the DPA in 1995, the governments of Bosnia, Croatia and Yugoslavia (Serbia and Montenegro) committed to peaceful settlement of conflicts, dealing with the legacies of the war and cooperation with the International Criminal Tribunal for the former Yugoslavia (ICTY). Furthermore, the European Union (EU) has defined the governments' cooperation with the ICTY as a precondition for advancing the accession process. However, in practice, there have been significant differences in terms of their willingness to cooperate with the ICTY. Above all, Croatia's and Serbia's policies regarding the extradition of suspected war criminals or evidence related to such cases have, at times, given cause for complaint.[3] Recent assessments by the ICTY and progress reports by the European Union[4] have stated that this policy has improved. The arrests and extradition of the fugitive Ante Gotovina (United Nations/ICTY, 2011) and, finally, Ratko Mladić and Goran Hadžić in 2011 were considered a 'milestone' in this respect.[5] The ICTY has taken the lead in prosecuting war crimes and crimes against humanity and in documenting facts in the region in a situation where domestic political leaders, legal and police institutions were unable or unwilling to conduct sound investigations and trials. Despite various criticisms of the ICTY or some of its practices, it was, from the outset, an important point of reference for state institutions, civil society actors,[6] and the domestic judiciary in the region

3 On the interaction between the Hague Tribunal, states and international organisations, see Zoglin, 2005; McMahon & Forsythe, 2008; Subotić, 2009; Subotić, 2011.

4 See, as an example, European Commission, 2010.

5 Address by ICTY President Patrick Robinson to the UN Security Council on 6 June 2011; online at www.icty.org/sid/10690.

6 For an overview of the development of CSOs' attitudes toward the ICTY, see Nettelfield, 2010, pp. 145–172; Stubbs, 2003.

(Petrović-Ziemer, 2013a) and has substantially contributed to capacity building for domestic judiciaries and to the establishment of institutions for war crimes prosecution in Bosnia-Herzegovina, Serbia and Croatia.

A section for war crimes of the Court of Bosnia-Herzegovina was inaugurated in 2005 as a permanent state-level organ designed to deal with grave breaches of international humanitarian law. With support from the ICTY, legislation was drafted to create this legal body, along with a Section for War Crimes within the Office of the Prosecutor, and a Registry. Designed as a hybrid court, it had an international staff, which was phased out after five years. Under a law adopted in 2004, a witness protection unit has been established within the Bosnia-Herzegovina State Investigation and Protection Agency.[7] In Croatia, four specialised war crimes chambers were set up in 2003 within the County Courts in Zagreb, Osijek, Rijeka and Split. The Croatian Parliament passed the Law on the Application of the Statute of the International Criminal Court and the Prosecution of Criminal Acts against the International Law of War and International Humanitarian Law. Croatia also made amendments to the Penal Code in 2004. A department for witness support was formed within the Ministry of Justice in 2005.[8] In Serbia, a specialised War Crimes Chamber of the Belgrade District Court and a War Crimes Prosecutor's Office were established in 2003.[9] The National Assembly of Serbia also passed a law to establish witness protection, and a special unit for this field of work was set up within Serbia's Interior Ministry (Fischer, 2011a, p. 61).

All these legal institutions will continue to take on a central role and responsibility with regard to fact finding and accountability. In terms of the effectiveness and reliability of the domestic courts, international experts and overseers agree that the above-mentioned courts operated with an ethnopolitical bias in their initial phase, but have substantially improved their practice in recent years, as outlined in our research report (Fischer and Petrović-Ziemer, 2013). Most of the international transitional justice experts interviewed in our research project (2010–2012) stated that the legal institutions in BiH, Serbia and Croatia have improved their performance in investigating and prosecuting war crimes in the past decade. According to these assessments, there was a clear shift from the practice of prosecuting only war crimes suspects from the other sides (often by *in absentia* trials) to increasing numbers of indictments and sentencing in cases where crimes were committed by members of their 'own' constituency, and to more advanced cooperation among courts in the region. Many *in absentia* trials have meanwhile been reviewed, and with the establishment of specialised war crimes chambers and prosecutor's offices, some of the previous problems have been overcome (Fischer, 2013b, p. 76). Nevertheless, with regard to their legitimacy the courts show similar

7 For an overview of the development of the judiciary in BiH, see Ivanišević, 2008; Mission to BiH, 2005; United Nations Development Programme, 2008.

8 For an overview of developments in Croatia, see Mission to Croatia, 2003; 2005.

9 For an overview of developments in Serbia, see Ivanišević, 2007; Organisation for Security and Cooperation in Europe mission to Serbia and Montenegro, 2003.

defects as the ICTY (Organisation for Security and Cooperation in Europe Mission to Serbia et al., 2009). Opinion polls have shown that those who disagree with the decisions and practice of the ICTY assume that the domestic courts are also biased (Organisation for Security and Cooperation in Europe Mission to Serbia, 2009; Fischer, 2013b). In some cases, policymakers also openly questioned the legitimacy of national institutions for war crimes prosecution. In BiH in particular, the Court of BiH suffered from a major lack of acceptance and support from the political leadership in the Republika Srpska (RS), which has presented an increasing challenge for the national BiH authorities and for policy making by the High Representative since 2007. The RS government, led by Prime Minister Milorad Dodik, has discredited this court and challenged its legitimacy, calling into question its authority to prosecute war crimes and economic crimes (corruption) falling within its jurisdiction.

Civil society experts acknowledge that there have been improvements in the practice of the domestic courts and some progress on sentencing in important war crimes cases (i.e. Ovčara[10] and Scorpions,[11] Glavaš,[12] Norac/Ademi[13]). However, compared with international representatives and representatives of transitional justice institutions, they express less confidence in these institutions (Petrović-Ziemer, 2013a) and still assume that there is a high degree of ethnopolitical bias and politicisation on the part of the domestic judiciary. Slowness of the trials and a lack of witness protection are the shortcomings most frequently mentioned in all three countries. Nevertheless, the field research conducted in 2010–2012[14] revealed that local human rights organisations and international actors all had a

10 At Ovčara near Vukovar in Eastern Slavonia, more than 200 men, mostly Croatians, were killed by Serbian forces in November 1991. In 2009, the District Court of Belgrade convicted 13 individuals responsible for the massacre and sentenced them to a total of 193 years. They were members of the Territorial Defence of Vukovar, part of the Yugoslav armed forces and members of the Leva Supoderica volunteer corps. See www.hlc-rdc.org/images/stories/pdf/sudjenje_za_ratne_zlocine/srbija/Miroljub_Vujovic_i_dr/Presuda-Ovcara-12_03_2009.pdf.

11 A Serbian paramilitary unit known as the Scorpions took part in the genocide at Srebrenica. In April 2007, four members were found guilty of the execution of six men and boys and sentenced by the Supreme Court of Serbia to a total of 58 years.
See www.hlc-rdc.org/images/stories/pdf/sudjenje_za_ratne_zlocine/srbija/Skorpioni%20Sl%20Medic/Skorpioni%20-20Presuda%20Vrhovnog%20suda%20Srbije%20-%2013.06.2008.pdf.

12 Branimir Glavaš was responsible for the defence of Osijek during the war in Eastern Slavonia. In May 2009, the County Court of Zagreb found him guilty of the torture and murder of Serb civilians. He was sentenced to eight years in prison; see www.centar-zamir.hr/index.php?page=article_sudjenja&trialId=50&article_id=48&lang=hr.

13 Mirko Norac was a former general in the Croatian army. Rahim Ademi was the former commander of the Gospić military district in Croatia. Both were indicted by the ICTY for crimes against humanity and violations of the laws and customs of war in south Croatia against Serb civilians in 1993. See www.icty.org/x/cases/ademi/ind/en/ade-ci040730e.htm. In 2005, the ICTY transferred the case to the County Court in Zagreb Organisation for Security and Cooperation in Europe. The trial at the County Court brought an acquittal for Ademi and a seven-year term of imprisonment for Norac. See www.centar-za-mir.hr/uploads/PRESUDA_Ademi_i_Norac.pdf.

14 The field research was related to the project 'Dealing with the Past and Peacebuilding in the Western Balkans'; for a project description, see footnote 2.

strong preference for legal accountability and further development of the capacities of the legal institutions. Most of the policy makers from the region who were interviewed also agreed that prosecution is necessary, although some of them clearly based this support on the argument that crimes had been committed on all sides and that only individuals and not collectives should be held responsible (Dvornik, 2013; Sejfija, 2013; Milićević, 2013). International actors emphasised that in Croatia in particular, considerable progress is needed on accountability, especially with regard to the events during and after Operation Storm, the military operation led by the Croatian army on the territory of the Krajina, at that time (1995) occupied by Yugoslav forces.[15] International monitoring agencies criticised the fact that until 2012, not a single member of the Croatian army was convicted for war crimes during and after Operation Storm, and although 33 trials were pending for the murder of civilians, they had not been taken up by the state attorney (Fischer, 2013b, p. 75). It was argued that the 'ultimate indication that Croatia is dealing seriously with its past will be the willingness to consider the 33 cases of murder and convert them into war crimes trials. Furthermore, the judiciary will have to find out what happened to the 677 civilians [killed in the aftermath of the military operation]. This is of particular importance because the ICTY will not pursue any other case in the context of Operation Storm' (Fischer, 2013b, p. 76).

2.2 Efforts to trace missing persons and fact-finding commissions

In the first years after the war(s), government activities to establish the fate of missing persons were organised either at a national level or, in the case of Bosnia, at entity level. In Bosnia, a Missing Persons Institute (MPI) was created in 2000 with international assistance, in response to an initiative launched by the OHR for a joint exhumation process that permitted the three former warring parties to conduct exhumations relevant to their own missing persons on the 'opposing side's' territory.[16] The International Commission on Missing Persons (ICMP)[17] was tasked to facilitate cooperation between the respective entity authorities, and in 2005 the Council of Ministers of BiH took on the role of co-founder of the MPI. Through the ICMP, cooperation was also enhanced on a regional level with

15 Figures relating to these events are highly contested. While human rights NGOs refer to 677 persons killed in the aftermath of the military operation, the state attorney argued that there were only 114 victims after 1995 and only recently accepted the number of 677 (Fischer 2013b, p. 75).

16 See www.ic-mp.org/icmp-worldwide/southeast-europe/bosnia-and-herzegovina.

17 The ICMP was established at the initiative of US President Clinton in 1996 to support the Dayton Peace Agreement. It has its headquarters in Sarajevo. Its primary role is to ensure the cooperation of governments in locating and identifying those who disappeared during armed conflict or as a result of human rights violations. Today, the ICMP is actively involved in assisting governments and other institutions around the world to address the issue of missing persons from armed conflict, human rights abuses, disasters and organised crime.

the establishment of the Commission for Missing Persons of the then Federal Republic of Yugoslavia and the Office for Detained or Missing Persons in Croatia. In January 2012, the EU decided that it would continue funding exhumation activities in the Western Balkans.[18]

Some regional cooperation among the institutions responsible for tracing the missing has developed, so some progress has been made in this area (Petrović-Ziemer, 2013a). Investigations, exhumations and identification of the missing could also count on continuous material and practical support from international organisations and bilateral donors from abroad. Thanks to these joint efforts, of the 40,000 persons missing as a result of the armed conflicts of the 1990s in the former Yugoslavia, over 70% have been accounted for, according to the figures presented by the Organisation for Security and Cooperation in Europe (OSCE) and the ICMP.[19] Facilitated by the OSCE and the ICMP, the Chairman of the Presidency of Bosnia-Herzegovina Bakir Izetbegović, the President of the Republic of Croatia Ivo Josipović, the President of Montenegro Filip Vujanović and the President of the Republic of Serbia Tomislav Nikolić signed a 'Declaration on the Role of the State in Addressing the Issue of Persons Missing as a Consequence of Armed Conflict and Human Rights Abuses' in Mostar on 29 August 2014.[20] The Declaration defines the role of states in accounting for the missing from conflict and human rights abuses. It highlights the primary responsibility of state authorities in addressing the issue of the missing and the need to ensure that mechanisms and methods employed conform to human rights standards and rule of law principles. In addition, it seeks to ensure that the rights of family members of the missing are upheld, and that survivors and civil society alike have access to information regarding the fate of their relatives and to a proper investigation, as well as to truth and justice. The Declaration seeks to ensure that past wrongs are addressed through accountable and just state institutions.[21]

Apart from allowing the establishment of legal bodies and tracing the missing, governments and parliaments have not been especially proactive in supporting further fact finding. Initiatives to set up commissions at a national level have been either half-hearted or lacking in political support. In 2001, in the then Federal Republic of Yugoslavia, President Vojislav Koštunica established a State Commission for Truth and Reconciliation as a top-down initiative. However, some of the designated members had such serious objections to the Commission's remit

18 See www.ic-mp.org/press-releases/eu-and-icmp-donation-agreement/#more-1493.

19 See www.ic-mp.org/icmp-worldwide/southeast-europe/bosnia-and-herzegovina.

20 See www.ic-mp.org/press-releases/bosnia-and-herzegovina-croatia-montenegro-and-serbia-sign-icmps-declaration-on-missing-persons/

21 ibid. The ICMP and OSCE have emphasised that the Declaration, whose first signatories include countries and successor states that signed the Dayton Peace Agreement in 1995, is seen as a precedent international instrument. The ICMP is keen to encourage other governments in the Western Balkans and other parts of the world (e.g. Argentina, Chile, South Africa and many others confronted with the issue of missing persons) to sign the Declaration.

and responsibilities that they refused to participate. The Commission was abolished in 2003, before it had held a single public hearing (Dimitrijević, 2008, p. 18).

In Bosnia-Herzegovina, two limited official initiatives have been undertaken with the investigations into the massacre in Srebrenica (Ivanišević, 2008, p. 38) and human rights abuses in Sarajevo.[22] In reaction to an initiative by families of victims, who brought an action against Republika Srpska before the Human Rights Court in Bosnia, a commission was established in 2003 to investigate the events in Srebrenica from 10–19 July 1995. The court awarded compensation to victims' relatives and ordered the RS authorities to pay around €1.8 million to the Foundation of Srebrenica Potočari, which built a memorial to the victims and a cemetery. The court also ordered the Bosnian Serb authorities to disclose all information in their possession about Srebrenica and to conduct a detailed investigation into the massacre.[23] A report was presented in 2005 in which the RS government finally acknowledged that more than 7,000 persons had been killed (correcting the figure of less than 2,000 presented up to that point). By contrast, the Sarajevo Commission never presented any results. A proposal to set up a truth and reconciliation commission at state level (Kritz & Finci, 2001), made by a Citizens' Association for Truth and Reconciliation with support from the US Institute of Peace, was rejected by parliamentarians from different sides (and also lacked support from victims' organisations).[24]

2.3 Initiatives to establish national strategies for transitional justice

Facilitated by international organisations (in particular the OSCE and United Nations Development Programme, UNDP), various initiatives were launched by parliaments and governments to advance more inclusive transitional justice processes. Both in Croatia and Serbia, journalists and CSO experts were involved in war crimes monitoring and reporting. In Bosnia, the Council of Ministers of BiH agreed a Transitional Justice Strategy in 2008 and is cooperating on its implementation with legal institutions, parliamentarians, journalists and experts from civil society. In both 2008 and 2009, consultations were held in Fojnica, Brčko and Mostar, to enhance dialogue on Transitional Justice issues together with victims' and veterans' organisations, women's groups, youth organisations, peace and human rights NGOs, and representatives of academic institutions and faith communities. As a result of participants' recommendations, the Council of Ministers

22 See Mirna Buljugić, 'No Progress for Sarajevo Truth Commission', www.bim.ba/en/51/10/2327/ (accessed 31 August 2012).

23 See http://newsvote.bbc.co.uk/mpapps/pagetools/print/news.bbc.co.uk/2/hi/europe/2828173.stm.

24 It was spearheaded by Jacob Finci from 1997 onwards, and backed by a coalition of the Forum of Tuzla Citizens, the Citizens' Alternative Parliament, Circle 99 and the Helsinki Committees for Human Rights from Sarajevo and Bijeljina; for details, see Hatschikjan, 2005.

issued a decision on forming an Expert Work Group responsible for drafting a Transitional Justice Strategy in BiH and an Action Plan for its implementation. Three pillars were defined: (1) verifying facts, (2) reparations and memorials, and (3) institutional reforms.[25] The initiative is an element of a broader project for a joint strategy for Supporting National Capacities in Transitional Justice Processes in BiH. In June 2009, the Ministry of Justice, the Ministry for Human Rights and Refugees and the United Nations Development Programme (UNDP) had agreed a document entitled 'Access to Justice: Facing the Past and Confidence Building for the Future'[26] in order to systematically address outstanding challenges, with a focus on increasing legal awareness, enhancing the system of free legal aid, and strengthening communication capacity in the judicial system, in cooperation with civil society organisations. Representatives of the Parliament of BiH, together with CSO activists and media experts, have undertaken fact-finding visits, such as study tours to memorial sites and museums addressing the Second World War and the Holocaust in Berlin, Germany, to discuss dealing with the past approaches. Although some progress has been made in setting up transitional justice institutions, the most important challenge is still to define who is officially accepted as a 'victim' and who deserves material compensation for war-related loss of property, health and economic prospects. Although some legislation has been developed for the compensation of former combatants who were injured or disabled by the war, there is still a lack of compensation schemes for civilian victims. Many victims (e.g. survivors of rape; see the chapter by Olivera Simić in this volume) have never received substantial support from state institutions.[27]

2.4 Official and 'unofficial' apologies: ambivalent policies by governments and parliaments

For almost two decades, the prevailing discourses in all three countries, not least in public statements by politicians and in the media, showed selective interpretations of the war events. While many politicians in Serbia regarded the conflicts of the early 1990s as a kind of civil war that caused suffering on all sides involved, politicians in Croatia largely took the view that their country was the victim of strategic aggression by Serbia; this position was also widely shared by Bosniak representatives in BiH (Subotić, 2009). As a consequence, the official politics of

25 For more details, see the *Transitional Justice Handbook for Bosnia and Herzegovina*, and the *Report on the Capacities of Courts and Prosecutor Offices* edited by UNDP (UNDP, 2009; UNDP, 2008).
26 See www.mpr.gov.ba/en/str.asp?id=397. See also UNDP, 2009.
27 This deficit was repeatedly mentioned by the former ICTY President Patrick Robinson. He suggested establishing a 'claims commission' in a speech before the UN Security Council in December 2009 (www.icty.org/sid/10280). In November 2011, he called upon UN Member States to support the establishment of a trust fund: 'The Tribunal cannot, through the rendering of its Judgements alone, bring peace and reconciliation to the region. Other remedies should complement the criminal trials if lasting peace is to be achieved, and one such remedy should be adequate assistance to the victims for their suffering.'

remembrance in all three countries has for a long time focused on the selective commemoration of war victims, each generally characterising its own 'constituency' as the main victim.[28] These discourses were largely determined by varying interpretations of the recent past, by experiences and narratives from the Second World War, or ancient myths (Popović, 2003).

Nevertheless, public apologies have been expressed by several governments, parliaments and political leaders in recent years, including moderate politicians from RS in Bosnia-Herzegovina, Serbia (or, until 2006, Serbia-Montenegro) and Croatia (Fischer, 2008; Horelt, 2011). In 2000, the Montenegrin President Milan Djukanović apologised for the shelling of Dubrovnik, in which troops from Montenegro were involved. From Croatia, a first step was taken by the Presidents of Croatia, Stjepan Mesić, and Serbia-Montenegro, Svetozar Marović, in September 2003, when they apologised for the actions of their citizens in the 1991–1995 war between the two countries. The apology was made during the Croatian President's first visit to Belgrade since the conflict that followed his country's declaration of independence from Yugoslavia.[29] Ivo Josipović, who became President of Croatia in 2010, followed this trend: he expressed regret for Croatian policy towards BiH during the 1990s and paid his respects to the victims of a massacre of Bosniak civilians in the village of Ahmići, committed by Croat forces in 1993.

After the ICTY had passed its verdicts in the case of Radislav Krstić, the wartime chief of staff of the Bosnian Serb army, finding him guilty of having participated in the genocide in Srebrenica,[30] the Bosnian Serb President Dragan Čavić publicly announced that there was a need to deal with the dark sides of his community's history, which was a first step in overcoming widespread denial. However, the Prime Minister of RS, Dragan Mikerević, made a statement that there was 'no collective responsibility of the Serbian people', although those individuals who had committed crimes should be held accountable (Horelt, 2011, p. 143). In November 2004, the RS government officially acknowledged the mass crime committed in Srebrenica for the first time and formally apologised in an official declaration, saying that the 'Bosnian Serb Government shares the pain of the families of Srebrenica victims, is truly sorry and apologises for the tragedy' (Associated Press, 11 November 2004). The question whether or not genocide took

28 See Kuljić, 2009; Ramet, 2007; Sajkas, 2007; Teršelić, 2008.

29 'As a president of Serbia-Montenegro, I want to apologise for all the evils any citizen of Serbia and Montenegro has committed against any citizen of Croatia' said Serbian President Svetozar Marović. Mesić apologised 'to all those who have suffered pain or damage at any time from citizens of Croatia who misused or acted against the law'. See http://news.bbc.co.uk/2/hi/europe/3095774.stm.

30 Krstić was Chief of Staff of the Drina Corps of the Army of Republika Srpska in July 1995. In 1998 he was indicted for war crimes related to Srebrenica. He became the first person to be convicted of genocide by the Tribunal and was sentenced to 46 years in prison. The sentence was subsequently shortened to 35 years by an appeal court, which upheld a lesser charge of aiding and abetting genocide.

place in Srebrenica remains a highly contested topic among Serb politicians. At the same time, the RS government announced that it would support prosecution of all those who had committed these crimes. However, the declaration followed the official report commissioned as a consequence of international pressure (by the High Representative Paddy Ashdown). The effect of this declaration was limited; authorities in Srebrenica expressed a low level of satisfaction, pointing to the fact that the declaration was mainly a consequence of international pressure rather than the political will of the RS leadership (Horelt, 2011, p. 146).

A similar dynamic could be observed after the declarations made by the President of Serbia with regard to the massacre in Srebrenica. On his first visit to BiH in December 2004, Tadić apologised to all citizens of BiH against whom crimes had been committed in the name of the Serbian people. But he also made clear that he made this statement as a private citizen and not in his official role, and he declared that 'these crimes were not committed by the Serbian people, but by criminals, individuals. It is not possible to charge a whole people because the same crimes were also committed against the Serbian people, so in that sense we all owe one another an apology. If I have to start first, well, here I am'.[31] Again, the reactions from the representatives of the Bosniak community were not very enthusiastic. Although the Bosniak Representative in the Presidency welcomed the apology, other political leaders were either sceptical or critical (Horelt, 2011). Bosniak politicians still seem very reluctant to apologise for crimes committed by Bosniak forces; this may be based in part on a discourse of Bosnia-Herzegovina being the main victim of the violence that marked the early 1990s.

Contradictory reactions also followed the declaration by the Parliament of Serbia on Srebrenica, which condemns the crime against Bosnian Muslims in Srebrenica but avoids the term genocide. In particular, the National Assembly of the Republic of Serbia stated that it 'most severely condemns the crime committed against the Bosnian population in Srebrenica in July 1995 (. . .) as well as the social and political processes (. . .) that led to the creation of awareness that realisation of personal national goals can be reached through the use of armed force and physical violence against members of other nations and religions, extending on the occasion condolences and apologies to the families of the victims that everything possible had not been done to prevent the tragedy'.[32] The declaration was adopted on 31 March 2010 and calls for all countries of the former Yugoslavia to adopt similar resolutions condemning crimes committed against Serbs during the war and to continue the process of reconciliation, based on the equality of nationalities and full respect for human and minority rights and freedoms. The declaration was a result of a very long process of negotiation within the political leadership and

31 See http://news.bbc.co.uk/2/hi/europe/4072949.stm.

32 Declaration of the National Assembly of the Republic of Serbia, 31 March, 2010. See www.parlament.gov.rs/upload/archive/files/eng/pdf/2010/deklaracija%20o%20srebrenici%20ENG.pdf.

Parliament of Serbia. A majority of 127 MPs (one more than the 126 required) voted in favour of the resolution. Representatives of the opposition Serbian Radical Party (SRS) and Liberal Democratic Party (LDP) did not vote; MPs from the opposition Democratic Party of Serbia (DSS), New Serbia (NS), and Serbian Progressive Party (SNS) voted against the resolution.[33] The Srebrenica declaration aroused a great deal of controversy, both in Serbia and Bosnia[34] and internationally.[35]

While international leaders (including the EU High Representative for Foreign Affairs, Catherine Ashton) welcomed it, the reactions in the Bosniak community, again, were mixed and not entirely positive. The prevailing arguments were that the declaration was a pragmatic gesture rather than an expression of genuine regret; victims' associations completely rejected it. Indeed, the declaration can be seen as ambivalent. The passive wording, characterising the crimes as the acts of individuals, not the outcome of policies undertaken by states or in the name of nations, again indicated a wish to evade political responsibility. Yet several politicians (including the Bosniak Representative in the Presidency of BiH, Bakir Izetbegović) recognised the 'stabilising effects' of the declaration.[36]

In sum, the public gestures mentioned so far in this chapter show that the official discourse is no longer marked by total denial. However, as most of the apologies were made by political representatives in their private capacity and not in an official role, motivated to a large extent by a desire to assign responsibility to individuals and avoiding any reference to genocide, there is clearly still a strong tendency to relativise the various sides' own involvement in the war by pointing to the involvement of others in acts of violence against their constituency. It is not surprising that the reparative effects on those addressed were quite limited, and reconciliatory effects almost entirely absent.

A new quality of gesture and a higher degree of reciprocity were observed with regard to the apologies made by the Serbian President in Croatia. In November 2010, Tadić apologised for the crimes committed in Ovčara, near Vukovar, and proposed 'reconciliation' – again highlighting the private and personal character of his apology and pointing out that there were missing persons and killings on both sides. The apologies were made during a joint visit, with symbolic gestures by the Serbian and Croatian Presidents Boris Tadić and Ivo Josipović. Both Presidents laid wreaths to honour Croat victims at a memorial in Ovčara. The two leaders

33 See www.b92.net/eng/news/politics-article.php?yyyy=2010&mm=03&dd=31&nav_id=66160.

34 For an analysis of the impact of the Srebrenica declaration on politics and society in the region, see Horelt, 2011, p. 147.

35 International reactions also varied. On the one hand, the declaration was regarded as a step in the right direction (see http://ictj.org/news/serbian-declaration-srebrenica-massacre-imperfect-important-step); on the other hand, it was criticised for failing to utilise the terminology of the International Court of Justice and the ICTY, both of which classed the killing of more than 7,000 civilians as genocide. See www.dw.de/dw/article/0,,5417176,00.html.

36 For a detailed analysis of the dynamics, see Horelt, 2011, pp. 146–147.

also visited a memorial to Serb civilians killed in the town of Paulin Dvor. Both towns were the scene of executions of prisoners and civilians during the war in 1991.[37] 'I am here to once again offer words of apology, to express regret and create a possibility for Serbs and Croats, Serbia and Croatia, to turn a new page of history,' said Tadić in Ovčara. Josipović expressed the belief that this event would help to boost the efforts to shed light on the fate of the missing persons and establish good-neighbourly relations, underscoring that a different policy, one of peace and friendship, was possible. In Paulin Dvor, Josipović said that the victims commemorated there 'deserve an apology'.[38]

Although Tadić's speech in Ovčara was very much in keeping with his previous statements, it was much more positively received than the statements he made in Bosnia. The Croatian government (in particular the then Prime Minster Jadranka Kosor) assessed it as a positive and significant moment in bilateral relations between Serbia and Croatia. It was reported that most Croatian politicians welcomed the Serbian President's visit to Vukovar and regarded it as an 'historic' event; only the far-right Croatian Party of Rights (HSP) organised protests.[39] This shows that the question of how gestures of apology are received and whether they are accepted or not depends on their wording and credibility, but also on the question of whether there is a political will for mutual rapprochement and normalisation of relations. Different from previous gestures, the joint visit by Tadić and Josipović was organised as a more symmetrical gesture. It was also well-received by the international media and the European Union, and it is likely that the international community was an important target group. It had a positive effect on the bilateral relations between Croatia and Serbia (Horelt, 2011, p. 149) and was interpreted as an important sign of hope and encouragement for local and international actors who are attempting to advance processes of transitional justice and reconciliation in the region; this was evident from the interviews conducted in 2010–2012 (Fischer & Petrović-Ziemer, 2013).

While some positive effects were reported in relations between Croatia and Serbia, the prospects for political reconciliation in BiH are less promising. The situation is much more complicated in this country, given that political and social life has not yet moved beyond the 'cold peace' (Ashdown 2004) that has marked the post-war period. No serious 'peace process' has been initiated so far, the political situation is still strongly polarised, and substantial initiatives for

37 In Ovčara near Vukovar, 261 Croat prisoners of war and civilians were shot and buried in a mass grave. 15 persons were found guilty of this atrocity and received a total of 207 years in prison in trials conducted in Serbia and at the Hague Tribunal. In Paulin Dvor near Osijek, Croat forces murdered 18 Serb civilians (see B92, Tanjug, www.b92.net/eng/news/politics-article.php?yyyy=2010&mm=11&dd=04&nav_id=70684).

38 For the full statement, see www.b92.net/eng/news/politics-article.php?yyyy=2010&mm=11&dd=04&nav_id=70684.

39 B92, Tanjug; see www.b92.net/eng/news/politics-article.php?yyyy=2010&mm=11&dd=04&nav_id=70684.

transforming the conflicts in this country are not in sight. Due to the absence of a broader political will for rapprochement and mutual understanding, it seems unlikely at present that policies of apology for war crimes will be developed at a national state level, as cultures of remembrance are still strongly based on separation, commemorating victims belonging to the 'own' constituency and excluding or ignoring those who belong to the 'other' side. The question of who has suffered most and who is most guilty continues to dominate the public discourse. Bosniak politicians often claim a role for Bosniaks as the exclusive victims, pointing to the asymmetry of suffering (i.e. the total of numbers of war victims), while RS representatives have constructed the narrative of the victimhood of Serbs who had to defend themselves against 'Muslim' attacks, and continue to deny that what happened in Srebrenica was genocide. Bosnian Croat politicians also show an ongoing tendency to cultivate their version of a defensive war and to relativise crimes committed in their names as excesses and exceptions for which individuals, not collectives, should be held responsible.

Against this background, it is remarkable, to say the least, and should be mentioned here, that at the time of writing this chapter, the President of RS, Milorad Dodik, had visited the Potočari Memorial Centre to lay flowers and pay respect to the victims of Srebrenica.[40] This gesture, again, might clearly be addressed to the international community as a massive international presence, including figures such as former US President Bill Clinton and Turkey's President Recep Tayyip Erdogan, is expected at the commemoration events in July 2015. Dodik's gesture prompted mixed reactions from politicians in BiH, ranging from positive remarks (e.g. from the mayor of Srebrenica, Camil Duraković, who welcomed Dodik's decision[41]) to harsh criticism (from the Vice-President of the RS National Assembly, Ramiz Salkić, who accused Dodik of hypocrisy

40 'It is true that a crime happened here and I am sorry for all the victims, but the fact is that this event is also being politicised a lot', Dodik said in Srebrenica on 17 April 2015 (see Jukić, 2015). Assessments of this gesture and its impact are difficult at this stage. Two problems should be mentioned: First, that Dodik's statement, apart from acknowledging the victims, encompasses a 'but'. Second, that the visit took place in a situation where polarisation is fostered by symbolic politics. On 17 April 2015 the RS National Assembly adopted a declaration warning that the state constitutional court has no right to rule on an appeal about the constitutionality of RS's official holiday (January 9, the date when Bosnian Serbs had declared an independent Serb state in Bosnia in 1992); two years ago, Bakir Izetbegović, leader of the influential Bosniak Party of Democratic Action, appealed to the court, arguing that this holiday, celebrated only by Serbs, is offensive to other ethnic groups. Both the ruling and opposition parties in RS have announced that they are not willing to implement any ruling in favour of Izetbegovic's appeal. International officials and observers warned that this would represent a dangerous challenge to the constitutional court's independence and see BiH entering another escalation of conflict and political tension (Panić, 2015).

41 'For me, this is a historical act, a positive visit which will significantly ease relations between the municipality of Srebrenica and the government as well as the entity of Republika Srpska', Duraković said; he also welcomed the RS government's offer to contribute €25,000 for the celebrations planned to mark the 20th anniversary of the Srebrenica massacres, which has never happened in previous years (see Jukić, 2015. p. 1).

as he still refuses to call the massacre in Srebrenica genocide).[42] The visit of the Prime Minister of Serbia at this place in July 2015 provoked similar reactions (see chapter 11).

However, whether apologies and gestures of acknowledgement can contribute to reconciliation depends very much on whether they are accompanied by policies that support fact-finding and additional acts of reparations for those who are suffering from the legacies of the war(s) and war crimes. Such policies are not in place at present, which means that most of the gestures mentioned above remain largely symbolic and do not provide strong incentives for a more fundamental process of conflict transformation within and among the societies in the region. The fact is that in many places policies of memorialisation still tend to emphasise the victimhood of the 'own' constituency, and there are still very few examples of acts of commemoration that include acknowledgement of the victims of the 'other side'; the same applies to discussions of reparations, which are often based on ethnically exclusive patterns (Banjeglav, 2013, p. 47). Finally, the prospects for reconciliation also depend on how these issues are discussed in wider society. Nevertheless, public apologies are still accompanied by very emotional debates and controversy in the respective societies. In order to create impetus for reconciliation, top-down and bottom-up initiatives must be mutually reinforcing. In this context, civil society actors have a crucial role to play.

3. Civil society engagement: fighting impunity and promoting restorative approaches to justice and truth recovery

In Bosnia, Serbia and Croatia, several CSOs have been working hard to counter the distortion of facts or biased politics of remembrance. They are involved in a range of activities.[43] They focus on fact-finding, human rights and victims' advocacy, and dealing with traumatised persons. Some of them have been working closely with the Hague Tribunal and national war crimes chambers, monitoring trials and providing legal, psychosocial or political advice for witnesses and victims. Their work includes collecting information and documenting facts about war victims, and supporting families who are searching for missing persons. Others focus on promoting inclusive cultures of remembrance, marking places of atrocities, and facilitating dialogue. Various cross-border initiatives have also been

42 Salkić (member of the Party of Democratic Action, SDA), criticised in particular that Dodik, on the one hand, denied that genocide took place in Srebrenica and on the other hand had recently proposed to the RS Assembly a declaration about the genocide of Armenians under the Ottoman Empire (Jukić, 2015, p. 1).

43 For an overview of CSOs' activities in the field of dealing with the past, see Fischer, 2011a; Rill & Franović, 2005; Franović, 2008; Rill, Smidling & Bitoljanu, 2007; Rangelov & Theros, 2009; Belloni & Hemmer, 2010; Balkan Civil Society Development Network, 2012; Rosandić et al., 2005.

launched, focusing on truth recovery, trust-building across borders or in local communities, and creating empathy for different narratives.

3.1 Human rights groups and victims engaged in fact-finding and prosecution of war crimes

CSO activities aim to complement fact finding and dismantle discourses marked by denial. In 2005, for instance, a video uncovered by the Humanitarian Law Center (Belgrade) provided evidence of the killing of several Bosniaks by members of a special police unit (Scorpions) under Slobodan Milošević's command. This revealed that the crimes around Srebrenica were not committed solely by Bosnian Serb militias but that forces from Yugoslavia were actively involved. The video was presented in evidence at the Hague Tribunal and was broadcast by all public TV stations in Bosnia. It was also shown in Serbia-Montenegro, triggering considerable public debate in both countries (Kandić, 2008, p. 64).

Another example is the Population Loss Project set up by the Research and Documentation Centre (IDC) in Sarajevo. The centre corrected the figures of an estimated 200,000 and 250,000 Bosnians killed, which were generally cited by official sources (Pupavac, 1997), and finally presented a total of 97,920 war-related deaths for which data have been verified and recorded (Tokača, 2008, p. 60). Data were collected and presented on the internet. The project has since become well-known as the 'Bosnian Book of Dead' (BBD database).[44] Although the initiative faced harsh criticism (especially from nationalistic Bosniak politicians) from the outset, it had an impact on the discourse, and most official institutions finally accepted the new figures.

In sum, CSOs have substantially supported fact finding and by doing so, have complemented the work of the ICTY and the domestic courts in establishing accountability. They have also supported the work of the courts in other ways, not least by systematically monitoring trials and reporting (together with investigative journalists and independent media experts, e.g. the Balkan Investigative Reporting Network). In some instances, they also played a key role in explaining the courts' verdicts to the public and correcting distorted media reports on the courts' activities.[45]

Women's groups have focused on gender aspects of transitional justice (Vušković & Trifunović, 2008). In BiH in particular, the fate of women who suffered rape and torture during the war was ignored and silenced by taboos. It was only after the

44 For an analysis of the methodology and impact, see Nettelfield, 2011.

45 This was particularly the case in Croatia in 2011 when the ICTY found the Croatian General Ante Gotovina guilty of having been involved in Operation Storm in 1995, which was described as a 'joint criminal enterprise' aimed at the expulsion of Serb citizens from Croatia. This verdict was misinterpreted by diverse news media, which implied that the ICTY's verdict had condemned Croatia's acts in the 1990s war in general, giving many people the impression that it was blamed as a nation and collective.

launch of the film 'Grbavica'[46] (which was awarded a Golden Bear at the 2006 Berlin Film Festival) that the Bosnian Parliament formally acknowledged raped women as 'war victims' or 'war invalids' and decided that they should receive compensation, similar to that payable to the men who fought in the war. The war shows how war-related trauma affects people's lives and how social taboos prolong their suffering and obstruct a constructive approach. After it was premiered in BiH, more than 100,000 people went to see the film. It was accompanied by a campaign by local and international NGOs which advocate for the rights of women and survivors of sexual violence.[47] The decision by the Bosnian Parliament that raped women should be recognised as war victims and receive compensation similar to that paid to ex-combatants was welcomed by human rights and women's organisations, although it should be added that many victims have gone away empty-handed or are still fighting for compensation.[48]

Women's groups have also pointed to the need to deal with the gender aspects of the 1990s wars and crimes committed during these wars (Sieber-Egger, 2011). Furthermore, in all three countries, a small number of activists from the lesbian, gay, bi- and transsexual (LGBT) movement also engaged for dealing with the past, pointing to the problematic impact of war-related identities based on militarised masculinity and their negative effect on today's human rights situation, which is marked by societal repression of sexual (and other) minorities.[49]

Furthermore, victims' groups, together with human rights activists, are engaged in searching for missing persons and empowering relatives. In BiH in particular, several associations of victims, detainees, displaced persons and relatives of missing persons contributed to fact finding after the 1992–1995 war (Gentile, 2008). Many of them support civilian war victims in their struggle for legal regulation of their rights of return, property restitution or compensation. Some of these organisations also provide psychosocial support for victims who decide to speak out as witnesses in war crimes trials. Victims' groups are influential in shaping discourses on dealing with the past. At the same time, they are often at risk of being manipulated for political purposes and ethno-nationalist discourses. However, several victims' associations and the different (Serb, Bosniak and Croat) constituencies have also

46 The film by Jasmila Žbanić tackles the relationship between a Bosniak woman who was raped during the war and her teenage daughter. Both are trying to cope with the past in post-war Sarajevo. The film outlines the individual trauma and existing taboos in society.

47 Under pressure from politicians, the screening was boycotted in Bosnia's Serb entity, Republika Srpska.

48 NGOs collected 50,000 signatures and campaigned for the official recognition of raped women and improvements in their situation. The NGO Medica Mondiale played an important role in this context. Draft legislation tabled in Parliament finally granted women an entitlement to compensation amounting to 50% of the payments made to men with war-related disabilities. Under pressure from the NGO campaign and the public, the decision was reviewed and women were granted a larger amount, similar to the figure paid to male ex-combatants (Baumann & Müller, 2006).

49 Examples are the Queeria Center in Belgrade and the Sarajevo Open Center; see www.queeria centar.org/index.php?option=com_content&view=article&id=8&Itemid=5; http://soc.ba/en/.

begun to overcome ethnic barriers and taken cautious steps towards cooperation; women's groups were the first to make efforts in this respect. The same applies to veterans' unions, which advocate for the rights of ex-combatants. Both victims' and veterans' groups also regularly participate in public commemorations.

3.2 The ambivalent roles of war veterans' groups

Veterans' unions engage as service-providing agencies and lobby organisations; they aim to improve their members' social and legal status. War veterans deal with the legacy of the conflict on a constant basis. Many of them inflicted violence during the war but are at the same time personally affected by violence (as war disabled, former prisoners of war or camp inmates, or displaced persons). Veterans' associations – with very limited funds – also try to assist families to trace missing soldiers, and provide social or legal care for those who were detained in war-time prisons or camps (Petrović-Ziemer, 2013b). Apart from their humanitarian activities, veterans groups are regularly involved in public commemorations of war events and some of them are eager to influence discourses and policies related to transitional justice (Schäuble, 2006; Schäuble, 2009; Pavlaković, 2010). In the past two decades, veterans often raised their voices in reaction to verdicts or decisions taken by the ICTY or domestic war crimes chambers, and were able to mobilise their membership in powerful demonstrations against transitional justice policies and reconciliation initiatives. Experience from the Balkans has shown that veterans can be both spoilers[50] and active supporters of peace building and reconciliation activities.

Protests were reported from the streets of Zagreb, Split and other cities in Croatia as a consequence of the first instance judgment of the ICTY against the Croatian commanders Ante Gotovina and Mladen Markač in April 2011.[51] Veterans were also vociferous during the celebrations held in November 2012 when the ICTY's Appeals Chamber finally decided to revise the first instance verdict and released both officers. Croatian ex-combatants also strongly opposed political initiatives for inter-communal reconciliation in Vukovar.[52] In February 2013, veterans' unions organised public protests against the government's decision to introduce Serbian (Cyrillic) script alongside Croatian after a census showed that nearly 35% of the inhabitants of Vukovar are Serbs.[53] Veterans' associations

50 On the debate on spoilers in peace building processes, see Stedman, 1997; Newman & Richmond, 2000; Greenhill & Major, 2003.

51 The indictment held both men responsible for targeting the Serb civilian population during Operation Storm in the Krajina region in 1995. For the significance of Gotovina as a political symbol in Croatia, see Pavlaković, 2010.

52 Vukovar (in the district of Eastern Slavonia on the border with Serbia) became a symbol of resistance for many Croatian fighters after it was destroyed by Serbian paramilitaries in 1991.

53 Croatia's law on minority rights states that a minority has the right to the official use of its script and language in areas where it makes up more than one-third of the population; ibid.

brought a suit against the minority rights law at the constitutional court. They organised a rally in which 20,000 of their members participated with slogans such as: 'Cyrillic never in Vukovar!', 'We died for Vukovar, Politicians Have Betrayed Us', 'Victory in War, Defeat in Peace', and 'Prime Minister, don't provoke the defenders of Vukovar!'[54]

In October 2014, veterans staged public protests in Zagreb, demanding improvements in their social and legal status. Led by the 'Association of 100 Percent Disabled War Veterans', around 1,000 veterans held demonstrations and established a protest camp and sit-ins in front of the Veterans Ministry, pushing for the dismissal of the Veterans Minister and a new constitutional law enshrining their rights. The protests were supported by the opposition Croatian Democratic Union (HDZ) and lasted for several weeks. Veterans also verbally attacked human rights activists for compiling a register of civilian war victims, to be used by the authorities. The leader of the protests, Đuri Glogoški, criticised the fact that the list might include 'individuals who participated in the aggression against Croatia', enabling them to receive the same reparations as Croatian victims. He also complained that the 'Law on Victims of Sexual Violence in the Homeland War' did not name the Yugoslav and Serbian armed forces as the aggressors.[55] Furthermore, the assistant of the Veterans Minister was attacked for saying that Serbian soldiers and civilians could also be suffering from Post-Traumatic Stress Disorder (PTSD) after the 1990s war. Campaigning veterans insisted that: 'We cannot allow ourselves to be compared with those who were involved in the aggression towards Croatia and who murdered and raped.'[56]

In Serbia and in RS in Bosnia, protesting and flag-waving war veterans could be seen when Radovan Karadžić (former 'president' of the self-proclaimed Bosnian Serb Republic) was arrested in 2008[57] and when the ex-commanders Ratko Mladić and Goran Hadžić were delivered to The Hague in July 2011. Both were celebrated as heroes (in a war in which Serbs had to 'defend' their people against Muslim dominance) by some ex-fighters' groups in Serbia and in RS.[58] Veterans' groups from BiH have also frequently been involved in public protests against decisions of the war crimes courts over the past two decades (Fisher, 2003, p. 84; Bojicić-Dželilović, 2006). They have also held public demonstrations for higher pensions and compensation. Since 2010, veterans have regularly held rallies in Sarajevo against the government's decision to cut the state benefits promised to ex-combatants in 2006. Several of the protests (for instance in March 2013) ended in clashes with police.

54 ibid. See also http://inavukic.com/2013/02/03/croatia-no-cyrillic-in-voukovar-thank-you/.
55 Balkan Insight, 6.11.14; www.balkaninsight.com/en/article/protesters-not-backing-up-explaining-their-demands-1.
56 Balkan Insight, 27.10.14; www.balkaninsight.com/en/article/protesting-croatian-war-veterans-not-giving-up.
57 See www.reuters.com/assets/print?aid=USL633267720080726.
58 See www.balkaninsight.com/en/article/bosnian-serbs-ready-major-rally-in-support-of-mladic.

In BiH in particular, some war veterans' organisations have 'slowed down the postwar transition by preserving the status quo and refusing to help the peace implementation process', according to assessments by the International Centre for Transitional Justice (Moratti & Sabić-El-Rayess, 2009, p. 30). Several of these associations have advocated against the return of displaced persons and refugees who belong to ethnic minorities, and opposed the strengthening of state institutions. However, not all of the public actions led by veterans were driven by nationalist attitudes. Surprisingly, in BiH in 2012, veterans' groups engaged in a rather unusual demonstration of solidarity when around 1,200 retired ex-soldiers in the Bosniak-Croat Federation of BiH decided to donate a percentage of their pensions to provide 300 veterans in RS with a monthly income, helping those from the 'other side' who were formerly regarded as enemies.[59] In addition, several representatives from veterans' groups in BiH decided to speak out about their experiences of the war and to enter a dialogue with former enemies. They also began to launch practical initiatives for inclusive cultures of remembrance, visiting atrocity sites and paying their respects to the victims from different sides (see Centre for Nonviolent Action, 2002; Fischer, 2007b).

In November 2012, a mixed group of veterans who had fought on different sides in the Bosnian war decided to pay their respects to the victims of Srebrenica. The ex-fighters visited Srebrenica on 17 November 2012 and laid flowers at the Potočari Memorial Centre, dedicated to the 8,000 Bosniak men who were massacred in Srebrenica in 1995.[60] The motives expressed by these veterans were:[61] the wish to 'raise awareness of the tragedy of war'; 'to prevent this from happening again'; 'to construct something better for future generations'; and to 'build peace and remember the recent past, but not forget the time after 1945 either'. Some of the ex-soldiers also mentioned the need for 'trust-building' and for 'bridging the divide in local communities.' They expressed the wish 'to establish dialogue between former enemies' and to 'question the rhetoric that we were victims and we were forced to participate in the war'. Several of the ex-combatants involved were representatives of war veterans' associations that are operating in local communities and started to visit atrocity sites in BiH on a regular basis, approaching local authorities and connecting to other veterans' groups in local communities. The group was empowered by the Centre for Nonviolent Action,[62]

59 See www.ctvnews.ca/bosnian-bailout-war-vets-send-cash-to-former-foes-1.761455.

60 See www.washingtonpost.com/world/europe/balkan-war-veterans-from-opposite-sides-pay-respect-to-bosnias-srebrenica-massacre-victims/2012/11/17/47d9fc26-30b1-11e2-af17-67abba0676e2_story.html. See http://nenasilje.org/en/2012/former-enemies-visit-srebrenica-memorial/.

61 See Fischer & Schroer-Hippel, 2013: statements by Avdija Banda, p. 15; Muhamed Azabagič, p. 17; Ivo Anđelovič, p. 16; Ibrahim Topič, p. 18; Novica Kostić, p. 18.

62 For an overview of CNA's cooperation with war veterans see Fischer, 2007b; Centre for Nonviolent Action, 2002; Wils, 2004; Franović, 2015. For an overview of CNA's general activities in the field of dealing with the past and nonviolent action, see Rill & Franović, 2005; Rill et al., 2007; see also the documentations of veterans' visits to atrocity sites online at www.nenasilje.org.

a group of cross-border peace activists based in Sarajevo and Belgrade. Further peacebuilding activities have been developed by the Center for Trauma in Novi Sad (Serbia) and war veterans, aimed at dialogue with youth on the past and peace education in schools (Simić & Milojević, 2014). Veterans have also been involved in cultural initiatives: the group 'Hajde da . . .' from Belgrade, for example, brought ex-combatants onto the stage in a theatre production (*Tanatos*) to share their combat-related experiences with a broader audience and open a space for a dialogue about the past, as Simić (2013) has shown.

The examples show that war veterans have both the potential to oppose or undermine and also to actively support initiatives aimed at reconciliation. Furthermore, the examples illustrate that transitional justice initiatives are a controversial issue in all three countries; the question of who is a victim and who is a perpetrator is highly contested and the discourse is based on collective attributions of guilt to 'Serbs', 'Croats' or 'Bosniaks/Muslims'. The reason is that ultimately, the wars of the early 1990s were *components of one overall scenario of conflict*: the dissolution of one single state (Yugoslavia) involved struggles between the successor states over sovereignty, with overlapping ethnopolitical communities in each of the three newly emerging states (e.g. Croats in Serbia and BiH, Serbs in Croatia and BiH, Muslims in Serbia and BiH), each with different claims relating to the location of borders and with different interests and levels of support for intervention by Croatia and Serbia in the violent conflict in Bosnia. This is the reason why many CSOs have come to the conclusion that reconciliation in the region needs to take place both within their respective societies and beyond, and that processes of dealing with the past need both local activities and cross-border approaches.

3.3 CSOs at a local and cross-border level: providing space for oral history and dialogue

Given that the 1990s war(s) had a regional dynamic, several peace and human rights organisations in BiH, Serbia and Croatia concluded that efforts for dealing with its legacies also had to consider the regional dimension. The Documenta Center (Zagreb), the Research and Documentation Centre (Sarajevo) and the Humanitarian Law Center (Belgrade) established cross-border co-operation on dealing with the past in 2004, aimed at documentation, training and awareness-raising. Several CSOs engage in facilitation of dialogues and exchange of narratives in oral history projects, both at a local and cross-border level. Examples are the Centre for Peace Studies (Zagreb), the Centre for Peace, Nonviolence and Human Rights (Osijek) and Miramida Centre (Groznjan), the Nansen Dialogue Centres (in Sarajevo, Banja Luka, Mostar and Osijek), and the youth group Odisej (Bratunac). Others advocate for peace education and alternative representations of history in schoolbooks or peace education (Dimou, 2009; Šebek, 2014). Some CSOs also focus on relationship building in divided communities or between people from different constituencies. One example of systematic cross-border engagement is the regional peace work of the Centre for Nonviolent Action (CNA) based in Sarajevo and Belgrade, which has developed training formats for non-violent conflict transformation, numerous dialogue and oral history projects across the borders, and pioneer initiatives focusing on the involvement of war veterans from different sides in peace activities (Fischer, 2007b; CNA, 2002). Initiatives for regional dialogue and reconciliation have also been supported by youth organisations, such as the Youth Initiative for Human Rights with teams in Novi Sad, Kragujevac, Niš and Sarajevo.

Religious and faith-based organisations have also provided incentives for regional dialogue and reconciliation (Brajović, 2007; Peuraca, 2003). They include the Inter-religious Council of Bosnia-Herzegovina, which was established by four religious leaders from the Catholic, Orthodox, Muslim and Jewish community in BiH in 2007. The leaders agreed on a Statement of Shared Moral Commitment, which was the first of its kind in the Balkans, opening windows of opportunity for rapprochement between the religious communities. The International Multireligious and Intercultural Centre and the Regional Address for Nonviolent Action in Croatia and BiH also engaged for inter-religious and cross-border dialogue.

However, all civil society organisations work under difficult conditions. Their work is tolerated by the governments and local authorities but is seldom actively encouraged and cannot count on material support. Although this work is extremely important, very few organisations are dedicated to transitional justice, reconciliation and peace building. Most activists continue to work in isolation and often risk being misunderstood by wider society (see also the chapter by Nikolić-Ristanović & Ćopić in this volume), or are the target of verbal attacks by nationalistic politicians. Most of these CSOs still depend on foreign funding for their activities. In the past decade, international donors have shifted their attention from the Balkans to other areas of crisis, creating a risk that the space for societal processes of dealing with the past in BiH, Croatia and Serbia will be narrowed.

3.4 The initiative for a regional truth commission ('RECOM-campaign')

In 2006, the Documenta Center (Zagreb), the Research and Documentation Centre (Sarajevo) and the Humanitarian Law Center (Belgrade) launched a campaign to establish a regional fact-finding mechanism for the countries of the former Yugoslavia. After a two-year consultation process (with regional forums held in Sarajevo, Zagreb, Belgrade and Priština), 108 local CSOs and 77 individuals from various countries signed an agreement in October 2008. The document stated that a Regional Commission for Truth-seeking and Truth-telling about War Crimes in the Former Yugoslavia (RECOM) should be established by the governments of Bosnia-Herzegovina, Croatia, Kosovo, Macedonia, Montenegro, Serbia and Slovenia, with the support of the United Nations and the European

Union.[63] It was argued that such a mechanism was needed to complement judicial proceedings, as 'at the current speed, courts in the region will be able to prosecute at most 1,200 war criminals by the end of 2020' and, therefore, 'an accurate overview of war crimes will not be provided, dignity to the victims will not be restored and trust between ethnic communities in the region cannot be built' (ibid.). Furthermore, it was argued that the various post-Yugoslav societies have 'different truths and historical accounts' and that 'denial of crimes perpetrated against others [and] acknowledgment of only one's own victims' still prevail (ibid.). A regional commission should counter this trend by establishing a record based on facts. The initiative established an internet forum, where victims' reports are published on a regular basis.

The initiative was organised in three phases. The first phase aimed to assess the needs of victims (or their organisations) and their expectations of a regional commission; in a second phase, participants were asked for suggestions on shaping the commission (in local, national and regional consultations); the third phase focused on drafting a statute (for a detailed analysis, see Kurze & Vukušić, 2013). Three years later, in March 2011, members of the coalition agreed a statute proposal for a 'Regional Commission for Establishing the Facts about War Crimes and other Gross Violations of Human Rights Committed on the Territory of the Former Yugoslavia in the period from 1991–2001'. One of the main objectives outlined in the RECOM Statute[64] is fact-finding about war crimes and other gross violations of human rights committed on the territory of the former Socialist Federal Republic of Yugoslavia (SFRY) in the period from 1991 until 2001, and clarifying the fate of the missing persons. Furthermore, it should help to acknowledge injustices inflicted upon victims, in order to help create a culture of compassion and solidarity, to contribute to the fulfilment of victims' rights, and to motivate the political elites and society in the region to accept the facts about war crimes and other gross violations of human rights. As an overarching aim, RECOM should help to prevent the recurrence of war crimes and other gross violations of human rights.

The coalition worked hard to gather signatures, which were to be delivered to the governments together with a request to pass a decree on the establishment of a commission. The initiative also gained the support of the Prime Ministers of Kosovo and Montenegro, the Presidents of Serbia and Croatia, 188 artists (in a joint letter), and a variety of international organisations such as the United Nations Development Programme (UNDP), the UN High Commissioner for Human Rights, the European Commission and European Parliament,[65] and the Council

63 Mission statement at www.webwiki.de/www.korekom.org.

64 Statute of REKOM (26 March 2011), Article 13; http://www.zarekom.org/Proposed-RECOM-Statute.en.html.

65 See www.europarl.europa.eu/sides/getDoc.do?pubRef=-//EP//NONSGML+MOTION+B7-2012-0188+0+DOC+PDF+V0//EN.

of Europe.[66] Although the coalition was marked by considerable fluctuation in the agencies involved, it has grown substantially.[67] At the time of writing, around 550,000 individuals have signed up in support of the initiative and 1,900 groups and individuals have become members of the coalition.[68]

As the RECOM campaign claimed to give a voice to the victims, there was considerable controversy among supporters concerning the question of who should be included in this category and what kind of policy towards victims would be appropriate. In RECOM's statute, it was stated that a regional truth commission should establish facts about human rights violations and war crimes and pay respect to all victims. However, several victims' organisations insisted that civilian victims should be the main focus, as war veterans across the region benefit from state pensions while civilian victims have largely been ignored. RECOM's membership includes more than 100 victims associations but only six veterans associations (including branches of the Association of Underage Volunteers of the Homeland War from Croatia, who do not receive support from the state) (Kurze & Vukušić, 2013, p. 211). As RECOM's strategy aimed to build bridges between different stakeholder groups, it did not adhere to the exclusive definition (victims = non-combatants) suggested by some victims' groups, such as the Mothers of Srebrenica (ibid.).

However, a number of human rights activists and victims' representatives are convinced that RECOM should also give a *voice to the victims* of war-related crimes. Nonetheless, the hearings held during the campaign have aroused controversy and are criticised by some of these actors (Petrivić-Ziemer, 2013a). In particular, the question of how to provide psychological support and protection for those who tell their stories in a public setting remains unresolved. The same applies to the question of how their testimonies can be verified and transformed into 'facts' that cannot be denied, so that they receive official acknowledgment.

Among peace practitioners and human rights activists, another strand of debate developed, based on the expectation that a regional commission would also enhance societal debate and dialogue on the past and help to establish an inclusive culture of remembrance. International promoters of the RECOM campaign also shared this expectation. Options expressed by the international supporters of a regional commission range from (a) establishing a shared view on the past, (b) providing a climate that enables people to accept that different views exist, (c) developing empathy for opposing narratives, and (d) providing a forum for alternative learning and debating of history.

However, some organisations have criticised the lack of transparency in RECOM's decision-making procedures, communication and invitation policies

66 See www.zarekom.org/news/index.7.en.html. However, it has also been reported that the UNDP and the EU are more reluctant to provide direct or financial support than the Council of Europe (see Kurze & Vukušić, 2013, p. 210).

67 For an analysis of the dynamic among the lead agencies from Croatia, Serbia and BiH, see Kurze & Vukušić, 2013, p. 207.

68 See www.zarekom.org.

(Petrović-Ziemer, 2013b). Although the RECOM initiative is supported by most of the Transitional Justice protagonists we interviewed in 2010–2012, they also express conflicting assessments of the *campaign* itself. Some criticism relates to the performance of the lead agencies and representatives. The most critical voices come from the group of CSOs interviewed, including both members and non-members of the RECOM coalition. Many of these interviewees perceived the process as highly conflictive. International actors shared this view. They observed that some of the leading personalities lacked the skills and sensitivity needed to deal with conflicts among different stakeholders (i.e. controversial positions and tensions among competing faith communities). There was also criticism of the formats chosen for the NGO consultations, which did not meet the standards of inclusivity (Petrović-Ziemer, 2013b). CSOs reported that, as a consequence of such deficits, several organisations that had co-initiated the campaign have left the coalition.

To sum up, Transitional Justice protagonists in all three countries pointed to a need to establish a set of undeniable facts relating to the recent war events, as a point of reference for a 'shared truth' and as a means to counteract denial of war-related crimes. Others argued that the societies in the region should also critically reflect on the misguided policies of the former Yugoslav regime, which paved the ground for a selective politics of remembrance by honouring partisans as heroes, silencing discussion of crimes committed in the Second World War and its aftermath, and largely ignoring the victims. Finally, many interviewees also suggested that earlier periods of history (World War II, and even before) must be considered. Furthermore, different opinions were expressed about the tasks, mandate and composition of a regional truth commission. The purpose of establishing dialogical and societal truth was definitely not seen as the first priority on the agenda of a regional commission. Instead, documenting the missing persons and gathering facts about the events of the war are clearly seen as preconditions for dialogue and societal debate on the past, and are therefore considered to be the most crucial task by all RECOM supporters. Most of the peace practitioners and human rights activists interviewed considered a regional fact-finding commission to be a useful mechanism to be established alongside the war crimes chambers, in order to complement and support the efforts of the courts. The interviews also revealed that no detailed concepts had been developed for the form that cooperation among legal and fact-finding institutions should take.

Most international actors also welcomed the regional approach. Those who promote the initiative all agree on one common denominator: that a regional commission should complement or support the courts' work and that it should mainly focus on *fact finding*. The majority of the international actors interviewed in all three countries expressed clear support for the RECOM campaign. Some of them have actively funded the campaign, while others do not provide financial assistance but support the aims and idea of establishing a cross-border commission. Only a minority questioned the sense or practicability of such a mechanism. Nevertheless, international representatives were most reluctant to express precise expectations or models for a regional commission. They emphasised that the process is as important as the goal, that RECOM is a 'home-grown' initiative, and that the local organisations should own both the process and the final decision on the scope of the commission. The principle of 'local ownership' was highlighted as a must in advancing the field of dealing with the past by almost all of the donors interviewed.

Representatives of the ICTY also welcomed an additional, non-judicial mechanism for fact-finding at a regional level (Petrović-Ziemer, 2013a). They were convinced that a regional commission can complement judicial proceedings and provide an open space for debate on different interpretations of the past. Representatives of the domestic judiciary were much more reluctant or even critical of the idea of establishing a regional commission. They pointed to the archives and facts already gathered by the ICTY and domestic courts, and were concerned that establishing RECOM might lead to a duplication of efforts. They recommended that instead of creating another mechanism, the right way forward is to start to systematise and analyse the existing material. Finally, they warned that public hearings that involve elements of story-telling might confuse and disappoint the victims, as victims who speak out in this context might expect legal prosecutions and compensation to result from this process (Petrović-Ziemer, 2013a). The most critical opinions towards RECOM were expressed by the Commissions for Missing Persons from all three countries, which argued that efforts would be duplicated and that establishing a regional commission might question and undermine the efforts made by the CMPs together with the courts, police and victims' organisations (ibid.). They also expressed concern that victims could be overloaded and involved in too many parallel activities, requiring them to tell their painful stories again and again.

In sum, we can conclude that the RECOM initiative offers much potential for restorative approaches as a complement to legal approaches. It also offers scope to engage a variety of actors: peace practitioners and human rights activists (including women's and youth groups), journalists and intellectuals, and veterans' and victims' groups (although only a small number of the latter are involved). At the same time, it seems that more discussion is needed to reach a consensus on the scope and mandate of a regional body and to convince more social groups and many more political leaders of the advantages of a regional approach.

4. Conclusions and challenges

As outlined in this chapter, some progress has been made in the field of transitional justice over the past two decades, notably as regards the tracing of the missing and support for accountability mechanisms from state actors in Bosnia, Serbia and Croatia. Although gestures of political reconciliation are rare, modest and often ambivalent, there are indications that some of the gestures by political leaders have helped to normalise relations. However, these gestures can be seen only as the first windows of opportunity and as minor elements of a broader wish list.

Fostering the capacities for war crimes prosecution and building on the achievements of the existing Transitional Justice mechanisms (Commissions for Missing Persons, international and domestic war crimes courts) remains an important challenge in future. First, the pending missing persons' cases have to be resolved. Second, support from state authorities is needed to strengthen the rule of law via functioning police forces and to improve the level of protection for witnesses and victims. Reliable witness protection mechanisms are one of the most important preconditions for effective war crimes prosecution. As many people have to travel abroad to testify in the courts of neighbouring countries, cross-border cooperation among authorities is needed. Witness protection systems need to be established and developed. Victims and witnesses who have to testify in the courts of other countries need police protection before, during and after the trials, both in their home country and at the places where they testify. More effective regional cooperation is therefore needed, which must involve the courts, state institutions, authorities in local municipalities and the police.

In all three countries, several thousand war crimes cases have still to be dealt with and concluded by domestic courts and prosecutors. Many suspects have left their former place of residence and are at large in their own or in other countries. As all three countries decided not to extradite fugitives, progress in this area will largely depend on governments' willingness to cooperate, as well as on monitoring by international actors, journalists and CSOs. Trial monitoring will remain an important task for CSOs in settings where international oversight has ceased, in particular in Croatia, where the OSCE mandate ended in December 2011 and where 677 murders of civilians during Operation Storm, which led to the expulsion of most of the Serb population in 1995, have to be investigated and prosecuted by local institutions. Pressure from the grassroots level will also be needed to push state institutions and local authorities to take additional measures in the field of Transitional Justice, including clear and unambiguous gestures of apology, inclusive forms of remembrance, symbolic reparations, and material compensation for the victims of war crimes and human rights violations.

Although official governmental discourses and declarations follow a less rigid rhetoric, they still remain ambiguous, and patterns of denial continue to prevail in the culture of some political parties and parliamentary spheres. It is obvious that many politicians in the region still shy away from expressing public gestures of apology as they fear a loss of authority among their audience or legal consequences. However, this reluctance is a significant hindrance to constructive forms of dealing with the legacies of the war. Due to a lack of initiative at the political level, no framework currently exists for civic trust-building and political reconciliation. This makes it difficult for bottom-up approaches driven by grassroots actors to advance trust- and relationship-building on an interpersonal and small-group level. Initiatives at the political and grassroots levels still do not dovetail in a way that creates strong synergies, and thus it is questionable whether these activities can actually be described as 'bottom-up' and 'top-down' approaches or are simply parallel endeavours. There are only occasional points of contact between them, mainly facilitated by international funding.

The RECOM project can be described as a bottom-up initiative as it was launched by CSOs and is intended to pressurise policy makers into establishing a joint mechanism to complement the work of the courts. It has received support from politicians, including presidents and prime ministers, in various countries. In this context, grassroots initiatives have shown a remarkable potential to dovetail with projects at the top level. But RECOM – although enjoying broad support in the region – has yet to be operationalised and implemented. It seems that in 2014/2015, the NGO coalition has made important steps forward towards this goal: after holding its seventh assembly in Belgrade on 17 November 2014, it amended the RECOM statute with a view to forming a future RECOM in 2015. It was agreed that, once established, RECOM will produce a definitive list of all those killed and missing, along with a list of camps and other places of detention during the armed conflicts from 1991 to 2001 in the region of former Yugoslavia. The Presidents of BiH, Croatia, Montenegro, Serbia, Kosovo and Macedonia undertook to present their joint initiative to the public and to the various national parliaments in January 2015. The initiative to change the statute came from the envoys of the Presidents, who are overseeing RECOM's formation on behalf of their countries. They also insisted that only state institutions and international courts – not the RECOM commission – should have the power to take repressive measures. The participants also agreed that all established facts should be incorporated into the education systems in the region, although it remains unclear to date what this means and which concrete political measures will be taken.[69] The seventh assembly also made changes to future financing. According to the new proposed statute, RECOM will be financed from domestic and foreign donations and not from state budgets. The various countries have made it clear from the outset that they do not want to be obliged to finance the commission.

The RECOM campaign has shown that CSOs in the region are able to develop a variety of activities for dealing with the past and to set up effective networking activities across countries and diverse stakeholder groups (peace groups, human rights organisations, including women's and youth groups, victims' associations and veterans' unions). The campaign was also successful, to a certain degree, in terms of its approach. However, due to changing government coalitions in BiH, Croatia and Serbia, the conditions for the campaign became much more imponderable. The political support is still very limited it remains to be seen whether RECOM evolves into a broader initiative based on long-term cooperation between political and civil society actors with an interest in dealing with the past, and whether it is able to pave the way to a new approach in transitional justice in the region.

69 See www.balkaninsight.com/en/article/transitional-justice-forum-opens-painful-topics/1455/6; RECOM Initiative!Voice, 20 February 2015, see www.zarekom.org.

A challenge is to balance limited financial and human resources and expertise in the long run in a way which allows CSOs to stay involved in the field of *justice*, monitoring of war crimes trials, *truth recovery*, fact-finding and story-telling activities in the scope of a RECOM. To avoid gaps, it will be necessary to forge effective alliances with independent media and journalists and thus establish a division of labour which allows all these fields to be covered. During the RECOM campaign, the CSOs involved have already proved that they can set up such cooperation and have thus created a solid basis that can be extended in future.

Civil society is still very fragile in the region (Dvornik, 2010; Stubbs, 2007; Belloni & Hemmer, 2010). It is apparently more developed in Croatia and Serbia, and remains quite fragmented in Bosnia, where a very large number of NGOs emerged as a consequence of international funding, but very few sustainable civil initiatives and structures have developed (Sejfija, 2007; Sejfija, 2008; Fischer, 2010). Nevertheless, numerous cultural reconciliation initiatives are ongoing, driven by local civil society actors, mostly with the support of international actors, both at a local community level and a regional level through cross-border cooperation. They will continue to need international support in the future. A particular challenge is to widen the scope of action and build alliances that go beyond the 'like-minded'. In this respect, joint activities, such as those developed between war veterans' representatives and peace activists, offer innovative space for advancing constructive approaches and more inclusive forms of remembrance that might contribute to bridge-building. Initiatives in arts and culture also have considerable potential to develop forms of coping with war-related experiences and inclusive cultures of remembrance. In view of the various deficits described above, it is essential that international actors support initiatives that aim to promote networking and cooperation across all levels, in order to increase the likelihood of convergence between bottom-up and top-down approaches. Programmes also need to be balanced in a way that supports both regional initiatives *and* activities in local communities, such as documentation, awareness-raising, trust- and relationship-building, peace education, and narrative and dialogical forms of dealing with the past.

For civil society to form a realm for top-down and bottom-up initiatives (White, 1996; White, 2004), CSO activists should acknowledge that networking across levels and establishing close working relations with alliance partners in parliaments, governments and local authorities are as important as horizontal networking at the grassroots level. At the same time, policy makers need to learn that trust-building in the region cannot simply be delegated to civil society initiatives; they themselves need to link in with these efforts and provide the framework for advancing peacebuilding and reconciliation at the grassroots level. As our field research revealed, many politicians in Bosnia, Croatia and Serbia now acknowledge that there is a need for reconciliation between nations and societies in the region (Dvornik, 2013; Sejfija, 2013; Miličević, 2013). At the same time, they continue to see initiatives for trust building and relationship-building mainly as a challenge for civil society actors rather than a task that they themselves should address. It is therefore important to raise awareness that restoring trust and relationships must be a specific item on their agenda and in their programmes. It is also important to sensitise politicians to the fact that reconciliation needs both cultural and political approaches and cooperation across levels. Although it is unlikely that ethno-nationalists can be won over to such an endeavour, there are moderate and open-minded politicians in political parties who offer the potential for cooperation. Civil society and policy makers in governments, parliaments and local authorities need to create opportunities for exchange in order to overcome mutual mistrust and advance joint learning.

References

Ashdown, Paddy (2004). 'Identifying Common Themes and Key Factors in Post-Conflict Reconstruction Processes'. In German Federal Foreign Office (Ed.), *Beyond Cold Peace: Strategies for Economic Reconstruction and Post-Conflict Management* (pp. 39–42). Conference Report, 27–28 October. Berlin: Edition Diplomatie.

Assefa, H. (2005). 'Reconciliation. Challenges, Responses and the Role of Civil Society'. In P. van Tongeren et al. (Eds.), *People Building Peace 2, Successful Stories of Civil Society* (pp. 637–645). London: Lynne Rienner.

Balkan Civil Society Development Network (2012). Donors' Strategies and Practices in Civil Society Development in the Balkans. *Balkan Civic Practices* No. 8, Skopje: BCSDN.

Banjeglav, T. (2013). 'Dealing with the Past in Post-war Croatia: Perceptions, Problems, and Perspectives'. In O. Simić & Z. Volčić (Eds.), *Transitional Justice and Civil Society in the Balkans* (pp. 33–50). New York: Springer.

Bar-On, D. (2007). 'Reconciliation Revisited for More Conceptual and Empirical Clarity'. In: J. Beč-Neumann (Ed.), *War Crimes, Genocide and Memories* (pp. 62–84). Sarajevo: Center for Interdisciplinary Postgraduate Studies of the University of Sarajevo.

Bar-Siman-Tov, Y. (Ed.) (2004). *From Conflict Resolution to Reconciliation*. Oxford/New York: Oxford University Press.

Bar-Tal, D. & Bennink, G.H (2004). 'The Nature of Reconciliation as an Outcome and a Process'. In Y. Bar-Simon-Tov (Ed.), *From Conflict Resolution to Reconciliation* (pp. 11–38). Oxford/New York: Oxford University Press.

Baumann, G. & Müller, N. (2006). *Vergangenheitsbewältigung und Erinnerungskultur in den Ländern Mittelost- und Südosteuropas*. Working Paper 164/2006, Berlin, St. Augustin: Konrad Adenauer Foundation, October. Online at www.kas.de/wf/de/33.9323.

Belloni, R. & Hemmer, B. (2010). 'Bosnia-Herzegovina: Civil Society in a Semi-protectorate'. In T. Paffenholz (Ed.), *Civil Society and Peacebuilding: A Critical Assessment* (pp. 129–152). Boulder (CO), London: Lynne Rienner.

Bloomfield, D. (2008). 'Reconciliation'. In V. Rittberger & M. Fischer (Eds.), *Strategies for Peace. Contributions of International Organisations, States, and Non-State Actors* (pp. 261–269). Opladen-Farmington Hills: Barbara Budrich Publishers.

Bloomfield, D. (2006). *On Good Terms. Clarifying Reconciliation*. Berghof Report No. 14, Berlin: Berghof Research Center.

Bojicić-Dželilović, V. (2006). 'Peace on Whose Terms? War Veterans' Associations in Bosnia and Herzegovina'. In E. Newman & O. Richmond (Eds.), *Challenges to Peacebuilding. Managing Spoilers During Conflict Resolution* (pp. 200–218). Tokyo: United Nations University Press.

Boraine, A. (2006). 'Transitional Justice. A Holistic Interpretation'. *Journal of International Affairs*, 60, 1, 17–27.
Brajović, Z. (2007). 'The Potential of Inter-Religious Dialogue'. In M. Fischer (Ed.), *Peacebuilding and Civil Society in Bosnia-Herzegovina. Ten Years After Dayton* (pp. 185–214). 2nd edn, Berlin, Münster: Lit-Verlag.
Centre for Nonviolent Action (2002). Four Views. How I Found Myself in War, How to Reach Sustainable Peace. Translation of special articles. *Vreme*, No 600, Belgrade, 4 July, 24–26. Online at www.nenasilje.org/publikacije/pdf/4pogleda/4views-02-sr-vreme.pdf.
Denti, D. (2013). 'Public Apologies in the Western Balkans. The Shadow of Ambiguity'. In D. Cuypers et al. (Ed.), *Public Apology between Ritual and Regret. Symbolic Excuses on False Pretenses or True Reconciliation out of Sincere Regret?* (pp. 103–122). Amsterdam, New York: Publishers Radopi B.V.
Dimitrijević, N. (2008). 'Serbia after the Criminal Past. What Went Wrong and What Should Be Done'. *International Journal of Transitional Justice*, 2, 1, 5–22.
Dimou, A. (2009). *Transition and the Politics of History Education in Southeast Europe*. Göttingen: V&R, Unipress.
Dvornik, S. (2013). 'Analysis of Interviews with Representatives of Political Parties in Croatia'. In M. Fischer & Lj. Petrović-Ziemer (Eds.), *Dealing with the Past in the Western Balkans. Initiatives for Peacebuilding and Transitional Justice in Bosnia-Herzegovina, Serbia and Croatia* (pp. 119–130). Berghof Report 18. Berlin: Berghof Foundation.
Dvornik, S. (2010). *Actors without Society. The Role of Civil Actors in the Post-communist Transformation. Democracy Series* 15. Berlin: Heinrich Böll Foundation.
European Commission (2010). *Serbia 2010 Progress Report. Enlargement Strategy and Main Challenges 2010–2011*. Online at http://ec.europa.eu/enlargement/pdf/key_documents/2010/package/sr_rapport_2010_en.pdf.
Fischer, M. (2013a). 'Summary Analysis'. In M. Fischer & Lj. Petrović-Ziemer, (Eds.), *Dealing with the Past in the Western Balkans. Initiatives for Peacebuilding and Transitional Justice in Bosnia-Herzegovina, Serbia and Croatia* (pp. 131–157). Berghof Report 18. Berlin: Berghof Foundation.
Fischer, M. (2013b). 'Analysis of Interviews with International Actors'. In M. Fischer & Lj. Petrović-Ziemer (Eds.), *Dealing with the Past in the Western Balkans. Initiatives for Peacebuilding and Transitional Justice in Bosnia-Herzegovina, Serbia and Croatia* (pp. 71–87). Berghof Report 18. Berlin: Berghof Foundation.
Fischer, M. (2011a). 'Struggling for Justice, Truth and Reconciliation in the Western Balkans'. In S. Buckley-Zistel & T. Kater (Eds.) (2011), *Nach Krieg, Gewalt und Repression. Vom schwierigen Umgang mit Vergangenheit* (pp. 59–80). Münster: Lit.
Fischer, M. (2011b). 'Transitional Justice and Reconciliation: Theory and Practice'. In B. Austin, M. Fischer & H. Giessmann (Eds.), *Advancing Conflict Transformation. The Berghof Handbook II* (pp. 405–430). Opladen, Farmington Hills: Barbara Budrich Publishers.
Fischer, M. (2010). 'Zivilgesellschaft und Friedenskonsolidierung. Erfahrungen in Bosnien-Herzegowina'. *Die Friedens-Warte, Journal of International Peace and Organization*, 85, 4, 77–97.
Fischer, M. (2008). *Friedens- und Versöhnungsprozesse im westlichen Balkan – Von den Schwierigkeiten des Umgangs mit gewaltsamer Vergangenheit*. Berghof Working Paper, 4, Berlin: Berghof Research Center.
Fischer, M. (Ed.), 2007a. *Peacebuilding and Civil Society in Bosnia-Herzegovina. Ten Years After Dayton*. 2nd edn. Berlin, Münster: Lit-Verlag.

(2007b). 'Confronting the Past and Involving War Veterans for Peace: Activities by the Centre for Nonviolent Action'. In M. Fischer (Ed.), *Peacebuilding and Civil Society in Bosnia-Herzegovina. Ten Years After Dayton* (pp. 387–416). 2nd edn. Berlin, Münster: Lit-Verlag.

Fischer, M. & Petrović-Ziemer, Lj. (Eds.) (2013). *Dealing with the Past in the Western Balkans. Initiatives for Peacebuilding and Transitional Justice in Bosnia-Herzegovina, Serbia and Croatia.* Berghof Report 18. Berlin: Berghof Foundation.

Fischer, M. & Schroer-Hippel, M. (Eds.) (2013). *'Horror Always Has the Same Face'. Cultures of Remembrance in the Balkans and Germany.* Documentation of the Workshop and Study Tour in Berlin with War Veterans from Bosnia-Herzegovina and Serbia, October 2012. Belgrade, Sarajevo: Centre for Nonviolent Action.

Fisher, S. (2003). 'Contentious Politics in Croatia. The War Veterans' Movement'. In P. Kopecký & C. Mudde (Eds.), *Civil and Uncivil Society? Contentious Politics in Post-Communist Europe* (pp. 70–88). London: Routledge Studies in Extremism and Democracy.

Franović, I. (2015). War Veterans in Constructive Process of Dealing with the Past. Belgrade: Centre for Nonviolent Action. Online at http://nenasilje.org/en/2015/text-war-veterans-in-constructive-process-of-dealing-with-the-past/ (accessed on 10 April 2015).

Franović, I. (2008). *Peacebuilding and Dealing with the Past in the Context of Ethnonationalism. The Case of Bosnia and Herzegovina, Croatia and Serbia.* Berghof Occasional Paper 29, Berlin: Berghof Research Center.

Gentile, V. (2008). *The Role of Civil Society in Post-Conflict Reconstruction: The Case of the Associations of Victims and Relatives of Missing Persons in Bosnia and Herzegovina.* SHUR Working Paper 5/08, Rome: Cersdu-Luiss University. Online at www.luiss.it/shur.

Greenhill, K. & Major, S. (2006). 'The Perils of Profiling. Civil War Spoilers and the Collapse of Intra-state Peace Accords'. *International Security* 31, 7–40.

Hatschikjan, M. (2005). 'Regional Overview. Western Balkans'. In M. Hatschikjan, D. Reljić & N. Šebek (Eds.), *Disclosing hidden History. Lustration in the Western Balkans* (pp. 23–32). Thessaloniki: CDRSEE et al.

Horelt, M. (2011). 'Durch Recht oder Symbolik zur Versöhnung? Ein Vergleich der Versöhnungswirkung des ICTY und politischer Entschuldigungen im ehemaligen Jugoslawien'. *Die Friedens-Warte, Journal of International Peace and Organization*, 86, 1–2, 131–154.

Ivanišević, B. (2008). *The War Crimes Chamber in Bosnia and Herzegovina. From Hybrid to Domestic Court.* New York: International Center for Transitional Justice.

Ivanišević, B. (2007). *Against the Current – War Crimes Prosecutions in Serbia 2007.* New York: International Center for Transitional Justice.

Jukić, E. M. (2015). 'Bosnian Serb Leader Pays "Historic" Visit to Srebrenica'. *Balkan Insight*, 17 April. Online at www.balkaninsight.com/en/article/bosnia-serb-hard-line-leader-pays-historic-visit-to-srebrenica?utm_source=Balkan+Transitional+Justice+Daily+Newsletter&utm_campaign=52bb2e5fb6-RSS_EMAIL_CAMPAIGN&utm_medium=email&utm_term=0_561b9a25c3-52bb2e5fb6-319706041 (accessed on 17 April 2015.

Kandić, N. (2008). 'Serbia without Monuments'. In Osservatorio Balcani e Caucaso (Ed.), *Bad Memories. Sites, Symbols and Narrations of the Wars in the Balkans* (pp. 63–67). Rovereto: Osservatorio Balcani e Caucaso & Provincia Autonoma di Trento.

Kriesberg, L. (2007). 'External Contributions to Post-Mass-Crime Rehabilitation'. In B. Pouligny et al. (Eds.), *After Mass Crime. Rebuilding States and Communities* (pp. 243–271). New York: United Nations University.

Kriesberg, L. (2004). 'From Conflict Resolution to Reconciliation'. In Y. Bar-Siman-Tov (Ed.), *From Conflict Resolution to Reconciliation* (pp. 81–110). Oxford/New York: Oxford University Press.

Kritz, N. J. (2009). 'Policy Implications of Empirical Research on Transitional Justice'. In H. van der Merwe et al. (Eds.), *Assessing the Impact of Transitional Justice. Challenges for Empirical Research* (pp. 13–22). Washington DC: US Institute of Peace.

Kritz, N. & Finci, J. (2001). 'A Truth and Reconciliation Commission in Bosnia and Herzegovina. An Idea Whose Time Has Come'. *International Law FORUM du droit international*, 3, 50–58.

Kuljić, T. (2009). *Umkämpfte Vergangenheiten: Die Kultur der Erinnerung im Postjugoslawischen Raum.* Berlin: Verbrecher Verlag.

Kurze, A. & Vukušić, I. (2013). 'Afraid to Cry Wolf: Human Rights Activists Struggle of Transitional Accountability Efforts in the Balkans'. In O. Simić & Z. Volčić (Eds.), *Transitional Justice and Civil Society in the Balkans* (pp. 201–216). New York: Springer.

McMahon, P. C. & Forsythe, D. P. (2008). 'The ICTY's Impact on Serbia. Judicial Romanticism Meets Network Politics'. *Human Rights Quarterly*, 30, 2, 412–435.

Meernik, J. (2005). 'Justice and Peace? How the International Criminal Tribunal Affects Societal Peace in Bosnia'. *Journal of Peace Research,* 43(3) 271–287.

Mertus, J. (2007). 'Findings from Focus Group Research on Public Perceptions of the ICTY. *Südosteuropa*', 55(1) 107–117.

Milićević, K. (2013). 'Analysis of Interviews with Representatives of Political Parties in Serbia'. In M. Fischer & Lj. Petrović-Ziemer (Eds.), *Dealing with the Past in the Western Balkans. Initiatives for Peacebuilding and Transitional Justice in Bosnia-Herzegovina, Serbia and Croatia* (pp. 105–118). Berghof Report 18. Berlin: Berghof Foundation.

Moratti, M. & Sabić-El-Rayess, A. (2009). *Transitional Justice and DDR: The Case of Bosnia and Herzegovina.* New York: International Center for Transitional Justice.

Nettelfield, L. (2011). 'Bridging the Divide with Numbers? The Case of the Bosnian Book of Dead (BBD)'. In P. Andreas & K.M. Greenhill (Eds.), *Sex, Drugs and Body Counts: The Politics of Numbers in Crime and Conflict* (pp. 159–187). London: Cornell University Press.

Nettelfield, L. (2010). *Courting Democracy in Bosnia and Herzegovina: The Hague Tribunal's Impact in a Postwar State.* Cambridge, Mass.: Cambridge Studies in Law and Society.

Newman, E. & Richmond, O. (Eds.), (2006). *Challenges to Peacebuilding. Managing Spoilers During Conflict Resolution.* Tokyo: United Nations University Press.

Organisation for Security and Cooperation in Europe Mission to Bosnia and Herzegovina (2005). *War Crimes Trials before the Domestic Courts of Bosnia and Herzegovina. Progress and Obstacles.* Sarajevo: OSCE.

Organisation for Security and Cooperation in Europe Mission to Croatia (2005). *Background Report: Domestic War Crime Trials 2004.* Zagreb: OSCE.

Organisation for Security and Cooperation in Europe Mission to Croatia (2003). *Background Report: Domestic War Crime Trials 2002.* Zagreb: OSCE.

Organisation for Security and Cooperation in Europe Mission to Serbia and Montenegro (2003). *War Crimes before Domestic Courts.* Belgrade: OSCE.

Osservatorio Balcani e Caucaso (Ed.), (2008). *Bad Memories. Sites, Symbols and Narrations of the Wars in the Balkans.* Rovereto: Osservatorio Balcani e Caucaso & Provincia Autonoma di Trento.

Panić, Katarina (2015). 'Bosnian Serbs Challenge Constitutional Court over Holiday.' *Balkan Insight*, 17 April. Online at www.balkaninsight.com/en/article/serbs-challenge-bosnia-s-constitutional-court-over-key-date?utm_source=Balkan+Insight+Newsletters&utm_campaign=5be6373eb0-BI_PREMIUM&utm_medium=email&utm_term=0_4027db42dc-5be6373eb0-319682977 (accessed on 17 April 2015).

Pavlakovic´, V. (2010). 'Croatia, the International Criminal Tribunal for the former Yugoslavia, and General Gotovina as a Political Symbol'. *Europe-Asia Studies*, 62, 10, 1707–1740.

Petrovic´-Ziemer, Lj. (2013a). 'Analysis of Interviews with TJ Institutions'. In M. Fischer & Lj. Petrovic´-Ziemer (Eds.), *Dealing with the Past in the Western Balkans. Initiatives for Peacebuilding and Transitional Justice in Bosnia-Herzegovina, Serbia and Croatia* (pp. 29–43). Berghof Report 18. Berlin: Berghof Foundation.

Petrović-Ziemer, Lj. (2013b). 'Analysis of Interviews with Civil Society Actors'. In M. Fischer & Lj. Petrović-Ziemer (Eds.), *Dealing with the Past in the Western Balkans. Initiatives for Peacebuilding and Transitional Justice in Bosnia-Herzegovina, Serbia and Croatia* (pp. 45–70). Berghof Report 18. Berlin: Berghof Foundation.

Peuraca, B. (2003). *Can Faith-Based NGOs Advance Interfaith Reconciliation? The Case of Bosnia and Herzegovina.* Special Report, March. Washington, DC: United States Institute of Peace.

Popović, T. (2003). *Die Mythologisierung des Alltags. Kollektive Erinnerungen, Geschichtsbilder und Vergangenheitskultur in Serbien und Montenegro seit Mitte der 90er Jahre.* 1st edn, Zürich: Pano.

Pupavac, V. (1997). 'Disputes over War Casualties in Former Yugoslavia'. In *Radical Statistics*, 69. Online at www.radstats.org.uk/no069/article3.htm.

Ramet, S. P. (2007). 'The Denial Syndrome and its Consequences. Serbian Political Culture Since 2000'. *Communist and Post-Communist Studies*, 40, 1, 41–58.

Rangelov, I. & Theros, M. (2009). 'Transitional Justice in Bosnia and Herzegovina. Coherence and Complementarity of EU Institutions and Civil Society'. In K. Ambos, J. Large & M. Wierda (Eds.), *Building a Future on Peace and Justice: Studies on Transitional Justice, Peace and Development. The Nuremberg Declaration on Peace and Justice* (pp. 357–389). Berlin: Springer.

Rill, H. & Franović, I. (2005). *Ne moze meni biti dobro ako je mom susjedu lose* [I cannot feel good if my neighbour does not]. Belgrade: Centre for Nonviolent Action.

Rill, H., Smidling, T. & Bitoljanu, A. (Eds.) (2007). *Twenty Pieces of Encouragement for Awakening and Change. Peacebuilding in the Region of Former Yugoslavia.* Belgrade: Centre for Nonviolent Action.

Rosandić, R. et al. (2005). *Peace by Piece. Peacebuilding Experience from the Local NGO's Perspective in the Regions of Former Yugoslavia.* Belgrade: Center for Antiwar Action.

Rush, P. & Simić, O. (Eds.) (2013). *The Arts of Transitional Justice. Culture, Activism, and Memory after Atrocity.* New York: Springer.

Sajkas, M. (2007). *Transitional Justice and the Role of the Media in the Balkans.* Discussion Paper. New York: International Center for Transitional Justice. Online at www.ictj.org/images/content/8/3/833.pdf.

Schäuble, M. (2009). 'Contested Masculinities: Discourses on the Role of Croatian Combatants During the 'Homeland War' (1991–1995)'. In C. Eifler & R. Seifert (Eds.), *Gender Dynamics and Post-Conflict Reconstruction* (pp. 169–198). Frankfurt a. M.: Peter Lang.

Schäuble, M. (2006). '"Imagined Suicide": Self-Sacrifice and the Making of Heroes in Post-war Croatia'. *Anthropology Matters Journal 2006*, 8, No. 1, 1–14. Online at www.anthropologymatters.com.

Šebek, N. (2014). 'The Development of Teaching Materials to Further Peace'. In B. Gruber (Ed.), *The Yugoslav Example. Violence, War and Difficult Ways towards Peace* (pp. 169–188). Münster, New York: Waxmann.
Sejfija, I. (2013). 'Analysis of Interviews with Representatives of Political Parties in Bosnia-Herzegovina'. In M. Fischer & Lj. Petrović-Ziemer (Eds.), *Dealing with the Past in the Western Balkans. Initiatives for Peacebuilding and Transitional Justice in Bosnia-Herzegovina, Serbia and Croatia* (pp. 89–103). Berghof Report 18. Berlin: Berghof Foundation.
Sejfija, I. (2008). *Historical Preconditions and Current Development of Civil Associations in BiH.* Sarajevo: Friedrich-Ebert-Foundation. Online at http://library.fes.de/pdf-files/bueros/sarajevo/06041.pdf.
Sejfija, I. (2007). 'From the "Civil Sector" towards a Civil Society?' In M. Fischer (Ed.), *Peacebuilding and Civil Society in Bosnia-Herzegovina. Ten Years After Dayton* (pp. 125–140). 2nd edn. Berlin, Münster: Lit-Verlag.
Sieber-Egger, A. (2011). *Krieg im Frieden. Frauen in Bosnien-Herzegowina und ihr Umgang mit der Vergangenheit.* Bielefeld: Transkript Verlag.
Simić, O. (2013). '"The Day After": Ex-Combatants Perform Live in Belgrade Theatre'. *History of Communism in Europe*, 4, 65–86.
Simić, O. & Milojević, I. (2014). 'Dialogues between Ex-Combatants and Youth in Serbia: A Constructive Use of War Experience'. *Peacebuilding*, 2(3) 2014, 322–335.
Simić, O. & Volčič, Z. (Eds.) (2013). *Transitional Justice and Civil Society in the Balkans.* New York: Springer.
Stedman, S. (1997). 'Spoiler Problems in Peace Processes'. *International Security*, 22(2), 5–53.
Stubbs, P. (2007). 'Civil Society or Ubleha?' In H. Rill et al. (Eds.), *Twenty Pieces of Encouragement for Awakening and Change. Peacebuilding in the Region of Former Yugoslavia* (pp. 215–228). Belgrade: Centre for Nonviolent Action.
Stubbs, P. (2003). 'Dealing with the Past in Bosnia-Herzegovina, Croatia, and Serbia & Montenegro. Post-Yugoslav Countries Programme, Regional Synthesis Report, Zagreb: Quaker Peace & Social Witness', September 4. Online at http://paulstubbs.pbwiki.com/f/stubbs_dealingwiththepast.pdf.
Subotić, J. (2011). 'Expanding the Scope of Post-Conflict Justice: Individual, State and Societal Responsibility for Mass Atrocity'. *Journal of Peace Research*, 48(2), 2011, 157–169.
Subotić, J. (2009). *Hijacked Justice. Dealing with the Past in the Balkans.* Ithaca and London: Cornell University Press.
Teršelič, V. (2008). 'Ascertaining Facts for combating ideological Manipulation'. In Osservatorio Balcani e Caucaso (Ed.), *Bad Memories. Sites, Symbols and Narrations of the Wars in the Balkans* (pp. 53–58). Rovereto: Osservatorio Balcani e Caucaso & Provincia Autonoma di Trento.
Tokača, M. (2008). 'The Importance of Every Victim'. In Osservatorio Balcani e Caucaso (Ed.), *Bad Memories. Sites, Symbols and Narrations of the Wars in the Balkans* (pp. 59–62). Rovereto: Osservatorio Balcani e Caucaso & Provincia Autonoma di Trento.
United Nations Development Programme (2009). *Transitional Justice Guidebook for Bosnia and Herzegovina.* Sarajevo. Online at www.undp.ba/index.aspx?PID=36&RID=88.
United Nations Development Programme (2008). *Solving War Crime Cases in Bosnia and Herzegovina.* Report on the Capacities of Courts and Prosecutor Offices' within Bosnia and Herzegovina to Investigate, Prosecute and Try War Crimes Cases. Sarajevo: UNDP BiH. Online at www.undp.ba/index.aspx?PID=36&RID=78.
United Nations/ICTY (2011). *Judgement Summary for Gotovina et al.*, The Hague, 15 April. Online at www.icty.org/x/cases/gotovina/tjug/en/110415_summary.pdf.

Vuškovic´, L. & Trifunovic´, Z. (Eds.) (2008). *Women's Side of War.* Belgrade: Women in Black.
Wils, Oliver (2004). *War Veterans and Peacebuilding in Former Yugoslavia. A Pilot Project of the Centre for Nonviolent Action.* Berghof Occasional Paper No. 24, Berlin: Berghof Reasearch Centre.
Zoglin, K. (2005). 'The Future of War Crimes Prosecutions in the Former Yugoslavia. Accountability or Junk Justice?' *Human Rights Quarterly*, 27, 1, 2005, 41–77.

All web-links mentioned in this study were accessed on 21 March 2015 (unless other dates are indicated).

Chapter 2

The ICTY after 20 years of experience – assessments from an insider's view[1]

Klaus Hoffmann

I. Introduction

My first personal experience with the work at the International Criminal Tribunal for the former Yugoslavia (ICTY) stems from 2001 when I worked for the Tribunal for several months as a junior lawyer. It was a very busy and interesting time as the first major cases were decided and new jurisprudence on sexual offences as war crimes and crimes against humanity evolved through various decisions and judgments. That new jurisprudence in itself was already a huge success. Soon thereafter we saw Milošević being arrested and transferred to The Hague. Later on, after five years of experience as a judge and prosecutor in Germany, I returned to The Hague and started to work for the Tribunal again in mid-2005. At that time I started to work as a Legal Officer for the Office of the Prosecutor (OTP). Among the most prominent cases we dealt with were the cases Šešelj,[2] Milošević,[3] and most importantly Stanišić and Simatović.[4] In this chapter I want to reflect on the experience gained from the various cases and comment on lessons to be learned from the Tribunal's work for future international trials. This contribution

1 The chapter presents only the author's view and does not necessarily reflect the views of the ICTY or the United Nations in general. The author wishes to thank Marie-Ursula Kind, former head of the ICTY Transition Team, for her thoughtful review and excellent suggestions.

2 A Serb politician and, since 1993, the President of the Serbian Radical Party (SRS), Šešelj was charged with crimes against humanity and war crimes in Croatia and BiH. He is alleged to have propagated a policy of uniting "all Serbian lands" in a homogenous Serbian state. He defined the so-called Karlobag-Ogulin-Karlovac-Virovitica line as the western border of the new Serbian state ("Greater Serbia"). He is alleged to have participated in a joint criminal enterprise through the recruitment of Serbian volunteers and massive hate speech and propaganda.

3 Milošević, President of Serbia as of December 1990 and President of the Federal Republic of Yugoslavia (FRY) from July 1997 to October 2000 (and, as such, also Supreme Commander of the Yugoslav Army), was charged with genocide and crimes against humanity in all three wars in Croatia, BiH and Kosovo. He died during his trial in detention on 11 March 2006.

4 The former head of the Serbian State Security Service and his assistant were charged with war crimes and crimes against humanity in Croatia and BiH from 1991 to 1995. They allegedly participated in a Serbian joint criminal enterprise, mainly by training, funding and otherwise supporting local Serbian troops and by sending special units who participated in the military operations in Croatia and BiH. Both were acquitted by the Trial Chamber in the judgment of 30 May 2013. The Prosecution Appeal is pending.

does not aim to add a systematic assessment of the Tribunal's work from a legal science perspective,[5] but rather offer a review that is written from an "insider's perspective" from that of a person who had a chance to be part of the processes and legal proceedings that were aiming at establishing justice after the wars in the region in the 1990s. This assessment aims to help readers to understand the work that has been done and is still ongoing at the Tribunal in The Hague. I also want to point to some lessons that, in my view, are key to the success of the work of international criminal courts in general and that should be considered in the further development of war crimes tribunals.

2. Contribution to reconciliation? Achievements and shortcomings of the ICTY's work

The question of whether the ICTY has made a contribution to reconciliation is very hard to answer. One has to bear in mind that the ICTY was established in response to the armed conflict that was ongoing in the 1990s and the atrocities committed in that context, which constituted, in the view of the UN Security Council, "a threat to international peace and security." The ICTY should put an end to such crimes and bring to justice the persons that are responsible for the crimes, thereby restoring and maintaining peace (UN Security Council Resolution 827, 1993). From the outset, it was hoped that the ICTY would and could contribute to reconciliation (Whiting, 2011, p. 88), a very ambitious goal for a criminal court that, as such, has to focus on findings of individual guilt. However, I would state that the Tribunal in various ways did, in fact, pave the way for a process of reconciliation. At the same time, I am fully aware that much more than judicial forms of justice are needed for a process of reconciliation; such a process is a long-term project which may take several decades and involve different generations. In the following section, I will list some of the ICTY's achievements.

2.1. Establishing adjudicated facts in order to counter denial

First of all, to be able to build up a new future for the war-torn societies, the facts of the past war crimes need to be established and adjudicated. There is an urgent need to find the missing. In many reviews and articles about the Balkan wars and the efforts in the region to rebuild, the immense negative impact of the constant denial of the horrible crimes of the past has been stressed (Hodžić, 2011, p. 116). In that sense, I think the Tribunal has done a great job by investigating in substantial detail and then rendering judicial findings on the events in the Balkan region since 1990. Thinking of the massacre of Srebrenica; there was constant denial by

5 A lot of relevant titles have been published in the past. For an overview, see for instance: Swart, Zahar & Sluiter, 2011; Steinberg, 2011; McIntyre, 2011, p. 293.

various nationalistic political groups and institutions—theories were spread to explain some of the deaths and victims were blamed for having made up a huge false story. It was only when, through the work of the Tribunal's experts, more and more victims were found and identified and matched with numerous witness statements, that no more serious denial was possible and more and more national politicians were ready to admit the heinous crimes committed in Srebrenica. Only such admittance seems to form the basis for any further steps in building up a new and peaceful society in the region.

I remember another massacre that occurred in May 1992 outside Bosanski Šamac when 16 people were killed. For many years, the mass grave could not be located and, again, we came up against constant denials that the massacre had ever taken place, despite the clear evidence of surviving witnesses. Our team put in great effort, in cooperation with the authorities of Bosnia-Herzegovina (BiH), to review statements and evidence and we were finally able to locate the grave sites. The bodies were exhumed and identified and thus the crime was confirmed.

Establishing adjudicated facts for the crimes of the past does not necessarily lead to reconciliation, but it is certainly a *necessary* basis for such a process to happen. The same applies to the need for apprehending those suspected of committing gross human rights violations or crimes against humanity, and establishing their individual responsibility.

2.2. Establishing individual responsibility

The procedure by which cases were selected by the prosecutor in the earlier days will be one point for historians to examine closely. However, there has always been harsh criticism of the number of cases against one ethnic group or the other. It is obviously a very tricky issue to select the cases to be brought before an international tribunal. I think that no matter how the decision is made and justified, there will always be criticism. Just looking at the huge number of persons (161) against whom procedures were initiated, it is clearly a great success that all these cases have been resolved one way or the other, although admittedly some judgments are still outstanding. We always felt that the arrest of the most prominent war crimes suspects is an indispensable prerequisite for establishing accountability and a precondition for any process of reconciliation to happen. There was a widespread opinion that with several of these fugitives still at large, the ICTY would not be able to complete its work and fulfil its mandate. It was then a huge relief—not only for the uncounted victims but also for the judiciary—when Ratko Mladić and Radovan Karadžić were finally arrested and brought to trial in The Hague.

2.3. Access to archives

One important step in the fact-finding mission of the Tribunal was gaining access to confidential archives, including those of the army and security services. Generally, such archives are not made public or even opened to a limited group of persons before some decades have passed. In the context of the ICTY—with strong political pressure from the European Union (EU)—our investigators and lawyers were finally granted access to many highly confidential archives in the Balkan countries, following the necessary political changes there. We found very important evidence that now forms the basis for the ICTY cases and judgments. Even if lots of that material is still treated confidentially, the core evidence has been brought to the attention and knowledge of the public through its inclusion in the judgments. As an example of such material, I would mention the monthly pay lists of the Serbian State Security (DB) that included many members of Serbian paramilitary units that fought in the Balkan wars.

2.4. *Giving victims a voice*

Throughout the dozens of cases, more than 5,500 witnesses and victims have testified before the ICTY. From the beginning, it had to concentrate on those most responsible for the war crimes and hence could not give all or even a majority of victims a voice in The Hague.[6] However, in every instance, it was a very important step for individual victims to be able to go to court, face the accused and tell the court and public what had been done to them.[7] Those thousands of witnesses and victims have not only spoken for themselves, but also for their families and other victims from their villages and homes. Their testimony has been recorded and mostly been made available to the public. Other uncounted witnesses have been interviewed and their statements recorded without being called to testify in The Hague; that was often surely a disappointment, however, their evidence is still available for the future work that needs to be done and those statements often formed the basis for domestic war crimes cases.

2.5. *Supporting domestic prosecutions and courts*

As the ICTY was, from the outset, forced and bound to concentrate on a small number of cases of those most responsible for the crimes, thousands of cases have been left with domestic prosecutors and regional courts. The close cooperation and exchange between the ICTY and domestic courts and prosecutors was a core issue from the early days. In our view, but also in that of our domestic counterparts (Vukčević, 2011, p. 260), the cooperation was extremely professional and exceptionally good. There was enormous mutual assistance over the years. Within the OTP, a Transition Team was formed, charged with organizing that cooperation and exchange with domestic judicial authorities. Although it should have been set

6 Unlike the International Criminal Court, the ICTY rules do not foresee distinct procedural rights for victims.

7 See also, on the importance for victims to testify, Hodžić, 2011, p. 118.

up much earlier, it played a vital role in the work of the ICTY, particularly in the final phase. However, the international practice seemed incoherent to me. A Legacy Conference was held in The Hague in February 2010.[8] At this meeting, I listened to victims but also to ICTY officials. I was surprised to hear ICTY officials talking about legacy, transitional justice, and the need for support of domestic courts and prosecutors while, at the same time, due to the completion strategy, the most important unit in the OTP in that respect, the Transition Unit, was reduced in staff when it should have been enlarged.

In the last years of The Hague Tribunal's existence, it seems to be most vital to lend all available support to domestic prosecutors and judges. The vast majority of cases are now pending before national courts and need all our support. Our team has cooperated very efficiently with some brilliant colleagues in Croatia and especially in BiH. One of the Prosecutors in Sarajevo told me that she had so many war crimes cases on her desk that she would be busy until she retired. This reminded me of the experience of my own country, Germany, where almost 70 years after World War II, investigations and trials related to crimes committed during the war are still ongoing. Looking back at this experience, one can easily understand that the judiciary in many successor countries of the former Yugoslavia will need years, and possibly decades, to investigate and complete all the pending cases of war-related crime in the region.

According to the State Attorney's Office of the Republic of Croatia,[9] 241 investigations were ongoing at 31 December 2013 and 613 cases were pending before first-instance courts. In a huge number of cases, the perpetrators have not yet been identified. According to the Organization for Security and Cooperation in Europe Mission to Bosnia-Herzegovina (OSCE, 2013) "current estimates indicate that BiH has over 1,200 cases involving some several thousand suspects in its backlog of war crimes cases". According to information from the OSCE Mission to Serbia, there are currently 11 cases pending before the High Court in Belgrade and four cases before the Court of Appeals. The Serbian War Crimes Prosecutor is conducting 20 formal investigations. The OSCE Mission estimates that some 1,100 cases are in the pre-investigative stage, while no official and detailed figures exist for Serbia.[10]

Key to the successful work of domestic judicial authorities was direct access to databases of the ICTY OTP since an agreement from July 2006 (Vukčević, 2011, p. 261). Lately, EU funding enabled an extended internship program for young lawyers from the Balkans to educate them to work on domestic cases and for Liaison Prosecutors from the Balkan States (Brammertz, 2011, p. 31) to work

8 The book edited by Steinberg, 2011 is based upon this conference.

9 See www.dorh.hr/.

10 The numbers for Serbia have been provided by members of the Organisation for Security and Cooperation in Europe mission in personal talks with the author in June 2014.

directly in the OTP, supporting domestic colleagues while having direct access to the ICTY evidence and staff. Overall, the ICTY has, through various measures (for example, assistance to national and regional prosecutors, provision of investigative material, training and educational programs), supported domestic investigators and courts and also fostered cooperation amongst the Balkan states in prosecuting war crimes cases (Brammertz, 2011, p. 28).

2.6. The "outreach program"

In the case of the ICTY, an outreach program was set up when it was realized that there was a huge deficit of acceptance of the work of the Tribunal and a lack of information among the populations in the region. With the ICTY far away from the Balkans, it should have been a task from the early days to actively inform and involve the public in various ways about its work.[11] It cannot be underestimated how important it is to create a proper outreach program for an international court that deals with war crimes and crimes against humanity.[12] The outreach program was only established in 1999 and was based on the initiative of Judge MacDonald—this decision was certainly far too late. By now, a huge program has been running for a number of years. Seminars on various issues are held in the region, classes are given at schools, and more and more information and various interactive presentations are made available, both online and offline.

Another important issue, related to the question of how to improve the Tribunal's outreach is the language of ICTY transcripts. There were good reasons to establish the Tribunal in a third country. However, I personally think it has been a major error not to have transcripts in the language of the region concerned. It was a political decision to have English and French transcripts. However, this was certainly not helpful in terms of reaching out to the people in the former Yugoslavia. Given its limited resources, the Tribunal should have opted for English and Bosnian-Croatian-Serbian transcripts (or, in the relevant cases, Albanian transcripts). This way, one also would have had the advantage of having the testimony of most witnesses transcribed in their original language, without possible misinterpretation. On multiple occasions, we had in-court discussions with parties and witnesses about the alleged misinterpretation of witness statements or previous testimony! But most importantly, all interested people in the countries concerned could have easily accessed and read the transcripts of all the cases. Due to the practice applied by the ICTY, it took several years until the first transcripts of the Milošević case were translated into the Bosnian-Croatian-Serbian language.

11 As to the context of the establishment of the program, see Hodžić, 2011, p. 116.
12 For more information, see www.icty.org/action/outreach/7.

3. Procedural issues and resources that have limited the Tribunal's work: lessons learned for the future

3.1. *Best legal procedure to choose?*

There have been many debates on the question of what would be the best legal procedure to be chosen for such trials. A huge body of legal literature was dedicated to this question.[13] It has also been claimed that the debate is unproductive and unnecessary and that the ICTY procedure would be neither common law nor civil law based (Whiting, 2011, p. 83). I will not go into too many details on that discussion, but I want to state that I would disagree on this point. I think the two concepts are clearly distinct; each has a different impact on the respective trials and even for the investigations that preceded the trials. The initial ICTY Statute and the Rules of Procedure and Evidence (RPE) were drafted mainly by a small team of American lawyers (Whiting, 2011, p. 92; Eser, 2011, p. 119) and they were elaborated in a setting far away from the region. Admittedly, the rules have been amended over time to achieve more expedient and efficient trials (Whiting, 2011, p. 92). In my view, some of the core issues were left untouched and should be widely discussed as they have a huge influence on the general impact and acceptance of the work of international courts.

I am in no position to categorically judge what procedural model is superior in general. However, given many years of experience in the ICTY trials, but also in domestic proceedings, my overall assessment is that the civil law-based and inquisitorial procedure would be better suited for such enormous trials at international level. In such a system, other than the practice at the ICTY, the actual Trial Chamber handling the case would be determined much earlier and could then prepare in detail for the trial. The leading role of the Chamber would also give rise to earlier and clearer decisions about what evidence is to be admitted, providing clear guidance to the parties.

One argument often put in favor of the common law system says that it would better ensure a fair trial for the accused. However, I think that in the context of the ICTY, the opposite is true. Several problematic aspects could be observed that should be mentioned. First, a procedural system was chosen completely unknown to the accused and—more importantly—unknown to domestic defense lawyers. The accused then had to either accept their trusted, domestic counsel, hoping that they would familiarize themselves with a completely new criminal procedure, or choose an international lawyer from abroad, with whom they could normally only communicate through interpretation and over distance. From a neutral point of view, I have to say that in some cases where only domestic counsel were defending the accused, clear disadvantages were noticed. Second, in the practised

13 See e.g. Eser, 2008, p. 206; Whiting, 2011; Ambos, 2011, p. 1; Schomburg, 2009, p. 108.

procedure, in cases where the defense counsel would do a bad job, the judge was in no position to "assist" without risking being held to be biased. In the civil law (inquisitorial) procedure, it quite often happens that where a suspect is not properly defended, the court will give additional advice to the defendant. With the main examination of witnesses done by the court in the civil law system, the quality of the defense lawyer is much less important and vital for the accused than in the common law system.[14]

3.2. The problematic consequences of the right to self-representation

Following the decision for a common law-based procedural system, the ICTY Statute does foresee in article 21(4) that the accused may defend himself in person or through legal counsel. That wording clearly establishes a right to self-representation for cases before the ICTY. This issue and the massive problems that arose from it were subject to many reviews and articles.[15] The problems started when Milošević was granted that right, but things really got worse in the Šešelj case.[16] Šešelj himself declared so many times that he would use any chance to abuse and obstruct the public proceedings that it should have been a straightforward decision to appoint legal counsel for him from the outset, in order to ensure a fair trial and that justice be done and not obstructed. When the Trial Chamber finally, upon our request, assigned counsel for Šešelj, he appealed and at the same time went on a hunger strike. In that situation, the ICTY as a whole came to its limits. In my view, the Tribunal lost a great part of its reputation and legitimacy when the Appeals Chamber, in a sudden decision and without really hearing the Prosecution, granted the appeal and dismissed the assignment of counsel (the appeal was mainly granted for procedural issues, and in general found that the assignment of legal counsel in the Šešelj case might be justified). With that new decision, the Trial Chamber had to restart with new judges and, at the same time, a Prosecution team that was, to a large degree, changed (Tuinstra, 2011, p. 374).

I do not want to repeat all the arguments brought up in the latest discussions. But what always struck me most was that an accused from the Balkans was granted a right that he or she would not have been given in any domestic trial. In most

14 On a side note, I have to mention that there were efforts to establish a common law-based criminal procedure in Croatia in the last few years. The inclusion of "cross-examination" in the Croatian criminal procedure code—only for some trials—was putting all participants on trial (i.e. prosecutors, defense lawyers and judges) in a very difficult situation. Given my experience in both systems, I was tasked through an EU Twinning project to train Croatian judges, prosecutors and lawyers in common law procedure in 2012 and 2013. Only recently, I learned that after many discussions and very critical feedback from all involved, the common law elements were again taken out of the Croatian criminal code.

15 For an overview, see e.g.: Tuinstra, 2011, p. 345; Zahar, 2008, p. 241; Jørgensen, 2006, p. 64.

16 Vojislav Šešelj is a Serbian lawyer and writer accused of being responsible for war crimes committed in Bosnia, Croatia and in the province of Vojvodina in Serbia. He is a founder and a former leader of the Radical Party in Serbia.

civil law-based procedural systems, the appointment of counsel is obligatory in more serious cases (Tuinstra, 2011, p. 348). In these legal systems, such obligatory appointment is seen as part of the fair trial right rather than as an exception to it. The prosecution team carried out various legal studies during the Milošević case, and especially during the Šešelj case, on the issue of self-representation. It became clear from jurisprudence in many common law countries that it is not an absolute right and each legal system does foresee exceptions. This is especially true for complex and difficult cases such as those before the international tribunals, but is also true when an accused attempts to abuse and obstruct proceedings. Self-representation also means that trials are proceeding very slowly as each accused needs the time to prepare each piece of evidence and witness himself, work that is normally done by a team of lawyers. Hence, already in the Milošević case, instead of a trial week with four to five days in court, hearings were held only twice or three times per week—it is easy to count to what extent that prolongs the whole trial.

Looking at the Tribunal's experience with the quality of self-defense, the incredible complexity of the cases, and the bulk of evidence, the right to self-representation can hardly be seen, in my view, as part of the right to fair trial[17]—it seems rather a right to an unfair trial (although self-chosen). No serious person would opt for self-representation in these cases, due to the vast number of exhibits and witnesses, the complex procedural issues, and the fact that both the Trial Chamber and the prosecution are composed of several experienced lawyers. One only needs to read a number of transcripts of cross-examination by Milošević or Šešelj to see that point. I am convinced that the rights of the accused always have to be balanced against the public interest to an efficient and expedient trial (including the rights of victims and witnesses). In the context of war crimes cases and other international criminal cases, the right to self-representation can never be an absolute right.[18]

Although there were many factors in the Milošević case that led to a fatal and disappointing outcome, I am convinced that granting him the right to self-representation was a major factor. Without a doubt, this case, as in the Šešelj case and the respective handling of the right to self-representation, will have a (negative) impact on the Tribunal's legacy (Tuinstra, 2011, p. 346). The experience of the ICTY should be a clear warning and I see a need to reconsider that issue and, in the future, find a better balance between the rights of the accused and all other parties involved. Choosing a civil law-based procedure would generally solve the problem. In the setting of large and complex international criminal trials, assignment of counsel should be, in any event, strictly obligatory.

17 Tuinstra, 2011, p. 347, refers to the right to self-representation as a minimum guarantee of the right to a fair trial. Reference is made to other international courts and article 6(3)(c) of the European Convention on Human Rights.

18 At least in theory, the ICTY Trial Chambers did come to the same conclusion. See Tuinstra, 2011, p. 352.

3.3. The pros and cons of witness proofing

The practice of so-called "witness proofing" at the ICTY has attracted a lot of criticism, particularly re-interviewing witnesses. However, I think that this practice first needs some explanation. Re-interviewing witnesses is, in fact, a standard procedure in all legal systems, especially when the need arises due to new evidence and new cases. In the case of the work of the ICTY there was a need for such a procedure for several reasons. The investigation and prosecution of war crimes and crimes against humanity are done in an extraordinary context many years, if not decades, after the actual crimes. Many witnesses were interviewed years ago, in some cases, more than ten years earlier. It is simply not practical to call such witnesses to court without verifying their earlier witness statements. To be very clear this procedure is in no way meant (and, to my knowledge from the prosecution, was never used) to "coach" a witness. But memory changes over the years, there may have been some misinterpretation and—maybe most important—the case knowledge at the early time of the interviews was very marginal or the focus of the interview was on a different case. Hence, various steps and measures were combined under the topic "witness proofing."

It seems that those criticizing the practice of witness proofing sometimes confuse the different steps when meeting a witness prior to his testimony in court. The most important step in my personal view was often a new interview with the witness which, as such, should raise no doubts or difficulties. Even in an inquisitorial (civil law-based) procedure, both the police and the prosecution can re-interview witnesses, if necessary. In the Stanišić/Simatović case, we did, in fact, call many witnesses who were interviewed much earlier for the Milošević case. At that time, the accused were hardly known to any of the investigators and the indictment had not even been filed; as such, we had to re-interview those witnesses. Due to practical reasons, this was sometimes only possible shortly before the trial hearing.

Another part of "proofing" was to make the witnesses familiar with the court proceedings. Had we had more time in court, we would have needed less time for "proofing." One has to bear in mind that many of the witnesses had never appeared in court before nor ever left their country or indeed their home village. Hence, these witnesses needed to become accustomed to the court procedures. We often took the witnesses to the court, at the weekends, showed them around and explained the respective roles of those present at trial and the court techniques. With the judges counting each minute of prosecution time in court, we could not "waste" our precious court time explaining these issues to the witnesses during the trial. In a more inquisitorial procedure, these aspects of witness proofing would be in the hands of the court staff who would have to take care of the witnesses before and during their stay and testimony in The Hague.[19] Due to

19 At the ICTY, the parties would end any contact with their witnesses only from the beginning of the actual testimony in court.

the strict time restrictions, witnesses often had no chance to really tell their story in court, at least in the more recent cases. It was then very important for the prosecution team to have additional time with the witnesses prior to the trial hearing to listen to them and make them feel they were being understood and taken seriously.

My conclusion is as follows: a civil law-based procedure would better allow the witnesses to tell their stories first before being examined by the court and the parties. My experience is that it is important for witnesses, even more so for victims, to be able to tell the court and the public in their own words and with the necessary time what was done to them. Under the common law procedure, and with the latest time constraints in the ICTY trials, many victims in the most important cases were only asked a very few questions or, often enough, were only cross-examined by the defense. One can easily imagine what impact this has on the witnesses and how much it damages the reputation of the Tribunal.

3.4. The need for safety: witness protection as a precondition for functioning accountability

A procedural issue with a huge impact on the outcome of trials is the one of witness protection. There has been repeated criticism that too much money was spent on ensuring a fair trial for the accused, but not enough money for the victims and that there was no obligation for national witness protection legislation and programs (Ramulić, 2011, p. 104). I certainly agree that national witness protection programs have to be in place. No international court or tribunal can manage witness protection over a long period in different countries. The core responsibility for this will always be with domestic programs.

A constant issue in any criminal trial is the balance between the rights of the accused and the rights of victims. As for the newly established international tribunals, it has been important to ensure fair trials and respect internationally recognized standards of the rights of accused persons. The whole project of international criminal tribunals is senseless if we try to achieve convictions at any cost. The international war crimes tribunals, and now the International Criminal Court (ICC), are meant to set and apply legal standards for criminal trials that clearly differ from the idea of quick revenge and from the unlawful situation of armed conflicts. We can only stress the importance of the rule of law if, in the tribunals, that rule is applied in the first place. While it is of core importance to guarantee safety for witnesses and victims, at the same time it is very difficult and demanding to ensure full witness protection in post-war situations which are marked by structures of organized crime. Too often, we have seen witnesses threatened, disappear, and not willing or able to testify. Unsurprisingly, these instances can lead to (partial) acquittals. The international community needs to put much more effort—and money—to establish more efficient witness protection programs in the future.

3.5. The need for acknowledgement: meeting victims' expectations?[20]

A difficult challenge is balancing the rights of the accused, the public interest in expeditious trials, and the expectations of victims (groups). There are often too high expectations and demands of victim groups that, in some cases, may prevent justice being done—or at least being done within a reasonable time.

In the Milošević case there were different factors relevant to the fatal end of the case. However, it may have been a poor decision to bring to trial all of the accusations related to the three wars in Croatia, BiH and Kosovo. Knowing that it is always easy to judge when looking back, it is not my intention in any way to criticize those making the decisions at that time. But critical reflection should enable us to make better decisions in the future. I do remember tough discussions at the time within the OTP, discussions that came up later again and again when looking back at the case. I remember even more the huge frustration of the whole team when we heard the news about Milošević's death. The team had invested so much energy and time into this trial and then only weeks before the end it all seemed in vain.[21]

I see a similar problem in the cases of Karadžić and Mladić as both are accused of a variety of crimes. It is quite understandable that each group wants to see their respective suffering included in the trial. However, if Mladić, for example, were only tried for the Srebrenica massacre and found guilty, he would certainly get a life sentence and one could have expected a judgment in a much shorter and more reasonable timeframe. That would serve justice far more, in my view. I also think that other ways could have been found for dealing with the additional crimes. These crimes and accusations could have been transferred to be tried by war crimes chambers in the domestic courts that would not then be excluded by limited international indictments. Alternative mechanisms like truth commissions could also be used to address these additional events and record facts related to other war crimes. It is important that victims can raise their voices and publicly report what has happened to them. However, I am not convinced that the only way to do this is by a criminal trial, with its narrow purpose and limited resources.

3.6. Sentencing and enforcement of sentences

There has been constant and repeated criticism of lenient sentences and the general practice of early release of convicted war criminals.[22] Article 24 of the

20 As to the participation of victims, see supra at 2.4 and 3.3.

21 Of course, after all, the trial was not in vain as so many facts were established and so many witnesses gave testimony in court, testimony that was used in later cases again. Not to be forgotten, the Trial Chamber already found in *Prosecutor v Milošević* (*Decision on Motion for Judgement of Acquittal*) (International Criminal Tribunal for the former Yugoslavia, Trial Chamber, Case No IT-02-54-T, 16 June 2004) (the 'Rule98*bis* decision') prior to the defense case that the prosecution had presented sufficient evidence on almost all counts of the indictment.

22 See e.g. Ramulić, 2011; Hodžić, 2011, p. 118.

ICTY Statute only mentions imprisonment as a penalty. Only very broad factors are to be considered in determining the appropriate sentence. Rule 101 of the RPE foresees sentences up to the remainder of a convicted person's life. Hardly any more detailed rules follow regarding the proper determination of individual guilt. One should certainly consider including a more detailed set of rules for sentencing to enable trial chambers to find a proper sentence in each case that is also comparable to other cases involving the same kind of charges. Looking back at some of the cases, I fully agree that some sentences seem inappropriately mild. If one takes into consideration that for a single murder under any national legislation, the accused will generally receive a life sentence (bearing in mind that a life sentence does not necessarily mean serving the rest of one's life in prison), it is hard to understand that for cases of war crimes and crimes against humanity, the ICTY has sentenced perpetrators to less than ten years in some cases.

It is indeed, not just for the victims, frustrating and disappointing that many convicted perpetrators have left prison by now through "early release" while efforts to properly and fully investigate the war crimes and search for missing persons is ongoing in the region. Thousands of victims are still waiting for justice to be done in their individual cases, witnesses remain at risk, and thousands of cases are pending in the domestic war crimes chambers. What a fatal signal it is when, at such times, war criminals convicted by international courts have already been released and return home, often (re-)entering a political career (as has happened in several cases). I would think and hope that a more detailed set of rules regarding the determination and enforcement of sentences would avoid both mild sentences and a too early release.

Under the ICTY Statute, the enforcement follows the rules of the enforcing state. The international department of the Dutch prison is only used for pre-trial and trial detention. After a final judgment, the ICTY Registrar concludes an enforcement agreement with a third country (not including the Balkan states). Even with a similar sentence rendered by the ICTY, the actual time of enforcement varies quite a bit depending on the enforcing state. An international scheme for the enforcement of internationally pronounced sentences would avoid arbitrary results as we have seen in the enforcement practice of the ICTY.[23]

3.7. *Qualification of staff*

One factor in assessing the legacy and impact of the Tribunal requires additional attention, that being the issue of the qualification of staff. Highly qualified staff are needed on all sides. As for judges, in my view, states should only send and mandate highly qualified lawyers who have long-standing practical experience in large criminal trials. This is at least most vital for the Trial Chamber and may be

23 For more detail, see Hoffmann, 2011, p. 838.

a bit different for the Appeals Chamber where more focus is on legal issues. The cases dealt with at trial are so complex and the perpetrators of the most outstanding crimes have been committed in such an organized manner that one really needs experienced judges. With all respect and not at all to criticize any particular judge, it is my personal conviction that the core issues at trial are how to handle the amount of evidence, difficult defendants and complex trial settings over a long period. Anyone who has followed some of the trials at the ICTY could easily, I am certain, distinguish between experienced judges and those judges who have been diplomats, ministry officials or even defense lawyers prior to their time at the ICTY. If we want international criminal courts to be successful, we need to send the most experienced judges who are well qualified for the demanding and difficult job expected of them. It is also as important to have highly qualified staff in the Prosecutor's Office. I would suggest this requires new and more systematic human resources management. In the first place, one needs lawyers who are both brilliant jurists and outstanding team leaders. That latter capability is very important in an office where colleagues from around the world work together, with many different social and cultural backgrounds, work attitudes, languages and ways of communication.

3.8. Problematic effects of "early completion" strategies

The experience with trials at the ICTY is in one way specific as its mandate was, from the beginning, limited in time and scope. Already in 2004, no new indictments could be filed. Soon thereafter the "completion strategy" started to kick in, which finally had a huge influence on the procedures in court. I can understand the desire of the international community, and especially the main contributors to the United Nations (UN) budget, to have the Tribunal finish its work as early as possible and in time. However, it has to be recognized that the "completion strategy" had very problematic effects. As a consequence of this strategy, the judges' plenary set new rules that allowed Trial Chambers to basically cut down indictments. Despite a more diplomatic wording in Rule73*bis* (D) ("the Trial Chamber . . . may invite the Prosecutor"), it was clear in practice that the Prosecution teams did have to follow such "invitations." Depending on the approach taken by the respective Prosecution team, the results were very different and often had no relation to the actual size, importance and complexity of the case. Hence, many of the indictments were cut by one third (and I can see good reason generally to cut indictments, as I have explained above). Even the hours for the Prosecution to present its case in court were dramatically reduced. In return, we would then take witnesses off the list or try to tender their testimony or statements in writing. With our witnesses in court, we had to count every minute and consider each single question. It is unbelievably difficult to sit in court with an important witness and to be forced to finish the examination-in-chief within two or three hours. Given the need for interpretation, one cannot ask that many questions in two hours. I do remember that I felt some frustration when I was criticized by the judge who told me that I had taken an extra three minutes beyond the granted two hours. Even more frustrating for me was the fact that it took the judge some ten minutes, if not more, to discuss this matter while I would have been grateful to have had these extra minutes with the witness.

The completion strategy also had an impact on the discussion of whether to first indict some accused for their most important crimes, knowing that there would probably be no "second go" for additional crimes, as there would be in a domestic context. Having been a member of the presidency of the ICTY Staff Union for two years, I have to mention one additional point that became enormously important during the last years. Following the completion strategy, the ICTY was forced to downsize its staff by quite some numbers while still operating at full speed in court. The Staff Union tried hard to convince officials, both at the ICTY and UN headquarters that a lot needed to be done to keep the most qualified staff members until the end of the respective cases. However, we were not able to get our message across and even received harsh criticism. During these years, staff would suddenly only receive short-term contracts and, often enough, a very late extension of their contracts. Staff who had family with children at school, a mortgage to pay and other obligations were understandably looking for job security. Hence, when the best qualified staff members had offers from other courts and UN agencies, they would, of course, leave. Many trial teams both in the OTP and Chambers were left abruptly without staff who knew the cases from the beginning.[24] Bearing in mind the complexity and length of the cases, this is no basis for professional, expedient, efficient and satisfactory work.

4. Conclusions and further perspectives

Despite the deficits outlined above, I am personally convinced that the work of the ICTY was, in general, a huge success. It has helped to establish the rule of law in the countries that have been at war with each other, it helped to establish special war crimes chambers and prosecutors' offices in these countries, it gave thousands of witnesses and victims a public voice, and it has established adjudicated facts that will form the basis for further debates in politics and society. The ICTY archive will not only assist the domestic courts and prosecutors in their work, but will also serve the future work of historians.

Over the last years, domestic politicians finally acknowledged the necessity of war crimes investigations in general and the work of the ICTY. As a consequence, and after some quite positive political developments in all these countries, the attitudes of both the political leaders and the public towards the ICTY became more and more positive and supportive (Šimonović, 2011, p. 293). As in any postwar society, it needs a lot of time and effort from all involved to overcome the

24 This was lately acknowledged in a different context in the Šešelj case: *Prosecutor v Šešelj* (*Concurring opinion of Judge Antonetti on decision on continuation of proceedings*) (International Criminal Tribunal for the former Yugoslavia, Trial Chamber II, Case No IT-03-67-T, 13 December 2013) pp. 37–38.

past, deal with it, and create a positive future.[25] In addition to this, I think that the work of the ICTY had an important impact on advancing international law and accountability mechanisms. I think it is fair to say that without the establishment and the work of the ICTY, it would not have been possible for the international community to set up the ICC through the Rome Statute in 2000. The ICTY (and the International Criminal Tribunal for Rwanda (ICTR)) set the context in which the creation of a permanent international criminal court was possible. For the success of the ICC it will now be most important to once again take a very close look at the lessons learned from these Tribunals and consider what changes to its work and procedure may be needed.

The establishment of the ICTY was clearly a huge step to end impunity and foster international criminal law. After all, it was the first international tribunal since Nuremberg and Tokyo. Despite high expectations, a lot has been achieved and all cases brought before the Tribunal have been resolved, one way or the other. The ICTY jurisprudence also contributed to the development of international criminal law, both procedurally and in terms of substantive law (Prost, 2011, p. 468).

Nevertheless, one has to admit that the latest judgments in the most important cases like Gotovina,[26] Perišić,[27] Haradinaj[28] and Stanišić/Simatović were a huge disappointment for any neutral observer. What message is left from the Tribunal if some of those most responsible for war crimes go unpunished and return to their countries, in some cases like national heroes? What is the impact on outstanding cases in the region? What does it mean for witnesses and victims? While most of these cases are final and even requests for a review and appeal was denied in each of these cases, there is still some hope that the Appeals Chamber will take a new and closer look at the evidence and the legal standards and come to different conclusions, at least in the Stanišić/Simatović case.[29] The outcome in the cases of

25 In the past, nationalistic propaganda by national media and politicians had a strong destructive and negative impact on the perception of the ICTY in the region; see e.g. Hodžić, 2011, pp. 115, 117.

26 The Croatian Military Commander, in charge of the military operation in the summer of 1995 known as "Operation Storm", was indicted for war crimes and crimes against humanity during that military operation.

27 Perišić served as Chief of the General Staff of the Yugoslav Army (VJ) from August 1993 until November 1998. He was charged with aiding and abetting war crimes in Croatia and BiH, and for failing to take necessary and reasonable measures to prevent or punish the commission of crimes by his subordinates. It was alleged that the VJ had direct influence on the Serbian troops in Croatia and BiH.

28 Haradinaj, Commander of the Kosovo Liberation Army (KLA), was charged with crimes against humanity in Kosovo during the war in 1998 and 1999.

29 Most remarkable is the clear voice raised in a separate opinion in *Prosecutor v Stanišić and Simatović (Judgment Vol. II, Dissenting Opinion of Judge Michèle Picard)* (International Criminal Tribunal for the former Yugoslavia, Trial Chamber I, Case No IT-03-69-T, 30 May 2013) pp. 852–867. Picard criticizes the majority for applying wrong legal standards leading to the full acquittal of both accused. Even more remarkable is the fact that the presiding judge felt the need to append yet another opinion to respond, trying to once again justify the acquittals (although the judgment itself should contain all reasons already).

Šešelj, Mladić and Karadžić also remains to be seen. The Šešelj case is certainly the longest ever trial at international level and sheds no good light on the procedure (for various reasons, some of which I have mentioned before). However, I also think that it is still one of the more important cases as it deals with the influence and impact of massive hate speech and propaganda. But it will be a difficult job to assess the criminal responsibility of a political leader like Šešelj. As has been demonstrated by similar convictions at the ICTR for instance—for example, the so-called *Media* case[30]—it is very hard for a Tribunal to prove any direct responsibility of individuals in genocide and crimes against humanity, even in cases where there is no doubt that they have actively been involved in propaganda campaigns that contributed to war and genocide.

Many books and reviews have been written about lessons learned from the ICTY. It will be most important to now find ways to implement and adopt changes in the current international tribunals to benefit from the long and sometimes painful experience of the ICTY. It is hard to imagine that the procedure at the ICC will be fully reinvented. However, I do hope that the state parties of the ICC will remain open to substantive changes that allow for more efficient and successful trials. After all, the establishment and work of the ICTY has been a historic step to end impunity and foster international criminal law. Still, there are many painful lessons to be learned, some of which I have outlined in this personal review. All of our colleagues were very dedicated to their work and the success of the Tribunal. In the interest of all victims, I do sincerely hope that the experience of the ICTY will lead to significant changes in future international criminal proceedings and also in the practice of domestic investigations and trials. I also hope for an open, result-oriented debate on the question of how to improve the human resources

30 *Prosecutor v Nahimana, Barayagwiza and Ngeze*, popularly titled the *Media* case, involved the prosecution of three persons alleged to have been initiators of a media campaign that invited the Hutu population to murder the Tutsi population in Rwanda in 1994. All accused were influential members of the "Comité d'Initiative" (the Steering Committee) which founded *Radio Télévision Libre des Mille Collines* ("RTLM") that, from July 1993 to July 1994, disseminated hate speech against Tutsis. In 2003, the Trial Chamber found all three defendants guilty of genocide, conspiracy to commit genocide, direct and public incitement to commit genocide and persecution and extermination as crimes against humanity. In 2007, the Appeals Chamber acquitted all three of conspiracy to commit genocide as well as extermination as a crime against humanity (see *Prosecutor v Nahimana, Barayagwiza and Ngez, 2007*). While Nahimana and Ngeze were still found guilty of direct and public incitement to commit genocide, Barayagwiza's verdict was reversed. Nahimana and Ngeze's sentences were reduced from life imprisonment to 30 years, and Barayagwiza's to 32 years. In this case, the Appeals Chamber laid down important principles and an interpretation of the law that has set standards for other cases to come, as Kagan (2008), p. 8 has outlined: "In rejecting the argument that inchoate crimes (or at least direct and public incitement to commit genocide) are continuous crimes, the Appeals Chamber has strictly limited the evidence that can be used to establish the guilt of an accused. Where, as in this case, accused are charged with having sown the seeds of hatred long before the genocide was unleashed, it will be harder for the prosecution to establish a case against such individuals. (. . .) Additionally, the Appeals Chamber has further delineated the difference between hate speech, direct and public incitement to commit genocide and persecution as a crime against humanity, though some ambiguities still remain."

management in order to guarantee that only the best qualified and experienced staff and judges will be sent to the international courts.

With regard to transitional justice in the region itself, I still hope that the final (appeal) judgments will bring long-expected justice to the people in the Balkans and send a strong signal of support to the domestic colleagues who bear the main responsibility for the bulk of outstanding cases and for ensuring the legacy of the Tribunal (Vukčević, 2011, p. 262; Robinson, 2011, p. 11). Finally, I hope that the question of where the database and archives of the ICTY will be stored and how they should be governed will be solved as soon as possible, in consultation and cooperation with the judicial authorities and relevant NGOs in the countries in the region.[31] Access to the database that has been created is a fundamental precondition for future initiatives for transitional justice in the region. It will remain an important point of reference for all those who want to enhance future processes of dealing with the past and reconciliation in the Western Balkans and beyond.

References

Ambos, K. (2003). 'International Criminal Procedure: "Adversarial", "Inquisitorial" or "Mixed"?' *International Criminal Law Review*, *3*(1), 1–37. Retrieved from www.brill.com/international-criminal-law-review-0.

Brammertz, S. (2011). 'The Legacy of the ICTY: Fair Trials and Cooperation with Local Courts'. In R. H. Steinberg (Ed.), *Assessing the Legacy of the ICTY* (pp. 27–34). Leiden, Netherlands; Boston, Massachusetts: Martinus Nijhoff Publishers.

Čekić, S. (2011). 'The Relevance of the ICTY Legacy for the Victims and Communities in Bosnia and Herzegovina'. In R. H. Steinberg (Ed.), *Assessing the Legacy of the ICTY* (pp. 107–110). Leiden, Netherlands; Boston, Massachusetts: Martinus Nijhoff Publishers.

Eser, A. (2008). 'The Adversarial Procedure: A Model Superior to Other Trial Systems in International Criminal Justice?' In T. Kruessmann (Ed.), *ICTY: Towards a fair trial?* (pp. 207–227). Vienna, Austria: Neuer Wissenschaftlicher Verlag.

Eser, A. (2011). 'Procedural Structure and Features of International Criminal Justice: Lessons from the ICTY'. In B. Swart, A. Zahar & G. Sluiter (Eds.), *The Legacy of the International Criminal Tribunal for the Former Yugoslavia* (pp. 108–148). Oxford: Oxford University Press.

Hodžić, R. (2011). 'A Long Road Yet to Reconciliation: The Impact of the ICTY on Reconciliation and Victims' Perceptions of Criminal Justice'. In R. H. Steinberg (Ed.), *Assessing the Legacy of the ICTY* (pp. 115–120). Leiden, Netherlands; Boston, Massachusetts: Martinus Nijhoff Publishers.

Hoffmann, K. (2011). 'Some Remarks on the Enforcement of International Sentences in Light of the Galić Case at the ICTY'. *Zeitschrift für Internationales Strafrecht*, *10*, 838–842. Retrieved from www.zis-online.com

31 There are differing interests as to the location of the archives. Čekić (2011, pp. 107–110), for example, makes a strong plea for the archives to be set up in Sarajevo. He also demands clear rules governing access to the public.

Jørgensen, N. H. B. (2006). 'The Problem of Self-Representation at International Criminal Tribunals: Striking a Balance between Fairness and Effectiveness'. *Journal of International Criminal Justice*, *4*(1), 64–77. doi:1O.1093/jicj/mqk003.

Kagan, S. (2008). *The "Media case" before the Rwanda Tribunal: The Nahimana et al. Appeal Judgement.* Retrieved from www.haguejusticeportal.net/Docs/Commentaries%20PDF/Kagan_Nahimana_EN.pdf.

McIntyre, G. (2011). 'The International Residual Mechanism and the Legacy of the International Criminal Tribunals for the Former Yugoslavia and Rwanda'. *Goettingen Journal of International Law*, *3*(3), 923–983. doi: 10.3249/1868-1581-3-3-mcintyre.

OSCE (2013). *Accountability for War Crimes: Domestic War Crimes Prosecutions.* Retrieved from www.oscebih.org/Default.aspx?id=70&lang=EN.

Prosecutor v Milošević (2004) (*Decision on Motion for Judgment of Acquittal*) (International Criminal Tribunal for the former Yugoslavia, Trial Chamber, Case No IT-02-54-T, 16 June 2004).

Prosecutor v Nahimana, Barayagwiza and Ngez (2007). *Appeals Judgment. International Criminal Tribunal for Rwanda, Appeals Chamber, Case No ICTR-99-52-A, 28 November.*

Prosecutor v Šešelj (2013). *Concurring Opinion of Judge Antonetti on Decision on Continuation of Proceeds.* International Criminal Tribunal for the former Yugoslavia, Trial Chamber II, Case No IT-03-67-T, 13 November 2013.

Prosecutor v Stanišić and Simatović (2013). *Judgment Vol. II. Dissenting Opinion of Judge Michèle Picard.* International Criminal Tribunal for the former Yugoslavia, Trial Chamber I, Case No IT-03-69-T, 30 May 2013.

Prost, K. (2011). 'The ICTY and its Relationship with National Jurisdictions: Powers, Limits and Misconceptions'. In B. Swart, A. Zahar & G. Sluiter (Eds.), *The Legacy of the International Criminal Tribunal for the Former Yugoslavia* (pp. 434–468). Oxford, England: Oxford University Press.

Ramulić, E. (2011). 'Victims' Perspectives'. In R. H. Steinberg (Ed.), *Assessing the Legacy of the ICTY* (pp. 103–106). Leiden, Netherlands; Boston, Massachusetts: Martinus Nijhoff Publishers.

Robinson, P. L. (2011). 'National Ownership: The Key Concept of the Tribunal's Legacy Vision'. In R. H. Steinberg (Ed.), *Assessing the Legacy of the ICTY* (pp. 11–12). Leiden, Netherlands; Boston, Massachusetts: Martinus Nijhoff Publishers.

Schomburg, W. (2009). 'Common Law versus Civil Law'. *Betrifft Justiz*, *99*, 108–112. Retrieved from www.betrifftjustiz.de/

Šimonović, I. (2011). 'The Effect of the ICTY on the Region'. In R. H. Steinberg (Ed.), *Assessing the Legacy of the ICTY* (pp. 293–296). Leiden, Netherlands; Boston, Massachusetts: Martinus Nijhoff Publishers.

Steinberg, R. H. (Ed.) (2011). *Assessing the Legacy of the ICTY.* Leiden, Netherlands, Boston, Massachusetts: Martinus Nijhof Publishers.

Swart, B., Zahar, A. & Sluiter, G. (Eds.) (2011). *The Legacy of the International Criminal Tribunal for the Former Yugoslavia.* Oxford, England: Oxford University Press.

Tuinstra, J. T. (2011). 'The ICTY's Continuing Struggle with the Right to Self-Representation'. In B. Swart, A. Zahar & G. Sluiter (Eds.), *The Legacy of the International Criminal Tribunal for the Former Yugoslavia* (pp. 345–376). Oxford: Oxford University Press.

UN Security Council Resolution 827, U.N. Doc S/RES/827 (22 May 25, 1993).

Vukčević, V. (2011). 'On Regional Cooperation, Progress, and the International Legacy of the ICTY'. In R. H. Steinberg (Ed.), *Assessing the Legacy of the ICTY* (pp. 259–262). Leiden, Netherlands; Boston, Massachusetts: Martinus Nijhoff Publishers.

Whiting, A. (2011). 'The ICTY as a Laboratory of International Criminal Procedure'. In B. Swart, A. Zahar & G. Sluiter (Eds.), *The Legacy of the International Criminal Tribunal for the Former Yugoslavia* (pp. 83–107). Oxford, England: Oxford University Press.

Zahar, A. (2008). 'Legal Aid, Self-Representation and the Crisis at the Hague Tribunal'. *Criminal Law Forum, 19*(2), 241–263. doi:10.1007/s10609-008-9063-z.

(All links mentioned in this chapter were accessed on November 30, 2014.)

Chapter 3

The micro legacy of the ICTY in Croatia—a case study of Vukovar

Tamara Banjeglav

1. Introduction

This chapter is concerned with the legacy of the International Criminal Tribunal for the former Yugoslavia (ICTY) in Croatia and the effects of its work on the local population. The chapter questions and examines two main issues: first, whether the local population in the eastern part of Croatia feels that post-war justice has been achieved through ICTY judgments and punishments of perpetrators of war crimes. Second, the chapter is interested in whether the local population accepts facts established during ICTY trials as "what actually happened" during the 1991–1995 war in Croatia. In order to examine this, the chapter focuses on the ICTY's micro legacy and on the impact it has had on the lives of people in the eastern part of Croatia (i.e. the town of Vukovar and its surroundings). The chapter is based on field work and semi-structured interviews with the local population.

While the existing research about the impact of the ICTY's work on the local population mostly focuses on Bosnia-Herzegovina (Clark, 2009, Meernik, 2005, Orentlicher, 2010, Clark, 2014, Simić, 2011, Delpla, 2013), this chapter takes Croatia as its case study and focuses on the area which has been most severely affected by the war and where judgments issued by the ICTY could have potentially had a significant impact on the local populations' process of dealing with the past. Although research has been done on the impact of the ICTY's work on reconciliation between Croats and Serbs in the town of Vukovar in particular (Clark, 2012, Čorkalo et al., 2004), this chapter does not focus on and does not try to measure the extent of reconciliation. Rather, it examines how people perceive and understand the work of the ICTY and whether they feel that its work has had an impact on their lives. The chapter takes a case-study approach informed by the belief that the effects and impact of transitional justice mechanisms cannot be fully understood without the inclusion of a grassroots perspective and without analysing the empirical data. As Eric Stover and Harvey M. Weinstein (2004, p. 4) argue:

> "many . . . astute writers and political leaders have extolled the virtues of criminal trials but seldom are such assertions grounded in empirical data.

> Indeed, a primary weakness of writings on justice in the aftermath of war and political violence is the paucity of objective evidence to substantiate claims about how well criminal trials or other accountability mechanisms achieve the goals ascribed to them."

As its main achievements, the ICTY lists, among other things, bringing justice to the victims and establishing facts about the wars in former Yugoslavia.[1] It argues that "by holding individuals responsible for crimes committed in the former Yugoslavia, the Tribunal is bringing justice to victims."[2] Moreover, the ICTY also stated that it "has established beyond a reasonable doubt crucial facts related to crimes committed in the former Yugoslavia."[3] This chapter questions these two claims by examining how the local population in the eastern part of Croatia perceives these ICTY achievements. The main argument of the chapter is that these two achievements have not really had a significant impact on the local population in the town of Vukovar and its surrounding area. To be specific, I argue that the ICTY had neither brought a feeling of justice to victims nor that the facts it established have affected people's perceptions of what had been happening during the war in Croatia. However, the chapter does not assume that concepts of "justice" and "truth" should be based on victims" perception only. Rather, it is interested in the relation between transitional justice and victims due to the lack of academic research on how the ICTY might have affected people's understanding of the past in Croatia in particular. Moreover, the chapter does not argue that the work of the ICTY has been unsuccessful altogether or that international criminal tribunals do not have the potential to achieve the above-mentioned aims.

Since the number of trials held before the ICTY related to crimes committed in Croatia (as well as the number of non-appealable judgments for committed war crimes) is relatively small,[4] this chapter aims to provide a deeper analysis of their impact on the local population. The area taken as the focus of this case study, the Vukovar area, was chosen for two reasons. First, this part of Croatia suffered great human and material losses and damages during the war. Second, it was chosen due to the fact that some important trials held before the ICTY, that of JNA major Veselin Šljivančanin[5] and President of the so-called Republic of Serbian Krajina Goran Hadžić,[6] are related to crimes committed in this area.

1 See www.icty.org (last accessed April 16, 2014).
2 ibid.
3 ibid.
4 There have been 13 trials held before the ICTY which included indictments for war crimes committed on the territory of the Republic of Croatia. Out of the 13, three trials were suspended due to the death of defendants (Slobodan Milošević, Janko Bobetko and Slavko Dokmanović), while in only seven cases non-appealable judgments have been issued so far. http://www.icty.org/sections/TheCases/KeyFiguresoftheCases (last accessed August 24, 2015)
5 See "Vukovar Hospital" Mrkšić et al. case information sheet at www.icty.org/x/cases/mrksic/cis/en/cis_mrksic_al_en.pdf (last accessed September 6, 2014).
6 See Goran Hadžić case information sheet at www.icty.org/case/hadzic/4 (last accessed September 6, 2014).

The chapter argues that the work of the ICTY did not have a great impact on the local population due to three factors: (1) the already mentioned small number of trials relating to perpetrators of crimes committed in Vukovar which have been held before the ICTY, as well as long duration of these trials; (2) the lack of strong political will of the Croatian government(s) to fully cooperate with the ICTY; and (3) the poor outreach activities of the tribunal. Each of these factors is discussed in more detail below and supported with examples obtained from semi-structured interviews with the local population.

2. Croatia and the ICTY: a short history of a complicated relationship

Croatia was among the first countries to request the establishment of an international criminal tribunal which would investigate and try war crimes committed during the wars in former Yugoslavia (Subotić, 2009). This request was made at the very beginning of the war, in 1991, when Croatia was attacked by Serb paramilitary forces and the Yugoslav National Army and when it assumed the role of victim in this war. However, at the time when the tribunal was finally established in 1993,[7] Croatia had another role in the conflict—that of a party involved in the war in neighboring Bosnia and Herzegovina (BiH).[8] During the 1990s and the Tuđman-HDZ rule,[9] Croatia was ready to cooperate with the ICTY only if it was recognized as a victim in the war and would refuse to cooperate when its role in the war in BiH or Croatian Army military operations "Flash" and "Storm"[10] were put into question and under investigation (Erözden, 2001). On March 5, 1999,

7 See the Resolution of the UN Security Council 827, dated May 25, 1993 at http://daccess-dds-ny.un.org/doc/UNDOC/GEN/N93/306/28/IMG/N9330628.pdf?OpenElement (last accessed April 18, 2014).

8 The Trial Chamber of the ICTY, in three different verdicts, described the war in Bosnia and Herzegovina as an international conflict, due to Croatia's direct intervention in the war. See *Prosecutor v Blaškić, Judgement: Trial Chamber, Case* IT-95-14-T, March 3, 2000 at www.icty.org/x/cases/blaskic/tjug/en/bla-tj000303e.pdf (last accessed April 18, 2014); *Prosecutor v. Kordić & Čerkez, Judgement: Trial Chamber Case*, IT-95-14/2, February 26, 2001 at www.icty.org/x/cases/kordic_cerkez/tjug/en/kor-tj010226e.pdf (last accessed April 18, 2014) and *Trial Chamber Judgment Summary for Jadranko Prlić and others*, May 29, 2013 at www.icty.org/x/cases/prlic/tjug/en/130529_summary_en.pdf (last accessed online April 18, 2014).

9 HDZ (Croatian Democratic Union) is a political party which won the first multiparty elections in Croatia in 1990, at the time when Yugoslavia was falling apart. The party was headed by Franjo Tuđman, who later became the first president of Croatia.

10 Operation "Flash" was a Croatian Army offensive conducted against forces of the self-declared Republic of Serbian Krajina (RSK) from May 1–3, 1995. The offensive was the first major confrontation after the ceasefire and economic cooperation agreements were signed between Croatia and the RSK in 1994. Operation "Flash" was a strategic victory for Croatia resulting in the capture of 558 km² of territory held by the RSK. Operation "Storm" was a Croatian Army military action which happened on August 4–5, 1995, during which almost the entire occupied Croatian territory was brought back under the Croatian constitutional and legal order. It was, together with operation "Flash," the key military operation which ended the 1991–1995 war. During the operation, some 10.400km² or 18.4 percent of Croatia's territory was liberated.

the Croatian Parliament adopted a resolution which declared that Croatian Army military operations "Flash" and "Storm" were under the jurisdiction of the Croatian judiciary and not the ICTY.[11] For this reason, in August 1999 the president of the ICTY Gabrielle Kirk McDonald reported Croatia to the UN Security Council for not cooperating and for refusing to collaborate in investigations of these military operations (Zambelli, 2010, p. 1668).

The new government, which came to power in 2000 and was led by Prime Minister Ivica Račan, was determined to cooperate with the ICTY in order to come closer to EU membership. On April 14, 2000 the new government passed the *Declaration on Cooperation with the International Criminal Tribunal for the Former Yugoslavia.*[12] The military operations "Flash" and "Storm" were no longer declared to be solely under the jurisdiction of the Croatian judiciary. The government agreed that the ICTY would investigate and determine responsibility of the Croatian Army forces for war crimes committed during the "Homeland War."

However, Croatia's relations with the ICTY deteriorated when several controversial war crime indictments against Croatian Army generals were issued. Mirko Norac was indicted in early 2001, Ante Gotovina and Rahim Ademi were indicted in mid-2001, and Janko Bobetko was indicted in autumn of 2002. The Croatian Government was hesitant to hand over the indicted Croatian generals because the government faced numerous criticisms from a large part of the Croatian public for its cooperation with the ICTY. Another indictment by the ICTY that resulted in a negative reaction and growing public resistance to cooperation with the court was that of general Ante Gotovina, who was perceived in public as a war-time hero rather than a criminal.[13] When Gotovina was arrested in December 2005 having spent four years in hiding, demonstrations were organized in nearly every major Croatian city. Gotovina, together with two other Croatian Army generals Ivan Čermak and Mladen Markač, was charged with being part of a "joint criminal enterprise," the aim of which was the ethnic cleansing of Serb civilians from Croatia's territory,[14] which directly undermined the widely accepted public narrative about the nature of the "Homeland War" as being exclusively defensive and not aggressive. Dissatisfaction with the ICTY culminated in April 2011 when Gotovina was sentenced in a first-instance judgment to 24 years in prison while Mladen Markač was sentenced to 18 years'

11 *Rezolucija o suradnji s Međunarodnim kaznenim sudom u Haagu* [Resolution on Cooperation with International Criminal Tribunal in the Hague], *Narodne novine* [The Official Gazette], 24/99, March 12, 1999 at www.nn.hr (last accessed April 18, 2014).

12 *Deklaracija o suradnji s Međunarodnim kaznenim sudom u Den Hagu* [Declaration on Cooperation with the International Criminal Tribunal in The Hague], *Narodne novine* [The Official Gazette], 41/2000, April 18, 2000 at www.nn.hr (last accessed April 18, 2014).

13 A poll conducted in 2011 for the purposes of research on the strategies of symbolic nation-building in South East Europe showed that 70.1% of respondents from Croatia thought that Croatian officials and soldiers indicted/sentenced by the ICTY and domestic courts were heroes and not criminals (Pavlaković, 2014, p. 40).

14 See Gotovina et al., "Operation Storm" indictment at www.icty.org/x/cases/gotovina/ind/en/got-amdjoind070517e.pdf (last accessed September 6, 2014).

imprisonment.[15] They were found guilty of participating in a joint criminal enterprise, the aim of which was to permanently remove the Serbian population from the Krajina region.[16] The ruling provoked protests (mainly by war veterans) as the verdict was perceived in the Croatian public as an indictment of the entire "Homeland War," and not just the accused generals. What sparked the protests was a wrong interpretation of the verdict, which was understood as labelling the entire "Homeland War" as "a joint criminal enterprise."

However, on November 16, 2012, the ICTY Appeals Chamber issued its non-appealable verdict reversing the Trial Chamber's findings and acquitted both Gotovina and Markač. The verdict immediately resulted in widespread celebrations throughout Croatia and was welcomed as the final recognition of Croatia's innocence and victimhood in the war. As the president of the association of parents and families of detained and missing Croatian war veterans "Mothers of Vukovar" stressed during her speech at the annual commemoration in Borovo Naselje, "November 16 is the day when the world finally recognized our innocence."[17]

The Croatian daily *Jutarnji list* reported on the occasion of the acquittal of generals Gotovina and Markač that no other issue had united Croats since the "Homeland War" as the release of the two generals. A poll conducted by *Jutarnji list* showed that 96 percent of respondents were happy with the final verdict, while only 0.3 percent did not agree with the verdict.[18] As *Jutarnji list* daily wrote, "the Hague judges' verdict, to a large extent, changed the perception of the tribunal in the eyes of Croatian citizens" (ibid.). The same poll, however, showed that when looking at the ICTY's work in general, almost 50 percent of Croatian citizens believed that the tribunal issued its judgments on the basis of political goals and influences and that only a third of the respondents felt that its work was based in evidence and facts (ibid.).

3. The ICTY cases related to Vukovar

At the time of writing this chapter, only one trial for crimes committed in the Vukovar area had been completed before the ICTY—"the Vukovar three"

15 Ivan Čermak was cleared of all charges.

16 The term "Krajina" comes from the name of the historical borderland of the Austro-Hungarian Empire, which existed up to the nineteenth century, and was called "Vojna krajina" ("Military frontier"). The Serbian "Krajina" entity to emerge after Croatia's declaration of independence in 1991 would include three kinds of territories: a large section of the historical Military Frontier, in areas with a majority of the Serbian population; areas such as parts of northern Dalmatia, that were never part of the Frontier but had a majority or a plurality of the Serbian population, including the self-proclaimed entity's capital, Knin; and areas that bordered Serbia and where Serbs constitute a significant minority (e.g. Baranja, Vukovar).

17 Manda Patko in a speech given at the annual commemoration in Borovo naselje, November 19, 2012. (The author attended the commemoration.)

18 Milovan, A. (November 18, 2012). 96% sretno presudom, 49% misli da je bilo zločina nakon Oluje [96% happy with the verdict, 49% think crimes were committed after "Storm"]. *Jutarnji list*, p. 6.

case.[19] The indictment against Mile Mrkšić, Miroslav Radić and Veselin Šljivančanin alleged that they participated in a joint criminal enterprise (JCE), the purpose of which was the persecution of Croats and other non-Serbs, after the fall of the city, through murder, torture, cruel treatment, extermination and inhumane acts. It was further alleged that on November 20, 1991, JNA soldiers removed some 400 non-Serbs from the Vukovar hospital.[20] Radić and Šljivančanin personally participated in the selection of detainees who were to be loaded onto buses. At least 264 of the captives were later killed at a farm building at Ovčara. Mile Mrkšić was found guilty of murder, torture and cruel treatment and was sentenced to 20 years in prison in September 2007, which was confirmed on appeal. Veselin Šljivančanin was sentenced, in the third non-appealable verdict, in 2010, to 10 years in prison for helping and supporting the crime at Ovčara, but was granted an early release from prison and released on July 5, 2011. Miroslav Radić was cleared of all charges.[21]

Two other cases related to crimes committed in Vukovar were still pending before the ICTY at the time of writing this chapter. Goran Hadžić, president of the government of the self-proclaimed Serbian Autonomous District Slavonia, Baranja and Western Srem and subsequently president of the Republic of Serbian Krajina, is indicted for crimes against humanity and violations of the laws or customs of war perpetrated, *inter alia*, in Vukovar. His trial started in October 2012.[22] Furthermore, Vojislav Šešelj, president of the Serbian Radical Party, is indicted for crimes against humanity, including the murder of Croats and other non-Serb civilians in the municipality of Vukovar, as well as for prolonged imprisonment of civilians in prison camps in Vukovar. He has been standing trial before the ICTY since 2007.[23]

4. Methodology of research

Research conducted for this case study was qualitative in nature. I conducted semi-structured interviews with 20 respondents from the town of Vukovar and the surrounding villages (Lovas, Negoslavci, and Stari Jankovci) at different intervals in the period between October 2012 and January 2014.[24] The interviewees were

19 See Mrkšić et al. 'Vukovar Hospital' case information sheet at www.icty.org/x/cases/mrksic/cis/en/cis_mrksic_al_en.pdf (last accessed April 27, 2014).

20 ibid.

21 See the Trial Chamber Judgment in the case Mrkšić et al. "Vukovar Hospital" at www.icty.org/case/mrksic/4#acjug. (last accessed September 6, 2014).

22 See Goran Hadžić case information sheet at www.icty.org/case/hadzic/4 (last accessed September 6, 2014).

23 See Vojislav Šešelj case information sheet at www.icty.org/x/cases/seselj/cis/en/cis_seselj_en.pdf (last accessed April 29, 2014).

24 All but one interview analyzed here were conducted during my employment with non-governmental organisation *Documenta*—Centre for Dealing with the Past, as part of *Documenta's* oral history project, *Unveiling Personal Memories on War and Detention*. See more about the project at www.croatianmemories.org. (last accessed August 2015).

all older than 18 and of both genders and from various social and ethnic backgrounds. Interviewees were, thus, of both Croat and Serb ethnicities, while one interviewee declared herself to belong to the German ethnic minority and one interviewee did not want to declare herself in terms of ethnicity. All interviewees signed a written consent agreeing for the interviews to be video recorded with a video camera,[25] but not all agreed for their identities to be revealed, which is why I do not quote any names in this study. The interviewees had been mostly identified and contacted through non-governmental organization *Documenta*—Centre for Dealing with the Past and with the help of *Documenta*'s local partner organisations[26] in Vukovar. Some interviewees were chosen with the use of purposive sampling[27] because they are well-known to the Croatian public due to their activities during the war (e.g. a war-time reporter and a doctor in Vukovar's war-time hospital). Some interviewees were also asked to provide further contacts among their friends or relatives, so the snowballing method was also used in some cases.

All interviews were conducted in Croatian and lasted between 30 and 90 minutes. The interviews usually took place at the interviewees' homes, but some were also conducted on the premises of local non-governmental organizations. The interviews were conducted with the use of a semi-structured questionnaire. Interviewees were asked about the origin of their family, the family's life in Yugoslavia before the war, relations with their neighbours during their life in Yugoslavia, and their life in general before the war. They were asked to describe changes that started happening in their home town/village at the end of the 1980s and the beginning of the 1990s, as well as to describe when they first noticed that social relations among people in their surrounding were changing and how the war started for them personally. Furthermore, they were asked to describe what happened to them and their families during the war (the loss of family members, the siege of the city, leaving their home, their experience as refugees), but also to comment on their return home and social relations with their neighbours after the war. In the second part of the interviews, the interviewees were asked about war crimes trials for crimes committed in their local surroundings. Did they know who was prosecuted and for what crimes? Had they followed (in newspapers or on TV) trials before domestic courts and the ICTY? Did they know about judgments issued in particular cases (e.g. about the "Vukovar three" case and Croatian generals Gotovina and Markač)? What did they think about these judgments? Finally, the interviewees were asked whether they believed that war crimes trials before the ICTY had brought justice to victims of war crimes and in what way, and whether they thought that justice could be achieved in some other

25 Only one interview was not recorded with a video camera, but with a voice recorder, since this interview was not conducted within the project *Unveiling Personal Memories on War and Detention*.

26 These include the organization *Europski dom Vukovar* [*European House Vukovar*] and association *Protiv zaborava* [*Against oblivion*].

27 A purposive sampling is one that is selected based on the knowledge of a population and the purpose of the study, so that the subjects of a study are selected because of certain characteristics.

way (other than through war crimes trials). The interviewees were also asked whether they knew what facts about the war were disclosed during these trials and whether they agreed with these facts. They were also asked if they thought that the "real truth" about the war would ever be known and, if yes, whether this "truth" could be established through war crimes trials or in some other way. In the end, the interviewees were asked who they thought was the most responsible for establishing the "truth" about the war.

Generally, the interviewees neither felt that the ICTY judgments would bring victims a feeling that justice was achieved nor believed that the ICTY would establish the "truth" about what happened during the war in Croatia. Examples of interviewees' reflections on the two main issues are discussed in more detail in the following sections.

5. "No justice was brought to anyone"

When talking to victims whose family members were either killed during the war in Vukovar or who were imprisoned in camps and had to endure the siege of the city, what could be heard is the overall dissatisfaction with the excessive duration of war crimes trials. Both Croat and Serb interviewees generally agreed that justice was "too slow" and that too much time had passed since the war, so that they did not really have the feeling that justice had been served. As one interviewee said, "they've waited for too long. The trials should have taken place immediately. That would have been much more effective."[28] Another interviewee even suggested that:

> "the Hague tribunal should have been set up like the Nuremberg tribunal after World War II. All trials should have taken place before the same court, from the lowest-ranking soldiers to the heads of states. But these trials have stretched for too long, so that some defendants have already died. I think there is no justice in these trials."[29]

Except for the general remark that the trials had taken too long and started relatively late, the interviewees also felt that not enough crimes committed in Vukovar had been prosecuted. One of the interviewees, who worked as a war-time reporter in Vukovar, was disappointed with the fact that the ICTY prosecuted only the crime at Ovčara, since, in her opinion:

> "to reduce the whole story only to Ovčara is shameless. Ovčara was a disaster, but cannot be separated from the entire context because if there had been no events preceding Ovčara, Ovčara would not have happened either. The judgement [of the 'Vukovar three'] was not even ridiculous. It was cynical.

28 Author interview VK_1331.
29 Author interview VK_1415.

> Other crimes that have been prosecuted, I don't know exactly how many there have been, considering their amount, are very small in number."[30]

The interviewees were also disappointed with the ICTY due to relatively lenient sentences given to the accused for very serious crimes. An interviewee whose family members were killed at the doorstep of their family home, did not believe the perpetrators would ever be punished since "even these bigger crimes are hard to prove. And if perpetrators are found guilty, they are given very low sentences for such serious and big crimes."[31] To another interviewee it was "not clear how someone who killed 200 people could only be sentenced to some 20 years in prison. That is really banal."[32] Moreover, when asked if she thought the judgments brought by the ICTY would give victims a sense of justice being served, an interviewee said "I don't know what kind of punishment could be given to someone who committed such crime as Srebrenica or Ovčara. What kind of punishment is appropriate in this case? Even if you sentenced them to death, it would be an easy way out. And life sentences in luxury prisons in Sweden with gyms and everything are even more absurd."[33]

Resentment was also expressed over people who were convicted for the committed crimes and over those who were not convicted. An interviewee who testified as a witness before the ICTY in trials related to Vukovar ("the Vukovar three", Šešelj, and Hadžić trials) was embittered that no one from the JNA leadership was convicted for crimes committed in Vukovar. Moreover, in her opinion, only local Serbs from Croatia were found guilty of crimes while Serbs from Serbia were cleared of all charges.[34] She thus believes that "the Hague tribunal is a political court. They are trying to equalise the guilt."[35] The belief that the ICTY was unfair was present among both Serb and Croat interviewees. Each side thought that higher sentences were given to members of their own ethnic group. A Serb interviewee complained of different treatment of Serb and Croat defendants, saying that only Serbs were ever found guilty and given prison sentences, while Croats were treated differently.[36] Moreover, another Serb interviewee did not believe in justice, because "judgments of Croats are different than judgments of Serbs for the same crimes committed. Everything is being done in order to avoid delivering justice."[37] Among Croats, similar opinions about injustice could be heard when conducting interviews after the first-instance judgment had been pronounced for Croatian generals Ante Gotovina and Mladen Markač, sentencing them to 24 and 18 years in prison respectively. An interviewee,

30 Author interview VK_1410.
31 Author interview VK_1332.
32 Author interview VK_1331.
33 Author interview VK_1410.
34 Author interview VK_1416.
35 ibid.
36 Author interview VK_1338.
37 Author interview VK_1413.

who was interviewed before the issuing of a non-appealable judgment to Gotovina and Markač, which cleared them of all charges, said that "they are trying our side which is not guilty of anything. Who attacked Serbia? Nobody. Our people are being tried and given high sentences, while they are getting such low sentences. The highest sentence is 20 years for killing so many innocent people!"[38] Another interviewee who was only a child when the war started considered it to be:

> "stupid to try the victorious army. Generals Norac, Gotovina, Praljak, Ademi and others are people who defended their country. They did not go to Serbia and attack Serbia, but were defending Croatia. I think it is outrageous that these people are even being tried. They were defending themselves. Take Šljivančanin for example, he was given a miserably low sentence. That is a disaster. (. . .) He was sentenced to only a couple of years in prison, while sentences given to our generals are a disgrace."[39]

An interviewee whose husband was killed at Ovčara said that "mostly Croats are given prison sentences, and not Serbs. It seems that they have not committed any crimes. Only our side committed crimes. Maybe we killed ourselves here in Vukovar. (. . .) To tell you the truth, I think that the Hague tribunal is irrelevant."[40] One interviewee summed up the issue of justice saying that "people relied on the tribunal to bring some kind of justice. But no justice was brought to anyone. Everybody is unhappy with the Hague tribunal."[41]

The above examples show how important it is that war crimes trials not only contribute to justice being done, but also that justice is *seen* to be done by those mostly affected by the crimes and judgments for these crimes. Thus, when assessing the work of the ICTY and its impact on societal change in the countries of former Yugoslavia, "it is not sufficient that justice is done from a formal legal perspective" (Clark, 2012, p. 404). What is also important is to consider "how local people perceive the ICTY and whether they associate its work with justice" (ibid.).

Other studies about the meaning of justice in ICTY trials similarly demonstrated that victims and witnesses generally supported war crimes trials but were uncertain whether justice could be rendered in these trials. Eric Stover (2004), in his study on witnesses who testified before the ICTY, found that people did not relate justice only to war crimes trials but that the term had other meanings for them as well:

> "For the witnesses, 'full justice' was far larger than criminal trials and the *ex cathedra* pronouncements of foreign judges in the Hague. It meant the return of stolen property; locating and identifying the bodies of the missing; capturing and trying *all* war criminals, from the garden-variety killers (the

38 Author interview VK_1347.
39 Author interview VK_1411.
40 Author interview VK_1417.
41 Autnor interview VK_1416.

> so-called 'small fry') in their communities all the way up to the nationalist ideologues who had poisoned their neighbours with ethnic hatred; securing reparations and apologies; leading lives devoid of fear; securing meaningful jobs; providing their children with good schools; and helping those traumatized by atrocities to recover."
>
> (Stover, 2004, p. 115)

It thus seems important when assessing the capacity of international criminal courts to provide people with a feeling of justice, to take into account that "justice" has a number of meanings and that it means different things to different people. Legal justice is not the only form of justice that people keep in mind when talking about post-conflict recovery of a society. This is because, as this chapter aims to show, legal justice is usually not fully understood by the local population of a post-conflict country, due to different factors. Furthermore, it is also not sufficient to try and convict perpetrators of crimes in order for victims to feel that justice has been served. For this reason, transitional justice mechanisms, such as war crimes trials, should be complemented and supported with other efforts to acknowledge the suffering of victims and help them recover from traumatizing experiences. These efforts include apologies for and acknowledgement of committed crimes, memorialization initiatives and commemorative practices, which provide victims with a type of symbolic reparations, as well as material reparations paid to victims' families as compensation for their loss and suffering.

Additionally, what should also be kept in mind is that, as one recent study showed, justice is to a large extent seen through a prism of group identity (David, 2014). This means that members of a group will have different standards in assessing a judgment as "just" when a person tried is a member of their own group, than when that person is a member of an out-group. The survey conducted in Croatia in 2008 revealed biased perceptions of justice and showed that "the perception of justice in a criminal case that condemns a member of the out-group is significantly lower than in the case of an in-group member" (David, 2014, p. 19). This means that the condemnation and punishment of in-group members is seen as injustice when compared to the condemnation and punishment of out-group members.

6. This is my truth, tell me yours

What emerged as an important topic during interviews were the interviewees' expectations that the "truth" about what was happening during the war would be established. However, interviewees generally felt that the entire "truth" about the war will never be known. When asked whether they thought that the ICTY will, through its judgments, establish facts that can reveal the "truth" about the war, the interviewees generally considered the tribunal's ability to establish what was done to them personally, who was responsible for their own personal losses and what was the nature of these crimes. One interviewee, whose son is still listed as missing, said she did not think the real "truth" about the war would ever be known, since "many of us have already died without ever finding out what happened to our sons."[42] Thus, rather than considering the "truth" about the entire war, the interviewees placed more importance on personal truths. This emphasis on personal losses and suffering is perhaps connected with strong victimization of oneself and one's own ethnic group, which is present with both Serbs and Croats in Vukovar. Since neither group's need for justice has been met, as Clark (2012) similarly noticed, stressing one's own victimization seems to provide people with an opportunity to demand recognition and acknowledgement of their own suffering.

Furthermore, the interviewees did not perceive the ICTY as crucial in revealing the "truth." For many, time proved to be an important factor in learning the "truth" about the war. Both Serb and Croat interviewees agreed that "time will tell" and that "after 40–50 years, when people who participated in the war die, someone will reveal the truth." [43] An interviewee who did believe that ICTY judgments would establish facts about the war also said that this did not matter, because "no one reads these judgments any more. Twenty-two years have passed."[44] Moreover, an interviewee remarked that, in order for her to know what facts have been established by the ICTY she would need to read transcripts from the trials:

> "I planned to read transcripts from the Ovčara trial, but this was too hard for me. So I can't say what facts have been established through these trials, but if someone takes these transcripts and reads them, maybe some new insights will become known. But I'm afraid that insights depend on people."[45]

This last observation points to the problem of who would read lengthy legal documents and in what way would facts determined during trials be interpreted. Since not many people are educated enough or have enough time and strength to read thousands and thousands of pages of transcripts from these trials, the interpretation of the established facts should have been a joint task of the ICTY, the media and the government. However, due to the ICTY's poor outreach activities, which will be discussed in more detail in the next section, the local population did not get a chance to hear an informed, accurate and non-biased explanation of the judgments. Moreover, the local population received their information about ICTY trials and judgments only through the reporting of local and national media, which were mostly biased and selective as to the information published. As one research of the Croatian national television and daily *Večernji list*'s reporting showed:

42 Author interview VK_1347.
43 Author interview VK_1345.
44 Author interview VK_1416.
45 Author interview VK_1410.

> "Croatian National Television"'s most watched news program and the highest circulation daily in Croatia covered ICTY-related events in a, conditionally speaking, selective manner and they gave considerably more attention to ICTY-related issues which do not have a negative background and which do not give rise to certain doubts and dilemmas regarding the war and the character of the crimes committed."
>
> (Obradović, 2001, p. 4)

Thus, Croatian citizens received very little (if any) information about the course of the trials, details about the raised indictments, accounts of witness testimonies or explanations of final judgments. As the next section will discuss in more detail, the problem of perceiving the facts established through ICTY trials as the "truth" about what was happening during the war lies in very selective information that people have about these trials and low level of familiarity and knowledge about the issued judgments.

However, even if they did know what facts have been established, some interviewees had problems both with accepting these facts and trying to accommodate them into their own experiences of the war. Thus, for example, when talking to a curator in Ovčara memorial museum, I was told that "we have to present in here the number of victims determined by the Hague tribunal. So we have displayed here 261 names of victims. But there are even more victims although not all have been found yet. There are some 400 victims, but the Hague tribunal determined there to be only 261."[46]

The interviewees also felt that the "truth" needs to come from direct participants of the war and not from an outside body (i.e. that both sides need to speak out about what they did and what happened to victims). One interviewee thought that "everybody who knows something should speak up. Why should things be kept secret? It turns out that we killed ourselves. It would be better to speak out about who did what."[47] For another interviewee, the truth will never be known, and the only way to find out what had been happening was "for everybody to speak up and say what they know. (. . .) Everybody is looking for their own truth."[48]

The "truth" was considered to be something private rather than public or generally accepted. As one interviewee said:

> "the truth will be known within families which have lost someone. I will tell my grandchildren what happened and what their grandmother went through. They will know the truth, because I will not distort it or blame someone who was not guilty. I will try to tell them objectively what had happened and then they will make their own conclusions."[49]

46 Author interview VK_2608.
47 Author interview VK_1346.
48 Author interview VK_1421.
49 Author interview VK_1417.

Another interviewee remarked that she knows "only one side, only what happened to me personally. (. . .) Other people certainly have their own truth."[50]

Previous examples show that, even if international criminal tribunals can establish facts about a conflict, this does not necessarily mean that people will accept these facts as "the truth" or that they will even be aware of the established facts. In Vukovar, both Serb and Croat interviewees adopted a very selective approach to the ICTY judgments and the established facts by accepting only those which confirmed their own (ethnic) narrative about the past, while rejecting those that did not.

However, many different factors, as shown in the examples quoted above, influence people's perception of the past, so that the ICTY's success in establishing "the truth" cannot be measured against the local population only. As the following paragraph argues, some of the reasons why the interviewees did not know of or accept the facts established through the ICTY's work, as well as why they did not feel that justice has been served through its judgments, are also due to the tribunal's poor outreach activities.

7. ICTY outreach in the former Yugoslavia and visibility of war crimes proceedings

As Vladimir Petrović (2011) rightly observed, "trials needed to be public, but they also needed to be publicized in the region of the former Yugoslavia, in order for the ICTY to achieve its purpose" (p. 21). This idea is not new in international criminal trials and was present already at the Nuremberg tribunal. One of the reasons why the Nuremberg trials stand out as *the* legal mechanism for punishing crimes of the Nazi regime is the high visibility of the proceedings (ibid.).

At first, the public in the former Yugoslavia was largely excluded from the ICTY's proceedings, as the trials were conducted in English or French and only some parts were translated into local languages. It was not difficult, for this reason, for the political elites back home to distort the image of the tribunal and create a negative public opinion about its work. The fact that the tribunal was located in The Hague, hundreds of kilometers away from the people concerned, did not help in bringing its work closer to those most affected. As a reaction to this, the ICTY recognized the need to make its work more visible and accessible to the population of successor states of former Yugoslavia, which is why an outreach program was developed and outreach offices opened in the capitals of the countries in the region (Belgrade, Pristina, Sarajevo and Zagreb). The aim of the program was to "communicate the work and relevance of the Tribunal, as well as forge partnerships with key bodies in the former Yugoslavia," and to "sustain close ties with the media, the legal community, governmental and non-governmental organizations, victims' associations, international organizations and diplomatic

50 Author interview VK_1421.

representatives."[51] However, as a former ICTY outreach officer noted, "it is much more difficult to dismantle already established misperceptions and propaganda than it would have been to start from the outset with updated and accurate information about the Tribunal" (as cited in Orentlicher, 2010, p. 102).

Furthermore, the Outreach Program was not set up until the end of 1999, six years after the tribunal was established.[52] Until that time, as Judge Gabrielle Kirk-McDonald noted, "the Tribunal had almost totally neglected its constituency in the countries of the former Yugoslavia" (as cited in Klarin, 2009, p. 96). Furthermore, as Mirko Klarin (2009) argued, ten years after the Outreach Program was established in 2009, the perception of the tribunal in Serbia, Croatia and Bosnia was even worse than when it was first set up (p. 96).

Today, although the ICTY judgments are available in local languages on its website, not everyone has access to the internet or the time and knowledge to read lengthy legal documents. While an ICTY outreach office was set up in Zagreb,[53] people who live in remote parts of Croatia, such as Vukovar, had little use for its services. Another problem with the Croatian Outreach office was, as Clark (2009b) noted, that for many years the Zagreb office had been staffed by just one person.

A good example of ICTY outreach activities is the "Bridging the Gap" project, which was set up in Bosnia-Herzegovina between May 2004 and June 2005 (Clark, 2009b, p. 102). Under this project:

> "once trial proceedings are completed (i.e., when there are no appeals proceedings ahead), ICTY officials and staff travel to the town where adjudicated crimes occurred and meet with local citizens and officials to explain how they investigated the crimes; to describe the outcome of cases, and to respond to questions."
>
> (Orentlicher, 2010, p. 103)

As Clark (2009b) also shows, the basic idea of the project was that local people could follow a case from start to finish. No such project, however, existed in Croatia. In the case of Vukovar for example, an outreach project similar to the one in BiH would have benefited the local population after the final judgment in the "Vukovar three" case was given. Such a project would have helped to explain the trial proceedings and its outcome to Vukovar's residents (most of whom were affected by the crimes for which Šljivančanin, Radić and Mrkšić stood trial). One of the interviewees for this study who testified before the ICTY in the Šljivančanin case,

51 ICTY Outreach Programme at www.icty.org/sections/Outreach/OutreachProgramme (last accessed April 19, 2014).

52 For a detailed discussion on the ICTY Outreach Program and challenges of outreach see Clark, 2009b.

53 The office closed on December 31, 2012.

told me: "you should see the documentation there. There exists a whole city of documents. Only about Vukovar they have documents that could fill this hospital. However, they, as all U.N. organizations, exist for their own sake."[54]

Moreover, the ICTY outreach office in Croatia closed before the final verdicts in the cases against Goran Hadžić and Vojislav Šešelj were pronounced, so no relevant explanation of the judgments can be communicated to the public. This, in turn, makes it easier for political elites and the media to misinterpret both the judgments and their meaning. During interviews I conducted it became clear that interviewees were not even informed about the ICTY's mandate, about which cases were tried before the court and which were left to the national judiciary. One of the interviewees told me he was invited to a meeting in Vukovar with "people from the Hague tribunal" at which "one of the Hague people asked: why don't you people here from the Balkans appreciate us? To that I replied: it is your own fault. You should not have taken an exclusive privilege to try someone, but the trials should have been left to domestic judiciary under your patronage."[55] Thus, it seems that despite the efforts directed at raising the visibility of the proceedings, expressed through the formation of outreach offices, the level of basic knowledge on the activities in prosecuting war crimes remained low. In an attempt to combat the low level of knowledge about its work in the region, the ICTY launched a series of conferences about its legacy, with the aim "to increase the knowledge of the target groups about the Tribunal's achievements and the potential impact this can have on wider process of reconciliation in post-Yugoslav states" (ICTY, 2012). The court recognized the importance of holding the legacy conferences, admitting that:

> "apart from the negative perceptions of the ICTY in post-Yugoslav states, other factors contribute to the underuse of its potential in the region: lack of knowledge about the ICTY's legacy and the ways to access it; lack of access to the internet or skills to use the website and online legal database; unavailability of most of the trial transcripts in the local languages, unavailability of large parts of the records to the public, to name but a few."
>
> (ibid)

However, the conferences were held as late as 2010 and 2011 and they took place again far from the region—in The Hague. Participants and invitees at these conferences included the tribunal's principals, judges, senior tribunal staff, the host country, representatives of the national jurisdictions in the former Yugoslavia, victim groups, non-governmental organisations and other stakeholders in the former Yugoslavia, international organisations, organs of the European Union,

54 Author interview VK_1416.
55 Autnor interview VK_1338.

legal counsel of embassies based in The Hague, think tanks, policy makers and international law scholars.[56]

A series of regional conferences was scheduled for 2012, and while those in Sarajevo and Zagreb[57] did take place, the one in Belgrade was postponed, never taking place. This was due to the extremely negative reactions of the Serbian public to the non-appealable judgment issued to Gotovina and Markač in November 2012, which, in my view, was a reason in favor of holding and not postponing the conference, because it could have been used as a chance to provide the public with an informed explanation on why the first-instance judgment was overturned on appeal.

Poor (and belated) outreach activities of the ICTY in the region created a significant gap between the tribunal and the people whom it was supposed to benefit. This lack of sufficient information and knowledge enabled a distorted image about the tribunal to be created through the media, and this was made even easier due to the governments' lack of effort to provide non-biased and clear explanations of its judgments.

As Mirko Klarin (2009, p. 90) argues:

> "unlike the victims and their families—whose attitude towards the Tribunal is primarily a function of their desire to get some form of redress for their suffering—public opinion in the former Yugoslavia is influenced very little by what the prosecution and the judges are actually doing in The Hague. Public perception is influenced to a much greater extent by the views of the local political, academic and cultural elites towards the ICTY and by the manner in which the local media depict proceedings at The Hague."

Thus, the ICTY is not the only one to be blamed for "not being appreciated" in the region of former Yugoslavia, since help from the governing elites was (and still is) much needed in combating the local perceptions that there is no justice at the ICTY.

8. Conclusion

Since the end of the 1991–1995 war, Croatia has been involved in transitional justice processes, such as truth-telling projects (the RECOM initiative), public

56 See Assessing the Legacy of the ICTY—2010 Conference at www.icty.org/sid/10293 (last accessed September 7, 2014) and the ICTY Global Legacy—2011 Conference at www.icty.org/sid/10405 (last accessed September 7, 2014).

57 However, the conference in Zagreb was attended mostly by governemnt officials and staff of local NGOs working on issues related to war crimes, who were all already well-informed about the tribunal and its work. (The author attended the conference.)

apologies, and memorialization practices.[58] One of the core elements of these processes is to establish the truth about human rights violations that took place during the war. The main transitional justice mechanisms employed in this particular case (as well as in the other post-war countries of the former Yugoslavia) have been trials against war crimes perpetrators held before the ICTY. In the course of these trials various facts about the serious crimes under international humanitarian law were publicly disclosed, thus openly opposing or challenging some of the statements of the dominant (ethno-nationalist) narrative of the war. For example, the trial of Croatian generals Gotovina, Čerkam and Markač challenged the dominant narrative of the "Homeland War" in Croatia, which is based on the assumption that the war was defensive and that no crimes were committed by the Croatian state.

However, as this chapter seeks to demonstrate with regard to the case study of the town of Vukovar and its surrounding area, these new findings have neither significantly changed the public perceptions of the war, nor have they contributed to the local population's feeling that justice has been served. It is not my intention, however, to claim that the ICTY has not succeeded in establishing facts about the 1991–1995 war. I rather try to show that these facts are not perceived or accepted by the local population as "the truth" about what had been happening in the war. Some authors argue that this can be explained by the ICTY's practice of producing historical narratives of their own, which collided with competing, well-established narratives from the region (Petrović, 2005). This failure of the international criminal trials to establish an undisputed truth of the past events that would change the public perceptions of the war can be additionally explained by the phenomenon of "hijacked justice" (Subotić, 2009). This concept describes how domestic elites tend to use international norms and institutions for achieving local political goals, thus reducing the effects of international justice projects, jeopardising their legitimacy and in that way preventing the social transformation from occurring (ibid.). In the case of Croatia, the governing political elites, in the early years of the ICTY's work, tried to paint a negative picture of the ICTY in cases when its decisions did not match the official narrative about the nature of the war in Croatia. Later on, although officially cooperating with the ICTY, the government did not engage in providing the local population with objective explanations of the ICTY, its mandate and its judgments. This was left to the media which, most often, presented the ICTY's work with very scarce and selective information, creating a negative attitude among the Croatian public towards the decisions made by the court. However, the task of revealing an authoritative and historically accurate "truth" is not only challenged by various practical obstacles, but also depends on a varying understanding of the concept of "truth," which, as this chapter attempted to show, means different things to different people. Similarly, the concept of

58 A detailed discussion on transitional justice mechanism in Croatia falls outside the scope of this chapter. For an extensive analysis see Banjeglav, 2013. See also Fond za humanitarno pravo, 2013.

"justice" also cannot be measured against the feeling of the local population, since "justice," according to people's opinion, can be achieved with the help of various different factors, and judgments for committed war crimes are perceived to be only one of these factors.

This chapter contributes to the academic research on how war crimes trials before international courts might affect people's understanding of the past, but also seeks to engage in wider discussions about whether international war crimes trials can and should be expected to establish a historical "truth" about the past. My conclusion is that, once facts about the past are established as factual truth, they require an interpretation and have to be given a meaning. This depends on a broader social effort and joint engagement by the court, decision-makers, civil society and the media in a country, each of which, in the case of Croatia, failed in performing this important task.

References and sources

Bibliography

Banjeglav, T. (2013). 'Dealing with the Past in Post-War Croatia: Perceptions, Problems and Perspectives.' In O. Simić and Z. Volčič (Eds.), *Transitional Justice and Civil Society in the Balkans* (pp. 33–50). New York, Heidelberg, Dordrecht, London: Springer.

Clark, J. N. (2009a). 'From Negative to Positive Peace. The Case of Bosnia and Herzegovina. *Journal of Human Rights*, 8, 360–384.

Clark, J. N. (2009b). 'International War Crimes Tribunals and the Challenge of Outreach'. *International Criminal Law Review*, 9, 99–116.

Clark, J. N. (2012). 'The ICTY and Reconciliation in Croatia. A Case Study of Vukovar'. *Journal of International Criminal Justice*, 10, 397–422.

Clark, J. N. (2014). *International Trials and Reconciliation: Assessing the Impact of the International Criminal Tribunal for the Former Yugoslavia*. New York: Routledge.

Čorkalo, D. et al. (2004). 'Neighbours again? Intercommunity relations after ethnic cleansing'. In E. Stover and H.M. Weinstein (Eds.), *My Neighbor, My Enemy: Justice and Community in the Aftermath of Mass Atrocity* (pp. 143–161). Cambridge: Cambridge University Press.

David, R. (2014). 'International Criminal Tribunals and the Perception of Justice: The Effect of the ICTY in Croatia'. *The International Journal of Transitional Justice*, 1–20. doi: 10.1093/ijtj/iju012.

Delpla, I. (2013). 'How Has the ICTY Changed Our Perceptions of War?' *Südosteuropa*, 61(4), 543–554.

Erözden, O. (2001). *Croatia &/v. ICTY: A difficult year of cooperation.* (Paper written for Blue Bird research group 'Future of the Nation State in SEE'). Retrieved from http://web.ceu.hu/cps/bluebird/pap/erozden1.pdf (accessed March 31, 2015).

Fond za humanitarno pravo. (2013). *Tranziciona Pravda u postjugoslovenskim zemljama. Izveštaj za 2010–2011 godinu.* Retrieved from www.hlc-rdc.org/?p=22665 (accessed March 31, 2015).

ICTY (2012). *Legacy of the ICTY in the former Yugoslavia. Concept Paper.* Retrieved from www.icty.org/x/file/. . ./2012_legacy_concept_en.pdf (accessed March 31, 2015).

Klarin, M. (2009). 'The Impact of the ICTY Trials on Public Opinion in the Former Yugoslavia'. *Journal of International Criminal Justice*, 7, 89–96.

Meernik, J. (2005). 'Justice and Peace? How International Criminal Tribunal Affects Societal Peace in Bosnia'. *Journal of Peace Research*, 42(3), 271–289.

Milovan, A. (2012, November 18). 96% sretno presudom, 49% misli da je bilo zločina nakon Oluje [96% happy with the verdict, 49% think crimes were committed after "Storm"]. *Jutarnji list*, p. 6.

Obradović, S. (2001). *ICTY Coverage on Croatian Television and in Vecernji list. Covering up The Hague?* Retrieved from www.mediaonline.ba/en/?ID=175 (accessed March 31, 2015).

Orentlicher, D. F. (2010). *That Someone Guilty Be Punished. The Impact of the ICTY in Bosnia.* New York: Open Society Institute.

Osiel, M. (2000). *Mass Atrocity, Collective Memory and the Law.* New Brunswick, London: Transaction Publishers.

Pavlaković, V. (2008). 'Better Grave than a Slave: Croatia and the International Criminal Tribunal for the former Yugoslavia'. In S. P. Ramet, C. Konrad, & R. Lukić (Eds.), *Croatia Since Independence. War, Politics, Society, Foreign Relations* (p. 447–477)). Munich: R. Oldenburg Verlag.

Pavlaković, V. (2010). 'Croatia, the International Criminal Tribunal for the Former Yugoslavia and General Gotovina as a Political Symbol'. *Europe-Asia Studies*, 62(10), 1707–1740.

Pavlaković, V. (2014). 'Fulfilling the Thousand-Year-Old Dream: Strategies of Symbolic Nation Building in Croatia'. In P. Kolsto (Ed.), *Strategies of Symbolic Nation Building in South Eastern Europe* (pp. 19–49). London: Ashgate.

Petrović, V. (2005). *Clio Takes the Stand: Historical Narratives in the International Criminal Tribunal for the Former Yugoslavia.* (Master's thesis, Central European University, Budapest, Hungary). Retrieved from www.library.ceu.hu/ETD.html.

Petrović, V. (2011). 'Gaining Trust though Facing the Past? Prosecuting War Crimes committed in the former Yugoslavia in a National and International Context'. *CAS Working Paper Series*, 4, 1–35. Retrieved from www.cas.bg/uploads/files/Shaken%20 Order/V.%20Petrovic.pdf (accessed March 31, 2015).

Simić, O. (2011). 'Bringing "Justice" Home? Bosnians, War Criminals and the Interaction between the Cosmopolitan and the Local'. *German Law Journal*, 12(7), 1388–1407.

Stover, E. & Weinstein, H. M. (Eds.) (2004). *My Neighbour, My Enemy: Justice and Community in the Aftermath of Atrocity.* New York, Cambridge: Cambridge University Press.

Subotić, J. (2009). *Hijacked Justice. Dealing with the Past in the Balkans.* Ithaca and London: Cornell University Press.

Vukušić, I. (2013). 'Judging their Hero. Perceptions of the International Criminal Tribunal for the former Yugoslavia in Croatia'. In J. Gow, R. Kerr & Z. Pajić (Eds.), *Prosecuting War Crimes: Lessons and Legacies of the International Criminal Tribunal for the Former Yugoslavia* (pp. 153–181). London: Routledge.

Zambelli, N. (2010). 'A Journey Westward: A Poststructuralist Analysis of Croatia's Identity and the Problem of Cooperation with the International Criminal Tribunal for the Former Yugoslavia'. *Europe-Asia Studies*, 62(10), 1661–1682.

List of Interviews conducted (October 2012–January 2014)

VK_1331, Stari Jankovci, October 18, 2012.
VK_1332, Stari Jankovci, October 18, 2012.

VK_1338, Vukovar, October 31, 2012.
VK_1345, Negoslavci, November 14, 2012.
VK_1346, Lovas, November 15, 2012.
VK_1347, Lovas, November 15, 2012.
VK_1397, Vukovar, May 23, 2013.
VK_1410, Vukovar, June 18, 2013.
VK_1411, Vukovar, June 17, 2013.
VK_1415, Vukovar, June 18, 2013.
VK_1416, Vukovar, June 19, 2013.
VK_1417, Vukovar, June 19, 2013.
VK_2608, Vukovar, August 26, 2013.
VK_1421, Vukovar, September 30, 2013.
VK_1423, Vukovar, October 1, 2013.
VK_1424, Vukovar, Ocotber 1, 2013.
VK_1426, Vukovar, October 2, 2013.
VK_1427, Vukovar, October 2, 2013.
VK_1440, Vukovar, January 14, 2014.
VK_1441, Vukovar, January 14, 2014.

Chapter 4

Rape, silence and denial

Olivera Simić[1]

1. Introduction

It is estimated that between 20,000 and 50,000 women were raped during the 1990s conflict in Bosnia and Herzegovina (BiH). The European Council first published these numbers in its report at the end of 1993, barely eight months into the war. While indicative, these figures remain an approximation due to a number of factors, including: timing, political interference, migration, displacement, killings, disappearance of victims, trauma and shame. Almost 20 years after the cessation of the war there is still no accurate data on the numbers of women raped and tortured in BiH today. Indeed, the number of rapes that actually happened will never be known (Thomas & Ralph, 1999, p. 203). The suggested estimates do not encompass women who were raped and tortured and then killed, women who disappeared, and women who never reported the crime. However, the fact that it is not possible to identify reliable data regarding wartime rape is not something unique to BiH. For example, the precise number of 'comfort women' who were sexually enslaved in military brothels in Japanese-occupied areas, both before and during World War II, likewise remains unknown (and is also the subject of much heated debate: Yoshiaki, 1995).

While ambiguous, statistics released by the European Council are often taken for granted and have become accepted fact. The statistics can be found in almost all official local and international documents, studies and media outlets that analyse the wartime rape in BiH. It is still questionable how many women have survived wartime rape, but according to Meznaric (1994):

> [o]ne could say that there is agreement in the sources concerning several important points: (1) mass rape had at least several thousand victims; (2) there have been many rapes of young girls between the ages of seven and fourteen;

1 I would like to thank Dr Melanie O'Brien, Dr Zala Volčič, Dr Martina Fischer and Associate Professor Elissa Helms for their comments and useful feedback on the previous draft of this chapter.

> (3) rape is often committed in the presence of the victim's parents/children and generally the rape victim is raped by several assailants.
>
> (p. 92)

Although victims were primarily of Bosniak ethnic origin, Bosnian Serb and Croat women were also subjected to horrific forms of sexual violence during the war. However, the academic and media focus has not been on all women survivors but survivors of a particular ethnic group – women who identify themselves as Bosniaks. While often acknowledging in passing that other women were victims of rape too: '[a]ll sides in the conflict used this terror tactic, but by most accounts, rape was most inflicted on Muslim women by Bosnian Serb men as part of their 'ethnic cleansing' campaign' (Simons, 1998), the majority of academic literature and media discuss rape only in relation to Bosniak women.

Some authors, such as Kohn (1994), go even further and claim that 'Serbian forces have raped an estimated 20,000 to 50,000 Bosnian Muslim women during the armed conflict which has accompanied the disintegration of the former Yugoslavia' (p. 199). It is due to the sheer number, brutality and transparency of rapes of Bosniak women that their suffering has become a symbol of authentic suffering of rape in BiH. Consequently, such reporting has made it difficult to acknowledge the complexity of Serb and other women's wartime experiences.

Although sexual violence in war is not a new phenomenon, partially due to widespread international attention to the war in BiH, and partially due to heavy lobbying by feminist activists, for the first time in history, rape has been recognised as a war crime, a crime against humanity and a crime of genocide before international criminal courts. Seventy-eight individuals in 24 different cases have been charged with crimes of sexual violence before the International Criminal Tribunal for the former Yugoslavia (ICTY) since 1993 (Mischkowski & Mlinarević, 2009, p. 27). As of September 2013, 36 cases of sexual violence have been prosecuted before the local courts in BiH, which saw 33 perpetrators convicted and 12 acquitted (Organization for Security and Co-operation in Europe, 2014, p. 14). According to the Organization for Security and Cooperation in Europe (OSCE), 111 cases involving sexual violence in an armed conflict have been addressed by the criminal justice system in the last decade, while many more cases are under investigation (OSCE, 2014). While this number may not seem that significant, in comparison with other countries and the ICTY itself, BiH domestic courts have processed the largest number of wartime sexual violence cases (OSCE, 2014).

The narrative of wartime rape is unavoidably shaped by the available statistics on the number of women raped during conflicts and by the prosecution of sexual violence pursuant to international, and to a lesser extent, domestic criminal law. Both the statistical accounting and the legal discourse contribute to the formation of a predominant narrative of wartime rape, which, for BiH, exists almost exclusively in relation to Bosniak women. As Karen Engle points out (2005), one of the most divisive feminist issues both at the time of the ICTY's establishment and in the immediate aftermath of the conflict was 'whether the rapes of Bosnian women in the war (Croatian women, early on) should be treated differently from the rapes of Serbian women and indeed, whether they should be treated differently from the rapes that happen in all wars' (p. 785).

This chapter interrogates the firmly established and unshaken ethnic hierarchy of wartime rape in BiH which has existed for the past 20 years. In particular, it seeks to problematise the silence surrounding Bosnian Serb women's experiences of rape. 'Rape camps', where women were often impregnated and kept in confinement until the last stage of their pregnancy, were mainly created by the Serb army but were used to a lesser extent by other warring parties. There were extensive rapes of Serb women in camps run by Muslim and Croatian authorities in several areas of BiH, in particular in 1992 at the very beginning of the war.[2] This is not to suggest that Bosniak women have received adequate redress or compensation for crimes of sexual violence or that attention should be diverted away from their suffering. Rather, the key aim of this chapter is to problematise binary and hierarchical representations of wartime sexual victimisation that further polarised and fastened on divisive nationalist discourse, while suppressing or discrediting the experiences of 'other' women (Copelon, 1994b; Henry, 2014).

As Doris Buss (2009) notes, the populist and legal notion of rape as 'a weapon of war' has had the effect of constructing some rapes as visible and paradigmatic, while obscuring, minimising and rendering invisible rapes that fail to meet the specific criteria for prosecuting rape under international criminal law (pp. 159–160). This chapter argues that the narratives of victimisation and rapes perpetrated against women belonging (and/or sympathetic) to so-called 'aggressor populations' are rendered largely silent and excluded in scholarly domains.

In the second section of this chapter, I briefly discuss feminist views on wartime rape in BiH, the establishment of the ICTY and its responses to rape. In the third section, the chapter adopts Ratna Kapur's notion of the 'authentic victim subject' in order to examine the way in which feminist scholars and activists have (or have not) sought to address 'non-paradigmatic' wartime rapes in recent history. In the fourth section, I examine the implications and consequences of the ethnopolitical hierarchies and the difficulties of Serb women in BiH to get recognition as victims of wartime rape, due to different legal regulations in the two Bosnian entities (Federation of BiH and Repulika Srpska). In the fifth and final section I conclude that the failure to acknowledge their victimhood has led to lack of legal, psychosocial and economic support for these women.

2. Rape and punishment

The contemporary international criminal courts have explicitly prohibited rape and other forms of sexual violence in their statutes. Since the establishment of the

2 For example, camp Dretelj-Capljina, camp Celebici, camp Strolit-Modrica, Odzak, Brod, Bradina, and camp Musala-Mostar. See, for example: Kerr, 2007; Nizich, 1994.

ad hoc international courts in the early 1990s, rape has been prosecuted as a war crime (torture), a crime against humanity and a crime of genocide, in contrast to historic war crimes tribunals that failed to adequately prosecute crimes of wartime sexual violence. Reporting on the large number of documented rapes during the armed conflict in BiH in 1993, the Special Rapporteur of the Commission on Human Rights, Tadeusz Mazowiecki, noted that rapes had been perpetrated by all sides of the conflict – against Croat, Muslim and Serb women. Other reports also recognised the ethnic dimension of rapes and victimisation across all ethnic groups but pointed to the fact that the majority of victims were Bosniak women and the majority of perpetrators were Bosnian Serbs. According to the United Nations (UN) Commission of Experts (1994), rape was part of a widespread and systematic campaign of 'ethnic cleansing' and an official strategy to remove and displace certain ethnic groups from an entire area through force, fear and intimidation (p. 36).

In response to the mass atrocities committed during the conflicts in the former Yugoslavia, the UN authorised the establishment of the first international war crimes court since the Nuremberg and Tokyo tribunals following the Second World War. The establishment of the ICTY in May 1993 signalled an 'historic opportunity' for prosecuting crimes of sexual violence that had long been ignored and silenced (Copelon, 1994a, p. 199). Feminist scholars began to debate the rules of evidence and the inclusion of rape in the ICTY statute as well as the strategies and legal arguments for including rape in the indictments and prosecuting these crimes within the courtroom (Engle, 2005, p. 785). After a long wait, rape was directly recognised as a crime deserving serious international attention and prosecution by the highest international court.

Hence, in both peace and war contexts, sexual violence has frequently been the subject of hierarchisation. It is well-known that in domestic criminal jurisdictions, rape by a stranger is pursued and prosecuted far more vigorously and successfully than acquaintance rape (Estrich, 1987). Stranger rape, for instance, is far more likely to succeed at trial, and victims who suffer sexual violence at the hands of a stranger are less likely to receive biased treatment, both inside and outside the criminal justice system. In comparing wartime and peacetime rape, some have commented on the contrastable gravity of war-related rapes. For example, William Hague (2012), on announcing a UK initiative on preventing sexual violence in conflict, noted recently:

> [s]exual violence is a problem found in every society in the world, and all countries have to do more to tackle it at home. But it is in the context of war and conflict that sexual violence is found to the most appalling degree, and on a scale most of us cannot imagine.

Similarly, Angelina Jolie – Hollywood celebrity and UN Goodwill Ambassador – noted recently during a conference in Sarajevo about sexual violence in war that the rapes in times of war are particularly vicious: '[t]his is rape so brutal, with such extreme violence, that it is even hard to talk about it' (quoted in Ninemsn, 2014). The hierarchy that is constructed around wartime rape as opposed to rape in peacetime is a product of the separation of ordinary and exceptional crimes. What makes a crime exceptional in its gravity and what makes a crime a crime against humanity, as David Luban (2004) describes it, are offences that violate a fundamental humanity – all 'humankind' (p. 90).

After rape was explicitly included as a crime against humanity in the ICTY statute in 1993, feminist scholars, legal professionals and activists were prompted to turn their attention to consider whether all rapes or only the 'worst ones' should be prosecuted in international war crimes courts. The acclaimed Western feminists and proponents of Bosnia's cause, Catharine MacKinnon and Alexandra Stiglmayer, knowingly or unwittingly found themselves embroiled in the internal struggle between feminist groups in the Yugoslav successor states. MacKinnon was openly hostile to Serbian feminists, despite their condemnation of Serb crimes towards Muslim and Croat women, accusing them of being pro-Serb nationalists (Kajevska, 2014). She called the rape of Bosniak women by Serb soldiers 'genocidal' rape, making such rape incomparable with the rape experienced by women at the hands of non-Serb soldiers:

> [s]ex has also been used before to create, mobilize, and manipulate ethnic hatred, from the Third Reich to *Penthouse* . . . [but] the world has never seen sex used this consciously, this cynically, this elaborately, this openly, this systematically, with this degree of technological and psychological sophistication, as a means of destroying a whole people.
>
> (1994a. p. 75)

Feminist scholars, such as Doris Buss, caution against ceasing our analysis of war rape at the point of strategic or 'genocidal' rape. In Rwanda, the widespread rape of Tutsi women was characterised by the International Criminal Tribunal for Rwanda (ICTR) as 'genocidal'. By framing rape as a weapon that one side uses against another, we enact a 'rape script' that 'naturalize[s]' sexual violence and ignores rapes that contradict the rape script (Buss, 2009, p. 155). According to the ICTR, 'genocidal' rape is defined as a crime against a particular group of women: Tutsi women. It thus renders some sexual violence and abuse invisible, such as the rape of Hutu women but also of Tutsi men and boys and Hutu boys for resisting violence. Buss (2009) argues that although such rapes did not occur with the same magnitude as the rape of Tutsi women, it is troubling that these victims were ignored by the ICTR (p. 155). This may similarly be argued for the Bosnian Serb women, largely neglected by the ICTY which has prosectued thus far only one rape case specifically addressing the Serb women victims.[3]

3 *Prosecutor v Zejnil Delalić and others* (The *Čelebići* Case), IT-96-21, *Judgement*, 16 November 1998.

Advocates of prosecuting 'genocidal' rape have argued that it is crucial to draw attention to 'who is doing what to whom' (MacKinnon, 1994b, p. 7). MacKinnon states emphatically that the problem is that the war in BiH was represented as a bilateral civil war with ethnic dimensions. She argues that:

> rapes in this war are not grasped as either a strategy in genocide or a practice of misogyny, far less both at once . . . What is happening here is first genocide, in which ethnicity is a tool for political hegemony: the war is an instrument of the genocide; the rapes are an instrument of the war.
>
> (p. 8)

Insisting on genocidal rape has been met with resistance from some feminist scholars and activists in the former Yugoslavia, who argue that the use of such a term implies that 'only certain victims count' (Kesic, 1994, p. 276; Helms, 2013, p. 63). As Helms (2013) suggests, 'the genocidal rape erases rapes perpetrated by those other than Serbs' (p. 259) and implies that only Serbs were capable of rape.[4] It reduces the dynamics of rape between Serb males and Bosniak and Croat females and, in turn, portrays Serbs as almost exclusive perpetrators (Nikolić-Ristanović, 1999, p. 63). The focus on the wartime mass rapes in BiH as unique, exceptional and even 'genocidal' paved the way, in part, for unprecedented global attention about the suffering of Bosniak women and helped to place rape on the prosecutorial agenda of international war crimes courts.

At the same time, such global attention on the rape of Bosniak women resulted in the construction of hierarchies of crimes, victims and perpetrators, which were based on ethnic identity. As Nancy Fraser (2000) writes, recognition based on identity has the effect of marginalising, eclipsing and displacing redistributive struggles – to 'drastically simplify and reify group identities . . . [encouraging] separatism, intolerance and chauvinism, patriarchalism and authoritarianism' (p. 108). In line with such critiques, some feminist scholars have been hesitant about distinguishing between rapes in peacetime and wartime contexts. Rhonda Copelon (1994a, p. 198), for example, noted that the condemnation of wartime rape has not been about the crime of gender but rather the mass rapes in the former Yugoslavia have only captured the world's attention because of the association with genocide or ethnic cleansing. The effect, she claims, is that a hierarchy around rape in wartime is created:

> [t]he focus on 'genocidal rape' as a means of emphasizing the heinousness of the rape of Muslim women in Bosnia is . . . dangerous. Rape and genocide are separate atrocities. Genocide – the effort to destroy a people based on its identity as a people – evokes the deepest horror and warrants the severest

4 The Human Rights Watch conducted interviews with Bosnian Serb women who were raped by Croatian forces in the municipalities of Bosanski Brod and Odžak: Human Rights Watch, 1995, p. 21.

> condemnation . . . to emphasize as unparalleled the horror of genocidal rape is factually dubious and risks rendering rape invisible once again.
>
> (1994, p. 198)

Although the ICTY was from the outset careful about pursuing the type of victor's justice reminiscent of both the Nuremberg and Tokyo trials following the Second World War (ICTY, n.d.), it has been perceived by Serbs as biased and anti-Serb (Obradović-Wochnik, 2014, p. 197). A substantial majority of cases have involved crimes of ethnic Serbs against non-Serb victims (Orentlicher, 2008, p. 86). While some Serbs deny these crimes, others acknowledge them; some think that crimes committed against Serbs are war crimes too and should not be treated as by-products or 'inevitable acts of war' (Orentlicher, 2008, p. 86). The hierarchy of crimes, including rape, against different ethnic groups reflects the hierarchy of victimhood which places Serbs, alleged perpetrators of the majority of war crimes, at its bottom. Such hierarchies bear the risk of Serb victims being regarded as somehow 'deserving of' those crimes and as such, less authentic and less worthy of protection than others (Askin, 1997).

3. The authentic victim subject

It has taken feminists decades to deconstruct problematic binaries and myths around rape in domestic contexts, however, the notion of the 'real' rape victim continues to hold sway. Feminist scholars have used Christie's 'ideal victim' (1986, p. 87) to explain apparent discrepancies in the treatment of victims of peacetime rape. Christie describes such a victim as 'a person or category of individuals who, when hit by crime, most readily are given the complete and legitimate status of being a victim' (p. 87). One of the characteristics of the 'ideal victim' is the implication that the offender was unknown to the victim.

Wartime rape, however, encompasses a different kind of dichotomy. What frequently sets rape victims of war apart is their ethnic or national identity, which is intimately connected to the notion of an 'ideal' or 'authentic' victim subject (Kapur, 2002, p. 2). Although Kapur situates her analysis within post-colonial feminist discourse, her argument is relevant to the creation of the 'authentic' victim subject in BiH and the role that local and international community played in that creation. Victimhood has become an important tool for building a new nation state and rape ethnic identity led to the creation of the 'real' or 'authentic' victim subject. Bosniak women's experiences of rape were appropriated for a nation-building project as an authentic representation of collective national trauma and suffering. While women victims of rape in the Federation of BiH (FBiH) have gained some benefits from this appropriation (such as modest financial reparation),[5] they have been largely disappointed by their government.

5 See, *Law on principals of social protection, protection of all civilian victims of war and protection of families with children* (Official Gazette of FBiH, no 36/99, 54/04 and 39/06).

According to Bakira Hasečić, a wartime rape survivor and the President of the Association of Women War Victims from Sarajevo:[6]

> [t]he Bosniak intellectuals are cowards, and I think that of most of Bosniak men too. It will stay written down and remembered that Bosniak women, a few of them, carried out the burden of proving the truth about suffering of Bosniak people . . . I think that in the whole Islamic world, such fight of Muslim women is precedent, after horrors that our women survived. After all the torture we survived in Chetnic camps, we stood up on the forefront of the fight and do not allow our killers to sleep in peace.
>
> (B. A., 2014)

Bosniak women survivors, such as Bakira, have been outspoken about their experiences and have drawn the attention of local and international media, while Serb women have received very little local or international coverage and scholarly attention. They have been perceived as a part of the 'perpetrator's nation' and, as such, there has been a failure to recognise, or attribute sufficient gravity to, atrocities perpetrated against this category of victims. In other wars, women who belong to such nations had similar experiences. For example, much controversy has surrounded the legitimacy of victimisation narratives of German women who were raped by advancing Soviet forces during the 1945 invasion of Berlin. In relation to sexual violence, some victims have been silenced as illegitimate or undeserving victims of war due to their identity not as women but as complicit members of an aggressor state or warring party (Buss, 2009).

There has been some discussion more recently amongst feminist scholars about the consequences of the heightened consciousness around wartime rape and its unintended effect of constructing a problematic hierarchy around victimisation (Henry, 2014; Buss, 2009). In the context of BiH, talking about Serb women as victims of rape is often interpreted as denying or minimising the same experiences of Bosniak women or, even worse, as justifying what was done by the Serb army and supporting Serb ultra-nationalist rhetoric.

Another reason for the exclusion and resulting silence of a subset of victims from the dominant legal and public narrative of wartime rape is related to the way in which governments seek to manipulate and politicise rape. Katherine M. Franke (2006) argues that one should be wary of the appropriation of women's 'stories, memories and experience' within the dominant and, only seemingly, ideologically neutral liberal democratic institutions (p. 823). She views with some discomfort the possibilities of 'popular identification with selected aspects of women's suffering' where, in particular, 'their sexual violation can stand for the nation's violation as a

6 The Association is a local NGO which has premises in Sarajevo, FBiH, and has a right to grant a status of 'civilian victim of wartime rape' after certain conditions have been met. Similar organisations do not exist in Republika Srpska.

whole' (p. 823). Franke expresses concern that the focus on the harms suffered by women will be instrumentalised in the service of an essentially patriarchal, albeit newly democratic, state. In BiH, women's experience of rape has been instrumentalised in the service of furthering ethno-nationalistic division.

Wartime rape is too often overlooked or subsumed within a larger category of crimes against civilians. Although it has been recognised as a crime against humanity, rape is still treated in BiH as less significant in comparison to other war crimes and the BiH government has been criticised by numerous organisations for not taking the issue of wartime rape seriously. In November 2012, UN human rights expert, Rashida Manjoo (OHCR, 2012), emphasised the long-lasting consequences of not dealing with this crime and linked these unresolved legacies of war to current violence that women in BiH experience, including domestic violence, poverty and post-traumatic stress disorder.

While the local women's movement has been the only interested party in keeping the issue of wartime rape alive and tirelessly demanding that assistance and recognition be given to women who survived the rape, the movement itself has been polarised in its fixation on sexual violence. Since the 1990s when much attention was directed towards understanding the complexities of wartime sexual violence, feminists have debated whether women were raped in wartime because of their sex or because they belong to a particular ethnic/religious group, and whether rape served as an 'ethnomarker' (Rejali, 1996, p. 368) or rather as an act of male violence against women that has no ethnic and religious boundaries.

By exclusively positioning and treating rape through ethnic lenses, feminist scholars unintentionally contributed to the further polarisation of rape discourses. As Pavlović (1999) argues, being a woman was subsumed under a particular national identity and 'attempts to express any form of solidarity and commonality with women across ethnic and national identity lines could be regarded as disloyalty' (p. 131). As Helms (2013) argues, the collective war narratives of innocence and victimhood are so sacred that people cannot allow themselves to think about anything that might disrupt them.

In such a complex political context, Serb women's experiences were often rejected, ignored or 'quantified' (in far lesser numbers), rendering their experiences insignificant. As Linda Grant (cited in Nikolić -Ristanović, 1999) argues, 'arguing how many women have been raped and why it was done has overshadowed another issue: What has happened to the women since the ordeal ended?' (p. 44). Such questions have been raised not to deny that Bosniak women were the most numerous among those who died or survived rape but, as Helms (2013) argues, to challenge existing and 'dominant representations' that portray them as 'the *only victims*' (p. 27; original emphasis). As a result, Serb and other women's experiences have been largely muted, invisible, misused and/or misinterpreted.

At the beginning of the war, when wartime rape started to receive international attention, feminist activists found themselves increasingly implicated within ethnic and nationalist discourse and often responded by taking refuge in universalism.

As early as 1992 there was debate among feminists as to whether aggressors/rapists should be singled out according to their ethnicity:

> [f]eminists and women's groups have been split into two relatively antagonistic groups: those who see rape as a universal problem of violence against women which needs to be identified and combated as such, and those who see the high incidence of rape in this particular war as being unique and the product of a contempt or hatred by one particular army (Serbian) for the women of a particular ethnic group (Muslim or Croatian).
>
> (Kesić, 1999, p. 194)

Feminists from Belgrade and Serbia issued a public appeal, protesting against an 'international campaign which instrumentalises women raped in Serbia and Croatia'. They issued a joint statement advocating for no distinction to be made between women according to their ethnic origin:

> [w]omen who are raped in war in Bosnia are not to be distinguished and valued differently with respect to their nationality to which they belong. The question of Serb, Croat, Muslim and women of all other nationalities has for us the same value.
>
> (Anti-ratni Bilten SOS-a, 1993, p. 3)

In 1993, a similar message was sent to the public by feminists from Belgrade:

> [s]ince the beginning of the war in Croatia and Bosnia, testimonies show that rape is widely spread; that victims of rape are of all nationalities, including Roma, Albanian and other women that do not belong to any warring parties. All the same, perpetrators belong to all military and para-military formations, as well as the civilian population.
>
> (Mlađenović, 1993, p. 111)

While there was no denying that women were the victims, in spite of these public proclamations, some feminists and scholars persistently argued that rape was only happening to 'certain women' (Helms, 2013, p. 61). Those feminists who insisted that rape is a universal act of violence by men against women were accused of downplaying the terror that Bosniak women suffered in the hands of the Serb army by holding this position. They were blamed for 'aiding the Serbian aggressors because they failed to single out "Croatian" and "Muslim" women as the victims' (Helms, 2013, p. 61); portrayed as disloyal and morally suspect, and exposed to public media accusations of 'concealing the Serbian rape of Muslim and Croat women' (Korać, 1994, p. 505).

The discourse on rape as a weapon of war in BiH has been – from the beginning of the war to the present – entirely positioned within the framework of ethnicity as a part of 'genocidal' strategy. Women, as Vesna Kesić (2003) argued a decade ago, were turned into metaphors: '[a] raped Croat or Bosniak woman stands for a raped Croatia or Bosnia'. But women were also raped because they 'belonged' to the 'bad guys', to the enemy; these women were raped by their 'own men' because they had partners or husbands on the 'other side'. Several women survivors who were detained in different rape camps confirmed that women from 'other' ethnic groups were detained and raped with them. Huzba Nukić, a 69-year-old Bosniak woman who was detained and repeatedly raped by Croatian military forces in Bosanski Brod, reportedly stated:

> I was raped first at the football stadium in Bosanksi Brod before the group of women by a Croatian soldier, named Lepar. Later, they were taking us in groups to Croatian soldiers who would rape us during nights . . . I remember a woman Kaća, a Croatian woman married to a Serb, who had two brothers in Croatian army . . . One night, nine Croatian soldiers raped Kaća in the warehouse of the Belgrade department store in Bosanski Brod. She could not stand on her feet for three days.
>
> (Čolić, 2002)

Testimonies such as this substantiate the feminist thesis that war is fought primarily over women bodies, regardless of their ethnicity. As Brownmiller (1976) argues, 'rape is directed against all women who belong to other men' (p. 181). It is used with an aim of dehumanisation and terror. Rada Borić ('Letter of Intention' quoted in Borić, n.d., p. 1) asserts too that:

> women were often raped because of real or invented behaviour of the male members of their family ('guilty for the sins of others') . . . rape was performed with an intention to punish male relative(s). And indirectly, to punish all male members of a women's ethnic group. In that manner, a woman's body ultimately becomes the place of interethnic 'communication'.

Despite these acknowledgments, rape in BiH was reduced exclusively to the dynamics between Serb males and Croat and Moslem women (Rejali, 1996, p. 366). Similarly, rapes have been constructed in the literature almost exclusively in this way: the body of a Serb man against the body of a Croat or Muslim woman. Any other bodily combination is excluded from the mainstream discussion. As a result, wartime rapes have become a symbol of primarily Bosniak and to some extent Croat women's suffering while the experiences of 'other' women were, at best, downplayed and, at worst, ignored. Rada Boric (n.d.) notes, we know that all women are exposed to rape, regardless of their ethnicities, but their gender and womanhood is inevitably 'blurred' by national/ethnic or religious 'representation' (p. 6). A few feminist scholars have noted that Serb women have not been on anyone's agenda (locally and internationally) because they were viewed as ultimately belonging to the 'Serb rapists' (Stiglmayer, 1993; Nikolić-Ristanović, 1999).

Since the experiences of Serb women as rape victims were largely silenced by the media, these women have been doubly victimised: once by soldiers or civilians who belonged to the 'other side', to the war enemy, who raped them and then by members of their 'own' constituency, who do not recognise their victimhood. International actors have also shown little interest in Serb women as victims. In 1994, Alexandra Stiglmayer reported why Serb women stayed muted and ignored by foreign journalists who flocked BiH in search of a 'good' story:

> [b]ecause of the suffering of Muslim and Croat rape victims, we frequently forget that Serbian women in Bosnia-Herzegovina are also being raped. Of course, they are not affected by rape as frequently as the Moslems . . . the real reason that Serbian women seldom appear in the reports of rapes in Bosnia might be a different one: they are the wives, sisters and daughters of the aggressors. There is hardly a journalist who feels motivated to seek them out, to check up on what has happened to them and thus offer propaganda material to the Serbian side – that is, the bad side, the side 'responsible for the war'.
>
> (p. 132)

Amnesty International in their recent country report offers an analysis of the situation of rape survivors but it admits that it 'did not talk to Bosnian Serb women survivors of rape and other sexual abuse crimes' because it is 'difficult for these women to come out in the public and speak up' (2012, p. 4). The fact is that the difficulty of talking about rape experiences is not something unique to Serb women but to any survivor of rape, regardless of ethnicity, race or any other identity determinator.

Similarly, one of the reasons why research into wartime rape is confined to Bosniak women has been offered by Skjelsbaek (2006):

> [w]hile it is a well-established fact that Serb and Croat women were also victims of similar forms of sexual violence during the war, this study draws its empirical findings from interviews with Bosniak women. There are pragmatic reasons for this choice. Though many of the local organizations I contacted aim to be multi-ethnic, there are simply more Bosniak women members of such organizations than members from other nationalities. It was therefore easier to get in touch with Bosniak women who were willing to talk than to contact similar women from other nationalities.
>
> (p. 378)

This statement is significant for two reasons. First, it suggests that there are few (if any) local organisations that represent non-Bosniak women survivors of rape in BiH.[7] Second, local organisations of women survivors are hardly multi-ethnic

7 According to some estimations, there are around 60 local women NGOs in FBiH that bring together women survivors of rape, torture and/or genocide.

since the researcher has struggled to find any other than Bosniak women survivors. As a result, even if researchers want to interview 'other' women, they have the hard or impossible task of attempting to reach them.[8] While there has been no women's non-governmental organisation (NGO) in the Republika Srpska (RS) entity bringing together women survivors of torture until recently (January 2013), if researchers wanted to reach these women they could do so indirectly through other local women's NGOs who have contact details for women willing to talk about their experiences.

4. Consequences of hierarchies

As a consequence of ethnopolitical perceptions that were framed along hierarchies of victimhood, testimonies of women from backgrounds other than Bosniak and Croat remain scarce and fragmented. There is a lack of knowledge about the scope of wartime rape and sexual abuse of Serb women.[9] The limited resources available on this topic have been scattered throughout various archives, court files and cases. A few documentary films made by The Association of Former Camp Inmates RS or journalists employed with the Radio Television RS (RTRS) are publicly available via the Internet. However, these movies are not commercialised; many are not transcribed into English or any other foreign language and so remain inaccessible to foreign journalists and researchers. The movies are difficult and painful to watch and, as such, are unattractive to local media. Further, these movies will not be taken up by anti-nationalist, anti-militarist or feminist groups since they promote nationalism and a 'one-sided' story of war that is not helpful for advancing peace and reconciliation. The failure to comprehensively report that Serb women were also raped, along with Croat and Bosniak women, had the effect of concealing the suffering and hardship experienced by Bosnian Serb women. This climate in BiH, in which the focus of media and academia, understanding and empathy turned towards one group of survivors only, resulted in delivering and developing an extensive psycho-social and legal support to primarily Bosniak women victims of rape living in FBiH.

Such polarised and strongly established view had enormous consequences on the lives of women survivors in both entities. During the war and in its aftermath, international organisations assisted in the establishment of dozens of NGOs in

8 The latest report on the position of women victims of wartime rape produced by Medica Zenica draws on interviews with 47 Bosniak, two Serb and two Croat women. See: Husić, Šiljak, Osmanović, Đekić & Heremić, 2014.

9 While Roma women had also been victims of rape, there has not been any research conducted into the experiences of these women. Such research is long overdue. So far, at least one case of mass killings and rape is known today – the *Skočić* case. At least three women and a 13-year-old girl were repeatedly gang raped by a member of the Serb paramilitary army called 'Sima Chetniks'. The 13-year-old girl, Zlatija Ribić, was later killed. See: Humanitarian Law Center. (26 February 2013). *Statement regarding the Conviction in Skočić Case* [Press Release]. Retrieved from www.hlc-rdc.org/?p=22549&lang=de, 12 August 2014.

FBiH that offer assistance to women survivors of wartime rape. Such support advanced women in FBiH in the sense that, at least, the government in this entity has shown some political will to move things, albeit slowly, on better. For example, as a result of a joint local and international feminist campaigns in 2006 women survivors now can exercise their right to material reparation as civilian victims of wartime rape. The government of FBiH has to pay reparation on a monthly basis for material and non-material harm to survivors who gain the status of 'civilian victim of war'.

On the other hand, support and assistance to wartime rape survivors who live in the RS entity, with the majority of the Serb population, are entirely missing. Women victims of rape living in this entity (regardless of their ethnicity) have not had any proper legal and financial support. International donors and aid agencies have shown no interest in developing programs to help them recover from trauma and regain their lives. As a result, today, almost 20 years after the war ended, there are no NGOs or governmental institutions in RS that have developed programs and strategies for the recovery and rehabilitation of wartime rape survivors. The polarised view and entrenched hierarchy of rape victims is an obstacle to donors developing projects and programs of assistance and rehabilitation to Serb and other women living in RS. Another problem is that to date many women have not succeeded in gaining the official status of civilian victim of war. Different treatment has led to diverging legal efforts within the two Bosnian entities and the status of victims of wartime rape differs substantially between the entities. In FBiH, rape victims are acknowledged as a special category of civilian victims of war and can achieve a status of victim that foresees monthly compensation while in RS victims of sexual violence have been treated as all other civilian victims of war. Women who applied for reparation in RS needed to provide medical evidence of physical disability: they could not request the status of victim with witness statements which is not the case in the FBiH. Popić and Panjeta (2010) noted that eligibility for compensation:

> is not based on the right that was violated. Instead, the right to receive compensation is based on the degree of physical disability, which may or may not reflect the experience of a victim of gross violations of human rights and serious violation of international humanitarian law.
>
> (p. 9)

It is not surprising that only 'a handful of women' received the status of civilian victim of war on the basis of wartime rape in RS because of the difficulties in obtaining the necessary medical documentation and proving that they suffered 60% of bodily harm, as required by RS law and because the deadline for applying for victim status had expired in 2007.[10] If a woman cannot meet such a high

10 Official correspondence with the Ministry of Labour and War Veterans of Republika Srpska, Banja Luka, 14 November, 2013. On file with the author.

threshold, but was nevertheless detained in a camp, beaten and/or tortured, she will not be entitled to any type of compensation in accordance with entity laws. To impose such a condition on rape survivors and completely disregard their psychological well being is unacceptable as it is well-known that experiences of sexual violence leave trauma that woman continue to live with.

5. Conclusion

Irrespective of their ethnicity, rape victims in BiH have been invisible and left with the feeling of shame and guilt for being (raped) (Mlinarević, Čaušević and Čaušević, 2012). Although victims of rape in the FBiH have more opportunities to exercise their human right, what is common to all women victims of rape in BiH is that they feel forgotten, stigmatised and left out from community, with no capacity to influence the political and social transformation of the country in which they live. They have collectively become 'collateral damage': an unfortunate by-product of war, faceless and nameless.

In 2013, the UN Committee on the Elimination of Discrimination Against Women (CEDAW) expressed its deep concern about the long delays in adopting measures to address the needs of a large number of women victimised by the conflict and their:

> inadequate and unequal access to compensation, support and rehabilitation measures for violations suffered during the war, including enforced disappearances, such as sustained psychological and medical support, as well as financial and social benefits, which are regulated differently in the entities.
>
> (para. 9c)

Almost 20 years after the war, one of the biggest obstacles to reconciliation and long-lasting peace in BiH that remains is ignorance about the experiences of thousands of women victims of sexual abuse and the discriminatory status these women have in respect to exercising their rights to material and symbolic reparation. Women victims of war still lack adequate medical, social and psychological support in BiH but in particular in RS where authorities have failed to recognise the rights of victims living in this entity. Women continue to wait for justice, recognition and support. Unfortunately many of them, due to age or ill-health, may not live long enough to receive the justice they deserve, unless the government fulfils its duties proscribed by law.[11]

11 Ljubica Lešić is one of the women survivors who died recently due to a heart condition. She was to appear as a witness in the first case against former Croatian soldiers indicted for rape and torture in 1992 in the Posavina region. See: Radio Slobodna Evropa (2014, April 21). Uhapšena Četvorica zbog ratnog zločina u Odžaku. *Slobodna Evropa*. Retrieved from www.slobodnaevropa.org/archive/news/20140421/500/500.html?id=25356995, 11 November 2014.

The Bosnian Serb women need to reclaim their voices and narrate their stories in order to realise their human rights and contribute to the process of truth recovery (Simpson, 2007). The authorities of RS, but also of BiH must, at the least, officially acknowledge that rape and other forms of sexual torture were committed during the war against all women. This will help create an atmosphere where public debate on this issue will thrive and survivors will feel confident to come forward, tell their stories and demand justice.

References

Amnesty International (2012). *Bosnia and Herzegovina: Old crimes same suffering: No justice for survivors of wartime rape in north-east Bosnia and Herzegovina* (Report). Bosnia and Herzegovina: Campaign for International Justice.

Anti-ratni Bilten SOS-a (1993, March 8). Broj 4, Beograd (SOS telefon za žene i decu žrtve nasilja).

Askin, K. D. (1997). *War crimes against women: Prosecution in International War Crimes Tribunals.* Netherlands: Martinus Nijhoff Publishers.

B. A. (2014, January 8). Bakira Hasečić Bošnjački političari i intelektualci su kukavice. *24 sata info.* Retrieved from www.24sata.info/vijesti/intervju/177029-bakira-hasecic-bosnjacki-politicari-i-intelektualci-su-kukavice.html.

Borić, R. (n.d.). *Gendered violence in the Balkans, sexualized violence against women.* Paper on file with the author.

Brownmiller, S. (1976). *Against Our Will: Men, Women and Rape.* Toronto: Bantam Books.

Buss, D. (2009). 'Rethinking rape as a weapon of war'. *Feminist Legal Studies, 17,* 145–163.

Christie, N. (1986) 'Ideal victim'. In E. A. Fattah (Ed.), *From Crime Policy to Victim Policy: Reorienting the Justice System* (pp. 17–30). Basingstoke, Hampshire: Macmillan.

Čolić, D. (2002, May 24). Tukli su me i silovanli. *Blic Online.* Retrieved from www.blic.rs/stara_arhiva/reportaze/27076/Tukli-su-me-i-silovali.

Committee on the Elimination of Discrimination against Women (2013, July 25). *Concluding Observations on the Combined Fourth and Fifth Periodic Reports of Bosnia and Herzegovina.* CEDAW/C/BIH/CO/4-5.

Copelon, R. (1994a). 'Surfacing gender: Reconceptualizing crimes against women in Bosnia-Herzegovina'. In A. Stiglmayer (Ed.), *Mass Rape: The War Against Women in Bosnia-Herzegovina* (pp. 197–218). London: University of Nebraska Press.

Copelon, R. (1994b). 'Surfacing gender: Re-engraving crimes against women in humanitarian law'. *Hastings Women's Law Journal, 5*(2), 243–265.

Engle, K. (2005). 'Feminism and its (Dis)contents: Criminalizing Wartime Rape in Bosnia and Herzegovina'. *American Journal of International Law, 99*(4), 778–816.

Estrich, S. (1987). *Real Rape.* Cambridge, Massachusetts: Harvard University Press.

Franke, K. M. (2006). 'Gendered subjects of transitional justice'. *Columbia Journal of Gender and Law, 15*(3), 813–828.

Fraser, N. (2000). 'Rethinking recognition'. *New Left Review, 3,* 107–120.

Hague, W. (2012, May 29). *Foreign Secretary announces UK initiative on preventing sexual violence in conflict.* UK: Foreign & Commonwealth Office. Retrieved from www.gov.uk/government/news/foreign-secretary-announces-uk-initiative-on-preventing-sexual-violence-in-conflict.

Helms, E. (2013). *Innocence and Victimhood: Gender, Nation, and Women's Activism in Postwar Bosnia-Herzegovina.* Madison, Wisconsin: University of Wisconsin Press.

Henry, N. (2014). 'The fixation on wartime rape: Feminist critique and international criminal law'. *Social & Legal Studies*, *23*, 93–111.

Human Rights Watch (1995). *The Human Rights Watch Global Report on Women's Human Rights* (Report). New York: Human Rights Watch.

Humanitarian Law Center (2013, February 26). *Statement regarding the conviction in Skočić Case* [Press Release]. Retrieved from www.hlc-rdc.org/?p=22549&lang=de.

Husić, S., Šiljak, I., Osmanović, E. Đekić, F. & Heremić, L. (2014). 'We are still alive': Research of the long-term consequences of war rape and coping strategies of survivors in Bosnia and Herzegovina. Germany: Medica Zenica.

ICTY (n.d.). *About the ICTY*. Retrieved from www.icty.org/sections/AbouttheICTY.

Kajevska, A. M. (2014). *Taking a stand in times of violent societal changes: Belgrade and Zagreb feminists' positionings on the (post-)Yugoslav wars and each other (1991–2000)* (PhD Thesis). University of Amsterdam, Netherlands.

Kapur, R. (2002). 'The tragedy of victimization rhetoric: Resurrecting the "native" subject in international/postcolonial feminist legal politics'. *Harvard Human Rights Journal*, *15*, 1–38.

Kerr, R. (2007). 'Peace through justice? The International Criminal Tribunal for former Yugoslavia'. *Southeast European and Black Sea Studies*, *7*(3), 373–385. doi:10.1080/14683850701565973.

Kesić, O. (1999). 'Women and gender imagery in Bosnia: Amazons, sluts, victims, witches, and wombs'. In S. P. Ramet (Ed.), *Gender and Politics in the Western Balkans: Women and Society in Yugoslavia and the Yugoslav Successor States* (pp. 187–202). University Park, Pennsylvania: Pennsylvania State University Press.

Kesić, V. (1994). 'A response to Catharine MacKinnon's article "Turning rape into pornography: Postmodern genocide"'. *Hastings Women's Law Journal*, *5*, 267–280.

Kesić, V. (2003, September 5). Muslim women, Croatian women, Serbian women, Albanian women. *Eurozine*. Retrieved from www.eurozine.com/articles/2003-05-09-kesic-en.html.

Kohn, E. A. (1994). 'Rape as a weapon of war: Women's human rights during the dissolution of Yugoslavia'. *Golden Gate University Law Review*, *24*(1), 199–221.

Korać, M. (1994). 'Representation of mass rape in ethnic conflicts in what was Yugoslavia'. *Sociologija*, *36*(4), 495–514.

Law on principles of social protection, protection of all civilian victims of war and protection of families with children (Official Gazette of FBiH, no 36/99, 54/04 and 39/06).

Luban, D. (2004). 'A theory of crimes against humanity'. *Yale Journal of International Law*, *29*, 85–167.

MacKinnon, C. (1994a). 'Turning rape into pornography'. In A. Stiglmayer (Ed.), *Mass Rape: The War against Women in Bosnia-Herzegovina* (pp. 73–81). London: University of Nebraska Press.

MacKinnon, C. (1994b). 'Rape, genocide and human rights'. *Harvard Women's Law Journal*, *17*, 5–16.

Meznaric, S. (1994). 'Gender as an ethno-marker: Rape, war and identity in the Former Yugoslavia'. In V. M. Moghadam (Ed.), *Identity Politics and Women: Cultural Reassertion and Feminism in International Perspective* (pp. 76–97). Boulder: Westview Press.

Mischkowski, G. & Mlinarević G. (2009, December). *'. . . and that it does not happen to anyone anywhere in the world': The trouble with rape trials – Views of witnesses, prosecutors and judges on prosecuting sexualised violence during the war in the former Yugoslavia* (Study). Köln: Medica Mondiale.

Mlađenović, L. (1993). Nacrt za projekta za centar za zene silovane u ratu. *Žene za Žene*, Beograd.

Mlinarević, G., Čaušević, J. and Čaušević, J. (2012). *Prosecution of wartime sexualized violence at the Court of Bosnia and Herzegovina: What happened to the interest of justice? An analysis and recommendations of gender sensitive trial monitoring for wartime sexualized violence cases in Bosnia and Herzegovina for the period 23/05/2011 – 25/05/2012* (Report). Sarajevo: Association Alumni of the Centre for Interdisciplinary Postgraduate Studies. Retrieved from http://www.acips.ba/bos/uploads/publikacije/ACIPS%20Prosecution%20of%20wartime%20sexualized%20violence.pdf.

Nikolić-Ristanović, V. (1999). 'Sexual violence'. In V. Nikolić-Ristanović (Ed.), *Women, Violence and War: Wartime Victimization of Refugees in the Balkans* (pp. 41–78). Budapest: Central European University Press.

Ninemsn (2014, March 29). Jolie moved to tears after meeting rape victims. *Nine News*. Retrieved from www.9news.com.au/entertainment/2014/03/29/09/27/jolie-moved-to-tears-after-meeting-rape-victims.

Nizich, I. (1994). 'Violations of the rules of war by Bosnian Croat and Muslim forces in Bosnia and Herzegovina'. *Hastings Women Law Journal*, *5*(1), 25–52.

Obradović-Wochnik, J. (2014). 'Revisionism, denial and anti-ICTY discourse in Serbia's public sphere: Beyond the "divided society" debate'. In J. Gow, R. Kerr, & Z. Pajic (Eds.), *Prosecuting War Crimes: Lessons and Legacies of the International Criminal Tribunal for the Former Yugoslavia* (pp. 182–203). London: Routledge.

OHCR (2012, November 5). *Violence against women, a war legacy in Bosnia and Herzegovina – UN Special Rapporteur* [Press Release]. Retrieved from www.ohchr.org/EN/NewsEvents/Pages/DisplayNews.aspx?NewsID=12747&LangID=E#sthash.G8d1rwFF.dpuf.

Orentlicher, D. F. (2008, May). *Shrinking the space for denial: The impact of the ICTY in Serbia* (Report). New York: Open Society Justice Initiative.

Organization for Security and Co-operation in Europe (OSCE) (2014, February). *Combating impunity for conflict-related sexual violence in BiH: Progress and challenges: An analysis of criminal proceedings before the Court of Bosnia and Herzegovina between 2005 and 2013* (Report). Sarajevo: OSCE Mission to Bosnia and Herzegovina. Retrieved from www.osce.org/bih/117051.

Pavlović, T. (1999). 'Women in Croatia: Feminists, nationalists and homosexuals'. In S. P. Ramet (Ed.), *Gender Politics in Western Balkans: Women and Society in Yugoslavia and the Yugoslav Successor States* (pp. 131–152). University Park, Pennsylvania: Pennsylvania State University Press.

Popić, L. & Panjeta, B. (2010, June). *Compensation, transitional justice and conditional international credit in Bosnia and Herzegovina: Attempts to reform government payments to victims and veterans of the 1992–1995 war* (Report). Bosnia and Herzegovina: Royal Norwegian Embassy in Bosnia and Herzegovina; Embassy of Switzerland in Bosnia and Herzegovina. Retrieved from www.norveska.ba/PageFiles/417487/Study_Linda_Popic_english.pdf.

Prosecutor v Zejnil Delalic and others (The Čelebići Case), Case No IT-96-21-T, *Judgment*, 16 November 1998.

Radio Slobodna Evropa. (2014, April 21). Uhapšena Četvorica zbog ratnog zločina u Odžaku. Slobodna Evropa. Retrieved from www.slobodnaevropa.org/archive/news/20140421/500/500.html?id=25356995.

Rejali, D. M. (1996). 'After feminist analyses of Bosnian violence'. *Peace Review*, *8*, 365–371.

Simons, M. (1998, March 10). An ex-Bosnian Serb Commander admits rape of Muslims in war. *The New York Times*. Retrieved from www.nytimes.com/1998/03/10/world/an-ex-bosnian-serb-commander-admits-rape-of-muslims-in-war.html.

Simpson, K. (2007). 'Voices silenced, voices rediscovered: victims of violence and the reclamation of language in transitional societies'. *International Journal of Law in Context, 3*, 89–103.

Skjelsbaek, I. (2006). 'Victim and survivor: Narrated social identities of women who experienced rape during the war in Bosnia-Hezegovina'. *Feminism and Psychology, 16*(4), 373–403.

Stiglmayer, A. (1994). 'The rapes in Bosnia-Herzegovina'. In A. Stiglmayer (Ed.), *Mass Rape: The War against Women in Bosnia-Herzegovina* (pp. 82–169). London: University of Nebraska Press.

Thomas, D. Q. & Ralph, R. E. (1999). 'Rape in war: The case in Bosnia'. In S. P. Ramet (Ed.), *Gender Politics in Western Balkans: Women and Society in Yugoslavia and the Yugoslave Successor States* (pp. 203–218). University Park, Pennsylvania: Pennsylvania State University Press.

UN Commission of Experts (1994). *Rape and sexual assault – Final report of the UN Commission of Experts.* UN Doc S/1994/674/Add. 2.28 December.

Yoshiaki, Y. (1995). *Comfort Women: Sexual Slavery in the Japanese Military during World War II.* New York: Columbia University Press.

All links mentioned in the list of references were accessed on 15 January 2015.

Chapter 5

Political memory as an obstacle to justice in Serbia, Croatia, and Bosnia-Herzegovina[1]

Jelena Subotić

1. Introduction

On his very first day in office in June 2012, the newly elected Serbian president Tomislav Nikolić said that no genocide took place in Srebrenica, and that, in any case, genocide was "difficult to prove in court" (B92, 2012). Right on cue, Bosnian Presidency Chairman Bakir Izetbegović responded that Nikolić's statement was "untrue and offensive for Bosniacs, especially for the survivors of Srebrenica genocide . . . Serbian leaders and Serbian people need to face the truth about crimes committed in Bosnia-Herzegovina in order to improve state relations and enable that the future in the region is better than its past" (B92, 2012). But this was not Nikolić's first foray into historical justice debates. Just before the second round of presidential elections, he declared that a "greater Serbia was [his] unrealized dream" and that "Vukovar was a Serbian town to which Croats should not return". While he quickly backtracked and denied this claim given in an interview to a German newspaper, his original statement caused an uproar in Croatia and was the subject of much passionate debate on Croatian TV. The Croatian president, Ivo Josipović, gave a stern response: "Croatia knew how to defend its sovereignty [in the past] . . . it will know how to defend it today."

Twenty years since the start of the Yugoslav wars, the countries of the region are stuck in public narratives of the past that are mutually exclusive, contradictory, and irreconcilable. I suggest that there is a direct link between ways in which different states remember their pasts and efforts to bring justice for past wrongs in the Western Balkans. In fact, instead of being productive instruments of transitional justice, official remembrance efforts in the region in the areas of history education and national memorialization have been largely used to further entrench mutually incompatible versions of the past and contribute to a renewed cycle of mistrust, untruth, and injustice. I suggest that memory projects need to be redesigned to include a much broader regional focus which would compel states in the region

1 This is a revised and updated version of an article that first appeared as Subotić, J. (2013). 'Remembrance, Public Narratives, and Obstacles to Justice in the Western Balkans' *Studies in Social Justice*, 7(2), 265–283.

to confront their pasts directly, and not dwell on their own victimization in isolation. Regional commissions of inquiry, comprehensive education reform, and multi-state memorialization projects should, therefore, not be thought of as secondary initiatives, but as critical steps in pursuit of regional justice based on trust, respect, and dignity. For this to happen, however, profound political change must first take place.

The chapter is structured as follows. I first present a brief argument about the relationship between justice and remembrance of the past. I then explore ways in which education and memorialization projects contribute to justice efforts. Following this, I illustrate the state of contemporary public debates about the past in Serbia, Croatia, and Bosnia with a focus on education and memorialization policies. I conclude by proposing mechanisms of public memory that would be more conducive to long-term reconciliation and regional justice, understood here as the basic tenets of transitional justice: reckoning with past wrongs, acknowledging victims' suffering, and repairing broken societies.

2. Justice and remembrance of the past

Transitional justice—a set of mechanisms aimed at addressing legacies of violence—has greatly expanded and deepened over the past twenty years as a field of inquiry. While early efforts at systematically addressing crimes of the past focused mostly on trials of perpetrators or truth commissions and were dominated by legal models and solutions, transitional justice as a field has broadened to include a much wider range of mechanisms, ideas, and policies (Bell, 2009). The principal assumption of transitional justice, however, remains that finding out the truth about past wrongs, identifying the perpetrators, and punishing them appropriately achieves justice by ending impunity (Mendeloff, 2004).

The claim that finding out the truth and remembering the past accomplishes justice is an ambitious one and can be broken down to a few analytical steps. First, the creation of a reliable record of past events—a credible truth commission report, for example—offers a platform for victims to tell their stories and restore the dignity of the victim. Second, truth finding and public remembrance can result in proposing legal or political remedies to avoid future violence, and also determine individual responsibility and punishment of perpetrators (a form of retributive justice). Finally, public remembrance can repair the injury suffered by victims through restitution, reparations, or apologies—a form of reparative justice (Minow, 1998). At the individual level, remembrance is thought to bring justice to individual victims by acknowledging their suffering, hearing their stories, and helping to heal the trauma that results from violence. Remembrance can also lead to justice by preventing revenge killing and instead placing retribution for atrocity within the framework of individual criminal accountability, and avoiding collective guilt. When justice is delivered through criminal prosecutions of individual perpetrators, it can break the cycle of violence by ending impunity.

At the public level, states can institutionalize a certain practice of remembrance through education, such as in history textbooks, but also through public commemoration practices such as monuments, museums, street names, memory sites, and national holidays. Public remembrance that produces a new, authoritative historical record of past violence can help create a new, shared history of groups in conflict, which then opens up the possibility for group reconciliation and more peaceful coexistence in the future. Public education is critical for this effort. Creating a credible account of past violence can provide an opportunity for society to learn from its criminal past and prevent similar atrocities from happening in the future (Hayner, 1994). Post-conflict education, therefore, has the potential to "demystify the past" and inculcate the public culture of human rights (Sarkin, 1999) or, even broadly, the culture of peace (Oglesby, 2007). Public education about the violent past is especially important for "perpetrator states," where society has yet to undergo a profound repudiation of the criminal past.

Changing entrenched narratives is clearly a difficult task. Uncontested public memories of past conflicts become salient because they are assimilated into public discourse and become very difficult to challenge, reproducing themselves over time, and taking on a life of their own (McGrattan, 2010). These public beliefs then become "deposited" into social institutions that act as "collective memory archives" for different political actors to draw upon (Aguilar, 2002). Public education after conflict is, therefore, important in order "to reduce the number of lies that can be circulated unchallenged in the public discourse" (Ignatieff, 1998, p. 173). Further, schools themselves are often spaces where profound systemic injustices are reproduced, through inclusion or exclusion of different groups, classes, and types of students and through teaching of stories of exclusion, separation, and isolation (Cole, 2007). Schools are, therefore, unique locations of a wider societal repair (Weinstein, Freedman & Hughson, 2007). School education, however, can also serve as an inculcator of intolerant ideologies and a disseminator of pernicious ethnic stereotypes (King, 2014).

History education in particular is critical to the success of a broader transitional justice project in post-conflict societies. How citizens understand history is crucial to a society's ability to deal with the difficult past and build a more just future (Cole, 2007). History education is an integral part of the larger transitional justice effort as it can deepen and personalize official acknowledgment of the harm done and suggest ways to embark on social repair.

Teaching about the past, however, is fraught with analytical, ethical, and interpretive minefields. History, especially at pre-college level, has traditionally been the most conservative area of education, focusing much more freely on the distant than on the recent past, and is therefore the area of education most scrutinized by the state (Cole, 2007). Further, history will and should always be contested, and the idea of multi-perspectivity is a growing trend in historical pedagogy. While this means that multiple interpretations of past events may be welcomed, it also means that a new reinterpretation of the past can be used for a renewed conflict in the future (Cole, 2007).

In the next section, I evaluate a few recent efforts at state remembrance of the past in the Western Balkans as preconditions for the pursuit of post-conflict justice in the region. The analysis of remembrance, broadly understood, is especially needed in the scholarship on the Balkans, since most of the transitional justice literature on the region has focused almost exclusively on the retributive justice efforts—trials for perpetrators of war crimes in front of domestic courts and the International Criminal Tribunal for the former Yugoslavia/ICTY (Nettelfield, 2010a; Orentlicher, 2008, 2010). The emphasis on retributive justice in Western Balkans scholarship has followed the same emphasis in international policymaking, as most international efforts and incentives were designed to jump start or improve existing trials of individual perpetrators. This focus on retribution has then effectively equated the larger field of transitional justice with just its one possible dimension—punishment—and has deemphasized many other available mechanisms that are designed to work on societal reparation or restoration. This is why in this chapter I focus deliberately on two other measurements of transitional justice: the teaching of history and national memorialization. My research shows that, instead of being used as instruments of transitional justice in the region, official remembrance projects in public education and commemoration have been used to further entrench mutually incompatible versions of the past and contribute to a renewed cycle of mistrust, untruth, and injustice.

3. Remembering the past in the Western Balkans

There are few better ways to reconstruct a state's remembrance of its past than by analyzing history textbooks. As Mendeloff has argued, history textbooks embody "lowest common denominator" history—"a distilled version of popular history and historical memory that appeals to the widest possible audience" (Mendeloff, 2008, p. 37). History textbooks are important barometers of dominant state remembrance because they are explicitly designed to inculcate particular views of the past into future generations. Memories of the past and the understanding and interpretation of history are always rewritten for the purposes of the political present. The problem with history education in the Western Balkans, however, is that this region's histories are multiple, contradictory, and mutually exclusive. Far from being a tool for social cohesion and healing, they continue to be instruments of political othering, alienation, and further injustice.

3.1. Serbia

After Milošević was removed from power in 2000, new, revised, history textbooks were developed in Serbia.[2] While the language was cleaned up and some of the

2 Some of the material covering history textbook debates in Serbia and Croatia is adapted from Subotić, 2013.

more overt hate speech from earlier textbooks toned down, the fundamental view about Serbia's past, especially as it relates to the breakup of the former Yugoslavia, remained mostly intact. The Serbian state continues to be represented as a victim, and Yugoslavia as a country destroyed by separatists in Slovenia, Croatia, and Bosnia, who worked against the interests of the Serbian nation (Stojanović, 2011). Serbian regional territorial aspirations, therefore, are interpreted not just as defensive, but also as preventive, to stop the inevitable crimes against the Serbian people. This narrative is what guides the new Serbian president Nikolić to recently warn of an "impending genocide against Serbs in Kosovo" (*The Guardian*, July 29, 2012).

This state effort at keeping silent about the Serbian criminal past has been largely successful. Surveys consistently show that the public mostly refuses to believe that Serbs had committed war crimes, and blamed other nations and ethnic groups for starting the wars (Ramet, 2007). In a recent large survey of popular knowledge about Serbian history, only 34 percent of the respondents correctly identified the victims of Srebrenica as Bosniacs, and only 10 percent reported that Croats, not Serbs, were killed in a mass atrocity in Ovčara, outside Vukovar, Croatia in 1991 (Manojlović Pintar, 2010, p. 97). It is difficult to ascertain whether this is simply ignorance of past events, or a more profound strategy of a "conspiracy of shame," where traumatic events for which we are responsible become a deeply buried "family secret," never to be discussed aloud (Ćurgus Kazimir, 2005).

While at the level of retributive justice, the transfer of last remaining war crimes fugitives to The Hague, and the ongoing trials before the Serbian War Crimes Chamber are very significant and demonstrate improved commitment to the rule of law, in terms of reparative justice and state apologies, Serbia has made a few contradictory moves. For example, the Serbian Parliament in March 2010 adopted the domestically controversial "Declaration on Srebrenica," which acknowledged the massacre at Srebrenica while never mentioning the term "genocide." This rhetorical strategy is an example of "interpretive denial," where crimes of the past are not denied as outright lies, but are interpreted in a manner that gives past events a very different meaning (Cohen, 2001). Another example of interpretive denial of the Srebrenica genocide is the shift in focus in the Serbian intellectual discourse. While the events at Srebrenica used to be flat out denied, they are now begrudgingly accepted as "real," but the number of victims is now dramatically lowered in most of the media reports (Helsinki Committee for Human Rights in Serbia, 2011). The Declaration, therefore, was a missed opportunity for the Serbian government to make a clean break and deconstruct the public remembrance of Serbia's past. Instead, it served to further entrench the dominant memory of the past in Serbia and foreclose on opportunities for engagement and dialogue with victims of Serbia's war effort.

What Serbia remembers most from the wars of the 1990s is, of course, its own victimization, the NATO intervention in 1999. The NATO war only further solidified Serbian feelings of victimhood and a great sense of injustice at the hands of great powers. In fact, a succession of Serbian governments post 1999, even after Milošević's ousting in 2000, consciously decided to promote the memory of Serbian victimhood during the NATO air war as if it were the central motif of the wars in the 1990s (David, 2013).

The evidence of this narrative is clear even with a cursory look at the official Serbian national calendar, "The State Program for Commemorating the Anniversaries of Historic Events of the Serbian Liberation Wars," which was adopted after much discussion and delay in March 2009. According to the official commemoration calendar, the wars of Yugoslav succession in the 1990s either never happened, or did not involve Serbia as a major participant. Various historical events representing Serbian victimhood or injustice suffered are, however, present in seven commemorative national holidays (David, 2012).[3] Similarly, the Serbian state embarked on a comprehensive project of renaming city streets, replacing all names associated with communist or antifascist heroes, which were abundant since 1945, with heroes or heroic events more broadly associated with Serbian "tradition," anticommunism, nationalism, and especially the Orthodox Church (Govedarica, 2012).[4]

What the state wants citizens to remember, therefore, are instances of loss, injustice, and pain inflicted on heroic Serbs of the past. What it wants them to forget are any memories of the Serbian state and its citizens inflicting pain or misery on others, or even acknowledge the suffering beyond its borders. Even what is considered the prime historical incidence of suffering—the Holocaust—is first memorialized as a crime against Serbs, and only then as a crime against Jews and others (Byford, 2007). The understanding of Serbia's past, therefore, continues to shape its future. Serbia's remembrance is not inclusive of the memory of others. It is exclusionary, isolating, and far from ready for the reconciliatory narrative reconstruction necessary for continuing justice efforts.

3.2. Croatia

The central tenet of Croatian remembrance of the past as derived from its history education is that, "Croats never fought aggressive, but only defensive wars" (Agičić & Najbar-Agičić, 2007, p. 204). This view is also reflected in the historical interpretation of Croatia's Homeland War of the 1990s, which is taught exclusively as being the consequence of Serbian aggression and terrorism, without any broader context of Yugoslav succession. Most textbooks dedicate considerable space to discussing Serbian crimes against Croatian civilians, but only one textbook even mentions, in passing, that thousands of Serbs were forced to leave Croatia in

3 The days in question commemorate Serbian victims of the battle against the Turks in 1809; Serbian losses in World War I and World War II, including at the Greek front in 1918; from German air attacks in 1941, and from Nazi genocide; and Serbian victims of the NATO air war in 1999.

4 The city of Belgrade alone has renamed 1,500 or about one-fifth of its street names since the early 1990s.

1995 during the ethnic cleansing campaign that accompanied Operation Storm (Agičić & Najbar-Agičić, 2007).

While the textbook market was liberalized and has been open to competition since 2000 (a process still not undertaken in Serbia), many of the books in circulation still use extreme nationalist language and concepts not much changed since the early 1990s. The fascist Independent State of Croatia is often glorified, and crimes of the ustasha regime marginalized or avoided (Mihajlović Trbovc & Pavasović Trošt, 2013). In fact, most of the Croatian textbooks currently in use "create in students the impression that Croatia has always been inhabited exclusively by Croats, while other ethnic groups appear as malicious newcomers and instigators of conflicts and problems" (Agičić & Najbar-Agičić, 2007, p. 212).

In 2005, a controversy erupted in Croatia regarding *Contemporary History Textbook Supplement*, a textbook written by a younger generation of Croatian historians, which included a critical analysis of Croatian efforts in the 1990s, as well as a statement that Croatian forces had committed war crimes against Serb civilians. The Croatian Education Ministry refused to approve the supplement, and a number of distinguished Croatian historians wrote open letters accusing the authors of a lack of patriotism. The authors were criticized for overemphasizing the suffering of Serbs, not using the terms "liberation" when discussing Operation Storm, and for painting it in a "negative light" (Agičić, 2011, pp. 361–362). The critics also offered this bold statement: "history textbooks must take into consideration not only scientific and pedagogic standards, but also national and state criteria" (Agičić, 2011, p. 362). It is hard to find more direct evidence of the role the teaching of history plays in nation-building projects than this attitude of the Croatian intellectual elite.

The Croatian Parliament had, on numerous occasions, actually legislated the memory of the war in Croatia and offered laws on how this event is to be commemorated, understood, and interpreted. Various Members of Parliament have put forward proposals for how to appropriately memorialize the war. In 2000, the Parliament adopted the "Declaration on the Homeland War," which compels "all officials and official organs of the Republic of Croatia to protect the fundamental values and dignity of the Homeland War" (Croatian Parliament, 2000). In practice, this meant discouraging any discussion of Croatian war crimes. The Declaration explicitly states that Croatia "led a just and legitimate, defensive and liberating, and not aggressive nor occupying war against any one; instead it defended its territory from Greater Serbian aggression within internationally recognized borders" (Croatian Parliament, 2000). In 2006, the Croatian Parliament adopted the "Declaration on Operation Storm," which requests from "the Croatian Parliament, Croatian scientific community, Croatian institutions of science and education, as well as media, to turn Operation Storm into a battle that will become part of Croatia's 'useful past' for its future generations" (Croatian Parliament, 2006).

Croatia's state remembrance is evident in many other official memorialization practices. For example, the Croatian government continues to finance commemorations to Croatian fascist ustasha troops executed by communists in 1945 at Bleiburg (Kolstø, 2010). The Croatian state also implicitly downplays the number of genocide victims killed during the World War II fascist-era Croatia, most notably in the way in which the contemporary exhibit is laid out and interpreted at Jasenovac concentration camp memorial site (Pavasović Trošt, 2012; Pavlaković, 2008).[5] Ironically, however, the former Croatian Prime Minister Ivo Sanader used the occasion of the Holocaust commemoration at Jasenovac in 2005 to make a remarkable equivalency claim between Croatian suffering during the Homeland War of the 1990s and the Holocaust: "We should not forget the aggression that Croatia endured because we too were victims of a terrible madness of Nazism and fascism, and we, Croatian citizens, Croats, know the best what it is like to suffer from aggression" (Banjeglav, 2012, p. 115). Obviously lost on the Prime Minister is the fact that the memorial site itself is a commemoration of the indigenous Croatian fascist movement and not of Croatian victimization.

The choice of Croatia's national holidays also demonstrates the official state strategy on what is to be remembered and how. There are three new national holidays that memorialize key moments in Croatia's "homeland war"—the Day of Victory and Homeland Thanksgiving (August 5, the date of the resolution of Operation Storm), Independence Day (October 8, the date Croatian Parliament declared Croatia's independence from the former Yugoslavia), and the fall of Vukovar (November 18). The August 5 celebration is especially significant in this context because, since 2004, the Croatian Government made it a practice for the entire Croatian political leadership (the President, Prime Minister and Speaker of the Parliament) to attend the memorial in Knin. The site of Knin is symbolic since it was historically the seat of the Croatian kingdom, and, during the 1990s war, the headquarters of the Croatian Serb rebellion (Pavlaković, 2010). It was during one of these commemorations, in 2006, that Prime Minister Sanader proclaimed that "'Storm' was not a crime; 'Storm' defeated the crime . . ." (*Jutarnji list*, August 6, 2006). In 2010, a youth organization erected a small plaque/monument for the Serbian victims of Operation Storm outside of Knin. The plaque was placed by the side of the road leading north of the city, to symbolize the thousands of Serb refugees who fled their homes during and after the military operation. Within a day, however, the plaque was removed by the Knin city authorities, who claimed that the plaque did not have the necessary permits, even though it was built with (subsequently denied) Croatian Government support (Banjeglav, 2012). The public remembrance of the city of Knin, therefore, is an example of the mutually exclusive power of memory: for Croatia, it is the site of triumph and independent statehood. For Serbia, it is the site of its failed Croatian project, and of the memory of Serbian exodus and loss.

5 The number of victims at Jasenovac varies fantastically from the minimal number offered by Croatian nationalists (40,000) to the vastly exaggerated number circulated by Serbian nationalists (700,000). Most comprehensive scholarly analyses put the probable number at somewhere between 70,000 and 100,000 dead (Graovac & Cvetković, 2005).

More broadly, the way in which the recent (and distant) past is remembered makes state narratives in Croatia and Serbia incompatible. Croatia remembers Operation Storm as the pinnacle of its fight for independence, an event that made the contemporary Croatian state possible. Serbia remembers Operation Storm as a site of Serbian defeat, a site of ethnic cleansing of Serb civilians. For the Croatian narrative, this criminalization of Operation Storm is inconceivable, because it criminalizes the Croatian state itself. The two narratives are speaking past each other; there is no discursive space in either of them for inclusion of an alternative, conciliatory, story. These are stories of exclusion and separation, not stories that build a sense of community. The fact that in November 2012 the ICTY acquitted two Croatian generals from any responsibility for the war crimes that followed Operation Storm (International Criminal Tribunal for the former Yugoslavia, 2012) has added further fuel to these narratives: in Croatia, of the purity and nobility of Operation Storm; in Serbia of another historical injustice against the Serbian people.

3.3. Bosnia-Herzegovina

In Bosnia, even more so than in Serbia or Croatia, history has developed an "ethnicity" of its own. In the aftermath of the Dayton Accords and the administrative partition of Bosnia, education policy has been decentralized and put in the hands of local authorities. Like everything else in postwar Bosnia, education has come to represent ethnic politics of the majority population in a particular region. Attempts at centralizing education platforms or unifying efforts in this sphere have failed, a consequence of the Dayton political reality that locked ethnic politics in its place and gave two major Bosnian political entities trappings of statehood (McMahon & Western, 2009; Perry, 2013).

What this means for the practice of history education is that not only are history narratives in Bosnia incompatible with those in Serbia and Croatia, but the three versions of the Bosnian past (Serbian, Croatian, and Bosniac) are incompatible within Bosnia itself. Bosnian students still use three very different sets of history textbooks: *Historija* for the Bosniac students printed in Sarajevo, *Povijest* for the Croatian students and imported from Croatia, and *Istorija* for the Serb students published in Belgrade, with an additional *Supplement* written specifically for the Bosnian Serb education market (Torsti, 2013). The absurdity of this ethnicization of education means that only the "Bosniac" textbook reflects the history of Bosnia in any systematic way, while the Croatian and Serbian versions refer to Croatia and Serbia, respectively, as ethnic "homelands" and mostly build on their historical narratives, different from, and largely opposed to, the narrative of the new Bosnian state. For example, the Bosniac textbook narrates the war of the 1990s through stories of Bosniac suffering, the unfair nature of war events, and the responsibility of outside powers for the conflict. It explains the cause of the war as aggression on the independent Bosnian state. The Serbian textbook, however, interprets the war as the result of Slovenian, Croatian, and Bosnian separatism that broke the former

Yugoslavia apart, while the Croatian textbook does not specify the cause of the war at all (Torsti, 2003).

Over the past 15 years, there have been multiple efforts—mostly driven by international actors—to reform the Bosnian education curriculum, especially in history and the social sciences. As part of the conditions for Bosnian admission to the Council of Europe in 1999, Bosnia was required to eliminate potentially offensive material from their textbooks. However, since they ran out of time to publish new textbooks, the education authorities instead agreed to redact the existing textbooks in sections deemed controversial. This rather absurd solution then led to equally absurd outcomes, such as student efforts to read the redacted "forbidden" text, further elevating their importance (Torsti, 2013, p. 218).

Almost two decades since the end of the war, these textbooks are still in circulation in Bosnia. The 2007 Open Society Institute review found that Bosnian history textbooks are "dividing and spreading hatred toward other national groups by relying on idealized autostereotypes of one's own groups and negative heterostereotypes of the other national groups," with Croatian and Serbian books being the biggest offenders (Torsti, 2013).

The problem with Bosnian education, however, is not only textbook content, but also the structural issues of segregation. It follows larger patterns of ethnic segregation in postwar Bosnia, and manifests itself in various models of physical segregation—demographic segregation that is the result of wartime ethnic cleansing and population displacement, the "separate but equal" model of "two schools under one roof," school busing policies that reinforce ethnic segregation by sending children to distant schools in order to educate ethnic groups "with their own kind," or mixed schools where minority students study "sensitive" national subjects (history, geography, language, religion) separately from everyone else (Perry, 2013). Integral to this effort of ethnicizing history is the obsession with language distinctions. Bosnian Serbs have come to use the Cyrillic alphabet exclusively to differentiate their written language from its Bosniac and Croatian counterparts, while the Bosniac and Croatian linguists have gone out of their way to construct increasingly separate language variants: the Bosniac version includes ever-more Turkisms, the Croatian version brings back old-Croatian elements—all in an effort to make the Serbo-Croatian language (historically the principal unifier of the region)—increasingly a marker of divergence and ethnic difference. These education strategies have created a new form of school geography, which is built on and further reproduces ethnic symmetry and division (Hromadžić, 2008).

The way in which the story of Bosnia is taught, therefore, serves to promote further ethnic division and politicization of the past in the country. The Bosnian political predicament influenced the teaching of history, but this also served to perpetuate the political status quo: the insistence on ethnic difference, the lackluster efforts at reconciliation, the victimization of one's group and the lack of acknowledgment of the suffering of others.

Aside from the ethnicization of education, the way in which Bosnia memorializes its past is also profoundly ethnically driven, serving a specific political purpose for each of the three major groups. For Bosnian Serbs, the past is remembered in museums, memorial sites, and contemporary books in a way that justifies claims to a separate political entity in Republika Srpska. For Croatians, memorialization efforts are used to emphasize the "Croatianization" of the Bosnian space, the affinity with Croatia as the principal "homeland," and the unique Catholic character of the Bosnian Croatian ethnic group (Torsti, 2004). For Bosniacs, the past is put to use to justify political projects of unitary, majority-Bosniac Bosnia, a state built on the memory of great injustice, victimization, suffering and genocide.

It is this particular narrative of Bosnia as a state victim of genocide that Bosniac political elites have tried so hard to maintain. The power of the narrative has been evident, for example, in another project aimed at memorializing Bosnia's past: the comprehensive database of Bosnian wartime losses, also known as the *Bosnian Book of the Dead*. This massive database project carried out over many years by the Bosnian nongovernmental organization, Research and Documentation Center, was meant to provide a narrative about every Bosnian victim, including known biographical information, family relations, and the circumstances of their death. When the project was completed in 2007, it provided evidence of close to 100,000 deaths, which, while still an incredibly high number, was much lower than the number of 200–250,000 deaths that has been circulating in the media for much of the past decade.[6]

Instead of providing a sense of relief, even solace, that far fewer people had perished in the war, the findings of the project unleashed a firestorm of hostility in Bosnia, including death threats against the project director (Nettelfield, 2010b). The main problem with the project was that the revised death toll figures conflicted with the predominant narratives of victimhood and the character of the Bosnian conflict, a narrative that Bosniac elites have a strong stake in. The curious fact, however, is that international courts have already settled the issue of genocide being committed in Bosnia—first in *ICTY v Krstić* and then in the *Bosnia v Serbia* genocide claim before the ICJ. Both of these cases provided convincing evidence that Bosnian Serbs—with Serbian support—had intended to destroy, at least in part, an ethnic group solely because of who they are—the very definition of genocide. In fact, the *Bosnian Book of the Dead* provided even more hard evidence for the Bosniac claim that the war was predominantly an anti-Bosniac endeavor, as the final ethnic breakdown of civilian victims—83 percent Bosniac, 10 percent Serb, and 5 percent Croat—showed clearly who had the majority of the victims.[7] In the light of this breakdown, how many total victims the war produced is much less significant—which makes the backlash against the project that much more bizarre. This behavior only makes political sense if the Bosniac political elite insisted on maintaining the inflated death toll numbers in order to argue for a unitary Bosnia and delegitimize Republika Srpska as a genocidal creation

6 The research findings have since been published in Tokača, 2013.
7 Data from Tokača, 2013.

(Nettelfield, 2010b). The memory of the past, again, is being used to advance the political needs of the present.

4. Existing efforts—RECOM and textbook reform

While official public space for reconciliation and justice projects has been constrained, civil society groups throughout the region have remained active and have put forward a series of proposals to deal with the legacy of violence. Among many projects that have been initiated since the end of the conflict, two merit special attention: the RECOM commission initiative, and the regional history textbook project.

The initiative for RECOM (Regional Commission Tasked with Establishing the Facts about All Victims of War Crimes and Other Serious Human Rights Violations Committed on the Territory of the Former Yugoslavia in the period from 1991–2001) was launched in 2004.[8] Today it brings together a network of more than 1,800 nongovernmental organizations (NGOs), associations, and individuals who represent and promote the effort to establish a lasting regional commission. RECOM is not the first attempt to create a truth/research commission to investigate the violence of the 1990s. Serbia, in fact, had a short-lived truth commission in the early 2000s, but this institution was quickly coopted by the government, and closed without issuing a report or hearing any witness testimonies. A few NGOs in Bosnia also attempted to create a truth commission there, but this initiative did not have broad support either (Subotić, 2009). Croatia never seriously debated a truth commission.

What makes RECOM different is the regional, not state-centered, aspect of the project, as well as it origins in the civil society sector in Serbia, Croatia, and Bosnia. The RECOM project is also different from current mechanisms of transitional justice in the region—international and domestic trials—in its emphasis on fostering public debate and shared testimonies about the past, not individual prosecution (Jeffrey & Jakala, 2012). Since 2004, RECOM has held dozens of conferences, multiple workshops and hearings around the region and collected half a million signatures demanding that states in the region officially recognize the commission and put its recommendations into state practice. Herein, however, lies the paradox. While building on the strength of civil society activism and expertise in multiple layers of addressing the injustice of the violent past RECOM also must rely on state institutions in order to make its recommendations official and hence, truly meaningful and broadly transformative. RECOM has already been hampered by internal obstacles within the organizational structure of the broader human rights movement which is not equipped and should probably not supplant investigative prosecutorial efforts of the state (Kurze & Vukusic, 2013). It has also faced significant resistance among civil society groups in Bosnia, where

8 Detailed information about RECOM is available at www.zarekom.org.

a focus on reconciliation instead of justice was often a hard sell (Rowen, 2012). At the same time, what the region needs is change in public remembrance practices, education policies, and enforcement of transitional justice mechanisms—all changes that need to come from state agencies in order to be implemented (Irvine & McMahon, 2013). Without official adoption of RECOM recommendations by regional governments, RECOM's worthwhile efforts will remain in the parallel sphere of civil society and human rights groups. They will remain aspirational, not operational.

Another regional initiative worth discussing briefly is the Joint History Project initiated by the Greece-based Center for Democracy and Reconciliation in Southeast Europe (CDRSEE) in 2005. This broader regional initiative aimed to offer four alternative history textbook supplements to teachers throughout the Balkans, focusing on different perspectives on the historical experience of countries in the region, including the conflicting memories of war and violence. While also placing itself within the larger body of reconciliation efforts, this project did not aim for a uniformed and mutually agreed-upon truth but, to the contrary worked from the premise that historical disagreement and dissent—managing difference—is itself a path to reconciliation (Johnson, 2012). While the textbook supplements were published and distributed, very few, if any, teachers in the region have adopted them. The obstacle to new textbook adoption primarily stems from the fact that textbook publishing and adoption remains heavily centralized and requires arduous bureaucratic approval by the ministries of education (Gasanabo, 2006). Being state agencies, education ministries are also reluctant to approve texts which are radically different in tone, language, narrative, and message than those that have been used for years. The state control of the textbook industry makes reform incredibly hard to initiate and maintain. History teachers, therefore, see no clear benefit to adopting textbook supplements that are neither sanctioned nor approved by the state and would, presumably, require them to do more work than if they only relied on official textbook materials.

5. Conclusion

This chapter provided snapshots of contemporary state practices of remembrance in Serbia, Croatia, and Bosnia, and made an argument for why these conflicting identities continue to be barriers to building a sustainable justice framework in the Western Balkans. The ways in which states remember their pasts are mutually exclusive. Serbian remembrance is built on the sense of Serbian victimization by Croats and Bosniacs, Croatian remembrance on liberation from Serbian aggression, and Bosniac remembrance on being survivors of the Serbian genocide. These histories cannot possibly all be true in their totality; parts of them are true, other exaggerated, yet others neglected. The region also faces a unique challenge in that victims and perpetrators no longer live with one another in the same country, a consequence of Yugoslav partition which has made domestic calls for justice much more difficult to push through official state channels. A related problem is that, in the Western Balkans, values continue to be defined "ethnically"—ethnic identity is still the ordering principle of political life, as witnessed in the efforts at education remembrance and memorialization projects. The past in the Western Balkans has an ethnicity of its own.

This pessimism, however, does not mean that nothing should be done. Quite the opposite, much needs to be done. There are multiple available mechanisms of dealing with the past that have yet to be systematically implemented in the region. In addition to retributive justice and individual war crimes trials, models of reparative justice (such as state apologies or restitution to victims) have not even been seriously considered. The Bosnian genocide claim in front of the ICJ was denied and that opportunity for reparations to victims and official state apology from Serbia has been squandered. However, a preferable mechanism would be for the state implicated in mass crimes to issue apologies or provide reparations on its own prompting, without the tools of international law. This would hold for Serbia and its crimes against Croatia and Bosnia, and for Croatia and its crimes against Bosnia. This idea may not be that far fetched. Willing to engage state responsibility for past violence can be useful for new governments politically, as they can use it to signal—domestically and abroad—a profound break with the past. Serbia and Croatia should also offer to either pay reparations to victims individually or through generous community gifts (roads, schools, parks, memorial sites).

Finally, all three states should implement comprehensive education reform, which includes textbook and curriculum reform that clearly presents evidence of crimes committed, the nature of the conflict, and the political environment that made the atrocities possible—even popular—among wide segments of society. They should promote media professionalization, specialization, and education in the field of transitional justice—how to investigate war crimes, how to write about them, how to present evidence, how to protect the victims. The states in the region—and this is especially important for Serbia and Croatia—should also create national days of memory for victims of atrocities their own troops have committed, and set up museums or other types of memorial sites to remember victims and survivors. Continuing efforts by human rights groups are important, but so are maintaining the interest of the media and, above all, the will of major political actors. This is not something that can develop overnight, but it is a social transformation that can be motivated by external incentives (e.g. a requirement for EU membership), or by subtle mechanisms of international socialization and persuasion.

These memorialization efforts are important in their own right, but they are a necessary component of a comprehensive postconflict justice framework. The states of the Western Balkans are far from creating sustainable justice architecture, but revisiting how they remember their pasts is a key starting point.

References

Agičić, D. (2011). 'Prikaz postanka suvremene Republike Hrvatske u hrvatskim udžbenicima' ['The Representation of the Creation of Modern Republic of Croatia in Croatian

Textbooks']. In T. Cipek (Ed.), *Kultura sjećanja: 1991. – Povijesni lomovi i svladavanje prošlosti [Culture of Memory: 1991 – Historical Clashes and Overcoming the Past]*. Zagreb: Disput.

Agičić, D. & Najbar-Agičić, M. (2007). 'History Teaching in 1990s Croatia'. In S. P. Ramet & D. Matić (Eds.), *Democratic Transition in Croatia: Value Transformation, Education & Media* (pp. 193–223). College Station: Texas A&M University Press.

Aguilar, P. (2002). *Memory and Amnesia: The Role of the Spanish Civil War in the Transition to Democracy*. Oxford: Berghahn Books.

B92. (2012, 1 June). Izetbegović: Nikolić vređa Bošnjake [Izetbegović: Nikolić is Insulting the Bosniacs], from www.b92.net/info/vesti/index.php?yyyy=2012&mm=06&dd=01&nav_category=11&nav_id=614859.

Banjeglav, T. (2012). 'Sjećanje na rat ili rat sjećanja?' In T. Banjeglav, N. Govedarica & D. Karačić (Eds.), *Re:vizija prošlosti: Politike sjećanja u Bosni i Hercegovini, Hrvatskoj i Srbiji od 1990. godine* (pp. 91–162). Sarajevo: ACIPS & Friedrich Ebert Foundation.

Bell, C. (2009). 'Transitional Justice, Interdisciplinarity and the State of the "Field," or "Non-Field"'. *International Journal of Transitional Justice*, *3*(1), 5–27.

Byford, J. (2007). 'When I Say "The Holocaust," I mean "Jasenovac"'. *East European Jewish Affairs*, *37*(1), 51–74.

Cohen, S. (2001). *States of Denial: Knowing about Atrocities and Suffering*. Cambridge: Polity Press.

Cole, E. A. (2007). 'Transitional Justice and the Reform of History Education'. *International Journal of Transitional Justice*, *1*(1), 115–137.

Croatian Parliament. (2000). *Deklaracija o domovinskom ratu [Declaration on the Homeland War]*. Zagreb. Narodne novine 102/2000.

Croatian Parliament. (2006). *Deklaracija o Oluji [Declaration on Operation Storm]*. Zagreb. Narodne novine 76–2000.

Ćurgus Kazimir, V. (2005). 'Zavera stida' ['Conspiracy of Shame']. In S. Biserko (Ed.), *Srebrenica: Od poricanja do priznanja [Srebrenica: From Denial to Acknowledgment]*. Belgrade: Helsinki Committee for Human Rights in Serbia (pp. 696–700).

David, L. (2012). *A Difficult Past in Serbia: The State-Sponsored Project of Remembering and Forgetting*. Paper presented at the Association for the Study of Nationalities World Convention, New York, NY, April 19–21.

David, L. (2013). *No-One's Memories and a Monument to No-One: The Process of Collective Memory Construction in Serbia after the Wars of the 1990s*. PhD, Ben-Gurion University, Beersheba, Israel.

Dimitrijević, N. (2008). 'Serbia After the Criminal Past: What Went Wrong and What Should be Done'. *International Journal of Transitional Justice*, *2*(1), 5–22.

Gasanabo, J.-D. n. (2006). *Fostering Peaceful Co-existence Through Analysis and Revision of History Curricula and Textbooks in Southeast Europe: Preliminary Stocktaking Report*. Paris: UNESCO.

Govedarica, N. (2012). 'Zemlja nesigurne prošlosti'. In T. Banjeglav, N. Govedarica & D. Karačić (Eds.), *Re:vizija prošlosti: Politike sjećanja u Bosni i Hercegovini, Hrvatskoj i Srbiji od 1990. godine* (pp. 163–234). Sarajevo: ACIPS & Friedrich Ebert Foundation.

Graovac, I. & Cvetković, D. (2005). *Ljudski gubici Hrvatske 1941–1945. godine: pitanja, primjeri, rezultati [Human Losses in Croatia 1941–1945: Questions, Examples, Findings]*. Zagreb: Zajednica istraživača dijalog.

Hayner, P. B. (1994). 'Fifteen Truth Commissions – 1974 to 1994: A Comparative Study'. *Human Rights Quarterly*, *16*, 597–655.

Helsinki Committee for Human Rights in Serbia. (2011). *Human Rights Reflect Institutional Impotence*. Belgrade: HCHRS.

Hromadžić, A. (2008). 'Discourses of Integration and Practices of Reunification at the Mostar Gymnasium, Bosnia and Herzegovina'. *Comparative Education Review*, *52*(4), 541–563.

Ignatieff, M. (1998). *The Warrior's Honor: Ethnic War and the Modern Conscience*. New York: Metropolitan Books.

International Criminal Tribunal for the Former Yugoslavia (2012). Appeals Judgement in Prosecutor vs. Ante Gotovina and Mladen Markač. The Hague: ICTY.

Irvine, J. A. & McMahon, P. C. (2013). 'From International Courts to Grassroots Organizing: Obstacles to Transitional Justice in the Balkans'. In O. Simić & Z. Volčič (Eds.), *Transitional Justice and Civil Society in the Balkans* (pp. 217–238). New York: Springer.

Jeffrey, A. & Jakala, M. (2012). 'Beyond Trial Justice in the Former Yugoslavia'. *The Geographical Journal*, *178*(4), 290–295.

Johnson, D. N. (2012). *Rewriting the Balkans: Memory, Historiography, and the Making of a European Citizenry.* MA Thesis, University of Massachusetts, Amherst.

King, E. (2014). *From Classrooms to Conflict in Rwanda*. Cambridge: Cambridge University Press.

Kolsto, P. (2010). 'Bleiburg: The Creation of a National Martyrology'. *Europe-Asia Studies*, *62*(7), 1153–1174.

Kurze, A. & Vukusic, I. (2013). 'Afraid to Cry Wolf: Human Rights Activists' Struggle of Transnational Accountability Efforts in the Balkans'. In O. Simić & Z. Volčič (Eds.), *Transitional Justice and Civil Society in the Balkans* (pp. 201–216). New York: Springer.

Manojlović Pintar, O. (2010). 'Rat i nemir' ['Peace and Uncertainty']. In D. Stojanović, R. Vučetić, S. Petrović Todosijević, O. Manojlović Pintar & R. Radić (Eds.), *Novosti iz prošlosti: Znanje, neznanje, upotreba i zloupotreba istorije [News from the Past: Knowledge, Ignorance, Use and Misuse of History]*. Belgrade: Belgrade Center for Human Rights.

McGrattan, C. (2010). *Northern Ireland, 1968–2008: The Politics of Entrenchment*. Basingstoke: Palgrave Macmillan.

McMahon, P. C. & Western, J. (2009, August 17). The Death of Dayton. *Foreign Affairs*. Online at https://www.foreignaffairs.com/articles/bosnia-herzegovina/2009-08-17/death-dayton

Mendeloff, D. (2004). 'Truth-Seeking, Truth-Telling, and Postconflict Peacebuilding: Curb the Enthusiasm?' *International Studies Review*, *6*(3), 355–380.

Mendeloff, D. (2008). '"Pernicious History" as a Cause of National Misperceptions'. *Cooperation and Conflict*, *43*(1), 31–56.

Mihajlović Trbovc, J. & Pavasović Trošt, T. (2013). 'Who Were the Anti-Fascists? Multiple Interpretations of World War II in Post-Yugoslav Textbooks'. In C. Karner & B. Mertens (Eds.), *The Use and Abuse of Memory: Interpreting World War Two in Contemporary European Politics* (pp. 173–192). New Brunswick, NJ: Transaction Publishers.

Minow, M. (1998). *Between Vengeance and Forgiveness: Facing History after Genocide and Mass Violence*. Boston: Beacon Press.

Nettelfield, L. J. (2010a). *Courting Democracy in Bosnia and Herzegovina: The Hague Tribunal's Impact in a Postwar State*. New York: Cambridge University Press.

Nettelfield, L. J. (2010b). 'Research and Repercussions of Death Tolls'. In P. Andreas & K. M. Greenhill (Eds.), *Sex, Drugs, and Body Counts: The Politics of Numbers in Global Crime and Conflict* (pp. 159–187). Ithaca: Cornell University Press.

Oglesby, E. (2007). 'Educating Citizens in Postwar Guatemala: Historical Memory, Genocide, and the Culture of Peace'. *Radical History Review*, *2007*(97), 77–98.

Orentlicher, D. F. (2008). *Shrinking the Space for Denial: The Impact of the ICTY in Serbia.* New York: Open Society Institute.

Orentlicher, D. F. (2010). *That Someone Guilty Be Punished: The Impact of the ICTY in Bosnia.* New York: Open Society Justice Initiative and International Center for Transitional Justice.

Pavasović Trošt, T. (2012). *Dealing with the Past: Identity Narratives among Serbian and Croatian Youth.* PhD Dissertation, Harvard University, Cambridge, MA.

Pavelić, B. (2012). 'Croatia and Nikolić: Shock Mixed with Irony'. *Balkan Insight.* 28 May. Retrieved from www.balkaninsight.com/en/article/croatia-shock-and-irony-about-nikolic.

Pavlaković, V. (2008). *Red Stars, Black Shirts: Symbols, Commemorations, and Contested Histories of World War Two in Croatia.* Seattle: The National Council for Eurasian and East European Research.

Pavlaković, V. (2010). 'Croatia, the International Criminal Tribunal for the former Yugoslavia, and General Gotovina as a Political Symbol'. *Europe-Asia Studies, 62*(10), 1707–1740.

Perry, V. (2013). 'Classrooms as a Battleground for Hearts and Minds: Efforts to Reform and Transform Education in Post-war Bosnia and Herzegovina'. In O. Listhaug & S. P. Ramet (Eds.), *Civic and Uncivic Values in Bosnia-Herzegovina: The Record Since Dayton,* (pp. 225–246). Ravenna: Longo Editore.

Ramet, S. P. (2007). 'The Denial Syndrome and Its Consequences: Serbian Political Culture since 2000'. *Communist and Post-Communist Studies, 40*(1), 41–58.

Rowen, J. (2012). 'Mobilizing Truth: Agenda-setting in a Transnational Social Movement'. *Law & Social Inquiry, 37*(3), 686–718.

Sarkin, J. (1999). 'The Necessity and Challenges of Establishing a Truth and Reconciliation Commission in Rwanda'. *Human Rights Quarterly, 21,* 767–823.

Stojanović, D. (2011). 'An Explosive Device with a Delayed Effect: Image of the Wars of the Nineties in Serbian History Textbooks (1993–2005)'. In T. Cipek (Ed.), *Kultura sjećanja: 1991.– Povijesni lomovi i svladavanje prošlosti [Culture of Memory: 1991 – Historical Clashes and Overcoming the Past].* Zagreb: Disput.

Subotić, J. (2009). *Hijacked Justice: Dealing with the Past in the Balkans.* Ithaca: Cornell University Press.

Subotić, J. (2013). 'Stories States Tell: Identity, Narrative, and Human Rights in the Balkans'. *Slavic Review, 72*(2), 306–326.

Tokača, M. (2013). *Bosnian Book of the Dead.* Sarajevo: Research Documentation Center.

Torsti, P. (2003). *Divergent Stories, Convergent Attitudes: Study on the Presence of History, History Textbooks, and the Thinking of Youth in Post-war Bosnia and Herzegovina.* PhD Dissertation, University of Helsinki, Helsinki.

Torsti, P. (2004). 'History Culture and Banal Nationalism in Post-war Bosnia'. *South East European Politics, 5*(2–3).

Torsti, P. (2013). 'Rival Histories and Textbook Reform in Bosnian Textbooks 1992–2009'. In O. Listhaug & S. P. Ramet (Eds.), *Civic and Uncivic Values in Bosnia-Herzegovina: The Record Since Dayton,* (pp. 205–223). Ravenna: Longo Editore.

Weinstein, H. M., Freedman, S. W. & Hughson, H. (2007). 'School Voices: Challenges Facing Education Systems after Identity-Based Conflicts'. *Education, Citizenship and Social Justice, 2*(1), 41–71.

All weblinks cited in this chapter were accessed on March 25, 2015.

Part 2

Obstacles and prospects for reconciliation

Chapter 6

Dealing with the past in Serbia – achievements in the past 20 years[1]

Vesna Nikolić-Ristanović and Sanja Ćopić

1. Introduction

This chapter presents results from the research project *Fostering victim-oriented dialogue in the multi-ethnic society*, which was undertaken during 2012 and 2013 by the Victimology Society of Serbia within the project consortium *Developing alternative understandings of security and justice through restorative justice approaches in intercultural settings within democratic societies – ALTERNATIVE.*[2] We present a general assessment of the activities and the discourse typical of state institutions in Serbia[3] in dealing with the inter-ethnic conflicts that emerged in the region of the former Yugoslavia in the 1990s. In its final section, the chapter also briefly looks at approaches by civil society actors. Due to the establishment of the International Criminal Tribunal for the former Yugoslavia in The Hague and international pressure, the transitional justice discourse is strongly influenced by legal approaches. In this analysis, we aim to identify the potential of restorative justice and possible pathways towards its broader use in Serbia.

The contribution is based on the qualitative analysis of academic publications, research reports, documents produced by governmental and non-governmental organisations, press clippings, website information, etc. Additional data was collected through group interviews with representatives of civil society organisations,

1 Parts of this chapter were published in Serbian in the following papers: Ćopić, S. (2013). 'Aktivnosti i diskurs državnih organa i institucija u Srbiji u bavljenju međuetničkim konfliktima' ('Activities and the discourse of the state agencies and institutions in Serbia in dealing with interethnic conflicts'). *Temida*, 3–4, pp. 61–94; Nikolić-Ristanović, V. & Šaćiri, B. (2013). 'Bavljenje međuetničkim konfliktima od strane organizacija civilnog društva u Srbiji: aktivnosti i diskurs' ('Dealing with interethnic conflicts by civil society in Serbia: activities and discourse'). *Temida*, 3–4, 27–60.

2 This chapter is based on the results of the research presented in *Dealing with interethnic conflicts in Serbia and the place of restorative justice and victims* (Nikolić-Ristanović and Ćopić, 2013), which is available on the website of the Victimology Society of Serbia www.vds.org.rs and the project ALTERNATIVE www.alternativeproject.eu (accessed on 25 March 2015). The research leading to these results has received funding from the European Union's Seventh Framework Programme (FP7-SEC-2011-1) under grant agreement No. 285368. The chapter reflects only the author's views and the European Union is not liable for any use that may be made of the information contained therein.

3 The term 'state institution' refers to legislative, executive and judicial institutions, as well as to the institutions at central (state) level and the level of the local communities.

state institutions and independent state agencies, undertaken in 2012 in the form of three round tables. Members of the research team from the Victimology Society of Serbia also collected data at press conferences, round tables, panels and meetings held by civil society organisations and state institutions in 2012–2013. The empirical material was collected using direct (participatory) observation and analyses of transcripts and video recordings of presentations and discussions. Additional information was obtained through electronic questionnaires.

For the purpose of this research, inter-ethnic conflict was defined very broadly and encompassed a wide range of problems in relationships between members of different ethnic groups from the territory of Serbia and other countries of the former Yugoslavia at the macro, meso and micro level. The term 'conflict' therefore refers to armed, societal, violent, cultural, religious, political, interpersonal, and group conflicts, etc. (Foss *et al*, 2012, p. 29). As the research and this contribution focus on inter-ethnic conflicts, it includes conflicts between Serbia and other countries of the former Yugoslavia,[4] as well as conflicts in Serbia itself (i.e. armed conflicts in Kosovo, during the 1990s).

In the next section we briefly analyse the socio-historical context of the conflicts in the former Yugoslavia. This is followed by an analysis of the approaches adopted by the state institutions in Serbia in dealing with the past over the last 20 years (Section 3). We elaborate on both the discourse and the state's policy and activities in dealing with the past, as well as on its impact on present-day inter-ethnic relations in Serbia. In addition, we briefly look at the debates and activities of civil society actors and explain the need for more inclusive and restorative approaches, which we call a 'third way' of dealing with the past (Section 4). In the conclusion (Section 5), we point out dilemmas that still exist and try to imagine possible further steps for broader use of restorative justice in dealing with the past.

2. The socio-historical context of the inter-ethnic conflicts

The wars in the former Yugoslavia in the 1990s and the way the Serbian state dealt with them had a strong impact on the dynamics of inter-ethnic relations within Serbia (Domonji, 2008; Nikolić-Ristanović & Ćopić, 2013). After the formal ending of the wars, numerous unresolved problems and conflicts remained, both at the state level (in terms of different political conflicts and confrontations) and between individual members of different ethnic groups. Even today, relationships and conflicts between members of different ethnic groups in Serbia are still very much affected by the legacies of the wars in the 1990s.[5] This is particularly visible

4 This refers to the armed conflicts in the territories of other republics of the former Yugoslavia (i.e. Slovenia, Croatia and Bosnia and Herzegovina) in the period between 1991 and 1995.

5 Contemporary conflicts are also influenced by other factors, such as: the current political and socio-economic situation, the new institutional framework, mechanisms and policies for dealing with discrimination, human and minority rights as well as crime and violence in general, past and

in areas with multi-ethnic populations, such as the territories bordering the other former Yugoslav republics and provinces where the armed conflicts took place: Croatia, Bosnia and Herzegovina (BiH) and Kosovo. We therefore argue that there is a connection between past violence and present conflicts and the way they are dealt with. As pointed out by some authors, the entire region of the former Yugoslavia shares a history of wars aimed at national liberation, with people from different ethnic groups waging war against each other without any attempt at reconciliation (Pavković, 2000). The region also has 'a history of denials and multiple truths (e.g. each ethnic group passing its own truth from generation to generation) as well as the history of exploitation of (their own people's) victimisation for feeding the cycle of violence' (Nikolić-Ristanović, 2006: 370). The main danger, however, lies in the fact that one-sided, partial truths, which include victim/offender binarism (Butler, 2004), still exist as 'ghosts in the bottle', and can be taken out and used to manipulate national sentiments and provoke war in the future (Nikolić-Ristanović, 2003).

Among the population of Serbia, there are victims (including refugees and internally displaced people[6] from other parts of the former Yugoslavia) and perpetrators of inter-ethnic crimes, as well as witnesses and bystanders. There is also an overlap between the roles of victim and perpetrator, which needs to be taken into consideration while looking for suitable mechanisms for dealing with inter-ethnic conflicts.[7] A large proportion of the male population were forced to participate in the war as soldiers. In many cases, their national sentiments and families' traumatic experiences from earlier wars were manipulated to convince them to fight. Consequently, these soldiers are also victims in a more direct way. Many people were victimised by different perpetrators from different communities and ethnic groups (e.g. Serbian refugees from Croatia, who later lived in BiH and then Kosovo). In addition, many people are multiple victims, due to a memory of victimisation from previous wars, or war trauma passed down to them by their parents or other relatives (e.g. Serbs from Croatia and BiH now living in Serbia, whose family members were killed by members of other ethnic groups during the Second World War, or Serbs whose family members were killed during and

present violence and crime in general, and problems in upholding rule of law etc. Inter-ethnic relationships in present-day Serbia are also strongly influenced by the international community, in particular in relation to the Kosovo problem, and by the trials before the International Criminal Tribunal for the former Yugoslavia and EU integration (Nikolić-Ristanović & Ćopić, 2013: 13).

6 In 1995, 250,000 people were expelled from a former Serb province in Croatia (Krajina); they moved to Serbia in a very short period of about two weeks. In 1999, about 230,000 Serbs from Kosovo came to Serbia under similar conditions (Mrvić-Petrović, 2000, p. 101). At the end of 1999, Serbia had almost 1 million refugees and internally displaced people, which made it the country with the highest number of refugees in Europe. Refugees came to Serbia in waves – the first big wave arrived in 1992, a second one in 1995 and the latest one in 1999, after the NATO bombing and the ending of armed conflict in Kosovo.

7 For a more detailed elaboration of this issue see Nikolić-Ristanović, 2003, pp. 246–247; Nikolić-Ristanović, 2006, p. 373, who emphasises the great complexity of victimisation and divisions, and points out several crucial features.

after the Second World War by other Serbs who belonged to different political/ military groups).[8]

Serbian society is marked by more than one division. Apart from divisions along ethnic lines (e.g. conflicts between Serbs and Albanians in parts of Serbia close to Kosovo, and between Serbs and Bosniaks in areas close to BiH), conflicts and divisions also exist among Serbs. Further tensions exist among and within other ethnic groups, as members of these minority groups are affiliated to different political and social groups. Ideological differences also contribute to the divide (e.g. between communists and anti-communists, between supporters of nationalist leaders and their opponents, between Serbs from Serbia and Serbs from other parts of the former Yugoslavia, between refugees and local communities, ex-combatants and those who did not participate in the wars etc.) (Nikolić-Ristanović, 2006, p. 373). Furthermore, people have experienced many different forms of war victimisation. The entire population of Serbia (Serbs but also other ethnic groups such as Roma, Albanians, Bosniaks, Hungarians, Croats etc.) were victims of both the immediate and the long-term consequences of NATO air strikes (Nikolić-Ristanović, 2003, p. 247).

As a post-conflict society which is also undergoing a painful transition from communism to neo-liberal capitalism, Serbia in general and its ethnically mixed border areas in particular constitute an unstable environment. These border areas are characterised by the 'continuous eruption of violence', which seriously jeopardises the security of citizens. Moreover, there is a 'post-conflict vacuum' in which 'the eruption of lawlessness, corruption and crime' is visible, while, as Rohne, Arsovska and Aertsen stressed (2008, pp. 12–13), 'post-conflict societies often lack mechanisms and institutions for upholding the rule of law and dealing with the past abuses'. As recent research suggests, this 'vacuum' further decreases the feeling of security and has particularly negative consequences for victims from ethnic minorities, whose prospects of protection and support are in doubt (Biro *et al*, 2002; Helsinki Committee for Human Rights in Serbia, 2004; Savković, 2010).

For the development of democracy, the rule of law and the security of citizens in Serbia, it is necessary, therefore, to face the past, but also to deal with past and present conflicts in their mutual interconnectedness (Pavković, 2000; Nikolić-Ristanović, 2003; Daskalovski, 2005; Guzina, 2005; Zdravković, 2005; Nikolić-Ristanović & Ćopić, 2013). There is a particular need to identify alternative, non-violent forms of dealing with the past, and to solve present inter-ethnic conflicts in order to prevent their future escalation. These alternative forms of dealing with the past must be based on the principles of restorative justice, in order

8 Two opposing inter-ethnic sides from the Second World War in Serbia (partisans and cetniks) were never reconciled. As noted by Đokić, although nationalist, Milošević never called for national reconciliation, with the result that this division became even more striking during his regime (Đokić, 2002).

to stop the cycle of violence, contribute to a process of reconciliation, and increase the security of all citizens.

3. Discourse and approaches of the state institutions in Serbia in dealing with the past

In this section, we provide an overview of the activities of the state institutions in dealing with inter-ethnic conflicts in Serbia and other parts of the former Yugoslavia. We also try to identify the discourse of the state institutions and the place of restorative justice in official policies relating to the past. We concentrate, first, on the way in which governmental institutions were dealing with the conflicts that occurred in the former Yugoslavia during the 1990s and affected the wider region. In a second step, we focus on conflicts in Serbia itself with reference to Kosovo. In addition, we analyse how Serbia dealt with inter-ethnic conflicts over time, focusing first on the 1990s and then on the period after 2000.

3.1 The period of violent conflicts in the 1990s

In the late 1970s/early 1980s, ethnicity became an important category of social differentiation (Blagojević, 2000), while 'nationalism was emerging as a synthesis of anti-communist fervour, on the one hand, and "blame-the-victim" and "scapegoat" ideologies, on the other' (Blagojević, 2005, p. 164). In the 1980s, ethnic tensions became visible in the countries of the former Yugoslavia, including Serbia, reinforcing nationalism: national identities were created, ethno-nationalistic movements were developed or strengthened, and the 'others' (primarily other ethnic groups but also other (political) opponents) were recognised as dangerous (potential) opponents and enemies, which, together with other factors, generated and further deepened the conflict (Blagojević, 2000; Guzina, 2005). This happened in the context of economic crisis, political disorientation and strong international influence, creating fertile ground for the manipulation of nationalistic attitudes and sentiments (Blagojević, 2000; Zdravković, 2005) based on 'the revival of old divisions and hostilities' (Nikolić-Ristanović, 2000, p. 11).[9]

Consequently, during the 1990s, a strong nationalistic discourse prevailed in Serbia. It was characterised by a 'partial "truth" about past and present conflicts' (Nikolić-Ristanović, 2006, p. 374), by 'narratives of victimisation' of its own ethnic group, by accusing 'others' of violence against 'us' (Serbs), and by considering members of other ethnic groups as threats to the security of the country and its citizens, labelling them as 'terrorists', 'extremists', 'secessionists' or 'fundamentalists' (Morrison, 2008, p. 3). Serbs were considered to be exclusive victims, more

9 A good example of this was the inflammatory nationalistic speech by Slobodan Milošević in 1989 in Gazimestan in Kosovo on the occasion of the 600th anniversary of the Battle of Kosovo (Pavković, 1999, p. 9).

victimised than members of other ethnic groups (hierarchy of victimisation), justifying the need for revenge for what 'others' (other ethnic groups or other opponents as enemies) did to 'us' and the idea that prevention was necessary (preventive or pre-emptive aggression), the thinking being that 'if we do not take some steps in defending ourselves (our own ethnic group), the "other" will attack us' (Blagojević, 2000, p. 7). In such a context, conflicts in the countries of the former Yugoslavia, but also inside Serbia, were justified as 'defensive' and were treated as just and inevitable. This pattern of legitimation strengthened national homogenisation (Raković, 2005, p. 72). This form of nationalistic discourse can therefore be characterised as a form of the security discourse which shaped the policy response to inter-ethnic conflicts in the countries of the former Yugoslavia and in Serbia itself, particularly in Kosovo, during the 1990s.

3.1.1 The role of the state institutions in dealing with inter-ethnic conflicts on the territory of the former Yugoslavia

During the 1990s, the Serbian state institutions' approach in dealing with inter-ethnic conflicts in the countries of the former Yugoslavia was ambivalent. On the one hand, the authorities adopted the 'not participating in the conflicts' rhetoric, denying that Serbia was at war, and thus denying its responsibility for generating conflicts, for war crimes, and for the suffering not only of other ethnic groups but also of Serbs in Serbia and other countries of the former Yugoslavia. On the other hand, the same authorities were mobilising Serbian citizens into the police and the military, sending them to war under the guise of protecting Serbs living outside Serbia, which was in line with the prevailing nationalistic discourse (Nikolić-Ristanović, 2006). The state institutions' policies mainly focused on repressive/retributive mechanisms, giving no space to any restorative approaches to conflict transformation. Reactions to the conflicts could be classified as follows: 'humanitarian' intervention, a policy of oppression and repression, waging war with numbers, selective prosecutions, and acceptance of and support to refugees and internally displaced persons.

Based on the policy of protecting Serbs who lived in territories outside Serbia during the 1990s (i.e. in Croatia and BiH) the authorities mobilised Serbian citizens, but also refugees from other former Yugoslav republics who came to Serbia, for the purpose of engaging in the war and military interventions on the territory of the former Yugoslavia, supposedly for humanitarian purposes. They aimed to protect Serbs from attack by other ethnic groups, but also to prevent the transfer of the conflicts to the territory of Serbia. These activities were presented as acts of pre-emptive intervention, which is a characteristic of the security discourse. In this process, the state authorities could rely on the mass media, which were completely controlled by the state. They have substantially contributed to making the 'victim game' possible (Blagojević, 2005, p. 175), strengthening the victim–perpetrator dichotomy or binarism (Butler, 2004) and further embedding nationalism. In the course of the violent escalation of the conflicts, a flow of refugees came to Serbia. Parliament had already passed the Law on Refugees in 1992,[10] and the Commissariat for Refugees was established, providing the legal and institutional framework for admission, care and support to refugees (this included temporary accommodation, at first in the collective centres and later in other facilities, food, health care and material support).

The policy of humanitarian intervention in areas beyond Serbia was closely linked with the policy of oppression and repression in Serbia itself. The repressive policy towards other ethnic groups in Serbia was legitimised by a rhetoric that considered these constituencies (such as Bosniaks in south-west Serbia) to be potential threats to security (Morrison, 2008, p. 3). Political opponents who advocated for the anti-war policy were also persecuted, which resulted in a series of political murders, some of which have not yet been fully investigated. State institutions also waged war with numbers, manipulating statistics on both military losses and victims (Nikolić-Ristanović, 2000, p. 12; Raković, 2005). Victims were not treated as individuals in need of assistance, protection and support, but as statistics, used solely to justify violence. Otherwise, victims were invisible, left on the margins of the system of support and protection.

During the 1990s, some war crimes cases were dealt with by national courts in Serbia, but they 'had been handled marginally and unprofessionally' (Ostojić, 2007, p. 114). A weak judiciary, lack of appropriate laws, a bad economic situation and strong political influence, together with pressure from the international community, created an unwillingness to try war criminals impartially. Consequently, it was mainly members of other ethnic groups who were sentenced, while Serb perpetrators were tried only occasionally, and lenient sentences were imposed (Ostojić, 2007, p. 114). In this way, the authorities actually denied any form of responsibility for, or involvement in, the crimes committed during the conflicts in the former Yugoslavia. This was the reason why the United Nations established the International Criminal Tribunal for the former Yugoslavia (ICTY) in 1993. However, at that time, the legitimacy of the ICTY was questioned in Serbia. There was considerable resistance to, and disapproval of, the Tribunal among political leaders, which resulted in the state institutions' failure to co-operate with it (Ostojić, 2007; Subotić, 2010).

A reluctance to deal with the conflicts from the 1990s was still present at the end of the 1990s, even during civil protests in 1996–1997, organised as a response to the electoral fraud attempted by Milošević's regime after the 1996 local elections. As Ilić (2005) observes, neither the political leaders nor the opposition parties were willing to accept responsibility for the conflicts in the 1990s. Consequently, by denying their own atrocities and not prosecuting (or by prosecuting selectively) those responsible for war crimes committed in the name of Serbia and the Serbian

10 Official Gazette of the Republic of Serbia, No. 18/92; Official Gazette of the Federal Republic of Yugoslavia, No. 42/2002.

people, the state institutions worsened the conflicts and even generated new conflicts on their own territory, which continue to this day.

3.1.2 Activities of the state institutions in dealing with the Kosovo conflict

As noted by several authors, in the post-communist countries such as Serbia, the concept of nationalism does not mean the struggle for one's own rights, but rather a struggle for denying and minimising the rights of the 'others' (Michnik, 1996, according to Hondus, 2007, p. 11), which results in a policy of intolerance, lack of respect for diversity, and exclusion. This was particularly visible in the conflicts in Kosovo. Although these conflicts started in the 1970s, it was only in the 1980s that they intensified, escalating into armed conflict at the end of the 1990s (Guzina, 2005; Zdravković, 2005). The dominant mechanisms for dealing with inter-ethnic conflicts in Kosovo at macro, meso and micro level were the policy of oppression and the use of repressive mechanisms, which was in line with the dominant nationalistic propaganda and security discourse promoted by political leaders in the 1990s (Arsovska, Valiñas & Fellegi, 2008; Nikolić, 2005; Zdravković, 2005). Therefore, in dealing with conflicts in Kosovo (or the 'Kosovo crisis' or 'Kosovo problem', as it was often referred to), the state institutions of Serbia actually undertook different activities that aimed to increase their control over Kosovo. That was done in two main ways: by suppressing any possible form of further strengthening of Albanians and their movement for independence, which can be considered as a 'policy of systematic exclusion of Albanians from the educational system, political and public life' (Janjić, 2005, p. 58)[11] and by increasing the repression over Albanian citizens and concentrating Serbian police and military forces in Kosovo (Daksalovski, 2005; Guzina, 2005).

Apart from repressive mechanisms, there were also some attempts to solve the Kosovo conflict through mediated dialogue – in 1992, and later in 1995 and 1996 (Burg, 2007, p. 24; Vukomanović, 1999). These were dialogues or, more accurately, discussions at the political level, which primarily focused on the issues of education and language. They were a mechanism deployed during the pre-election campaign, not a serious attempt to transform the ongoing conflicts. These potentially restorative mechanisms failed to bring a solution to the Kosovo crisis, with the result that in the late 1990s, violence escalated into armed conflict and gross violations of the human rights of both Albanians and Serbs.

Pressure from the international community helped to bring about a shift in the governments' reactions to the conflicts in Kosovo. Milošević decided to stop police

11 Such as arrests and political hearings of Albanians, segregation of Albanians in schools, closure of Albanian schools and universities, dismissals of Albanian state and military officials, prohibition of the use of Albanian as the official language and the use of Serbian as the only official language, ban on media coverage in the Albanian language etc. (Arsovska, Valiñas & Fellegi 2008; Nikolić 2005; Zdravkovic 2005; Guzina, 2005).

and military operations in Kosovo and to prepare for dialogue with Albanians. However, a direct dialogue between the conflicting parties was never established. This would have been a precondition for this activity to develop a restorative character and potential for finding solutions that would have been acceptable to both sides. Instead, the international community organised the so-called peaceful negotiations in Rambouillet in France in 1999, which were a form of 'shuttle diplomacy'. Although negotiation is considered to be 'a basic means of getting what you want from others' and is oriented towards an outcome or agreement (Berghof Foundation, 2012, 49), it could have some restorative potential and could possibly be transformed into a dialogue process. Nevertheless, these negotiations were far from being a possible restorative practice based on dialogue:[12] both parties were forced to participate in negotiations, being blackmailed by the international actors – either to sign the agreement or to be destroyed (Chomsky, 2000, according to Zdravković, 2005, p. 75; Dauphinee, 2005). The principles were set forth by the international community (the Contact Group) and were, in effect, non-negotiable (Arsovska, Valiñas & Fellegi, 2008, p. 84). This showed the failure of the international community to facilitate conflict transformation; indeed, as noted by some authors, the international community contributed to the failure of the negotiations from the outset (Dauphinee, 2005; Zdravkovic, 2005, p. 76). This resulted in 79 days of NATO air strikes against the Federal Republic of Yugoslavia (Serbia and Montenegro), which directly contributed to the resurgence of the feeling of suffering among Serbs and the image of victim, while the state institutions increased their war propaganda and the level of violence in Kosovo escalated dramatically (Nikolić, 2005, pp. 62–63; Zdravković, 2005, p. 76). This showed once again how the use of repressive mechanisms and the failure of potentially restorative approaches fed the spiral of violence and deepened the conflict, eliminating any prospects of coexistence between different ethnic groups in Kosovo (Nikolić, 2005, p. 64).

3.2 The period of transition: activities and the discourse of the state institutions after 2000

After the collapse of the Milošević regime, a period of transition toward a market economy, democracy and the rule of law commenced. However, the new (transitional) government was confronted with two crucial challenges on its way towards democratisation: on the one hand, there was strong pressure from the international community for the state institutions and society in Serbia to deal with

12 From the restorative justice point of view, dialogue is seen as an inclusive, open-ended process of constructive, two-way communication that puts the participants into interaction. Dialogue participants are cooperating, working towards a common understanding. Dialogue is primarily a relationship-orientated process, rather than problem solving. It tries to transform the relationship by promoting empathy and enlarging possibilities for participants to change their views and to understand the other side. For more information, see Nikolić-Ristanović *et al.*, 2012.

the atrocities committed by Serbia during the ethnic conflicts in the 1990s, while on the other hand the government was confronted with opposition and obstruction from Milošević's supporters and nationalists (Nikolić-Ristanović, 2006, p. 369). The new ruling coalition was also overburdened with internal divisions in respect to dealing with inter-ethnic conflicts in the former Yugoslavia (Subotić, 2010), resulting in a lack of political consensus on this issue.

The international community showed little interest in restorative approaches to dealing with the past and the legacies of the inter-ethnic conflicts in the countries of the former Yugoslavia (Nikolić-Ristanović, 2006, p. 372), focusing instead on judicial mechanisms, pressing Serbia to intensify its cooperation with the ICTY and eliminating impunity for gross human rights violations. Generally speaking, during the past decade, cooperation with the ICTY has been one of the main or even the key indicator of respect for international justice (Subotić, 2010, p. 65). It could therefore be argued that in the period after 2000 the so-called Hague discourse on dealing with inter-ethnic conflicts from the 1990s became dominant in Serbia. It divided the ruling coalition, but also politics, civil society and the public in Serbia into two main streams: pro-Hague and anti-Hague-orientated forces and individuals (Nikolić-Ristanović, 2006, p. 372). This division actually corresponded to two other opposite discourses visible on the political scene in Serbia: nationalistic vs. reformist or pro-European.[13] The nationalistic discourse of the anti-Hague-orientated structures – in which there was a lot of Milošević's supporters who were still embedded in the state institutions, primarily in the police and judiciary[14] – was characterised by opposition to, and obstruction of, any form of cooperation with the ICTY. It also protected and glorified war criminals as heroes, created a victim-oppressor/aggressor and friend-enemy dichotomy, and relativised Serbia's own responsibility for the inter-ethnic conflicts (Pavković, 2000). At the other end of the spectrum in the Hague discourse were the pro-European factions, who advocated for cooperation with the ICTY in order to pave the path for Serbia's European integration; this cooperation was motivated more by political and economic reasoning than by a desire to achieve reconciliation.

This situation still continues today. There have been constant changes in policy towards cooperation with the ICTY, depending on political conditions in Serbia. Any intensification of this cooperation (primarily arrests and extraditions) has reinforced the right wing and further strengthened nationalism and nationalistic

13 For example, Prime Minister Zoran Đinđić was committed to cooperating with the ICTY and the international community in general, while the President of the FR Yugoslavia Vojislav Koštunica was not willing to take any radical steps in facing the past atrocities.

14 In this regard, it is important to mention that in 2003 the Serbian Parliament adopted the Law on Accountability for Human Rights Violations (i.e. the Law on Lustration) (Official Gazette of the Republic of Serbia, No. 58/2003 and 61/2003), and the Commission for examining responsibility for violations of human rights was established. However, this Commission never worked, this vetting law was never applied and lustration has never been done. Ten years later, in June 2013, the Law was repealed.

discourse in Serbia, resulting in new divisions, tensions and protests. Any search for the accused and their arrest and extradition were seen by nationalist hardliners as 'an attack on their people, raising the prospect of renewed violence' (Liebmann, 2007, p. 362). Such a climate offered little scope for an alternative discourse or restorative approaches to dealing with the legacies of the past and inter-ethnic conflicts in the countries of the former Yugoslavia. Nonetheless, there have been sporadic attempts at dialogue, reconciliation and relationship building, as well as apologies for the crimes committed and the condemnation of war crimes. Even so, it seems that these restorative (or at least potentially restorative) mechanisms have remained on the margins in efforts to deal with the legacies of the inter-ethnic conflicts from the 1990s, and have been overshadowed by the dominant discourse that was almost exclusively fixated on the activities of the Hague Tribunal.

To sum up: the prevailing Hague discourse substantially shaped the state's policies in dealing with inter-ethnic conflicts in the countries of the former Yugoslavia. Notwithstanding the absence of a systematic approach to dealing with conflicts from the 1990s, we may argue that in comparison to the period before 2000, the state institutions at least intensified their commitment to support prosecutions of war crimes. Some non-judicial mechanisms are visible as well.

3.2.1 Judicial mechanisms

Since 2000, under strong pressure from the international community, Serbia has focused almost exclusively on the criminal prosecution of war crimes (legal justice): (a) on legal proceedings before the ICTY and cooperation with the Tribunal; and (b) on establishing a legal and institutional framework for prosecutions of war crimes in Serbia.

(A) COOPERATION WITH THE ICTY

Although the period from 2001 to 2003 was marked by many acts of obstruction and disagreements in the ruling coalition, under Prime Minister Đinđić's government the state institutions began to cooperate more intensively with the ICTY.[15] Consequently, Đinđić was targeted by nationalists and supporters of Milošević, which resulted in his assassination. This was followed by a broad police campaign whose aim was to identify, uncover and arrest the perpetrators of the assassination and their collaborators. This revealed links between war crimes and crimes committed against Milošević's opponents in Serbia, which to some extent

15 The Decree and, later, the Law on the Cooperation of Serbia and Montenegro with the International Tribunal for Criminal Prosecution of Persons Responsible for Serious Crimes against International Humanitarian Laws Committed on the territory of the former Yugoslavia since 1991 (Official Gazette of FR Yugoslavia, No. 18/2002, and Official Gazette of Serbia and Montenegro, No. 16/2003) were adopted, arrests and extraditions of the accused individuals to the Tribunal were performed, evidence was provided for the ICTY etc.

also 'contributed to lessening the denial of war crimes committed by Serbs' (Nikolić-Ristanović, 2006, p. 372). However, the official response to Đinđić's assassination was framed in terms of a 'war against organised crime' and 'moral panic', prioritising 'selective repression over uncovering the entire truth and, in this way, missed a unique opportunity to establish grounds for political consensus about the past' (Nikolić-Ristanović, 2006, p. 372).

After 2001, the global war on terrorism and the security discourse prevailed over international law. The state authorities in Serbia increasingly abused this situation as grounds to minimise or postpone cooperation with the ICTY (Subotić, 2010, p. 62). In addition, right-wing political parties became stronger and the nationalistic discourse prevailed. Consequently, the cooperation with the ICTY 'suffered a downturn' (Ostojić, 2007, p. 113), and a policy of benevolent surrender, which involved providing moral and material support to indicted persons who surrendered to The Hague voluntarily, and to their families was advocated (Subotić, 2010). With their failure or unwillingness to fulfil their obligations to the ICTY, the state institutions in Serbia reduced the level of cooperation to formal, passive cooperation. However, under renewed pressure from the international community in general and the European Union in particular, Serbian authorities intensified their cooperation with the ICTY from 2005 onwards, for the very pragmatic reason of gaining favour with the international community.

(B) PROSECUTION OF WAR CRIMES BEFORE THE NATIONAL COURTS

Establishing a national legal and institutional framework for the investigation and prosecution of war crimes was another approach to dealing with the legacies of the 1990s' conflicts. This began in 2003 with the Serbian Parliament's adoption of the Law on the Organisation and Authorities of the State Agencies in War Crime Procedures[16] and the establishment of special units for uncovering and prosecuting war crimes within the police, prosecution authorities (Office of the War Crimes Prosecutor) and the judiciary (Chamber for War Crimes of the Belgrade Higher Court). This was meant to contribute to more impartial prosecutions and to establish improved mechanisms for the protection of victims and witnesses. Both the Office of the War Crimes Prosecutor and the Chamber for War Crimes intensified their work, particularly after 2005.[17] They established cooperation with relevant institutions in the former Yugoslav republics (Croatia, BiH and Montenegro) and the UN Mission in Kosovo (UNMIK). Many efforts were made by the Serbian judiciary to improve the criminal justice process, although the Prosecutor's office and the Chamber for War Crimes are operating

16 Official Gazette of the Republic of Serbia, Nos. 67/2003, 135/2004, 61/2005, 101/2007 and 104/2009.

17 More information on the number of prosecutions, charged and convicted persons, investigations, victims etc. can be found on the website of the Office of the War Crimes Prosecutor www.tuzilastvorz.org.rs/html_trz/predmeti_eng.htm (accessed on 25 March 2015).

in 'an atmosphere of threats and intimidation from some members of the public', and with 'limited political support and even obstruction by some political parties' (Council of Europe, 2012, p. 18).[18]

Since 2005, several legal reforms in Serbia have helped to improve the legal position of victims of crime, including victims of war crimes, establishing the basis for their better protection both from secondary victimisation and re-victimisation, intimidation and threats (Ćopić, 2011; Nikolić-Ristanović, 2011). In practice, positive steps were made with the establishment of the Service for the Protection of Victims/Witnesses within the Chamber for War Crimes in 2006 (Nikolić-Ristanović, 2011; Peković, 2011). It provides logistical and emotional support for victims and witnesses in war crimes cases. The Service has established cooperation with similar services in BiH and Croatia. However, as one recent research study suggests, there is a lack of cooperation between it and other victim support services in Serbia (Nikolić-Ristanović, 2011, p. 112). The Service thus operates outside the broader system of support for victims of crime, with the result that victims are left without any further protection and assistance after giving evidence in court.

Although there are still many inconsistencies in the existing legislation, and victim protection and support need to be improved, we may argue that the state institutions took important steps in dealing with the legacies of the 1990s conflicts at the judicial level. This seems particularly important if we keep in mind that the authorities still operate in a very unstable political context, facing diverse obstacles and forms of obstruction. Nevertheless, the prosecution of war crimes by the police and legal institutions in Serbia and continuation of the cooperation on this issue with other countries in the region of the former Yugoslavia will form part of the negotiations on Serbia's accession to the EU.[19] It can thus be expected that the

18 Among the problems these agencies face are: (a) a lack of support from the police and the media, which is contrary to the support the media provides for the agencies authorised to deal with the cases of organised crime, minimising the work of the Office of the War Crimes Prosecutor; (b) inadequate cooperation with the police unit responsible for uncovering and prosecuting war crimes and with the unit for the protection of witnesses (particularly in regard to the protection of the members of the police and army who are ready to testify about crimes committed during the 1990s, to whom this unit is not willing to provide protection); (c) a lack of understanding of the complex process of war crimes prosecution (problems in obtaining material evidence, unwillingness of the victims and witnesses to testify, fading memories etc.); and (d) a lack of consensus on the question of the exact time period to be considered. These problems were identified by the War Crimes Prosecutor Vladimir Vukčević at the conference 'Dostignuća i pozicije tranzicione pravde u pregovorima Srbije sa EU' ('Achievements and positions of transitional justice in Serbia's negotiations with the EU'), hosted by the Balkan Research Network (BRN) in Belgrade on 14 November 2013.

19 This was emphasised by Pierre Mirel, responsible for the Western Balkans in the European Commission's Directorate-General for Enlargement in a statement at the conference 'Dostignuća i pozicije tranzicione pravde u pregovorima Srbije sa EU' ('Achievements and positions of transitional justice in Serbia's negotiations with the EU'). This event was hosted by the Balkan Research Network (BRN) in Belgrade on 14 November 2013. Similar thoughts were expressed by Oskar Benedikt, the Deputy Head of the EU Delegation to Serbia at the conference 'Tranziciona pravda u procesu pristupanja Srbije Evropskoj uniji' ('Transitional justice in the process of accession of Serbia to the EU'), which took place in Belgrade on 26 June 2014: he stated that transitional justice is an integral part of fundamental rights.

discourse on transitional justice will continue to focus particularly on judicial mechanisms in future.

Although criminal justice is often seen as the best and necessary means to 'undo past state justice and to advance the normative transformation of these times to a rule-of-law system' (Teitel, 2000, p. 28), there are three crucial objections to trials as the main form of dealing with the legacies of inter-ethnic conflicts: retroactivity, politicisation and selectivity of cases (Minow, 1998, pp. 30–31); this is evident in the case of Serbia. Criminal proceedings are designed in such a way that they primarily focus on the relationship between the offender (usually represented by his/her attorney) and the state (represented by the public prosecutor) (Nielsen, 2001, p. 151). These parties to the proceedings are engaged in a competition to prove their case, to defeat their opponent and to emerge as the winner. In such a context, the victim, who is directly or indirectly affected by the concrete conflict, is invisible: the victim is neglected, marginalised and not treated as a party. In other words, the 'owners' of the conflict are actually excluded from the process of conflict resolution; no space is left for their (constructive) communication and interaction. Trials generally offer no scope for 'interaction between dissimilar voices', which is the essence of the 'dialogical/restorative justice' (Foss *et al*, 2012, p. 47) and is particularly important in the process of victim recovery and restoration of justice.

Most of those who testified before the War Crimes Chamber in Belgrade were victims/witnesses from BiH, Croatia and Kosovo, but due to the Service's insufficient capacities to protect victims/witnesses, they have often been unable to access assistance and support. In addition, many victims are still reluctant to come to Serbia and give evidence, either because they live far away or because they fear threats and intimidation.[20] Victims are often dissatisfied with the decisions of both the ICTY and the national courts, because they do not fulfil their expectations of tough sentences for perpetrators. These expectations are created through the strong influence of the dominant repressive discourse, and the insistence of both the state institutions and civil society organisations that trials and punishments are the main forums for dealing with the legacies of the wars from the 1990s. Although an important element of transitional justice, the criminal justice system also deepens the conflicts, leading some authors to argue, correctly, that legal justice is little more than 'symbolic justice' (Liebmann, 2007, p. 362) and needs to be complemented with non-judicial forms of justice which are more victim-orientated, aimed at conflict transformation and closing the cycle of violence, instead of deepening the existing conflicts.

3.2.2 Non-judicial mechanisms

In addition to the retributive (criminal) justice mechanisms, some restorative approaches can be observed, notably fact-finding and truth-seeking mechanisms,

20 Conference of the project 'Justice and war crimes', May 2011. Available at: www.slobodnaevropa.org/content/region_sudjenja_svedoci/24093744.html (accessed on 5 February 2012).

public apologies and condemnation of atrocities, and victim-orientated initiatives in local communities (particularly memorials). In addition, it is important to mention the dialogues, or rather the negotiations, about the Kosovo problem, which can be considered a form of peaceful resolution of the problems that emerged after the formal end of the conflict in Kosovo.

(A) TRUTH-SEEKING MECHANISMS

Two important steps were taken by the state authorities in respect to truth-seeking processes: the establishment of the Commission for Missing Persons, and the appointment of the Truth and Reconciliation Commission.

The Commission for Missing Persons was set up by the government in 2006. Its work is important in establishing the circumstances surrounding the fates of persons who have been missing since the conflicts in the former Yugoslavia, primarily in Croatia and BiH, and in Kosovo. Finding the missing is a precondition for the healing process and is of great importance to their families. The Commission's mandate includes: monitoring, exploring and developing proposals for solving missing person cases; collecting data and providing information about missing persons; coordinating the work of relevant agencies and organisations in the procedure for finding missing persons; and cooperation with authorised agencies, families and associations of missing persons. In its work, the Commission has adopted an inclusive approach, meaning that it focuses not only on Serbs as victims, but also on members of other ethnic groups who have disappeared. The Commission cooperates with similar bodies (commissions or working groups) in Croatia, BiH, Montenegro and Kosovo, as well as with the International Commission on Missing Persons.[21]

In terms of restorative justice and its main principles, including active participation by victims (survivors) and their relatives in the truth-seeking process, truth commissions play an even greater role. They provide an official forum to allow both direct and indirect victims, as well as perpetrators, to be heard, to tell their stories and express their feelings, and 'give evidence of human rights abuses' (Liebmann, 2007, p. 363). From the victims' perspective, this is an important step in their process of recovery, empowerment and restoration. Truth and Reconciliation Commissions are therefore considered to be restorative mechanisms, although the level of their restorativeness may depend on the extent to which they try to actively involve victims and provide support and symbolic reparations, involve the community etc. (Liebmann, 2007, p. 381).

21 For some data on the work of the Commission please visit www.kirs.gov.rs/docs/komisijazanestalalica/prezentacije/Komisija%20za%20nestala%20lica.pdf (accessed on 17 November 2014). In addition, as pointed out on the website of the International Commission on Missing Persons, 'Serbia continues in its efforts to find missing persons on its territory. To date, approximately 1,100 persons have been found of whom almost 900 were missing from the Kosovo conflict and the remainder from the conflicts of 1991–1995.' Available at: www.ic-mp.org/where-we-work/europe/western-balkans/republic-of-serbia/ (accessed on 17 November 2014).

In Serbia, the Truth and Reconciliation Commission (TRC) was established by the Decree of the President of the Federal Republic of Yugoslavia, Vojislav Koštunica, in 2001. Its mandate was defined as follows: to organise research work on recovery of records about social, international and political conflicts which led to the war, and to establish causal links between events; to inform the domestic and international public about its work and results; and to cooperate and exchange experience with similar commissions and bodies in neighbouring and other countries. Nineteen persons from different professional backgrounds, political affiliations and profiles were appointed as members of the TRC, but no non-governmental organisations were invited to participate. It was a matter for Commission members to define the basic concept and strategy for their work. However, the Commission's mandate remained unclear and there was no clear concept on how it should cooperate with other agencies and organisations. As noted by Ilić (2005, p. 63), from the text of the President's Decree on the TRC it was difficult to understand the reasoning behind its establishment, who was supposed to reconcile with whom and why.

The Serbian TRC never started work and was abolished just two years after its establishment, without producing any significant results (Ilić, 2005). There appear to be two main reasons for this. First, the TRC was established unnecessarily quickly and without being preceded by broader discussions involving different stakeholders, including NGO representatives; there was also no consensus about the focus of its work (Nikolić-Ristanović, 2003; Subotić, 2010). Second, the mandate of the TRC was disputable: it was rather broad, but essentially did not concentrate on what the role of a TRC is supposed to be – a 'tool for enabling truth-telling and public engagement to take place' (Ostojić, 2007, p. 123). In this respect, it was not clear how the public would be involved, and whether and how the perspectives of the victims would be included. Consequently, it is argued that by establishing a TRC, the new government wanted to gain political credit from abroad, creating an image of its readiness to face the legacies of the 1990s conflicts, but actually wanting to reduce external pressure and to convince the international community that the TRC should be given priority over the prosecutions before the ICTY. It has been argued that the government's policy was mainly intended to minimise cooperation with the ICTY and prevent further extraditions (Ilić, 2005, p. 71; Nikolić-Ristanović, 2006, p. 376). It therefore seems likely that the Commission's establishment was not motivated by a political decision to contribute to a more inclusive process of conflict resolution that would actively involve all parties, including victims, but was primarily a way of complying with the international community's demands (Subotić, 2010).

(B) PUBLIC APOLOGIES AND SYMBOLIC REPARATIONS

State institutions and political leaders have made some effort to make symbolic gestures and reparations, including public apologies, the condemnation of atrocities and some victim-orientated initiatives, often with local authority support, such as setting up monuments (as a form of symbolic reparation) and implementing programmes for refugees and internally displaced persons. However, material reparations were and still are outstanding, preserving a hierarchy of victims.

Public apologies from state officials[22] are important in decreasing ethnic tensions and facilitating the process of reconciliation (Biro, 2001). Nevertheless, these steps produced different reactions, sometimes being criticised as too formal and insubstantial. For example, reactions in Serbia after the public apologies by Boris Tadić differ: the apology given in Sarajevo in 2004 for the crimes committed by Serbs in BiH was strongly criticised, reinforcing the existing polarisations in the ruling structures and political parties regarding cooperation with the ICTY. By contrast, the apology given in Zagreb in 2007 to the people of Croatia was better accepted in Serbia, even among some (softer) right-wing political parties, some of which were serving in the governing coalition. From the perspective of the state institutions and most political parties, this apology was seen as a correct and timely political act and was important in improving Serbia's position and mobilising support for efforts to solve the Kosovo conflict. It was viewed positively by civil society, too, largely because President Tadić accepted Serbia's responsibility, which was interpreted as a political decision to intensify cooperation with the ICTY and help secure the convictions of the accused. Therefore, it seems that the gesture of apology, which is considered to be one of the possible restorative outcomes, was in fact viewed pragmatically as a way to gain political points and strengthen judicial mechanisms in dealing with past atrocities.

In 2010, after several years of resistance and controversial debates, the Serbian Parliament adopted the Declaration on Srebrenica, which was a positive move in the process of dealing with the legacies of the 1990s conflicts. In the Declaration, the Serbian Parliament condemned atrocities committed in Srebrenica in 1995 and apologised to the families of the victims for all their suffering. Apart from this official document, the government and the President of Serbia condemned all war crimes committed on the territory of the former Yugoslavia, as well as the celebration of war criminals as heroes, all forms of fascism, anti-Semitism and discrimination. Similar to apologies, these steps could be analysed from two different standpoints: They are important for victims and their families, because they can be seen as acknowledging their losses and suffering and can help in their recovery, empowerment and restoration, meaning that they have at least a partly restorative character. However, similar to apologies, the Srebrenica Declaration cannot be seen as a completely restorative initiative as it was not accompanied by restorative processes based on encounter and active participation of all those who were directly or indirectly involved in the conflicts, and on dialogue, which should 'involve an effort to recognize the value of the other – to see him/her as an end

22 President of Serbia and Montenegro Svetozar Marović apologised in 2003 for crimes committed by Serb forces against Croatians and Bosnians, while the President of Serbia Boris Tadić apologised in 2004 for war crimes committed on behalf of Serbia and the Serbian people in Bosnia and Herzegovina, as well as in 2007 and 2010 for the crimes committed in Croatia.

and not merely as a means to achieving a desired goal' (Kent & Taylor, 2002, p. 22). It is also important to emphasise that these initiatives led to divisions in Serbia, given that a political consensus about the role of Serbia in the conflicts in the countries of the former Yugoslavia and the nature of the crimes committed during the conflicts was still lacking. This contributed to a constant recurrence of a discourse that emphasises nationalistic values and narratives of victimisation of one's own ethnic group (Serbs in this case), jeopardising the process of democratisation.

The Declaration on Srebrenica reflects the existence of the two different discourses: one is visible in the Declaration itself in its condemnation of the atrocities committed in Srebrenica, its acknowledgement of all victims, and its expectation that other countries in the region will condemn atrocities committed against Serbs (inclusive approach). The other discourse, advocated by some political parties and civil society organisations, suggests that representatives of the state need to clearly condemn the atrocities committed in Srebrenica as genocide. The crimes committed in Srebrenica were not described in the Declaration as genocide, but Parliament referred to statements made in the judgment of the International Court of Justice. According to this judgment, Serbia was not directly responsible for the Srebrenica genocide and was not complicit in it, but is responsible for the breach of the Convention on the Prevention and Punishment of the Crime of Genocide by failing to prevent the Srebrenica genocide, by not cooperating with the ICTY in punishing the perpetrators of the genocide, and by violating its obligation to comply with the provisional measures ordered by the Court.[23]

Finally, tributes, memorials and commemorations can also be regarded as forms of symbolic reparation. Unfortunately, they are quite sporadic and primarily initiated at the local level (in local communities). Some of them have been successful, resulting, for example, in memorials to the victims of atrocities (e.g. in Prijepolje).[24] Other initiatives were less successful for various reasons (a place for the monument was not defined, threats, obstruction etc.). Monument-building initiatives can also have counterproductive effects. An example is the decision to set up a memorial in 2012 in the central part of Belgrade, which is dedicated to 'all victims of wars and defendants of the homeland from 1990 to 1999' (as stated on the monument). It was set up without any broader dialogue (restorative process) that included all stakeholders, including representatives of victims' organisations. The victims still remain invisible in this monument: it is not clear to

23 Information on the judgment of the International Court of Justice in the case Bosnia and Herzegovina v. Serbia is available at www.icj-cij.org/docket/index.php?p1=3&p2=2&case=91&code=bhy&p3=5 (accessed on 6 February 2013).

24 In 2009 a monument was unveiled in Prijepolje in south-west Serbia, dedicated to nine persons (Bosniaks) who were among 19 persons kidnapped and killed in Štrpce in 1993. The names of the victims are inscribed on the monument, along with words emphasising that 'whoever forgets what happened in 1993 gives up on the future'.

which conflicts it refers, there are no names of victims, and victims are put together with those who participated in the wars. This kind of initiative cannot be considered to be restorative; rather, it fits into the nationalistic discourse of justifying conflicts from the 1990s as defensive and provides another example of acknowledging victimisation of only one's own citizens.

As to material reparations, there is still a lack of a reparation mechanism for all victims of the inter-ethnic conflicts, which is a direct consequence of the attitude of the authorities towards the conflicts from the 1990s and results in the hierarchy of victims. Some victims (e.g. war-disabled persons and families of those killed in an armed conflict or deceased as a result of injuries suffered in connection with the conflict) have been able to obtain administrative compensation, while many others are excluded (e.g. victims whose injuries or loss of life resulted from actions of Serbian state agencies), and some have been compensated but under certain conditions (e.g. former camp detainees, victims of sexual violence, and victims of torture but only if the abuses against them resulted in bodily infirmity above a certain threshold) (Council of Europe, 2012: 28). In addition, the state representatives have not yet recognised the status of civilians as victims of war; consequently, they are also excluded from the reparation mechanisms. Victims in the excluded categories can seek redress for material and non-material damages only through regular (civil) court procedures, which are long-lasting, expensive and with uncertain outcomes. Redress for the victims remains a crucial issue, along with the care for refugees and displaced persons. After the conflicts ended, the state institutions continued to support and assist refugees and internally displaced persons either with reintegration in Serbia (by giving them Serbian citizenship, providing accommodation, building new flats and moving refugees and internally displaced persons from the collective centres and reducing the number of collective centres, providing material support etc.) or with return.[25]

(C) MEDIATED DIALOGUE WITH THE GOVERNMENT OF KOSOVO

Although led on a political level, mediated dialogues or, more accurately, facilitated negotiations between Belgrade and Pristina can be regarded as an attempt to solve the consequences of the Kosovo conflict in a peaceful way. The authorities are actually trying to protect Serbs in Kosovo and prevent further conflicts that are still emerging. Initial attempts to start the dialogue were made in 2001, soon after political changes took place in Serbia, but these efforts failed. Only after 2005, when the UN Security Council gave the green light for the start of negotiations on the status of Kosovo, did the process of facilitated negotiations start, commencing in 2006 and continuing throughout 2007. However, it proved ineffective due to

25 More information on this issue can be found on the website of the Commissariat for Refugees of the Republic of Serbia: www.kirs.gov.rs/articles/onama.php?lang=ENG (accessed on 5 February 2013).

the completely opposing attitudes of Belgrade and Pristina representatives about the status of Kosovo. This was followed by the unilateral proclamation of the independence of Kosovo in 2008, with subsequent diplomatic recognition of Kosovo as an independent state by a number of countries. This provoked protests throughout Serbia in 2008.[26]

There was renewed scope to begin a process of negotiations in 2010. The process started in March 2011 and has continued until the present. This is a political dialogue facilitated by the EU. The dynamic of the dialogue is changing, going forwards and backwards, depending on the political circumstances. At the beginning of 2013, the Serbian Parliament adopted the Resolution on Kosovo and the Platform for further political dialogue with the Kosovo institutions.[27] It stated that one of the crucial aims of the dialogue is to provide security and protect the human rights of Serbs and other ethnic groups who live in Kosovo. In April 2013, the Brussels agreement on the normalisation of relations between Belgrade and Pristina was signed; this envisaged the establishment of the Association/Community of Serb-majority municipalities in Kosovo and defined its competences, and opened the way for the integration of the police forces and the judiciary. Nevertheless, there are still tensions between Serbs and Albanians in Kosovo, which from time to time escalate into violence. This reinforces the perception of Serbs living in Kosovo that they are unsafe and not sufficiently protected.

4. The limitations of civil society and the need for a 'third way' of dealing with the past

Civil society organisations (CSOs)[28] played a very important political role in activities against the war and against human rights violations and the regime of Slobodan Milošević.[29] During the 1990s, the common denominator of CSOs was their political (anti-war and anti-government) orientation, regardless of their specific mission and activities. Civil society organisations and a large number of individuals were involved in peaceful demonstrations during the 1990s, sending

26 For more information see http://en.wikipedia.org/wiki/2008_protests_in_Serbia (accessed on 6 February 2013).

27 More information can be found on the website of the National Assembly of the Republic of Serbia, www.parlament.gov.rs/upload/archive/files/lat/pdf/ostala_akta/2013/RS1-13Lat.pdf (accessed on 10 February 2013).

28 The term 'civil society organisation' has been used in Serbia more frequently over the last several years, whereas in the 1990s until the mid-2000s, they were mostly referred to as non-governmental organisations. We use 'civil society organisations' (CSO) throughout this chapter as a generic term for all local organisations.

29 Although CSOs, as organisations with autonomy in relation to the state, had appeared in Serbia during communist times, their development primarily coincided with the political and economic transition in the late 1980s and early 1990s. Development of CSOs was intensive, particularly during the wars in Bosnia and Herzegovina and Croatia. This development was further intensified after opposition parties took power at the local level in major cities in Serbia (1996–1999) and particularly after the final defeat of the Miloševic regime and political change in 2000 (Milić, 2002; Nikolić-Ristanović, 2002; Lazić, 2005).

clear messages about the strength and potential of a non-violent approach to conflict resolution, as a contrast to violence and repression as the state's way of dealing with conflicts. The protests started in 1991, and also included large student rallies and protests against falsified local election results in 1996. The massive protests that developed during 2000 finally resulted in mostly peaceful political change (with some violent episodes) in September 2000.

After the end of the armed conflicts in the former Yugoslavia and political change in Serbia, the activities of the CSOs continued to have a political component, but many changed their focus. Over time, the issue of 'dealing with the past' was either added to the agenda or replaced the anti-war and anti-government activities. CSO activities fell into the following categories:[30]

- awareness-raising (mainly raising awareness of war crimes, ICTY, human rights and minority rights violations);
- monitoring and advocacy, mainly relating to criminal prosecutions for war crimes, human rights violations and related political crime in Serbia;
- psychosocial support and assistance for victims;
- research, publications and education;
- mediation and activities that aim to promote inter-ethnic and intra-ethnic dialogue; and
- cultural and artistic activities (films, exhibitions, literature, theatre, street performances) and religious events, such as regular prayers for peace (Nikolić-Ristanović & Šaćiri, 2013).

After the political changes in Serbia, the political conflict shifted. The conflict between the democratic opposition and Milošević's regime was replaced by the conflict between the nationalist forces arguing against cooperation with the Hague Tribunal, on the one hand, and the pro-Hague groups and individuals, on the other. Two extreme discourses regarding the past have prevailed, not only among political parties and policy-makers, but also among civil society actors.[31] While the extreme nationalistic discourse recognises only victimhood of Serbs and considers war criminals national heroes, the extreme anti-nationalist discourse addresses non-Serbs exclusively as victims and Serbs as war criminals (Nikolić-Ristanović, 2006). Both these discourses may be recognised as forms of the security discourse, which appeared to be counterproductive and created new conflicts rather than solving old ones.[32] Within this discourse, the inter-ethnic conflicts are addressed in

30 This classification is based on findings of available research (Blagojević & Milenković, 2004; Rosandić, Milenković & Kovačević, 2005; Fischer & Petrović-Ziemer, 2013), and on information obtained from CSO material and interviews with CSOs representatives.

31 Nationalistic views were promoted by right-wing organisations and by some victims, particularly refugee organisations influenced and manipulated by right-wing political parties.

32 For an excellent critical analysis of the security discourse of some civil society organisations, developed in relation to dealing with the past, and its contribution to solidifying divisions and producing rather than reducing conflicts, see Stephenson & Zanotti (2011).

a very abstract way and the debate on the past comprises mostly Serbian collective guilt and high numbers of depersonalised victims, rather than dealing with the suffering, responsibilities, needs and conflicts of real people. Both approaches are based on selective remembrance and therefore have to be regarded as problematic. In this way, they do not open space for other views, dialogical truth and 'communicative memory' (as defined by Assmann, 1992). Nevertheless, some CSOs recently modified their security discourse by including Serb victims in their public statements, activities and advocacy, or by becoming critical towards the release of Croats and Albanians accused of war crimes. However, their discourse is still very exclusive and does not allow space for different views. The evident tension between the prevailing security discourse on the one hand and restorative justice mechanisms and activities used by some organisations on the other (for some examples: Putnik, 2004; Fond za humanitarno pravo, 2006; Stephenson & Zanotti, 2011) is therefore an ongoing issue and a challenge that needs to be addressed in Serbia.

In sum, although elements of restorative justice are present in the discussions of civil society actors, retributive and security discourses prevail. There is no clear understanding of what restorative approaches might look like. The public discourse of CSOs in Serbia is mainly about criminal prosecutions and punishments, lustration, and police and judicial reform, and to some extent reparation of victims. It rarely includes dealing with the accountability of the perpetrators in its interconnectedness with the consequences for victims and the needs of both parties. Constructive approaches to conflict transformation, based on listening and understanding all those who were directly or indirectly involved in the conflict, are still lacking. Consequently, the use of the term 'reconciliation' tends to be avoided (Fischer & Petrović-Ziemer, 2013).

As a response to the extreme and exclusive approaches to dealing with the past, described above, the Victimology Society of Serbia initiated the 'third way', which was elaborated within an informal initiative known as Joint Action for Truth and Reconciliation (ZAIP). The 'third way' accepted restorative discourse as a result of the efforts to find a new model which would try to stop or mitigate existing and prevent future conflicts (Nikolić-Ristanović & Hanak, 2006; Nikolić-Ristanović & Srna, 2010).

ZAIP currently has 113 members. The main characteristics of the *third way*, as defined by participants attending a series of seminars held in 2007 and 2008 (Nikolić-Ristanović & Srna, 2008), are as follows:

- non-conflict two-way communication about the past, involving people with different war experiences and focusing on mutual recognition, support and non-accusation;
- an inclusive relationship toward crimes, victims and perpetrators and inclusive discourse about the past (speaking about all crimes, victims and perpetrators regardless of their ethnic and other identity and features);
- respect for human rights, empowerment and reintegration of all persons affected by conflict;

- use of a wide range of methods in truth-seeking and reconciliation; and
- a pro-active approach in dealing with the past.

The explicit or implicit recognition of the existence of various types of truths, or interpretations of truths (factual or forensic, personal or narrative, social or 'dialogue', restorative and healing truth) as identified by the South African Truth and Reconciliation Commission (Cohen, 2003, 227), is accepted as the basis of the third way. Dialogue and restorative/healing truth are regarded as especially important for reconciliation in post-conflict society. The third way was recognised as leading to 'positive peace'[33] by bridging the gap between people with different war experiences and closing the conflicts/cycles of violence.

Inter-group contact and communication are important in dealing with inter-group conflict in post-conflict societies, including the Western Balkan countries. Moreover, the existing literature suggests that optimal contact and constructive communication are crucial in overcoming divisions and inter-group conflicts, particularly in societies striving to come to terms with a violent past (Allport, 1954; Pettigrew, 1998; Amir, 1998; Janoff-Bulman & Werther, 2008; Foss *et al*, 2012, p. 47). However, widespread monolithic and authoritarian communication is one of the main obstacles to constructive communication about the past in Serbia. The third way as a form of restorative dialogue[34] and as a pluralistic and democratic approach to truth, reconciliation and conflict management is therefore needed.[35]

5. Conclusion

Dealing with the legacies of the inter-ethnic conflicts from the 1990s is very important for democracy, social justice, security, peace and reconciliation in the entire region of the former Yugoslavia, including Serbia. Without facing the past, it is hard to understand the present and the conflicts between members of different ethnic groups that exist in Serbia today, which are still influenced by the dynamics of these wars. Nevertheless, recent political instability in Serbia and the strong nationalistic discourse have created unfavourable conditions for dealing with the past effectively. The analysis of the activities and the discourse of the state

33 This term is originally conceptualised by Quinney as part of his critique of the criminal justice system in which he views peacemaking criminology as part of the movement toward 'positive peace' (Quinney, 1997, quoted by Bierne & Messerschmidt, 1999, p. 233).

34 Similarly, White speaks about reconciliation dialogue, which is inclusive of all opinions and constituencies to the conflict, non-judgmental, voluntary and supportive of all at the psychological level (White, 2003).

35 According to Bloomfield, democracy 'is a system for managing conflict. This process of conflict management involves debate, argument, disagreement, compromise and cooperation, all within a system that permits opposing points of view to coexist fairly without recourse to violence' (Bloomfield, 2003, p. 10). This definition of democracy derives from the paradigm of restorative justice and acknowledges the existence of different perspectives and the possibility of more than one truth.

institutions suggest that there is still a lack of a clear political will to deal with the responsibility for the interethnic conflicts and to speak openly about the role of the Serbian authorities and the people involved in the wars of the 1990s. In general, the policies pursued by the state institutions in Serbia in dealing with these legacies were greatly influenced by the international and European community; it could thus be argued that these policies were mainly motivated by the need to comply with the international community's demands and achieve favourable political and economic conditions, rather than by the wish for reconciliation.

Serbia's policies for transitional justice were and are primarily focused on judicial mechanisms (i.e. on legal justice). This is in line with the dominant international security discourse and the overall policy of penal populism (Garland, 2001), which is visible in Serbia as well (Soković, 2012). However, the nationalistic discourse and a lack of rule of law, together with the policy of penal populism, created fertile ground for political obstruction and misuse of the criminal justice system, which undermines existing efforts to bring perpetrators to justice. On the other hand, it is hard to imagine that every individual who committed crimes during the wars in the former Yugoslavia will ever be prosecuted. Therefore, although criminal prosecution is seen as an important transitional justice mechanism, whose role will be emphasised during negotiations on Serbia's accession to the European Union, it has its own limitations, as shown in this chapter. As long as victims are not actively involved in conflict transformation but remain passive observers of the process, particularly of the criminal justice proceedings, they will not be able to participate actively in conflict transformation. There appears to be a need to create more space for restorative justice approaches and dialogical truth in dealing with the past, which should be seen as adding value to the judicial mechanisms. Although the state institutions in Serbia have made some efforts (e.g. the TRC, public apologies, condemnation of war crimes etc.) we argue that they were just sporadic attempts on the margins of the state's efforts to deal with the past. However, these attempts also suggest that at least some potential for the use of restorative justice by state institutions exists. They need to be further developed and improved.

Although civil society organisations contributed significantly to dealing with the past in Serbia in terms of war crimes monitoring, advocacy for human rights and support for victims, dialogue and educational work, they were not able to send strong and convincing messages about the past to Serbian citizens. The security discourse also had a strong impact on civil society organisations and continues to provoke resistance and hostile attitudes rather than contributing to dialogue and resolving existing conflicts. Nevertheless, the potential for non-violent conflict resolution and restorative justice is evident in civil society. This was particularly visible during the peaceful demonstrations against the Milošević regime and contributions to peaceful political change.

However, so far, restorative activities have not been sufficiently recognised and applied by the state and civil society organisations. It is partly due to a lack of awareness and knowledge of its potential. There is thus a need to educate representatives of both sectors on this issue and for further work to develop and implement mechanisms of transitional justice based on the principles of restorative justice: active participation, dialogue, respect, inclusion, empowerment and restoration (Vanfraechem, 2012, p. 14). It is therefore important to encourage cooperation between the state institutions and civil society and to focus more on 'communicative memory' (i.e. on the memory-related activities based on restorative dialogue, which must be inclusive and allow for the plurality of truths and opinions). As a precondition, the state institutions must put more effort into acknowledging the status of all the victims and war veterans, eliminating any discrimination and hierarchy. In addition, it is important for the state to acknowledge the status of civilians as victims of war. Extending recognition of victim and war veteran status to certain categories of persons who are currently excluded would open the way for reparations as one of the important restorative outcomes. This would also create space for them to be included in conflict transformation and in prevention of future conflicts. Finally, we would argue that there is a need to develop restorative approaches in the local communities in Serbia in order to solve existing and prevent future conflicts between members of different ethnic groups. This would be one of the paths towards peaceful coexistence and increased security for all citizens.

References

Allport, G. W. (1954). *The Nature of Prejudice*. Reading, MA: Addison-Wesley.

Amir, Y. (1998). 'Contact Hypothesis in Ethnic Relations'. In Weiner, E. (Ed.), *The Handbook of Interethnic Coexistence* (pp. 162–181). New York: Continuum Publishing.

Arsovska, J., Valiñas, M. & Fellegi, B. (2008). 'Prologue to the Kosovo Drama: Causes and Consequences of a Violent Ethno-political Conflict'. In Aertsen, I., Arsovska, J., Rohne, H.-C., Valiñas, M. and Vanspauwen, K. (Eds.), *Restoring Justice after Large-scale Violent Conflicts* (pp. 75–98). Devon, UK: Willan Publishing.

Assmann, J. (1992). *Das kulturelle Gedächtnis. Schrift, Erinnerung und politische Identität in frühen Hochkulturen*. München: Beck.

Beirne, P. I. & Messerschmidt, J. (1999). *Criminology*. Boulder: Westview Press.

Berghof Foundation (Ed.) (2012). *Berghof Glossary on Conflict Transformation – 20 notions for theory and practice*. Berlin: Berghof Foundation Operations GmbH.

Biro, M. (2001). 'Kako pomiriti Srbe, Hrvate i Bošnjake?' *Nova srpska politička misao* 1–4, 111–122.

Biro, M., Mihić, V., Milin, P. & Logar-Durić, S. (2002). 'Da li su društveno-političke promene u Srbiji promenile nivo autoritarnosti i etnocentrizma građana?' *Psihologija* 1–2, 37–47.

Blagojević, M. (2000). 'Prebrojavanje mrtvih tela: viktimizacija kao samoostvarujuće proročanstvo'. *Temida 2*, 5–10.

Blagojević, M. (2005). 'War on Kosovo: A Victory for the Media?' In Bieber, F. & Daskalovski, Z. (Eds.), *Understanding the War in Kosovo* (pp. 163–180). London: Frank Cass.

Blagojević, M. & Milenković, N. (2004). *Suočavanje sa prošlošću: Izveštaj za Srbiju i Crnu Goru*. Quaker Peace and Social Witness.

Bloomfield, D. (2003). 'Reconciliation: an Introduction'. In Bloomfield, D., Barnes, T. & Huyse, L., *Reconciliation after Violent Conflict: A Handbook* (pp. 10–18). Stockholm: International IDEA.

Burg, S. (2007). 'NGOs and Ethnic Conflict: Lessons from the Work of the Project on Ethnic Relations in the Balkans'. *Negotiation Journal* 1, 7–33.

Butler, J. (2004). *Precarious Life: The Powers of Mourning and Violence*. London and New York: Verso.

Ćopić, S. (2011). 'Položaj i zaštita žrtve u krivičnom postupku'. In *Prava žrtava i EU: izazovi pružanja pomoći žrtvama*, edited by Nikolić-Ristanović, V. & Ćopić, S., *Prava zrtava i EU: izazovi pruzanja pomoci zrtvama* (pp. 136–160). Beograd: Viktimološko društvo Srbije: Prometej.

Ćopić, S. (2013). 'Aktivnosti i diskurs državnih organa i institucija u Srbiji u bavljenju medjuetničkim konfliktima'. *Temida* 3–4, 61–94.

Council of Europe (2012). *Post-War Justice and Durable Peace in the Former Yugoslavia*. Strasbourg: Commissioner for Human Rights.

Daskalovski, Z. (2005). 'Claims to Kosovo: Nationalism and Self-Determination'. In Bieber, F. & Daskalovski, Z. (Eds.), *Understanding the War in Kosovo* (pp. 11–27). London: Frank Cass.

Dauphinee, E. A. (2005). 'Rambouillet: A Critical (Re)Assessment'. In Bieber, F. & Daskalovski, Z. (Eds.), *Understanding the War in Kosovo* (pp. 99–119). London: Frank Cass.

Domonji, P. (Ed.) (2008). *Vojvodina's Multiethnic Identity: Challenges in 2007–08. Helsinki Files No. 27*. Belgrade: Helsinki Committee for Human Rights in Serbia.

Đokić, D. (2002). 'The Second World War: Discourses of Reconciliation in Serbia and Croatia in the late 1980s and early 1990s'. *Journal of Southern Europe and the Balkans* 4:2, 127–140.

Fischer, M. & Petrović-Ziemer, Lj. (Eds.) (2013). *Dealing with the Past in the Western Balkans. Initiatives for Peacebuilding and Transitional Justice in Bosnia-Hercegovina, Serbia and Croatia. Berghof Report No. 18*. Berlin: Berghof Foundation.

Fond za humanitarno pravo (2006). *Izveštaj o tranzicionoj pravdi u Srbiji, Crnoj Gori i na Kosovu 1999–2005*. Beograd: Fond za humanitarno pravo.

Foss, E., Marius, H., Cecilie, S. Hydle, I., Seeberg, M. L. & Uhrig, B (2012). *Deliverable 2.1.: Report on conflicts in intercultural settings*. ALTERNATIVE Collaborative Project (unpublished).

Garland, D. (2001). *The Culture of Control – Crime and Social Order in Contemporary Society*. Oxford: Oxford University Press.

Guzina, D. (2005). 'Kosovo or Kosova – Could It Be Both? The Case of Interlocking Serbian and Albanian Nationalisms'. In Bieber, F. & Daskalovski, Z. (Eds.), *Understanding the War in Kosovo* (pp. 29–49). London: Frank Cass.

Helsinki Committee for Human Rights in Serbia (2004). *National Minorities in Serbia: In Conflict With a State Ethnic Identity*. Annual Report 2004.

Hondus, P. (2007). 'Mogu li Srbi i Albanci živeti zajedno?' *Bezbednost Zapadnog Balkana* 4, 4–12.

Ilić, D. (2005). 'Jugoslovenska komisija za istinu i pomirenje'. *Reč 73.19*: 53–79.

Janjić, D. (2005). *The Crisis in South Serbia. Occasional Paper No. 11*. Belgrade: Belgrade Centre for Civil-Military Relations.

Janoff-Bulman, R. & Werther, A. (2008). 'The Social Psychology of Respect: Implications for Delegitimization and Reconciliation'. In Nadler, A., Malloy, T. & Fisher, J. D (Eds.), *The Social Psychology of Intergroup Reconciliation* (pp. 145–170). Oxford: Oxford University Press.

Kent, M. & Taylor, M. (2002). 'Toward a Dialogic Theory of Public Relations'. *Public Relations Review* 28, 21–37.

Lazić, M. (2005). *Promene i otpori*. Beograd: IP Filip Visnjic.

Liebmann, M. (2007). *Restorative Justice: How it Works*. London: Jessica Kingsley Publishers.

Milić, A. (2002). *Ženski pokret ma raskršću milenijuma*. Beograd: Institut za sociološka istraživanja Filozofskog fakulteta.

Minow, M. (1998). *Between Vengeance and Forgiveness – Facing History after Genocide and Mass Violence*. Boston: Beacon Press.

Morrison, K. (2008). *Political and Religious Confict in Sandzak*. Shrivenham: Defence Academy of the United Kingdom.

Mrvic-Petrović, N. (2000). 'Problemi zbrinjavanja i socijalne adaptacije izbeglica'. *Temida* 2, 101–109.

Nielsen, B. (2001). 'Repressive, Restorative and Reflexive Criminal Law'. In Ezzat, F. & Parmentier, S., *Victim Policies and Criminal Justice on the Road to Restorative Justice* (pp.145–166). Leuven: Leuven University Press.

Nikolić, L. (2005). 'Ethnic Prejudices and Discrimination: The Case of Kosovo'. In Bieber, F. & Daskalovski, Z. (Eds.), *Understanding the War in Kosovo* (pp. 51–76). London: Frank Cass.

Nikolić-Ristanović, V. (2000). 'Žrtve ratova u bivšoj Jugoslaviji: obim, struktura i obrasci viktimizacije'. *Temida* 2, 11–21.

Nikolić-Ristanović, V. (2002). *Social Change, Gender and Violence: Post-Communist and War-Affected Societies*. Dordrecht, Boston, London: Kluwer Academic Publishers.

Nikolić-Ristanović, V. (2003). 'Possibilities for Restorative Justice in Serbia'. In Walgrave, L. (Ed.), *Positioning Restorative Justice* (pp. 239–255). Devon: Willan Publishers.

Nikolić-Ristanović, V. (2006). 'Truth and Reconciliation in Serbia'. In Sullivan, D. & Tifft, L. (Eds.), *Handbook of Restorative Justice* (pp. 369–387). Oxon: Taylor & Francis.

Nikolić-Ristanović, V. (2011). 'Izazovi pružanja pomoći žrtvama u Srbiji' ('Challenges of victim support in Serbia)'. In Nikolić-Ristanović, V. & Ćopić, S. (Eds.), *Prava žrtava i EU: izazovi pružanja pomoći*, (pp. 163–178). Beograd: Viktimološko društvo Srbije: Prometej.

Nikolić-Ristanović, V. & Ćopić, S. (2013). *Dealing with inter-ethnic conflicts in Serbia and the place of restorative justice and victims* (unpublished) Available at: www.vds.org.rs/File/Deliverable_6_1_Research_report_on_dealing_with_conflicts_by_NGOs_and_the_state.pdf (accessed on 25 March 2015).

Nikolić-Ristanović, V. & Hanak, N. (2006). 'Truth, Reconciliation, and the Serbian Victimology Society'. *Peace Review: A Journal of Social Justice* 3, 379–387.

Nikolić-Ristanović, V. & Šaćiri B. (2013). 'Bavljenje međuetničkim konfliktima od strane organizacija civilnog društva u Srbiji: aktivnosti i diskurs'. *Temida* 3–4, 27–60.

Nikolić-Ristanović, V. & Srna, J. (2008). 'Mogući put ka pomirenju u Srbiji: Zajednička akcija za istinu i pomirenje' ('Possible way to reconciliation in Serbia: Joint Action for Truth and Reconciliation'). Belgrade: Victimology Society in Serbia and Prometej.

Nikolić-Ristanović, V. & Srna, J. (2010). 'Pomirenje sa sobom i drugima: od pristupa ka modelu' ('Reconciliation with ourselves and others: from approach to model'). *Temida* 1, 43–58.

Nikolić-Ristanović, V., Ćopić, S., Petrović, N. & Saciri, B. (2012). *Draft research report 6.1*. Belgrade: Victimology Society of Serbia (unpublished document).

Ostojić, M. (2007). 'Beyond Transitional Justice: Coming to Terms with the Past in Post-Milošević Serbia'. *Slovo* 2, 103–123.

Pavković, A. (1999). 'Kosovo: a Land of Conflicting Myths'. In Drezov, K., Gokay, B. & Kostovicova, D. (Eds.), *Kosovo–Myths, Conflict and War* (pp. 4–12). Keele University, United Kingdom: Keele European Research Centre.

Pavković, A. (2000). 'A Reconciliation Model for the Former Yugoslavia'. *Peace Review* 1, 103–109.

Peković, S. (2011). 'Podrška žrtvama i svedocima u sudskim postupcima za ratne zločine'. In Nikolić-Ristanović, V. & Ćopić, S. (Eds.), *Prava žrtava i EU: izazovi pružanja pomoći žrtvama*, (pp. 189–198). Beograd: Viktimolosko drustvo Srbije: Prometej.

Popović, D. (2005). *Etničke zajednice na Kosovu 2003 i 2004*. Beograd: Fond za humanitarno pravo.

Pettigrew, T. (1998). 'Intergroup Contact Theory'. *Annual Review of Psychology*, 49, 65–88.

Putnik, K. (Ed.) (2004). *Nasilna društva u tranziciji: alternativni dijalog Kosovo-Srbija*. Beograd: Inicijativa mladih za ljudska prava.

Raković, S. (2005). 'We are not like Them: Denial of the Other in Serbia, Croatia and Bosnia-Herzegovina'. In Pajnik, M. & Kuzmanić, T. (Eds.), *Nation-States and Xenophobia: In the ruins of Ex-Yugoslavia,* (pp. 63–74). Ljubljana: Peace Institute.

Rohne, H.-C., Arsovska, J. & Aertsen, I. (2008). 'Challenging Restorative Justice – State based Conflict, Mass Victimisation and the Changing Nature of Warfare'. In Aertsen, I., Arsovska, J., Rohne, H.-C., Valiñas, M. & Vanspauwen, K. (Eds.), *Restoring Justice after Large-scale Violent Conflicts* (pp. 3–46). Devon, UK: Willan Publishing.

Rosandić, R., Milenković, N. & Kovačevic, M. (2005). *Teži put – mirovne akcije na tlu Jugoslavije.* Beograd: Centar za antiratnu akciju.

Savković, M. (2010). 'Kontekst i implikacije huliganskog nasilja u Srbiji'. *Bezbednost Zapadnog Balkana* 18, 91–99.

Soković, S. (2012). 'Penitersijarne statistike: mera kriminaliteta i/ili više od toga?' In Nikolić-Ristanović, V. (Ed.), *Evidentiranje kriminaliteta iskustva iz sveta i Srbije* (pp. 83–104). Beograd: Prometej.

Stephenson, M. & Zanotti, L. (2011). 'Implementing the Liberal Peace in Post-conflict Scenarios: The Case of Women in Black-Serbia'. *Global Policy* 1, 46–57.

Subotić, J. (2010). *Otimanje pravde: suočavanje s prošlošću na Balkanu.* Beograd: Beogradski centar za ljudska prava.

Teitel, R. (2000). *Transitional Justice.* Oxford: Oxford University Press.

Vanfraechem, I. (2012). *Deliverable 8.1: Work document on operationalisation of theoretical concepts, ALTERNATIVE-Project,* Leuven: KU Leuven (unpublished document).

Vukomanović, D. (1999). 'Kosovska kriza – upravljanje etničkim sukobom'. *Nova srpska politička misao* 3–4, 35–59.

Zajović, S. (2007). 'Suočavanje s prošlošću – feministički pristup. Iskustva Žena u crnom'. *Genero* 10/11, 61–71.

Zdravković, H. (2005). *Politika žrtve na Kosovu: identitet žrtve kao primarni diskurzivni cilj Srba i Albanaca u upornom sukobu na Kosovu.* Beograd: Srpski genealoški centar.

White, I. (2003). 'Victim–Combatant Dialogue in Northern Ireland'. In Bloomfield, D., Barnes, T. & Huyse, L. (Eds.), *Reconciliation after Violent Conflict: A Handbook* (pp. 89–96). Stockholm: International IDEA.

Chapter 7

Young adults' perspective of social reconstruction in three post-war communities in Croatia and Bosnia-Herzegovina[1]

Dinka Čorkalo Biruški and Dean Ajduković

1. Introduction

War leaves behind devastating consequences for individuals, families, communities and for the overall social order. Its impact on the psychosocial well-being of survivors has been well documented (Ajduković, 2004; Čorkalo, Ajduković, Weinstein, Djipa, & Biro, 2004; Barber, 2009; Jones & Kafetsios, 2005). It is also well-known that war is not over when the arms have been laid down. This is certainly a precondition for stopping the enmity and open conflicts; however, at this point the very long process of dealing with the legacy of the war only begins. The present chapter deals with a crucial post-war social process—social reconstruction. In the post-conflict context of the 1991–1995 war in Croatia and Bosnia and Herzegovina (BiH) we asked a second generation of survivors, young adults, how they felt about rebuilding the relations with the former adversary group. Our Croat and Serb participants found themselves on different sides of the conflict though they were too young to fight in the war. Nevertheless, as young children in the war period and as young adults in the present, they have to cope with the consequences of the war, their ethnic group identity, painful collective victimization and exclusive group narratives of who-did-what-to-whom-and-when. In their particular contexts they have to rebuild their own communities and reach out to the "other side." In this respect, the present study is among a few that examine the post-conflict context the young people were raised into and its influences in shaping their attitudes towards the social reconstruction.

1 Acknowledgement: The preparation of this manuscript was supported by the Ministry of Science, Education and Sports of the Republic of Croatia, grant no. 130–1301422–1418. We also gratefully acknowledge use of the services and facilities of the Kroc Institute for International Peace Studies at the University of Notre Dame during the fellowship granted to the first author.

2. Post-conflict social recovery: Social reconstruction and reconciliation

Our approach to social recovery builds upon previous theorizing on the improvement of post-conflict intergroup relations. Much of this literature is about intergroup reconciliation (Bar-Tal, 2008; Kriesberg, 1998; Lederach, 1997; Long & Brecke, 2003; Nadler, 2002; Nadler, Malloy, & Fisher, 2008; Staub, 2006), and ideas aiming to reach this *final stage* of recovery in a very long process of advancement of post-conflict intergroup relations. This is reflected in how the authors have defined the concept of intergroup reconciliation. Though most scholars use the same term, the processes that are assumed are often somewhat different. For example, some authors talk about reconciliation even when the result is only a "relatively amicable relationship" (Kriesberg, 1998, p. 184), while others understand reconciliation as a "genuine peaceful relationships between societies" (Bar-Tal, 2008, p. 365; Bar-Tal & Bennink, 2004), or positive and cooperative relationships that go a step further than the process of forgiveness (Deutsch, 2008). Nadler and colleagues assumed the processes of removing emotional obstacles that are conflict-related and prevent "the ending of intergroup conflict" (Nadler & Shnabel, 2008, p. 39).

Nevertheless, most definitions of intergroup reconciliation imply a process that requires a profound psychological change of the social actors (Staub, 2006). In that sense the intergroup reconciliation has been postulated as a sort of a psychological makeover that includes cognitive, motivational, emotional and behavioral changes related to the past, present, and future relations of the conflicting parties (Nadler, Malloy & Fisher, 2008; Staub, 2006; Bar-Tal, 2008). Furthermore, some concepts of reconciliation emphasize that the changes need to be so profound that they imply changes in the participants' identities (Kelman, 2008), or should respond to different needs of the parties involved (Nadler & Shnabel, 2008).

Besides intrapersonal changes, some authors place at the core of reconciliation a restoration of trust between parties that is accomplished through "mutually trustworthy behaviors of the participants" (Worthington, Sandage & Berry, 2000, p. 229). Nadler & Liviatan (2004) also consider trust to be critical for successful reconciliation. They found that if there is trust in the other group, an expression of empathy and apology would be perceived more favorably and relations in the future would be seen as more promising than if trust in other groups was low. We also recently found that intergroup trust was positively related to positive outgroup emotions and negatively related to negative emotional orientation toward the other group (Čorkalo Biruški, 2014). A recent meta-analysis corroborated that a strong positive relationship between trust and forgiveness is an element of reconciliation (Van Tongeren, Burnette, O'Boyle, Worthington, & Forsyth, 2014). In our understanding of the post-conflict intergroup processes we also assume trust as a precondition for more demanding forms of emotional intergroup exchange and thus believe that trust precedes reconciliation (cf. Deutsch, 2008; Kelman, 2008; Nadler, 2002).

Finally, some scholars emphasize that it is not only psychological change that is needed (assuming an individual level of analyses), but also a change in "sociopsychological infrastructure" (Bar-Tal & Rosen, 2009), implying changes that go further and beyond an individual are directed to a group level of analysis (Čorkalo Biruški, 2012) and advocating a contextual determinant of intergroup violence and the recovery of intergroup relations (Ajduković, 2004; Bar-Tal & Bennink, 2004; Lederach, 1997; Verdeja, 2009).

Taking into account a variety of approaches and processes that are implied by the term reconciliation, we propose that instead of using the final outcome (i.e. reconciliation) as a label for revealing what happens in the long process of post-conflict improvement of intergroup relations, a more humble but, we argue, a more accurate term for describing the process should be used. We named this process *social reconstruction* (Ajduković, 2004), and assume it as an overarching concept that includes post-conflict processes at various instances and phases of post-conflict relations between opposing parties. In our earlier theorizing we defined social reconstruction as a "process within the community which brings its damaged social functioning to a normal level of interpersonal and group relations, and renews the social fabric of the affected community" (Ajduković, 2004, p. 128). In other words, we propose that social reconstruction goes from separation and estrangement of the conflicting parties, through cooperation, interdependence and building of trust, towards the most demanding processes of intergroup relations like apology and forgiveness. At some point it can reach the level of reconciliation between groups that have been hurt. As we pointed out elsewhere (Čorkalo Biruški, 2012), the social reconstruction processes are not related only to those happening within the community; the processes *around* the community are also important in determining the pace and dynamic of the social repair. In operationalizing the construct we hypothesized few interrelated aspects encompassing the post-conflict improvement of intergroup relations: intergroup rapprochement, intergroup trust and need for apology from the other side (Čorkalo Biruški, Ajduković, & Löw Stanić, 2014).

3. Social reconstruction after community violence

The processes of post-conflict recovery are much more complex, demanding and longer when former enemies have to continue living together on the same territory, in the same state and even in the same community (Govier, 2002; Nadler, 2002; Long & Brecke, 2003; Nadler & Shnabel, 2008; Deutsch, 2008). It is not that these processes are categorically different from those between separated groups; it is that they are more complex, and they include more layers of past relations that have to be re-built. Moreover, they are more likely, even if being repaired, to be fragile and easier to break again. When the intergroup violence happened in the same community, the violation of trust, a deep sense of betrayal and fragmentation of previous social network make social recovery and rebuilding of the relations between the groups extremely difficult (Ajduković, 2004; Ajduković & Čorkalo,

2004; Čorkalo et al., 2004; Staub, 2006). The intra-communal violence is more likely to take the pattern of intractability (Bar-Tal, 2007) and to be historically fed by narratives of past defeats and victimization (Gödl, 2007). The "intimacy of violence"—to borrow a metaphor from Staub (2006)—makes the trauma more devastating for the worldview of survivors and their recovery much slower. This is true not only for psychological recovery of the traumatized victims, but the changed worldview influences also the survivors' readiness to approach and trust the other side (Čorkalo Biruški, Ajduković, & Löw Stanić, 2014).

If there is one consequence that may be singled out as the most prominent and the one that has most fundamentally changed the social landscape of the context where the violence happened and where the post-conflict recovery should take place, then it is a loss of a dense social network, i.e. loss of community (Čorkalo Biruški, 2012). A close-knit web of relations was very typical for most communities, especially small ones, in prewar Croatia, BiH and, for that matter, most of the similar communities in the former Yugoslavia. Besides the relational connections (cf. loss of communality by Erikson, 1976) that were destroyed during the war, leaving the communities isolated and deserted, the very nature of the communities had also been lost. From social networks of relatives, friends, neighbors and co-workers where ethnic membership was an irrelevant element for inclusion in the communal "circle of trust," ethnicity has become a dominant characteristic of the community divide and a major element for managing relationships (Ajduković & Čorkalo, 2004; Čorkalo et al., 2004; Freedman Warshauer & Abazovic, 2006). War has changed the structure of social relations among adults and even "nationalized children's identity" (Povrzanović, 1995). Growing up in the context of an ethnic divide makes ethnicity an important social marker and profoundly shapes the social relations. This is why we assumed that ethnicity and ethnic identity would not be only a sociodemographic fact, but also an important factor in determining how young adults feel about re-establishing relations with the former adversary group.

4. Group identity and social reconstruction

In designating ethnic identity as an important feature of post-conflict community that influences ingroup–outgroup relations we followed the Social Identity Theory (SIT, Tajfel & Turner, 1986) and the Social Categorization Theory (SCT, Turner, Hogg, Oakes, Reicher, & Wetherell, 1987). Both theories describe processes of how people define themselves in terms of their group membership and how they attach significance to it. A basic postulate of both theories is that our social world is structured around categories; by comparing the position of the group to which we belong with the position of other groups, we also orient ourselves in our social environment. By defining who we are and who we are not, we define our social world and give meaning to it. SIT also suggests that a part of our self-esteem is derived from the groups we belong to: when social comparison favors our group, we feel good about ourselves (i.e. our self-esteem rises). When the group is not positively evaluated in comparisons with other groups, members may engage in various esteem-boosting behaviors in order to enhance the self-image and the social standing of their group—psychologically and/or realistically.

In the present work we assume ethnic identity as a special form of social or collective identity, derived from one's membership to an ethnic group. As Turner et al. (1987) pointed out, the social context determines the salience of social categories and their relevance for social relations. Moreover, Ashmore and colleagues emphasized social embeddedness as a distinguished dimension of collective identity based on how much it is relevant in everyday social encounters (Ashmore, Deaux, & McLaughlin-Volpe, 2004). Intergroup conflict exaggerates the importance and embeddedness of an ethnic aspect of the social identity; moreover it may even "reduce" an individual to an ethnic being. In our study the context of post-war communities struggling with the consequences of war makes ethnicity a salient category that overwhelmingly influences the social life of individuals and groups.

Building group identity of communities during the war in the former Yugoslavia had gone through processes of identity deconstruction (abandoning identification with the collapsing state, Yugoslav identity and ideology of "brotherhood and unity") and new identity formation through firm bonding with a particular ethnic group and newly formed states (Sekulić, Massey, & Hodson, 1994; Majstorović & Turjačanin, 2013). These processes were psychologically demanding for many adults (Keel & Drew, 2004) and were not much easier for the second generation of survivors, born in one state, but being brought up in another, often after severe war experiences, uprooting, and resettlement (Hjort & Frisen, 2006; Jones & Kafetsios, 2005). The mixture of ethnicities in most former Yugoslav republics meant that some ethnic groups became a dominant group in one newly born state, but a minority in another. War circumstances and post-war resettlement made this new identity building particularly difficult for individuals who lived through displacement, resolved their refugee status by receiving dual citizenship and who have developed a mixture of group identities and loyalties (Correa-Velez, Gifford, & Barnett, 2010; Keel & Drew, 2004; Majstorović & Turjačanin, 2013). Many of our participants went through similar processes. We explored intergroup social reconstruction of Croats and Serbs from Croatia: (1) the majority Croat group; (2) the Serbs ethnic minority who remained living in Croatia; and (3) the Serbs who fled from Croatia because of the war, and resettled in Republika Srpska which is the majority Serb entity in BiH. We looked at how their group membership and strength of ethnic identity relate towards reconstruction of the relations with their former adversarial group: for Croats towards Serbs and for Serbs towards the Croats.

The power relations and social status among those three groups are obviously different: Croats were a victorious but more victimized majority group during the war still holding grudges against a rebellious and defeated Serb minority. However, two Serb groups differ in their status: the Serbs living in Croatia are clearly a minority group for whom supporting social reconstruction with Croats is the most reasonable and adaptive reaction—this minority is not in the position to react differently. However, expatriate Serbs who fled Croatia and live in another country, have more options. They used to be an ethnic minority in Croatia, but are a majority in their new country (Republika Srpska entity in BiH) which is a status that gives them more social freedom regarding readiness for social reconstruction with Croats in their home country. This complex web of dynamics of war experiences, post-war power and group social status may have created a "residual negative affect" (Harris & Fiske, 2008) and hinders social reconstruction processes.

5. Group victimization and social reconstruction

For most of our participants, by virtue of their group membership, the ethnic identity transformation also overlapped with their group victimization, even if they did not suffer personally. As with the other group-based phenomena, group membership makes it possible to feel in-group victimization, to think about it as if we have been hurt personally and to act upon the premises of this depersonalized, but collectively felt victimization. People identify with the suffering of their in-group and victimization of in-group members becomes "ours" (Bar-Tal, Chernyak-Hai, Schori, & Gundar, 2009). In this regard, many scholars use the term *collective victimhood* to describe the phenomenon and related consequences (Nadler, 2002; Smyth, 2003; Noor, Brown, & Prentice, 2008a, 2008b). A sense of collective victimhood is a group-shared belief that members of the group have suffered (only) because of their group belonging and that this harm has been inflicted intentionally and unjustly (cf. Bar-Tal et al., 2009). As Bar-Tal et al. (2009) pointed out, it is not only a real objective harm that defines the group sense of victimization; the social interpretation of the harm, the way it is experienced, interpreted and transformed within society is what makes it socially shared, pervasive and historically embedded.

Notions of victimization affect strongly the course of the conflict, its resolution, and finally, the process of reconciliation (Bar-Tal et al., 2009). Previous work proved it as a factor that may hinder or ameliorate intergroup reconciliation (Noor, Brown, & Prentice, 2008a). This is even more true when belligerent groups transform the in-group suffering into being "exclusive" (i.e. each group claims that it has suffered more and has been the major victim of the war or other form of intergroup conflict) (Bar-Tal et al., 2009). This *entitlement to suffering* prevents groups, communities and whole societies facing the troubled past and envisioning a more peaceful future. As such, the groups perceive only their own suffering with no or little capacity to acknowledge the suffering of the other side. Specifically, *competitive victimhood*, a belief held by each group in the conflict claiming that one's own group suffered more (Nadler, 2002; Noor et al., 2008a, 2008b) is negatively associated with intergroup forgiveness and other apects of reconciliation (Smyth, 2003). As we postulated in our previous work, this perception of exclusive victimhood may influence biased processing of past events in terms of how they are remembered, interpreted and transformed into collective narrative (Čorkalo et al., 2004).

A typical example of this process is what we have called *ethnization of memory*, where memory itself and interpretation of the past become ethnically exclusive. A narrative of one's own group victimization is certainly a part of this process. In the present paper we hypothesized that perceived in-group victimization would influence attitudes towards social reconstruction

6. Social context of the present study

Our research sites were at three locations—two in Croatia (cities of Vukovar and Knin) and one in BiH, Republika Srpska entity (city of Banja Luka). All three cities have their unique meaning and significance in the context of the recent war, and two of them—Vukovar and Knin—are the key symbols of the Croatian homeland war. Knin is the place where the rebellion of Serbian minority started after Croatia had declared independence from the former Yugoslavia in 1991. The city was under the control of the Serbian forces until August 1995 when it was liberated by Croatian military forces (*Operation Storm*). As such, Knin is a symbol of a military victory that became celebrated as a national holiday. However, during the Croatian military operation, hundreds of thousands of Serbs fled the area in fear, some were killed at their homes and some in the process of fleeing. Those who abandoned their homes became refugees mostly in Serbia and part of BiH controlled by Serbian forces. Thus, for Croats the city of Knin is a symbol of a great victory when a large part of the country was liberated. For Serbs the same event is mourned as a cause of their suffering, displacement and political and military defeat. In the following years many Serbs returned to Knin, but this process has been very slow and hindered by Croatian authorities over several post-war years. Today Serbs in Knin are a minority of about 23 percent, compared to 82 percent in 1991 (Državni zavod za statistiku/Croatian Bureau of Statistics, 2013). It has been estimated that between 1995 and 2014 about 25 percent of the pre-war Serb population in Knin had returned permanently and continued to live in the area. Additionally, estimates are that about 80 percent of the pre-war Serb population in the same area requested and were issued with Croatian personal identification documents (UNHCR Field Office in Knin, personal communication, October 8, 2014). This is qualified by the State Office for Reconstruction and Housing Care, reporting that about 78 percent of returnees in the area are minority Serbs (spokeperson I. Preskar, Državni zavod za obnovu i stambeno zbrinjavanje/State Office for Reconstruction and Housing Care, personal communication, October 11, 2014).

On the other hand, Vukovar had suffered a three-month siege of Yugoslav Army forces and Serbian paramilitaries in 1991, remained under their control until 1997 and was finally and peacefully reintegrated into Croatian borders under the auspices of the United Nations. During the siege the city experienced tremendous destruction of buildings, housing and infrastructure, with over 1,500 people killed (Žunec, 1998). After the Serbian forces took over the city, the non-Serb population was expelled, transported to prisoner-of-war camps and many people were killed. The major grievance was the removal of over 260 wounded Croatian soldiers and civilians from the hospital and their execution at the nearby farm Ovčara. Their bodies were secretly buried in a mass grave that was discovered in 1992; the place is today the most important site for commemorating victims of the Homeland war. The return of Croats started in 1997, but the city has never reached its pre-war population. Today Serbs make up one-third of the inhabitants and Croats are the majority with 57 percent (Državni zavod za statistiku/Croatian Bureau of Statistics, 2013); their proportions have not changed much compared to pre-war Vukovar. However, unlike the situation before the war, almost 20 years after reintegration the city is very much divided along ethnic lines.

Banja Luka became the administrative center of Republika Srpska, after BiH was divided in two parts (entities) by the Dayton Accords: Federation, ruled by Bosniaks and Croats, and Republika Srpska as the Serbian entity. The last census in BiH took place in 2013; however, official data have not been released yet. Before the war Serbs had about 49 percent of inhabitants and were a relative majority in Banja Luka. During the war most of the non-Serbs citizens were expelled from the city, their properties looted, confiscated or destroyed. It is estimated that the vast majority of Banja Luka inhabitants today are Serbs. Many of them came to the city during the war as refugees from Croatia and other parts of BiH.

7. Research design

7.1. Research questions and aim of the study

As far as we know, no study has yet examined social reconstruction tendencies by comparing the perspectives of majority and minority groups on different sides of the conflict in the former Yugoslavia. The present study fills this gap by comparing three samples of young adults whose homeland was the same (Croatia), but who ended up on different sides of the conflict. Their current status is very different: they are either majority (Croats) who won the war, minority Serbs who remain living in the country, but by group membership are linked to the defeated group, or Serb expatriates who fled Croatia, settled in Serb-dominated part of BiH and who have grievances over ethnic defeat and uprootedness. Their displacement as well as the displacement of many more people in the wars of the former Yugoslavia has continued to be a source of instability and challenge for newly formed societies (Daiute & Turniski, 2005; Jones, 2002).

The young adults in the present study are the second generation of the survivors of war: they were preschoolers or school-age children during the 1991–1995 war. We ask how the legacy of growing up in the context of group violence shaped their attitudes and beliefs about getting closer to their former "collective enemy." We compare the same generation with similar experiences, but with very different outcomes due to their life circumstances. Who they are collectively was passed down to them by family, school, their peers and significant adults, community, media etc. The variety of influences was combined in a narrative about war and collective destiny. We were specifically interested in how the narrative on victimhood has shaped youth tendencies towards social reconstruction. Being a part of collective "shared beliefs" (Bar-Tal, 2000), the narrative of victimhood is not only a historical discourse; it is a living part of collective identity (Bikmen, 2013), and a narrative of the group (Ashmore et al., 2004) with a potential to be (re)activated as needed and direct group behavior.

The present study linked the group membership of majority and two minority groups, perceived collective victimhood and ethnic identity in order to unfold their independent and interactive relations in shaping the views regarding post-conflict social reconstruction among the young adults. We assumed that perception of victimhood would have a strong impact causing less readiness for social reconstruction in those who felt their in-group had suffered more in the last war. We also hypothesized that those who identified more with their in-group would be less ready to relate with the other side. Finally, we expected the more powerful majority group (Croats) to be less supportive of social reconstruction than the minority (Serbs living in Croatia). However, we did not expect the expatriated minority who continue to live as an ethnic majority in another country (Serbs) and the Croat majority to differ regarding the social reconstruction of their relations.

7.2. Instruments

The tendency for social reconstruction was measured by a three-component 21-item scale SORS-21 (Čorkalo Biruški et al., 2014). The three components encompass items describing various aspects of getting closer to a formerly belligerent group (Croats and Serbs). Intergroup Rapprochement Scale consists of nine statements (α=.87) that indicate willingness for more positive intergroup relations (e.g. *I think it is important for our children to cooperate*; or *I believe that the other side also suffered during the war*). Intergroup Trust Scale also consists of nine items (α=.83) describing beliefs about rebuilding trust between groups (e.g. *I think that trust between Croats and Serbs has been lost forever*; or *I don't think it is possible to overcome ever the wounds from the past war*). Need for Apology Scale includes three items (α=.60) that describe beliefs that apology is necessary for improving intergroup relations (e.g. *It is important for me that the other side offers an apology*; or *I would like the other side to show remorse for our victims*). Response format was from 1 (strongly disagree) to 5 (strongly agree), and scores were calculated as a mean of the relevant responses. A total score based on all 21 items indicates a general readiness for social reconstruction. However, in order to study specificities and mechanisms that we believe highlight the process of social reconstruction, scores for each component of social reconstruction were also used.

Ethnic identity was assessed by combining 10 items (α=.83) measuring in-group identification (e.g. *I am glad to be a member of my group*), nationalism (e.g. *Members of the same nation should always stick together*), and the absence of in-group belonging (e.g. *I do not feel that I belong to any particular nation*) (Čorkalo & Kamenov, 2003).

Collective victimization was measured by an item asking the following: *When I think about the last war, I consider: (a) my group to be a greater victim, (b) the other group to be a greater victim, (c) both groups were equally victimized.* Only two participants chose the other group to be a greater victim, so their answers were omitted and results were formed as a dichotomous variable. Higher score indicates a stronger belief in in-group collective victimization.

Finally, a group membership was designated as being majority (Croats living in Vukovar or Knin), domicile minority (Serbs living in Vukovar or Knin) or expatriated minority (Serb refugees living in Banja Luka).

7.3. Sample and procedure

A total of 440 young adults participated in the study from Vukovar ($N = 148$), Knin ($N = 190$) and Banja Luka ($N = 102$), aged from 18 to 34 years ($M = 23.76$, $SD = 3.64$). No age differences were found among subgroups, $F(1, 24) = 2.13$, $p > .05$. The proportion of women in the samples were from 59 percent to 64 percent, with no significant difference among subsamples, $\chi^2(2, N = 439) = 0.94$, $p > .05$. At the outbreak of war the participants were children. Specifically, 62 percent were pre-schoolers (six years and younger), 33 percent were in their late childhood (between 7 and 12 years old), and only 5 percent were adolescents, between 13 and 17 years old.

In the Vukovar subsample there were 70 Croats (47%) and 78 Serbs, in Knin there were 93 Croats (49%) and 97 Serbs, and in Banja Luka all of the participants were of Serb ethnic background. Since there were no differences in the variables of interest between two Croat samples, we treated them as being homogenous and compared their results to Serbs living in Croatia (from Vukovar and Knin) and Serb refugees from Croatia (expatriates)[2] currently living in Banja Luka. In this regard we labeled our groups as majority Croats ($N = 163$), domicile Serbs ($N = 175$) and expatriate Serbs ($N = 102$).

The method of recruitment was snowballing because we searched for participants of a certain age and specific experiences who were difficult to locate. Though this sampling method might be a source of bias, it is useful when members of the target populations are difficult to reach (Hoyle, Harris, & Judd, 2009). Giving the sensitivity of a topic under study, we chose this sampling strategy as appropriate given the circumstances in the field. The data collection started in Vukovar and demographics of that particular sample were later used to guide sample composition in two other cities. The first ten participants in each sample were approached by a trained psychologist or a senior student in psychology

2 The vast majority of our Banja Luka participants (73%) declared they did not think about moving back to Croatia. In terms of their citizenship 49 percent held dual citizenship (of both Croatia and Bosnia and Herzegovina), while 2 percent held only Croatian citizenship. The rest of the respondents were Bosnia and Herzegovina citizens only. None of the participants held Serbian citizenship, though they were ethnic Serbs. These data illustrate nicely only one of the complexities of ethnicity and citizenship issues in newly formed states of the former Yugoslavia.

through a network of personal contacts and acquaintances. These participants served as entrance points into the study population. After they filled out the questionnaire they handed it in a sealed envelope to the recruiter and were asked to help in recruiting new participants who matched characteristics relevant for the target sample of young adults. The same procedure was applied as long as a target number of participants in each of the communities were reached. All participants handed in their questionnaires in a sealed envelope; in that sense the survey was anonymous. Each participant was assured of anonymity and confidentiality, which helped considerably in recruiting the participants.

8. Research results

First we tested differences in our samples regarding the level of ethnic identity and perceived collective victimhood.

After that we tested effects of ethnic identity, perceived collective victimhood and group membership on the results of the readiness for social reconstruction. We first analyzed the total social reconstruction score, then its three components separately. Considering a size range of the correlation coefficients among three component of the social reconstruction in this sample, ($r(440)$ Intergroup Rapprochement, Trust = .57, $p < .001$; $r(440)$ Trust, Apology = −.18, $p < .001$ and no correlation between intergroup rapprochement and apology $r(440)$ Intergroup Rapprochement, Apology = −.00, $p > .05$;), we decided to perform analysis of variance (ANOVA) instead of multiple analysis of variance (MANOVA) in order to test the effects of the selected factors on the social reconstruction outcomes.

8.1. Ethnic identity and collective victimhood in three groups

A vivid illustration of how the participants from the three samples perceived their group victimization is shown in Figure 1. While over 80 percent of domicile

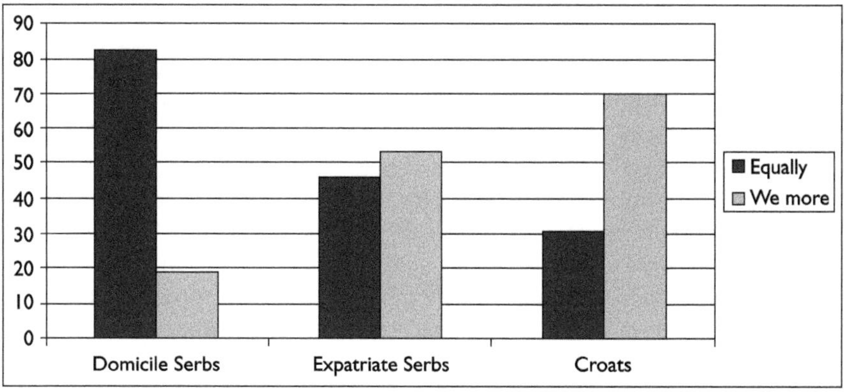

Figure 1 Perception of collective victimhood among three groups of youth

minority Serbs believe that both groups suffered equally, the majority in two other samples, 54 percent Serb expatriates and almost 70 percent Croats believe that their in-group was the major victim.

One-way analysis of variance showed a significant effect of the group membership $F(2,404) = 52.65$, $p < .001$ on the victimhood. A post hoc Tukey test indicated differences among all three groups. As expected, majority Croats scored the highest ($M = 1.69$, $SD = 0.46$), followed by Serb expatriates $M = 1.54$, $SD = 0.50$) and domicile minority Serbs ($M = 1.19$, $SD = 0.32$). The difference between majority Croats and Serb expatriates was the smallest ($p < 0.05$), indicating competitive victimhood phenomenon between these groups.

A similar pattern of ethnic identity differences corroborates a hypothesis of competition among the groups. Here ANOVA also showed a significant effect of the group membership $F(2,404) = 52.65$, $p < .001$. Post hoc comparisons indicated that domicile minority Serbs scored lower ($M = 35.35$, $SD = 8.67$) than expatriate Serbs ($M = 39.67$, $SD = 5.47$, $p < 0.001$) and majority Croats ($M = 37.39$, $SD = 8.02$; $p < 0.05$). The difference between the latter two groups was also significant ($p < 0.05$). In sum, all three groups scored high on the measure of ethnic identity, and clearly above the neutral point of the scale of 30 (the smallest difference from the neutral point of 30 was in the Knin sample and appeared to be significant $t(175) = 8.17$, $p < .001$).

8.2. Social reconstruction and group membership, ethnic identity, and collective victimhood

In order to determine whether a tendency to re-establish social relations with the former adversary group after a severe conflict differed as a function of a group membership, ethnic identity and collective victimhood, four analyses of variance (ANOVA) were performed. Group membership (majority Croats, domicile minority Serbs, minority Serb expatriates), ethnic identity (low vs high) and victimhood (in-group seen as more vs equally victimized) were treated as between-subjects factors.

Regarding the *general tendency for social reconstruction*, all three main effects were significant (Table 1). As for group membership, Tukey post-hoc comparison showed that domicile minority Serbs were most ready for social reconstruction ($M_{adj}=3.92$)[3] compared to Croats ($M_{adj}=3.69$), and Serb expatriates ($M_{adj}=3.52$). No difference was found between Croats and Serb expatriates. Also, those with less strong ethnic identity were more ready for social reconstruction ($M_{adj}=3.92$) than strong ethnic identifiers ($M_{adj}=3.50$). Finally, participants who saw their in-group as more victimized in the last conflict were less ready for social reconstruction ($M_{adj}=3.52$) than the participants who perceived both groups as equally victimized ($M_{adj}=3.90$). However, a two-way interaction of group membership and ethnic

3 Estimated marginal means.

Table 1. Significant F-ratios and effect sizes of main effects and interactions in group membership x ethnic identity x perceived collective victimhood ANOVA of social reconstruction tendencies

	Independent variables: main effects						*2-way interactions*						*3-way interactions*	
	Group membership		*Ethnic identity*		*Perceived collective victimhood*		*Group membership x ethnic identity*		*Group membership x collective victimhood*		*Ethnic identity x collective victimhood*		*Group membership x ethnic identity x collective victimhood*	
	F	η^2	*F*	η^2	*F*	η^2	*F*	η^2	*F*	η^2	*F*	η^2	*F*	η^2
SORS-21	11.20***	.054	40.80***	.094	32.77***	.077	3.74*	.019					2.73+	.014
Rapprochement	5.01**	.025	5.97**	.015	30.33***	.072	9.20***	.045	2.97*	.015			2.95*	.015
Trust	18.91***	.088	39.35***	.091	15.38***	.038								
Apology			22.16***	.053			2.41++	.012						

Note: SORS-21=Total score in social reconstruction tendency; Rapprochement=Intergroup rapprochement; Trust=Intergroup trust; Apology=Need for apology as a precondition for social reconstruction
*$p<0.05$
**$p<0.01$
***$p<0.001$
+$p=.07$
++=.09

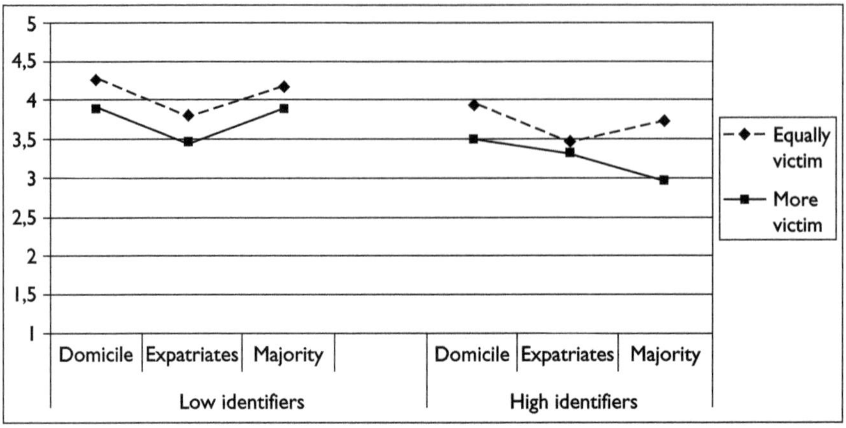

Figure 2 Readiness for social reconstruction as a function of group membership, ethnic identity and perceived group victimhood

identity broadened interpretation of the main effects. Simple effects tests were performed by using a Bonferroni adjustment to hold the alpha level at .05. High identifiers were less ready for social reconstruction compared to their low identified in-groups. Among low identifiers, Serb expatriates were the least ready for social reconstruction, compared to both domicile minority Serbs and majority Croats. No difference was found between domicile Serbs and majority Croats. On the contrary, among high identifiers, Serb expatriates and majority Croats did not differ, but they both differed from domicile minority Serbs.

The results are even more complicated by a marginally significant three-way interaction showing that collective victimhood modified relations between group membership and ethnic identity (see Figure 2). Among low identifiers, only majority Croats differed depending on how they saw their in-group victimization: those who perceived their in-group as a bigger victim were less ready for social reconstruction. Two other groups of Serbs scored equally, regardless of how they perceived the collective victimhood. However, among high identifiers, only Serb expatriates did not differ in their readiness for social reconstruction depending on how they perceived their in-group victimization. In two other cases, those who perceived that their group suffered more were also less ready for social reconstruction.

Further analysis showed that when they identified low with their ethnic group and perceived their in-group as being as equally victimized as the out-group, Serb expatriates were the least ready for social reconstruction and differed in this regard from both Croats and domicile minority Serbs. No difference between Croats and domicile Serbs was found. When the in-group was perceived as being the major victim, the only difference was found between expatriate Serbs and majority Croats, with Croats being more ready for social reconstruction. When highly identified but convinced that the in-group and out-group suffered equally, both groups of Serbs differed from Croats, but domicile minority Serbs were more ready for social reconstruction than were expatriates. However, when the in-group was perceived as the major victim, highly identified Croats were the least ready for social reconstruction, and differed from both groups of Serbs who did not differ.

As regards to *intergroup rapprochement* all three main effects were significant (see Table 1). Post-hoc comparisons showed that domicile minority Serbs were most ready for rapprochement (M_{adj}=4.40), more so, though marginally significant, than Serb expatriates (M_{adj}=4.21) and significantly more than majority Croats (M_{adj}=4.08). Serb expatriates were also more ready for intergroup rapprochement than majority Croats. Youths with stronger ethnic identities were less ready for rapprochement (M_{adj}=4. 13) than those less identified (M_{adj}=4.33). Further, those who believed their in-group suffered more scored lower (M_{adj}=4.01) then those who believed that both groups suffered equally (M_{adj}=4.46). These main effects were obtained in the context of a significant three-way interaction (see Table 1; Figure 3). These complex relationships were analyzed by looking at how the interaction of the group membership and ethnic identification was modified by the perceived victimhood. Bonferroni adjusted simple effects tests with alpha level at .05 were used. Among low identified Serbs (both domicile and expatriates), there was no difference in tendency for rapprochement between those who believed in exclusive victimization and those who believed that groups suffered equally; for Croats, however, those low identifiers who perceived their groups suffered more were less ready for rapprochement than those who perceived a more equal "distribution" of suffering. However, the importance of the perceived victimhood was more obvious among high identifiers. Here, only among expatriated Serbs did victimhood not matter—they were equally ready for intergroup rapproche-ment. Among domicile minority Serbs and even more so in majority Croats,

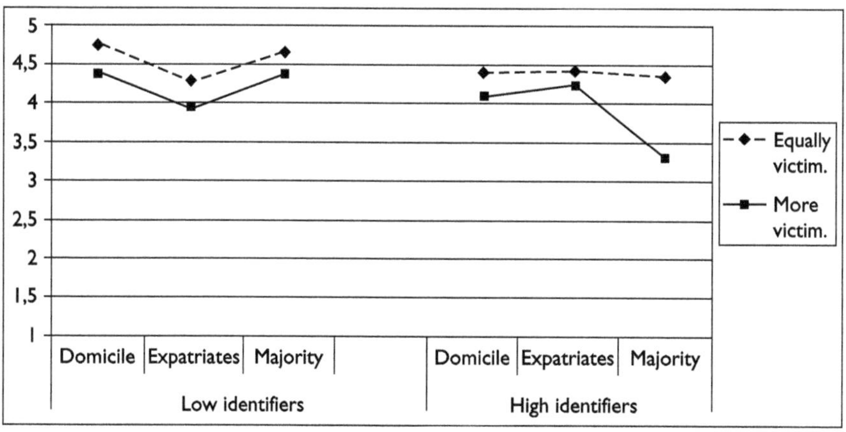

Figure 3 Intergroup rapprochement as a function of group membership, ethnic identity and perceived group victimhood

those who believed they were more victimized were also less ready for approaching the other side.

Further, low identifiers from three groups who believed they suffered more did not differ in their readiness to approach the other side regardless of their group membership. When they believed that their in-group was victimized as equally as the other group, domicile Serbs were more ready to approach the other side than were the expatriate Serbs. No other differences among low identifiers were found. Perception of victimization mattered more for the high identifiers. While those who did not compete over victimhood were equally ready for rapprochement, regardless of their group membership, more victimized Croats were less ready for rapprochement than both Serb groups. There was no difference between the two Serb groups.

In analyzing the effects of selected factors on *intergroup trust* only the main effects appeared to be significant (see Table 1). Group membership determines significantly the level of trust towards others, being the highest in domicile minority Serbs ($M_{adj} = 3.89$), than in majority Croats ($M_{adj} = 3.74$), and the lowest in expatriates Serbs ($M_{adj} = 3.18$). Further, high ethnic identifiers scored lower on trust ($M_{adj} = 3.30$) than those who identified less with their ethnic group ($M_{adj} = 3.91$). Finally, the participants who believed that both groups suffered equally during the conflict were more trustful ($M_{adj} = 3.80$) than those who perceived their in-group as being the major victim ($M_{adj} = 3.41$).

The third component of social reconstruction—a *need for apology* as a precondition for improvement of intergroup relations—proved to be determined only by the strength of ethnic identification (Table 1). Those who identified more with their ethnic group needed the apology from the other side more ($M_{adj} = 3.80$) than those who identified less ($M_{adj} = 3.29$). A marginally significant group membership by ethnic identity interaction also is worth a comment (see Table 1 and Figure 4). It clearly shows that ethnic identity played an important role in

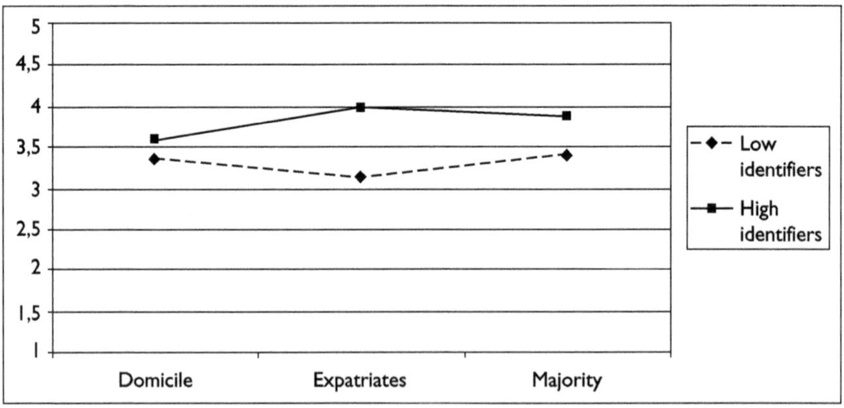

Figure 4 A need for apology from the other side as a function of the group membership and ethnic identity

shaping the need for apology from the other group in both majority Croats and expatriate Serbs. In both groups, high identifiers sought apology more than low identifiers. No such influence of ethnic identification was found in domicile minority Serbs ($p>0.05$). Furthermore, while low identifiers did not differ in their need for apology, regardless of which group they belonged to, among highly identified participants only domicile Serbs showed lower need for apology. There was no difference between highly identified Serb expatriates and the majority Croats.

9. Discussion of the results

The present study explored how group membership of being majority, domicile ethnic minority or expatriated minority, perceived group victimhood and ethnic identity determine readiness for social reconstruction with the former adversary group. Social reconstruction was defined through three components: readiness for intergroup rapprochement, readiness for trustful relations with the other group and a need for apology for the past wrongdoings. Our analyses tell a complex story of independent and interactive influences of the factors under study in shaping various aspects of improving intergroup relations after a severe conflict.

For general social reconstruction the results showed that interaction of the ethnic identity and perceived victimization is not the same in three subgroups. Though this three-way interaction was marginally significant, the patterns of results may indicate important implications. When not identified strongly with their in-group, Serb young adults, both domicile and expatriates, do not differ in how they feel about social reconstruction regardless of how they perceive their in-group victimization. For Croats, however, perceived victimization makes a difference even for low identifiers: those who feel their in-group has suffered more are less ready for social reconstruction. For the highly identified Croats the difference between those who perceived their in-group suffering differently is even larger.

In sum, it seems that for the majority of Croats perceived victimization is a major determinant of how both low and high identifiers feel about social reconstruction—if the group is perceived as the major victim, both high and low identified Croats are less ready for social reconstruction and for high identifiers this difference is even bigger than for low identifiers. Among the domicile minority Serbs, only those with high in-group identification showed lower readiness for social reconstruction if they believed their in-group suffered more. Hence, it seems that in-group identification and perceived victimhood interact more systematically in determining social reconstruction attitudes for the majority than for the minority.

The same patterns of results appeared when analyzing interaction of the variables in determining the readiness for intergroup rapprochement. Here again, among majority Croats (and again to some extent for domicile minority Serbs), high identification brought about even more differences in rapprochement between those who believe their groups suffered more and those who believed in the "equal share" of suffering.

Both patterns of results—for the overall social reconstruction and for intergroup rapprochement—suggest that perceived victimhood may play an important role in shaping group identity (Bar-Tal et al., 2009; Bikmen, 2013; Smyth, 2003). If the group is also a dominant group in the society, and as such "owns" a public space for talking about group victimization, as is the case for the Croat group in our sample, then the story of victimhood could easily become a part of a public discourse and a "shared belief" around which a common identity could be built and maintained. The suffering of the other (defeated) side within the same state, let alone the expatriates who have fled, has much less space, if any, for being presented and shared. Consequently, the (dominant) in-group suffering is hermetic and hegemonic and, with no challenge for its exclusivity, may be adopted as a part of a (dominant) group identity. This sort of *victimhood entitlement of winners* may seriously prevent the society to critically examine the recent past, face its own injustices and wrongdoings, and acknowledge also the suffering of those who were on the other side of the conflict, especially as civilians. This kind of one-sidedness may fuel grievances and feelings of humiliation on the other side and plant the seed for future misunderstandings and even conflict (Lind, 2008). Vamik Volkan's concept of a "chosen trauma" and the process of mythologizing in-group defeats and/or heroism is a nice illustration of the phenomenon (Volkan, 1997). If these processes are not worked through and challenged with engagement and participation of various segments of the society, they may prolong and even prevent social reconstruction and intergroup reconciliation (Bar-Tal et al., 2009).

With regards to intergroup trust, as expected, those highly identified with their in-group, and those who believed that their in-group suffered more are also less ready to trust the other side. The group membership effect showed that domicile minority is the most trustful, majority Croats are more trustful than Serb expatriates who had fled the country during the war. These results may contradict the claim of some scholars (e.g. Nadler, 2002; Nadler & Shnabel, 2008) that for the groups who do not "share" the same society but are separated it is easier to rebuild relations than for the groups who have to live in the same society after the conflict. If this were the case, expatriate Serbs would be expected to be more trustful than the Serbs who remained living in Croatia. Our results showed the opposite. However, there is another aspect that should be taken into account when interpreting these findings. Expatriate Serbs may have more grievances towards Croats in Croatia and feel that Croats as a group are responsible for their uprootedness. Moreover, we specifically asked the young adults in Banja Luka to give their responses with regard to the Croats in Croatia; in that sense we actually asked them to respond as Croatian compatriots and members of Croatian society. Furthermore, we cannot rule out the possibility that the youth (at least some of them) in Banja Luka may still want to go back to Croatia and consider it as their real home. Here we highlight results of our analysis on the citizenship of Banja Luka sample and their declared intention to go back to Croatia some time in the future. Their indicative responses showed that while the vast majority of the participants did not have any plans to go back to Croatia, more than a quarter of them (26%) did consider this possibility. Since nearly half of the Banja Luka participants had dual citizenship (of both Croatia and BiH), and a small percentage had only Croatian, we assume they have maintained some bonds with the country of origin. The data we presented are suggestive in indicating that Serbs from Banja Luka may not look at their relationships with Croats as relationships with the separated out-group. They may blame Croats for their suffering and displacement, but they also see them as the group they shared the same social environment with in the past and may want to share it in the future. It is possible that their attitudes would be quite different if Banja Luka Serbs had been asked about their attitudes towards the Croats in BiH. More research is needed to unfold the bonding of expatriates of different republics of the former Yugoslavia in order to understand the identity processes those groups have gone through and to be able to recommend strategies for the most successful integration of the formerly belligerent groups. What is even more challenging is to clarify the role of competing narratives in the process of identity building and what mechanism could be most useful in opening a space for a dialogue about the recent collective histories that were painful for all sides. It would not serve to create a narrative of an "equal share of guilt," but is necessary to move affected societies a step closer to a mutually acceptable narrative of the recent past that all sides can live with.

Finally, regarding probably the most demanding aspect of intergroup social reconstruction—a need for apology from the other group—the results showed only ethnic identity to be an important independent factor of influence. Those who identified more with their in-group also showed more need for an apology from the other side. However the influence of in-group identity was modified by group membership: while low and high identifiers among domicile Serbs did not differ in their need for apology, highly identified Serbs expatriated and majority Croats showed a bigger need for apology than their low identified in-groups. Here, again, two highly identified and competing groups, both from their "comfort zone" of being entitled to claim more victimhood (Croats in Croatia and expatriates in Serb-dominated Banja Luka) seek apology from the other side, probably very convinced in their sense of self-righteousness. Though being a popular tool for ameliorating complex post-conflict intergroup relations (e.g. Verdeja, 2009; Lind, 2008), apologies may not be so successful in promoting intergroup reconciliation (Lind, 2008; Philpot & Hornsey, 2008). Furthermore, the usefulness of this apology has also been questioned due to ambiguity about the processes involved at the intergroup level (Čorkalo Biruški, 2012; Philpot & Hornsey, 2008; Verdeja, 2009). If an apology is not accompanied by other constructive processes aimed at healing and rebuilding wounded societies, its effectiveness in helping societies to move forward may be even more questionable.

Though the present study gives an indicative insight in group-based determinants of social reconstruction, the study has certain limitations. For example, we did not control for the influence of war-related traumatic events that our participants might have experienced. This information could be useful for at least two reasons. For one, it would provide an opportunity to analyze possible differences in readiness for social reconstruction depending on the intensity and nature of the traumatization. Second, these experiences might also have shaped the participants' ideas about collective victimization. Furthermore, we evaluated collective victimization by a relatively simple one-item measure, while the concept is probably much more complex. It is for further research to refine the measure of collective victimization which could be used in analyzing more thoroughly its influences in social reconstruction processes.

In sum, our study showed that three variables under study were all important in determining the readiness towards social reconstruction. Their independent effects were more prominent than their mutual interplay, showing especially strong effects of ethnic identity and collective victimhood. In this regard our study corroborates earlier theorizing and research findings that salience and the importance of ethnicity and ethnic identity are contextually dependent (Ruben & Richard, 1997; Hjort & Frisen, 2006). War and post-war circumstances often reduce the complexity of identity to a single dimension of an ethnic being and its high salience persists long after the conflict has ended (Hjort & Frisen, 2006). Similar processes are described in the recent study with Palestinian and Bosnian youth (Barber, 2009). Studies show convincingly how youth in post-conflict settings are trapped in their ethnicity and how their relations with others are determined by their ethnic belonging (Ajduković & Čorkalo Biruški, 2008; Daiute & Turniski, 2005; Freedman Warshauer & Abazovic, 2006; Jones, 2002; Majstorović & Turjačanin, 2013). These factors may be particularly strong in our sample. The majority of our participants were children during the war, they were brought up mostly in ethnically divided communities, many of them were uprooted because of their ethnicity. It is only to be expected that this part of their social identity has been particularly salient in shaping their overall social world and may continue to influence (negatively) their future social relations even in their adult years. The patterns found for the perceived collective victimhood corroborate earlier studies in post-conflict and/or highly divided society that found negative influences of collective victimhood on intergroup reconciliatory processes (Bar-Tal et al., 2009; Noor et al., 2008a; Noor et al., 2008b; Van Tongeren et al., 2014).

10. Conclusions

The present research showed that majority and minority young adults who were children during the war hold a strong sense of victimization of their own group and are strongly identified with their ethnicity. Both variables are important in shaping their attitudes towards various aspects of relationships with the other side. Our participants' views were probably shaped by their first-hand experiences, experiences of their families and communities, and also by group narratives and stories about own-group victimization. Transforming these stories in order to make them palatable for both sides is the work that needs be done. There is no doubt that transgenerational transmission of the experiences and narratives was unavoidable, and it would be unrealistic to expect that social experiences could be relevant only for the time and context in which they happened.

By their transmission families and whole communities shape own histories and make sure that the past will not be forgotten. However, facing history is not about what should not be forgotten; it is about how it should be remembered. If remembered as a constant remainder of what "they" did to "us" or had been doing over the course of history, the present is tainted and the future even more so. If remembered by paying tribute to the victims and taking care of those who survived with empathy and determination that their voices should be heard, the past could be faced with more wisdom, with more "lessons learned" for the future.

Tools have been developed showing that even unimaginable encounters between people from opposing sides are possible. Dan Bar-On's TRT approach ("To Reflect and Trust") where German and Jewish "second generation" groups met and discussed their personal and collective histories proved that "getting closer" is possible. Further studies revealed that a similar process is possible with groups whose conflicts were not situated in the far past, but were their everyday experience (Bar-On, 2002). The very same approach, however, tells another story: the process is difficult, emotionally challenging, time demanding, very slow and needs to be led and managed with the utmost care. This is exactly the message for the processes of facing history: they are demanding in many ways, but they are possible and necessary and may have a healing effect not only for victims and perpetrators, but also for future generations.

Our results clearly showed that *perceived* victimization is not without *real consequences*: how young adults perceive their present and future intergroup relations. These results more than suggest that *competition over victimhood* perpetuates the "conflicting ethos" (Bar-Tal, 2007) and keeps it alive, building around it even more than "ethos." It creates the *culture of conflict* with the potential to sweep out the legacy of decades of former peaceful living (Ajduković & Čorkalo, 2004; Čorkalo Biruški, 2012; Sekulić, 2014) as fewer and fewer people remember that it had been possible. Our previous work corroborates that young people are less equipped for approaching the other side than adults (Ajduković & Čorkalo Biruški, 2008). Unlike their parents, who have memories of well-integrated communities, they have only experienced the reality of division created by conflict. While the painful recent past cannot be changed, what we do with it in the present can be—for better or for worse.

References

Ajduković, D. (2004). Social contexts of trauma and healing. *Medicine, Conflict, and Survival, 20*(2), 120–135. doi:10.1080/1362369042000234717.

Ajduković, D. & Čorkalo, D. (2004). Trust and betrayal in war. In E. Stover & H. Weinstein (Eds.), *My neighbor, my enemy: Justice and community in the aftermath of mass atrocity* (pp. 287–302). Cambridge: Cambridge University Press.

Ajduković, D. & Čorkalo Biruški, D. (2008). Caught between the ethnic sides: Children growing up in a divided post-war community. *International Journal of Behavioral Development, 32*(4), 337–347. doi:10.1177/0165025408090975.

Ashmore, R. D., Deaux, K. & McLaughlin-Volpe, T. (2004). An organizing framework for collective identity: articulation and significance of multidimensionality. *Psychological Bulletin, 130*(1), 80–114. doi:10.1037/0033-2909.130.1.80.

Barber, B. K. (2009). *Adolescents and war: How youth deal with political violence.* B. K. Barber, (Ed.), New York: Oxford University Press.

Bar-On, D. (2002). Conciliation through storytelling: Beyond victimhood. In G. Salomon & B. Nevo (Eds.), *Peace education: The concept, principles, and practices around the world* (pp. 109–116). New Jersey.

Bar-Tal, D. (2000). *Shared beliefs in a society: Social psychological analysis.* Thousand Oaks: Sage.

Bar-Tal, D. (2007). Sociopsychological foundations of intractable conflicts. *American Behavioral Scientist, 50*(11), 1430–1453. doi:10.1177/0002764207302462.

Bar-Tal, D. (2008). Reconciliation as a foundation of culture of peace. In J. de Rivera (Ed.), *Handbook on building cultures of peace* (pp. 363–378). New York: Springer.

Bar-Tal, D. & Bennink, G. H. (2004). The nature of reconciliation as an outcome and as a process. In Y. Bar-Siman- Tov (Ed.), *From conflict resolution to reconciliation* (pp. 11–38). Oxford: Oxford University Press.

Bar-Tal, D. & Rosen, Y. (2009). Peace education in societies involved in intractable conflicts: Direct and indirect models. *Review of Educational Research, 79*(2), 557–575.

Bar-Tal, D., Chernyak-Hai, L., Schori, N. & Gundar, A. (2009). A sense of self-perceived collective victimhood in intractable conflicts. *International Review of the Red Cross, 91*(874), 229–258. doi:10.1017/S1816383109990221.

Bikmen, N. (2013). Collective memory as identity content after ethnic conflict: An exploratory study. *Peace and Conflict: Journal of Peace Psychology, 19*(1), 23–33. doi:10.1037/a0031472.

Čorkalo Biruški, D. (2012). Lessons learned from the Former Yugoslavia: The case of Croatia. In D. Landis & R. D. Albert (Eds.), *Handbook of ethnic conflict: International perspectives* (pp. 327–348). New York: Springer.

Čorkalo Biruški, D. (2014). Determinants of trust: lessons from a divided post-conflict community. Paper presented at the *Conference on Trust in Conflict Resolution.* Tel Aviv, January 8–9.

Čorkalo Biruški, D., Ajduković, D. & Löw Stanić, A. (2014). When the world collapses: Changed worldview and social reconstruction in a traumatized community. *European Journal of Psychotraumatology*, 5, Sep. 2014. Available at: www.ejpt.net/index.php/ejpt/article/view/24098. Date accessed: 12 Oct. 2014.

Čorkalo, D., Ajduković, D., Weinstein, H., Djipa, D. & Biro, M. (2004). Neighbors again? Inter-community relations after ethnic violence. In E. Stover & H. Weinstein (Eds.), *My neighbor, my enemy: Justice and community in the aftermath of mass atrocity* (pp. 143–161). Cambridge: Cambridge University Press.

Correa-Velez, I., Gifford, S. M. & Barnett, A. G. (2010). Longing to belong: social inclusion and wellbeing among youth with refugee backgrounds in the first three years in Melbourne, Australia. *Social Science & Medicine, 71*(8), 1399–1408. doi:10.1016/j.socscimed.2010.07.018.

Čorkalo, D. & Kamenov, Ž. (2003). National identity and social distance: Does in-group loyalty lead to outgroup hostility? *Review of Psychology, 10*(2), 85–94.

Daiute, C. & Turniski, M. (2005). Young people stories on war in Croatia. *Narrative Inquiry, 15*(2), 217–240.

Deutsch, M. (2008). Reconciliation after destructive intergroup conflict. In A. Nadler, T. E. Malloy & J. D. Fisher (Eds.), *The social psychology of intergroup reconciliation* (pp. 471–485). Oxford: Oxford University Press.

Državni zavod za statistiku/Croatian Bureau of Statistics (2013). *Popis stanovništva, kućanstava i stanova 2011. Stanovništvo prema državljanstvu, narodnosti, vjeri i materinskom jeziku/Census of population, household and dwellings 2011. Population by citizenship, ethnicity, religion and mother tongue.* Zagreb: Državni zavod za statistiku Republike Hrvatske/Croatian Bureau of Statistics.

Erikson, K. (1976). Loss of communality at Buffalo Creek. *American Journal of Psychiatry*, 133, 302–305.

Freedman Warshauer, S. & Abazović, D. (2006). Growing up during the Balkan Wars of the 1990s. In C. Daiute, Z. Beykont, C. Higson-Smith & L. Nucci (Eds.), *International perspectives on youth conflict and development* (pp. 76–91). Oxford: Oxford University Press.

Gödl, D. (2007). Challenging the past: Serbian and Croatian aggressor-victim narratives. *International Journal of Sociology*, *37*(1), 43–57. doi:10.2753/IJS0020-7659370103.

Govier, T. (2002). *Forgiveness and revenge.* London: Routledge.

Harris, L. T. & Fiske, S. T. (2008). Diminishing vertical distance: Power and social status as barriers to intergroup reconciliation. In A. Nadler, T. E. Malloy & J. D. Fisher (Eds.), *The social psychology of intergroup reconciliation* (pp. 301–317). Oxford: Oxford University Press.

Hjort, H. & Frisen, A. (2006). Ethnic identity and reconciliation: Two main tasks for the young in Bosnia-Herzegovina. *Adolescence*, *41*(161), 141–163.

Hoyle, R. H., Harris, M. J. & Judd, C. M. (2009). *Research methods in social relation.* Toronto: Wadsworth Publishing.

Jones, L. (2002). Adolescent understandings of political violence and psychological well-being: a qualitative study from Bosnia Herzegovina. *Social Science & Medicine*, *55*(8), 1351–1371. Retrieved from www.ncbi.nlm.nih.gov/pubmed/12231014.

Jones, L. & Kafetsios, K. (2005). Exposure to political violence and psychological well-being in Bosnian adolescents: A mixed method approach. *Clinical Child Psychology and Psychiatry*, *10*(2), 157–176. doi:10.1177/1359104505051209.

Keel, M. R. & Drew, N. M. (2004). The settlement experiences of refugees from the Former Yugoslavia. *Community, Work & Family*, *7*(1), 95–115. doi:10.1080/1366880042000200316.

Kelman, H. (2008). Reconciliation for a social-psychological perspective. In A. Nadler, T. E. Malloy & J. D. Fisher (Eds.), *The social psychology of intergroup reconciliation* (pp. 15–32). Oxford: Oxford University Press.

Kriesberg, L. (1998). Coexistence and the reconciliation of communal conflicts. In E. Weiner (Ed.), *The handbook of interethnic coexistence* (pp. 182–197). New York: The Continuum Publishing Company.

Lederach, J. P. (1997). *Building peace: Sustainable reconciliation in divided societies.* Washington, D. C.: United States Institute of Peace Press.

Lind, J. (2008). *Sorry states: Apologies in international politics.* Ithaca: Cornell Unniversity Press.

Long, W. J. & Brecke, P. (2003). *War and reconciliation: Reason and emotion in conflict resolution.* Cambridge: MIT Press.

Majstorović, D. & Turjačanin, V. (2013). *Youth ethnic and national identity in Bosnia and Herzegovina.* New York: Palgrave Macmillan.

Nadler, A. (2002). Post-resolution processes: Instrumental and socio-emotional routes to reconciliation. In G. Salomon & B. Nevo (Eds.), *Peace education: The concept, principles, and practices around the world* (pp. 127–141). New Jersey: Lawrence Erlbaum Associates.

Nadler, A. & Liviatan, I. (2004). Intergroup reconciliation processes in Israel: Theoretical analysis and empirical findidngs. In N. Branscombe & B. Doosje (Eds.), *Collective guilt: International perspectives* (pp. 216–235). Cambridge: Cambridge University Press.

Nadler, A. & Shnabel, N. (2008). Instrumental and socioemotional path to intergroup reconciliation and the needs-based model of socioemotional reconciliation. In A. Nadler, T. E. Malloy & J. D. Fischer (Eds.), *The social psychology of intergroup reconciliation* (pp. 37–56). Oxford: Oxford University Press.
Nadler, A., Malloy, T. E. & Fisher, J. D. (Eds.) (2008). *The social psychology of intergroup relations.* Oxford: Oxford University Press.
Noor, M., Brown, R. & Prentice, G. (2008a). Precursors and mediators of intergroup reconciliation in Northern Ireland: a new model. *The British Journal of Social Psychology*, *47*, 481–495. doi:10.1348/014466607X238751.
Noor, M., Brown, R. & Prentice, G. (2008b). Prospects for intergroup reconciliation: Social-psychological predictors of intergroup forgiveness and reparation in Northern Ireland and Chile. In A. Nadler, T. E. Malloy & J. D. Fisher (Eds.), *The social psychology of intergroup reconciliation* (pp. 97–114). Oxford: Oxford University Press.
Philpot, C. R. & Hornsey, M. J. (2008). What happens when groups say sorry: the effect of intergroup apologies on their recipients. *Personality & Social Psychology Bulletin*, *34*(4), 474–487. doi:10.1177/0146167207311283.
Povrzanović, M. (1995). War experience and ethnic identities in Croatia. *Collegium Antropologicum*, *19*(1), 29–39.
Ruben, O. & Richard, L. (1997). The effects of ethnic identity, ethnicity, and gender on adolescent well-being. *Journal of Youth and Adolescence*, *26*(5), 503–516.
Sekulić, D. (2014). Ethnic intolerance as a product rather than a cause of war: Revisiting the state of the art. In D. Spini, G. Elcheroth & D. Čorkalo Biruški (Eds.), *War, community and social change: Collective experiences in the Former Yugoslavia* (pp. 45–62). New York: Springer.
Sekulić, D., Massey, G. & Hodson, R. (1994). Who were the Yugoslavs? Failed sources of a common identity in the Former Yugoslavia. *American Sociological Review*, *59*(1), 83. doi:10.2307/2096134.
Smyth, M. (2003). Putting the past in its place: Issues of victimhood and reconciliation in Northern Ireland's peace process. In N. Biggar (Ed.), *Burying the past: Making peace and doing justice after civil conflict* (pp. 125–153). Washington, D. C.: Georgetown University Press.
Staub, E. (2006). Reconciliation after genocide, mass killing, or intractable conflict: Understanding the roots of violence, psychological recovery, and steps toward a general theory. *Political Psychology*, *27*(6), 867–894. doi:10.1111/j.1467-9221.2006.00541.x.
Tajfel, H. & Turner, J. C. (1986). Theory of intergroup behavior. In S. Worchel & W. G. Austin (Eds.), *Psychology of intergroup relations* (pp. 7–24). Chicago: Nelson-Hall Publishers.
Turner, J. C., Hogg, M. A., Oakes, P. J., Reicher, S. D. & Wetherell, M. S. (1987). *Rediscovering the social group. A self-categorization theory*. Oxford: Basil Blackwell.
Van Tongeren, D. R., Burnette, J. L., O'Boyle, E., Worthington, E. L. & Forsyth, D. R. (2014). A meta-analysis of intergroup forgiveness. *The Journal of Positive Psychology*, *9*(1), 81–95. doi:10.1080/17439760.2013.844268.
Verdeja, E. (2009). *Unchoping a tree. Reconciliation in the aftermath of political violence*. Philadelphia: Tempel University Press.
Volkan, V. (1997). *Blood lines: From ethnic pride to ethnic terrorism.* Boulder: Westview Press.
Worthington, E.L., Jr., Sandage, S. J. & Berry, J. W. (2000). Group interventions to promote forgiveness: What researchers and clinicians ought to know. In M. E. McCullough, K. I. Pargament & C. E. Thoresen (Eds.), *Forgiveness: Theory, research, and practice* (pp. 228–251). New York: Guilford Press.
Žunec, O. (1998). Rat u Hrvatskoj 1991.-1995. 1. dio: Uzroci rata i operacije do Sarajevskog primirja. *Polemos*, *1*, 57–87.

Chapter 8

Educating citizens in Bosnia-Herzegovina – experiences and contradictions in post-war education reform

Briony Jones

1. Introduction

In societies which have experienced war and violence a crucial question which arises is who will play a role in engaging with the war-to-peace transition and thus who will create a common future. Children are often the focus of internationally led post-war reforms designed to transform attitudes and the classroom is seen as a space and opportunity to enact change. As Cole has recently articulated, 'despite being a truism, it bears repeating that children and youth are the future citizens of society. In places psychologically, economically, politically, and socially damaged by war or violently unjust systems, the young, especially the rising generation that was not directly involved in the conflict, may represent the only hope for a post-war reality' (Cole, 2011, p. 335). This chapter addresses this 'truism' and seeks to understand the dynamics of the intersection between education–citizenship–transition in the particular case of Bosnia-Herzegovina (BiH). Looking back over the last 20 years since the Dayton Peace Accords we have an opportunity not only to continue our reflections on past violence but also to think about whether international expectations and hopes for the future of BiH are being realised. Each statement that what happened in the past was wrong is at the same time a statement about what the future should look like. In the BiH case such statements and aspirations have been closely related with controversial opinions about the type of state and society which is imagined by different groups. It is through the concrete practices of post-war reform that the dynamics between these different visions of BiH can be seen and analysed. Accordingly this chapter focuses on education reform and investigates aspirations to educate Bosnia's post-war citizens in a way that contributes to peaceful change and political transformation. The work presented in this chapter is based on qualitative fieldwork that was conducted in BiH (and in particular Brčko District) from 2007 and 2008[1] and more recent reflections in the context of a research network on contemporary

1 This fieldwork was generously funded by the United Kingdom Economic and Social Research Council.

politics in BiH (from 2010 until time of writing), and on a research project on higher education in BiH[2] (from 2011 until 2014). Drawing on prior work on this topic,[3] this chapter's contribution to this volume is certainly a place where the author can reflect on education reform, models and possibilities with the benefit of fresh analysis and perspectives.

The chapter is structured in four parts. Following this introduction Part 2 discusses the intersection between education–citizenship–transition on a conceptual level. Part 3 focuses on developments in BiH and current challenges regarding education and its role in the post-war transition. In section 3.1 I will outline international initiatives and understanding of educational reforms as a tool for constructing peace. In section 3.2 I will then analyse a model of reform that has been implemented in Brčko District, and relate these experiences to the challenges identified in the previous sections. Some concluding remarks in Part 4 highlight the porous boundaries of the classroom which exists in, and is part of, the forging of a workable and inspiring post-war social contract for BiH.

2. Education, citizenship and transition

Post-war transition towards peace, justice and democracy, involves many different kinds of transformations in the relationships between people living in the society undergoing transition. Such relationships will be shaped by the intersection between 'victim' and 'perpetrator' identities forged through violence with historical social and political categories such as an urban/rural divide or religious faith. In addition the relationships between people and the state, which are often complicit in or accused of violence, require transformation in order to address, among other issues, structures which have encouraged or allowed violence and to ensure accountability for those most responsible for human rights abuses. As part of such transformations education reform is often highlighted as vital. The role it can play is multi-faceted, but commonly discussed themes are: its role in challenging dominant narratives of past violence, bringing children from previously opposing 'sides' together, promoting reconciliation, and educating a new generation of peaceful citizens willing to play a role in democratic society (Weinstein et al., 2007). A series of debates inform such work and it is worth highlighting the most relevant ones for the chapter here before moving onto the specifics of the case of BiH.

A first strand of debate looks at the *potential of new generations as agents of change*. As illustrated in the quote from Cole used in the introduction, the figure of the (school) child is often imbued with a sense of hope for the future when a society is gradually emerging from a history of violence and oppression. The belief which

2 This project was generously funded by the Swiss National Science Foundation through their SCOPES funding instrument and ensured that additional field trips to BiH were possible as well as exchanges with Bosnian academics.

3 Such work will be cited where relevant.

informs such a hope is that the new generation will act as some kind of new start, almost a *tabula rasa* upon which the values of a post-war society – read justice, peace, and democracy – can be written. Such a description of this type of approach may be deemed rather simplistic, but if we look at concrete policies and programmes its key elements become visible. For example, Hart has criticised advocates of education for peace building and reconciliation, whom he understands as failing to see the ways in which children have learned and have been socialised through their own experiences of violence (Hart, 2011, p. 16). Using the case of the Occupied Palestinian Territories, he demonstrates through anthropological fieldwork with children that the Israeli advocates of education reform for 're-education to peace and reconciliation with the state of Israel' (Burdman, cited in Hart, 2011, p. 19) place too much emphasis on the ability of curriculum and classroom praxis to change attitudes (ibid). This, Hart argues, does not fit with the lived experience and conditions of the children themselves meaning, in fact, that education programmes will be less effective in their intended outcomes (ibid., p. 26). In other work, Evans writes of the surprise expressed by the staff of international organisations running education programmes for Bhutanese refugee children living in camps in Nepal, when the children were seemingly contradictory in their practice of simultaneous engagement with human rights and peace promotion as well as with political parties advocating violence (Evans, 2008). That children are active social, economic and political agents inside and outside of educational experiences is too often not factored into such post-war education programmes. An overly optimistic expectation that education will easily imprint onto children the values and practices which are believed to be more peaceful by its advocates has thus led to poorly conceived and implemented programmes.

A second strand of debate emphasises *context*, and asks how the environment which surrounds the classroom shapes the ways in which post-war education reform plays out in practice. It seems somewhat obvious to state that the education experience does not exist in a vacuum, but for the discussion which follows in this chapter it is important to remind ourselves of the different ways in which context might be relevant for the issues being debated. Weinstein et al. (2007) state that it is necessary to view schools as part of an overall process of social change (in the context of transitions), and this is particularly the case when the curriculum and classroom are the focus of explicit reforms aimed at educating a new generation of peaceful citizens. The wider context for education in societies undergoing transition is that of trauma, political pressure and resource limitations, all of which are factors determining how pupils learn and how teachers teach (Cole, 2007, p. 120), reminding us that the identities of 'pupil' and 'teacher' are but one of the many identities held by individuals who may also be 'victims', 'perpetrators', 'young', 'old', 'Christian', and 'Muslim' among others. Such wider contexts and personal histories come into the classroom affecting the way in which post-war education reforms are negotiated and shaped in the realities of post-war life. Examples of this can be found in two well-researched cases, Northern Ireland and Israel, where integrated schooling programmes have been analysed for their impact. In reference to these cases in particular different aspects of context have been found to be relevant, for example that social and cultural norms influence the result of contact between students in integrated schools (Donnelly & Hughes, 2009) and that community attitudes and political discourse affect the ways in which policy is enacted as practice in the everyday life of the classroom (Bekerman, 2009; Salters & McEwan, 1993). If the lives of pupils and teachers are embedded in complex contexts, all influencing how post-war education reform is perceived, negotiated and practised, then it is important to reflect on the stated purposes of education for peace, reconciliation and democracy in societies undergoing transition.

A third strand of debate focuses on the *universal versus the particular*, or rather to what extent the values promoted by post-war education reform should be universal, and to what extent they should speak directly or indirectly to the everyday lives of the pupils and teachers who are the target of such reforms. Unsurprisingly, this debate turns on similar issues as those raised in relation to the role of context. Education reform which aims at promoting and/or producing peace/reconciliation/democracy must necessarily have been designed by actors who (a) hold a position with regards to what these broad terms mean, and (b) who believe that the values of a certain way of life encapsulated in these terms are better than others. This is a normative question: if one educates for a certain goal then the goal to which one aims has been judged to be of value. A quote from Minow illustrates the power of the idea of change through education towards 'the better':

> 'Education offers the chance to shape minds, hearts and behaviours of succeeding generations. Educational responses [to intergroup conflict] express this hope: if we can educate young people to respect others, to understand the costs of group hatreds, to avoid stereotypes, to develop tools for resolving disputes, to choose to stand up to demagogues, and to be peacemakers, we might hope to prevent future violence.'
>
> (Minow, 2003, p. 214)

The abstract goals described in this quote are difficult to argue with in principle, but it is their interpretation which is the key to understanding how and why post-war education reforms are designed and practised in the way that they are. Cole & Murphy write that 'The essential goal of education is to transform children into citizens, into adults who can function beyond the circle of the family in society, the workplace, the polity' (Cole & Murphy, 2011, p. 336). If we add to this goal the elements of a *peaceful, democratic* citizen, then the terms under which transformation takes place are somewhat narrowed. Indeed, it is often frameworks perceived to be universal by their designers that underpin human rights, peace and citizenship education in post-war contexts (Paulson, 2011, p. 182). Not only does the application of universal frameworks fail to speak to the complexities of the everyday lives of children in such contexts (Hart, 2011) but the supposed neutrality which comes from such universality may, in fact, entrench unequal and conflict-producing relationships. Oglseby (2007) argues that in Guatemala the liberal constructs of personhood contained within democracy and human rights curricula create a universalised, idealised subject while at the same time obscuring concrete contexts of social, political and economic subordination. Given that post-war education reform is taking place in societies where membership of a political and social community has been violently contested, it might be problematic to engage directly with such contested terms as 'citizen' and 'democracy' and instead easier to opt for a more universalised and sanitised version of civic education. But this does not have to be the case, as Cole and Murphy argue, for: 'It is a constant paradox of history education reform that progressive history writing and pedagogy oppose the creation of a single, hegemonic narrative, yet the goals of transitional justice – to facilitate public recognition of an accountability for major human rights abuses – at some level assumes something like that' (Cole & Murphy, 2011, p. 348).

At the core of these debates is a single question: how can education reform play a positive role in war-torn societies and contribute to the transition towards peace and democracy while at the same time retaining sensitivity to context and relevance for the everyday lives of pupils and teachers? Here the idea of education as a tool to produce change (i.e. to educate the new generation of peaceful and democratic citizens) intersects with the complicated realities of being a citizen in a transition context. Dominant thinking on post-war transition has been accused of too often taking a de-contextualised and ahistorical approach to the societies for which, and in which, programmes are designed (e.g. see Fletcher, Weinstein & Rowen, 2009, p. 31 who write specifically of transitional justice). Education reform as part of war-to-peace-transition is no exception to this, as we can see in the case of BiH.

3. Educating citizens in Bosnia-Herzegovina

BiH provides a rich and rewarding case study both in terms of post-war education reform and in terms of its intersection with a complex landscape of citizenship and transition. Furthermore, within BiH there exist some of the 'worst' and 'best' examples of post-war education in terms of the normative goals outlined above. First we will reflect on the more general landscape of post-war education in BiH in order to set the scene for the discussion of models, claims and experiences to follow.

It is estimated that the three-year war in BiH (1992–1995) resulted in over 1 million refugees, over 1 million internally displaced people (Bieber, 2006, p. 29) and 97,000 deaths.[4] Extremely high levels of international funding during and following the signing of the Dayton Peace Accords in 1995 have accompanied a

4 According to statistics of the Istraživački Dokumentacioni Centar Sarajevo (accessed on 25 March 2015), see www.hrarchives.org/directory/name/g-k/idc-ba/.

triple transition from war to peace, from Communism to parliamentary liberal democracy and from the Socialist Federal Republic of Yugoslavia to independence (Bieber, 2006, p. 35). The Dayton Peace Accords established a consociational democracy, meaning that BiH is now a rare case of a post-Communist federal state in which each citizen has a state level and sub-state level citizenship (Štiks, 2011, p. 246).[5] The logic behind such an arrangement is that the three main ethno-national groups[6] are able to share political power safe in the knowledge that their specific group interests are protected. This arrangement has been criticised for being an ethnopolis, that is 'a political context where a person's citizenship is predetermined by her or his kinship, or her or his belonging to this or that group of mutual blood origin' (Mujkić, 2008, p. 20). The implications of such an arrangement are that minority ethnicities are not formally politically represented, that individual rights are often secondary to group rights, and that the results of ethnic cleansing of the war period have been crystallised in a political arrangement based on units of overlapping political territorial and ethnic identities.

Social reality in BiH's post-war transition is still marked by diverse conflicts and tensions which arise not only from the experiences of violence but also from the nature of the peace settlement. Whilst the consociational political arrangements have been criticised for the primacy they place on ethno-national categories of identity, international actors such as the Office of the High Representative[7] have at the same time supported a nation building and state building process which is designed to develop a consensus over an understanding of a what it is to be a Bosnian citizen (Sejfija, 2006). As Kostić describes: 'external nationbuilding measures in B-H have included the building of state institutions as well as the state identity through the creation of a flag, an anthem and a coat-of-arms. These identity-building measures have a twofold task; first, to foster popular legitimacy for the state institution, and second to enhance social integration' (Kostić, 2008, p. 390). It is not a coincidence that the Office of the High Representative in particular viewed these symbols of the state as vital to such a project: 'The flag, coat of arms, anthem, state holidays, etc. are typically products of history often reflecting the identity of a country and its population. They are among the symbols aimed at creating and/or maintaining a feeling of belonging to a state (vertical relation), as well as a feeling of community towards all other citizens of that state (horizontal relation). At the same time, they draw a border (either imaginary or real) separating the citizens of one state from citizens of other states' (Stojanović,

5 This means citizenship of the state of BiH and of one of the two entities of the Federation of BiH (occupying 51% of the territory) and the Serb Republic (occupying 49% of the territory). Citizens of the third entity Brčko District select citizenship of either of the other two entities.

6 Bosniaks, Bosnian-Serbs and Bosnian-Croats.

7 This is the civilian office mandated with overseeing the peace process and ensuring that the terms of the Dayton Peace Accords are met. Since 1997, the Office of the High Representative has held powers, referred to as the 'Bonn Powers' which allow the High Representative – an international, not a Bosnian citizen – to remove elected officials and to pass laws on the basis that such actions are in line with the terms of the peace accords.

2008, p. 1). The type of citizen and type of state which is imagined in these reforms are quite specific. According to Coles:

> 'The openly formulated goal of the international community is to touch and change the political, social and economic life of BiH as a state and Bosnians as a people in such a way that the country and its citizens become modern, democratic and capitalist with regard for human rights and rule of law.'
>
> (Coles, 2007, p. 257)

Debates over, and concerns with, the 'stateness' problem in BiH, whereby a significant proportion of the population does not accept the territorial boundaries of the state, or see it as a legitimate political unit to which they owe allegiance (Bose, 2005, pp. 323–324), have continued for the 20 years after the signing of the Dayton Peace Accords. As Mujkić observes: 'all that remains of the citizen is mere individualism in its primordial form – egoism' (Mujkić, 2008, 34). The Dayton Peace Accords created an ethnopolis through which the citizen is only known as part of an ethnic group, narrowing political identity in the formal political space, and limiting the opportunity for ongoing contestations over the everyday lives of people and their social and political membership (Jones, 2009; Jones, 2011). This is a particularly pertinent issue in the context of contemporary BiH where we have seen (primarily externally led) sustained nation- and state-building processes but where, after 20 years of 'peace', the people of BiH have spoken out against continued low standards of living, political and official corruption, and a lack of economic prospects. Thc transitional 'moment of exception' belies a historical and ongoing struggle over who is and can be a member of the citizenry, and how such a citizenry can make demands on a state. It is in the broader story of violence and transition that post-war education reform has targeted Bosnian children as the bearers of the possibility for change. A focus on integrated schooling and lessons on democracy and human rights all imply that education reform is seen as part of a solution to the problems of ethno-nationalism and lack of identification with the current state of BiH. In the following sections we will explore this further, first with background on the current state of education in BiH and then by looking at one 'success' story of Brčko District. The reflections will speak to the role of education in the broader story of social and political communities in BiH, bearing in mind ongoing contestations over this issue.

3.1. Education as a tool for constructing peace?

The issue of education has been the subject of heated debate and attempted reform since the signing of the Dayton Peace Accords. In particular, different international actors have considered education reform to be vital in the fight against ethno-nationalism (which has been seen by many external and domestic observers as a significant cause of the violence) and the efforts to build a Bosnian nation. The dominant narrative about post-war education reform is thus that of a space in which ethno-nationalism battles multi-ethnicity and, in addition, that if education reform is successful, integrated schools will be able to educate a new generation of peaceful and democratic citizens of BiH. 'The reform of this system is widely regarded as critical to the country's long-term stability' (OSCE http://www.osce.org/bih/106652). 'In BIH, separate education systems are based on political and religious/cultural division promoting ethnic separation and distrust' (UNICEF http://www.unicef.org/bih/education_1029.html); and 'there can be no true security without a commitment to democracy and human rights. Addressing the roots of discrimination in education as a consequence of former conflict is therefore essential for promoting co-existence and sustainable peace' (OSCE http://www.oscebih.org/Default.aspx?id=3&lang=EN). Following this logic it makes sense that education reform is not only about quality of education, but is also about broader transformations as a part of BiH's ongoing post-war transition. As one scholar writes, 'Social cohesion within schools can have effects far beyond the classroom and students' immediate lives and relationships with one another. This is because social cohesion within the classroom is related to and influences social cohesion throughout the greater society' (Hill, 2011, p. 157).

According to Hromadžić (2008), the current education system in BiH reflects the consequences of the destruction of the war, the paradoxes of the Dayton Peace Accords and the weaknesses of the Bosnian constitution. Following the war, education in BiH was decentralised into thirteen education policy making authorities, making coordination at the state level difficult (Smith & Vaux, 2002, p. 24). There is no state-wide curriculum, but a core of subjects whose teaching has been agreed upon by each entity, as well as a set of national subjects (history, literature, geography, religion, language, art and music) which have been controversial in the post-war period and which are taught according to the preferences of the dominant ethno-national group in the territory where the school is based (Perry, 2003). The country still struggles with a legacy of segregated schooling, whereby pupils of different ethno-national backgrounds are taught in different classrooms according to different curricula. Such a system has been described by one scholar as 'a retrograde phenomenon that works contrary to all contemporary international aims and the efforts of various organizations to promote educational progress' (Pašalić Kreso, 2008, pp. 358–359). Local efforts to counter segregated education can be seen in a 2012 ruling by a court in Mostar stating that ethnic separation of students in some schools amounts to discrimination, and a demand that two schools abolish the practice and establish mixed classes for Bosniak and Croat children (Radio Free Europe, 2012). However, despite a wide range of such public condemnation from academics, activists and international actors, segregation in education continues, and children 'fail to learn that they are all citizens of BiH' (Pašalić Kreso, 2008, p. 360).

Despite not being included as a special topic in the Dayton Peace Accords (Torsti, 2009, p. 72), post-war education reform has been a significant focus of the work of international non-governmental organisations in BiH. The numbers working on education and training as part of their activities has been in the hundreds, leading to problems with coordination, impact and donor dependency in this area (Hill, 2011, p. 166). Since 2002, international efforts in post-war education reform have been coordinated by the Organisation for Security and Cooperation in Europe (OSCE), but with a limited impact in terms of changes in practices and attitudes (Torsti, 2009, pp. 69–70). Such efforts have been working against established pedagogic practices from the pre-war era which 'centred mainly on transmission learning and lecturing with very little interaction between teachers and students' (Kasumagić, 2008, p. 380), historical tendencies for education to be used by those in power to 'limit, not enable; dominate, not liberate; indoctrinate, not enlighten; restrict, not free' (McCreight, 2002, p. 135) and the current overall segregation that divides children into three ethno-national groups, whether in terms of the school building or the teaching of the national subjects (Torsti, 2009, p. 66). Accordingly, much of the education reform promoted by the OSCE and other organisations working in this area has been on democracy, human rights, civic education and peace education. This fits very well with the narratives identified in the debates in Part 1 of this chapter. First, education is seen as a 'solution' to ethno-nationalism which is perceived to be a primary cause of the violence. Second, children are seen as a new possibility to move on from the past and 'wipe the slate clean' by educating a generation of peaceful and democratic citizens. Third, the content of the curricula focuses on universal values such as democracy and human rights; these are seen to stand 'above' those of ethno-national identification.

Whilst in many parts of BiH the same problems with education continue 20 years after the end of the war, there has been a 'success story' which is lauded as a model for the rest of the country. In Brčko District the education system has been integrated with pupils and teachers of different ethno-national groups sharing the same classroom space and curricula. As one commentator observes, 'For people whose lives had been destroyed by tribal hatred, Brčko became a chance to experiment in multi-ethnicity' (Geoghegan, 2014). This experiment has been broadly seen as a success by Bosnian and international commentators alike, but fieldwork conducted by the author suggests that daily practice and experiences of education reform are complicated by context, ongoing tensions and the avoidance of issues central to the current debates regarding what it means to be Bosnian in BiH today.

3.2. Experiences of successful education reform: the example of Brčko-District

Situated in the northeast of BiH, on an internal border between the two entities of the state and on the international border between BiH, Croatia and Serbia, Brčko District is strategically significant. Since a Final Award in 1999[8] it has been

8 The Dayton Peace Accord negotiations almost stalled over the question of which entity would have control of Brčko District. This was due to its geographically strategic position between the two

held in condominium by both entities and has its own international supervisor presiding over the multi-ethnic institutions of a district assembly, police, judiciary, and school system. In this context, education in Brčko District stands in stark contrast to the rest of the country and its reform has been central to a project of post-war transition to democracy which is directly opposed to a project of ethno-national citizenship (Fischer, 2006).

In Brčko District, education reform was imposed by the district supervisor[9] following opposition from the Serb Democratic Party and the Serbian Orthodox Church, which had blocked the process of the new law through the District Assembly (ICG, 2003). Following promulgation on 5 July 2001, of the Single Law on Education and Harmonized Curriculum, three different education systems servicing Bosniaks, Bosnian-Serbs and Bosnian-Croats were integrated (Perry, 2003) meaning each school was to have an ethno-national mix of both pupils and teachers. To support this change, religious iconography has been banned from classrooms, students are taught together for most of their classes and each student has the right to be taught in and to use their preferred language and script (OSCE, 2007). According to the district government, this 'aims to respect the integrity of national values of all communities' (Brčko District Government, 2007, p. 20). Underpinning such functional changes is a set of normative values. Students, through design, are taught to be multi-ethnic in their outlook and to see themselves as joint citizens within a multi-ethnic society. This is supported by a new subject on democracy and human rights designed by local and international actors (OSCE, 2007, p. 16). As the author has argued elsewhere, by delegitimizing ethno-national affiliation and emphasizing democratic norms, students are encouraged to share a (liberal democratic) vision of political and moral community which requires mixing between ethno-national groups and the public acceptance of an overarching civic identity (Jones, 2012, p. 138).

In many ways the integration of the three different school systems into one integrated system has been a success. In the Final Award for Brčko District it was stated that 'the Supervisor will integrate the District's educational system, harmonize curricula within the District, and ensure the removal of teaching material which the Supervisor considers to be inconsistent with the objective of creating a democratic, multi-ethnic society within the District (Annex to the Final Award, 18 August 1999, point 11). Six years after the schools were integrated the OSCE claims that '[in Brčko District] students of different ethnicities go to school together, receive instruction in their own languages in the same classroom, and

entities, its place on the borders with Croatia and Serbia and the fertile land on which it lies. A decision was delayed until 1999, when an internationally arbitrated Final Award decided that the territory should be held in condominium by both entities, but will remain only accountable to the state level and the OHR. This provided an opportunity for extensive intervention and the crafting of a multi-ethnic space outside of the constraints of the two ethnic entities discussed earlier in this chapter.

9 The District Supervisor is always a non-Bosnian.

retain their individual cultural identities . . . The evidence suggests that, with sufficient political will, it can [serve as a model for the rest of BiH]' (2007, p. 5). This view was repeated by many teachers interviewed, as these excerpts illustrate: 'when he enters the school he becomes a student and they all have the same rights' (Head Teacher, Brčko District, 14 March 2008) and 'The integration process has been completed successfully and today we have quite a high level of tolerance' (Teacher, Brčko District, 25 March 2008).

In previous work on student protests which accompanied the announcement of the integration of the school systems in Brčko District, the author has argued that the meaning of education reform was shaped not just by pedagogic principles and priorities but also by feelings of disempowerment amongst the pupils, of fear over international control of Brčko District, and of the unknown impact of all of the other changes made possible by education reform, such as minority return[10] to the District and increased competition for housing and jobs (Jones, 2011b). One head teacher, responsible for sensitisation around the imposed law on education reform, expressed it in this way: 'I agree that you have been fighting in order that your children are not together with anybody else, so have your fathers and so on . . . but there is one thing that speaks against you and that is the signature of your political leader who signed the treaty. Which means that you are all free to accept the law as it is and decide to live in Brčko district, or you don't have to accept it but you also don't have to live here as part of Brčko district government' (Head Teacher, Brčko District, 14 March 2008). Whilst only one quote, its sentiment is consistent with the concerns expressed by Jeffrey (2013) and by the author when previously analysing the data (Jones, 2012, p. 140): 'Choice and debate about the boundaries and content of social and political communities was sacrificed in order to ensure that Brčko was reformed in a way which was consistent with internationally recognized standards of democracy and human rights . . . Ordinary people thus had to decide whether they were "in" or "out", rather than being able to contribute their opinions legitimately on the terms under which the boundaries and form of the district were decided.' Such concerns, which can be summarised as a struggle over decision-making power in post-war Brčko District, continue today where ongoing frustration with the political elite and dissatisfaction with everyday political, social and economic situations elicited an outpouring of anger in February and March 2014.

On 4 February 2014 protests began in the northern town of Tuzla during which several hundred redundant workers from large privatised companies which had been subsequently shut down, took to the streets. These protests turned violent and spread to other towns such as Zenica, Mostar and Sarajevo; buildings were burnt and there were clashes on the street between protesters and police (Jukić, 2014). Protests were observed in Brčko, although they were non violent. The protests

10 In the context of Brčko District this means the return of Bosniaks and Bosnian-Croats who were former residents of the district.

evolved into plenums which were established in the same towns as direct democratic assemblies in which citizens could voice concerns with the political elite, corruption, economic mismanagement and lack of prospects in terms of standards of living (Keil, 2014), despite years of external intervention and funding for BiH's transition. Indeed, the events in early 2014 have shown that the democratic life of citizens in Brčko District seems to be alive and well with the protests and plenum movement. With the first plenum held on 11 February 2014 citizens of Brčko District, while small in number, came together to demand a change in the current political and economic situation including the resignation of the whole of the current District Government (Cerić, 2014). However, the ability of citizens to actively take part in public political debate and to affect change faces a number of constraining factors. Jeffrey has written of the pursuit of democracy through non-democratic means in Brčko District, meaning the suspension of elections and individual power held by the office of the District Supervisor, as well as the gentrification of non-governmental organisations which are increasingly professionalised in their reproduction of donor priorities rather than the creation of spaces of alternative political action (Jeffrey, 2013, Chapters 4 and 5). The types of changes demanded by the citizens in the protests and plenums are more radical than those 'allowed' by the narrow liberal democratic space constructed by international actors such as the OHR in particular. This leaves us with a complex set of questions on the role which education can play in engaging with the current questions which are pertinent for democratic life in Brčko District today.

In reference to the plenum movement in general, and as cited above, part of the dialogue surrounding this recent citizen action has been a contest over where the real divisions between people in BiH lie. The dominant narrative about the war and post-war period in BiH has been an almost exclusive emphasis on ethno-national division with multi-ethnicity as a solution, hence the choices about content in the new democracy and human rights classes in Brčko District. However, there is an increasingly vocal part of Bosnian society which argues that the real divisions lie between the 'haves' and 'have-nots'; between the 'corrupt political elite' and the 'ordinary people'. These current and pressing concerns are not being addressed in a classroom space where pupils and teachers are treated either as members of ethno-national groups to be brought closer together, or as 'neutral' liberal democratic citizens with equal rights. The curricula on democracy and human rights certainly do not contain discussions on the role or legitimacy of the OHR and its 'Bonn Powers' (see footnote 7), or on whether the state of BiH in its current form can adequately protect its citizens and fulfil their needs. In fact, teachers would also need much more training and empowerment in order to tackle such difficult questions and to overcome their fear of the consequences (Jones, 2012).

International programmes and education reformers explicitly aimed to help create a democratic society in BiH by educating a new generation of peaceful and democratic citizens. These ambitions, and the content of the reforms, simply do not seem to match up with the kinds of political discussions which are ongoing amongst the citizenry. Looking at the example of Brčko District, where education reform is lauded as a success, the difficult questions raised by imposed education reform and the nature of democracy in this context, are either avoided or excluded from discussions over how to educate the 'new generation'.

4. Concluding remarks on educating citizens

The protests and plenums established in early 2014 spoke to a concern over the way in which the violence in BiH, and the following transition, have been dominantly understood: 'The problem has never been one of ethnic nationalism and ancient hatreds, as it is sometimes portrayed; it lies in the fact that the elites have been able to manipulate the public discourse so that it appears that everything is about Serbs not wanting to part of Bosnia, Muslims wanting to control Serbs and Croats wanting their own entity' (Keil, 2014).

If indeed it is 'not ethnic nationalism that divides Bosnia [but] social inequality and political dissatisfaction [that] unite the people of Bosnia' (Keil, 2014) then it is important to reflect on the way in which such issues are dealt with at times of transition. Transitional justice processes, concerned with dealing with the past as part of a political transition towards democracy (Arthur, 2009), have been critiqued for the tendency to view transitions as linear processes towards specified end-goals of peace, democracy and justice. In scholarship on the 'transition' in transitional justice we learn that 'transitional justice is not only about human rights violations; it is a process to shape citizens' understanding of justice and a re-foundation of democracy' (Arenhövel, 2008, p. 580). However, the very term 'transition' implies a beginning, middle and end as one state (i.e. violence, war, authoritarianism) turns into another (i.e. peace, justice, democracy). Because of this, scholars have identified a 'common trope that transitional justice allows countries to "start over" by settling accounts with the past' (Fletcher, Weinstein & Rowen, 2009, p. 207). It is this framing which implies that transition is a temporary moment of exception, following a rupture in a pre-democratic state which is able to be repaired and in so doing lead to a set of pre-identified outcomes. This framing, in which the past is the target of a transition designed to (re)turn to a future, has the effect of dislocating transitional justice processes from longer-term historical contexts of struggle. However, much of the literature to date takes a more contemporary view of the immediate events preceding a transitional justice process and the dynamics and impacts of the process itself. McEvoy & McGregor (2008, pp. 4–6), in their work on transitional justice from below, importantly remind scholars to keep in mind the social and political struggles which have placed dealing with the past on the political agenda in the first place.

International efforts on education reform have been guided by the idea of improving inter-ethnic relations and democratisation, at the same time as avoiding difficult topics such as continuing inequalities, the role of certain actors in the violence, and more radical political projects. Certainly it is unrealistic to expect teachers and pupils to be thrust into potentially explosive subject matter immediately after war or violent episodes. However, in the case of BiH, the ongoing debates over what it means to be Bosnian are a relevant part of people's lives inside and outside the classroom. This will affect how education reform is enacted and perceived, and therefore the chances of it having the kind of impact hoped for. We can go further than this though and ask whether or not education reform in BiH might be missing some opportunities with its continued emphasis on ethno-national divisions rather than tackling some of the more contentious aspects of democracy and human rights education. This is not to say that integrated schooling is not a worthwhile goal to strive for, but rather that education reform must always seek to be relevant to the contexts of people's lives in order to avoid becoming irrelevant to or complicit in continued injustices. Today, 20 years after the end of the war, many Bosnians feel a high degree of frustration and anger over the continued political corruption, lack of economic progress, international intervention and lack of adequate social welfare protection. It is not the role of education to 'solve' all of the post-war challenges which Bosnians face. However, the claims and ambitions of education reformers need to be analysed and understood in a much broader context.

References

Arenhövel, M. (2008). 'Democratization and Transitional Justice'. *Democratization, 15*(3), 570–587.

Arthur, P. (2009). 'How "Transitions" Reshaped Human Rights: A Conceptual History of Transitional Justice'. *Human Rights Quarterly, 31*(2), 321–367.

Bekerman, Z. (2009). 'The Complexities of Teaching Historical Conflictual Narratives in Integrated Palestinian-Jewish Schools in Israel'. *International Review of Education*, 55(2–3), 235–250.

Bieber, F. (2006). *Post-war Bosnia: Ethnicity, Inequality and Public Sector Governance.* Basingstoke and New York: Palgrave Macmillan.

Bose, S. (2005). 'The Bosnian State a Decade after Dayton'. *International Peacekeeping, 12*(3), 322–335.

Brčko District Government (2007). *Brčko District of BiH, 2000–2007.* Brčko: Brčko District Government.

Cerić, I. (2014). 'Report Back from First Brčko Plenum'. *Bosnia-Herzegovina Protest Files* 12 February 2014. Retrieved from: http://bhprotestfiles.wordpress.com/2014/02/12/reportback-from-first-brcko-plenum/.

Cole, E. A. & Murphy, K. (2011). 'History Education Reform, Transitional Justice, and the Transformation of Identities'. In A. Paige (Ed.), *Identities in Transition: Challenges for Transitional Justice in Divided Societies* (pp. 334–367). New York: Cambridge University Press.

Cole, Elizabeth, A. (2007). 'Transitional Justice and the Reform of History Education'. *International Journal of Transitional Justice, 1*(1), 115–137.

Coles, K. (2007). 'Ambivalent Builders: Europeanization, the Production of Difference, and Internationals in Bosnia-Herzegovina'. In X. Bougarel, E. Helms & G. Duijzings (Eds.), *The New Bosnian Mosaic: Identities, Memories and Moral Claims in a Post-War Society* (pp. 172–255). Aldershot: Ashgate.

Council of Europe (2000). *Education in Bosnia and Herzegovina.* Report Document 8663. Retrieved from http://assembly.coe.int/ASP/Doc/XrefViewHTML.asp?FileID=8874&Language=EN.

Donnelly, C. & Hughes, J. (2009). 'Contact and Culture: Mechanisms of Reconciliation in Schools in Northern Ireland and Israel'. In J. R. Quinn (Ed.), *Reconciliation(s): Transitional Justice in Postconflict Societies* (pp. 147–173). Montreal: McGill-Queen's University Press.

Fischer, M. (2006). 'Introduction: Moving out of the Dayton Era into the Era of Brussels?' In M. Fischer (Ed.), *Peacebuilding and Civil Society in Bosnia-Herzegovina: Ten Years after Dayton* (pp. 7–43). Münster: Lit.

Fletcher, L., Weinstein, H. & Rowen, J. (2009). 'Context, Timing and the Dynamics of Transitional Justice: A Historical Perspective'. *Human Rights Quarterly, 31*(1), 163–220.

Geoghegan, P. (2014). 'Welcome to Brčko: Europe's Only Free City and a Law Unto Itself'. *The Guardian* Wednesday 14 May. Retrieved from www.theguardian.com/cities/2014/may/14/brcko-bosnia-europe-only-free-city.

Hart, J. (2011). 'Young People and Conflict: The Implications for Education'. In J. Paulson, (Ed.), *Education and Reconciliation: Exploring Conflict and Post-conflict Situations* (pp. 11–31). London and New York: Continuum.

Hill, K. (2011). 'Possibilities for Social Cohesion in Education: Bosnia-Herzegovina'. *Peabody Journal of Education, 86*(2), 155–170.

Hromadžić, A. (2008). 'Discourses of Integration and Practices of Reunification at the Mostar Gymnasium, Bosnia and Herzegovina.' *Comparative Education Review, 52*(4), 541–563.

International Crisis Group (June 2003). *Bosnia's Brčko, Getting In, Getting On and Getting Out.* Sarajevo, Brussels: ICG.

Jeffrey, A. (2013). *The Improvised State: Sovereignty, Performance and Agency in Dayton Bosnia.* West Sussex: Wiley-Blackwell.

Jones, B. (2012). 'Exploring the Politics of Reconciliation through Education Reform: The Case of Brčko Distric, Bosnia and Herzegovina'. *The International Journal of Transitional Justice, 6*(1), 126–148.

Jones, B. (2011a). 'Who does this District Belong to? Contesting, Negotiating and Practicing Citizenship in a Mjesna Zajednica in Brčko District'. *Transitions, 51*(1–2), 171–191.

Jones, B. (2011b). 'Understanding Responses to Postwar Education Reform in the Mutiethnic District of Brčko, Bosnia-Herzegovina'. In J. Paulson (Ed.), *Education and Reconciliation: Exploring Conflict and Post-conflict Situations* (pp. 81–102). London and New York: Continuum.

Jones, B. (2009). *Examining Reconciliation's Citizen: Insights from the Multi-Ethnic District of Bosnia-Herzegovina.* Doctoral Thesis submitted to the University of Manchester.

Jukić, E. M. (2014). 'Bosnian Plenums Offer "New Model of Democracy"'. Retrieved from www.balkaninsight.com/en/article/bosnian-plenums-offer-new-model-of-democracy.

Kasumagić, L. (2008). 'Engaging Youth in Community Development: Post-war Healing and Recovery in Bosnia and Herzegovina'. *International Review of Education, 54*(3/4), 375–392.

Keil, S. (2014). 'Whatever Happened to the Plenums in Bosnia?' Retrieved from www.balkaninsight.com/en/article/whatever-happened-to-the-plenums-in-bosnia.

Kostić, R. (2008). 'Nationbuilding as an Instrument of Peace? Exploring Local Attitudes towards International Nationbuilding and Reconciliation in Bosnia and Herzegovina'. *Civil Wars, 10*(4), 384–412.

McCreight, R. (2002). *Education in Bosnia: Language, Religion and Control.* Stillwater: New Forums Press Inc.

McEvoy, K. & McGregor, L. (2008). 'Transitional Justice from Below: An Agenda for Research, Policy and Praxis'. In K. McEvoy & L. McGregor (Eds.), *Transitional Justice from Below: Grassroots Activism and the Struggle for Change* (pp. 1–13). Hart Publishing: Oxford and Portland.

Minow, M. (2003). 'Education for Coexistence'. In A. Chayes & M. Minow (Eds.), *Imagine Coexistence: Restoring Humanity after Violent Ethnic Conflict.* San Francisco, Jossey-Bass.

Mujkić, A. (2008). *We, the Citizens of Ethnopolis.* Sarajevo: Centar za ljudska prava Univerziteta u Sarajevu.

Oglesby, E. (2007). 'Educating Citizens in Postwar Guatemala: Historical Memory, Genocide, and the Culture of Peace'. *Radical History Review*, *97*(winter), 77–98.

Organisation for Security and Co-operation in Europe. Retrieved from www.oscebih.org/Default.aspx?id=3&lang=EN.

Organisation for Security and Co-operation in Europe Mission to BiH Education Department (October 2007). *Lessons from Education Reform in Brčko.* Sarajevo: OSCE.

Pašelić Kreso, A. (2008). 'The War and Post-War Impact on the Educational System of Bosnia and Herzegovina'. *International Review of Education*, *54*(3/4), 353–374.

Paulson, J. (2011). 'Conclusion: Assumptions and Realities'. In J. Paulson (Ed.), *Education and Reconciliation: Exploring Conflict and Post-conflict Situations* (pp. 178–184). London and New York: Continuum.

Perry, V. (2003) *Reading, Writing and Reconciliation.* Flensburg, Germany: European Centre for Minority Issues.

Radio Free Europe (30 April 2012). 'Bosnian Court Rules against Ethnic Segregation in Schools'. Retrieved from www.rferl.org/content/bosnian_court_rules_against_ethnic_segregation_schools/24565464.html.

Salters, J. & and McEwan, A. (1993). 'Doing Something Different: "Integrated Parents" in Northern Ireland'. *Research in Education*, *49*(May), 53–62.

Sejfija, I. (2006). 'From the "Civil Sector" to Civil Society? Progress and Prospects'. In M. Fischer (Ed.), *Peacebuilding and Civil Society in Bosnia-Herzegovina Ten Years after Dayton* (pp. 125–140). Berlin: Lit.

Smith, A. & and Vaux, T. (2002). *Education, Conflict and International Development.* London: Department for International Development.

Štiks, I. (2011). 'Being Citizen the Bosnian Way: Transformations of Citizenship and Political Identities in Bosnia-Herzegovina'. *Transitions*, *51*(1–2), 245–267.

Stojanović, N. (2008). 'The Road to the Disintegration of Society? State Symbols in BiH'. *Puls Demokratije.* Retrieved from www.pulsdemokratije.ba/index.php?l=en&id=686.

Torsti, P. (2009). 'Segregated Education and Texts: A Challenge to Peace in Bosnia-Herzegovina'. *International Journal on World Peace*, *26*(2), 65–82.

UNICEF (n.d.). Retrieved from www.unicef.org/bih/education_1029.html.

Weinstein, H. M., Warshauer Freedman, S. & and Hughson, H. (2007). 'School Voices: Challenges Facing Education Systems after Identity-based Conflicts'. *Education, Citizenship and Social Justice*, *2*(1), 41–71.

All weblinks were accessed on 25 March 2015, unless otherwise indicated.

Chapter 9

Discrimination: from construction to deconstruction – an essay on the prospects of reconciliation in Bosnia-Herzegovina 20 years after Dayton

Miodrag Živanović

1. Introduction

Discrimination has been a significant characteristic of the social reality in Bosnia-Herzegovina (BiH) in the past two decades. This results from social construction and structural disorders of society that mark both the political system and the subjective sphere of society, which encompasses collective and individual awareness, political ideology, as well as social norms and values. Specifically, BiH is marked by a deep contradiction as the internal organisation of its society clashes with the objectives of the transition process that was introduced by the international community. I call this the 'paradox of Bosnia and Herzegovina'. In this country, social and political relations are formed by segregation that is based on the construction of 'three ethnos', defining the Bosniak, Bosnian-Croat and Bosnian-Serb population as three different constituent nations. The Constitution of BiH and Annex IV of the Dayton Peace Accords have contributed to foster this process of segregation.

Ethnicity was not a decisive factor in pre-war BiH; today, 20 years after Dayton, we exist no longer as citizens, but exclusively as Serbs, Croats and Bosniaks. Our entire lives have been reduced to this ethnic matrix, which is supported by the current political structure. At the same time we go through a process of transition driven by international actors that aims to install the model of Western liberal capitalism which is very much based on the idea of citizenship and individualism. Undoubtedly, this objective is not compatible with the normative and real structure of our society that is based on tribalism. This represents a paradoxical base for the forms of social relations evolving in BiH. The paradox generates various forms of discrimination and numerous problems in social relations.

This chapter addresses some of these contradictions. First, it illustrates the paradox of BiH's political system in more detail. Then the chapter outlines why and how the political system and the normative sphere contribute to the discrimination that generates from the underlying ethnic matrix. The chapter then explains how ethnicity and nationality determine collective identities, perceptions of the 'self' and the 'others'. It also shows that BiH is a 'pre-political state' and outlines the needs for democratic transformation. Finally, it gives an analysis of the international contributions to the 'construction' of ethnic categories and their deficits in setting up strategies for overcoming the structures that have been established by the Dayton Peace Accords. The chapter concludes with a clear appeal that renaissance is needed instead of reforms, in order to pave the way for any process of reconciliation in this country.

2. The paradox of Bosnia-Herzegovina's political system

The political system in BiH has been established in a way that has contributed to a very asymmetric organisation of its political power. There are two levels of government in the entity of Republika Srpska (51% of the territory): entity level and municipal level. In the other entity, the Federation of BiH (49% of the territory), there are three levels of government: municipality, canton and entity. In sum, BiH has 14 different state administrations, namely: two entities, ten cantons, one district (Brcko) and, in addition to this, the institutions that operate on a national level. The political organisation of the state is asymmetric; such disorder enables each institution to function independently. The state institutions of Republika Srpska are based on a high degree of autonomy and each of the cantons can function that way, too. BiH is not a decentralised state, but rather a state with a polycentric organisation. The fact that all the institutions of the political system are based on ethnic principles, in almost ethnically homogenous territories, has to be considered as very problematic. Accordingly, the key characteristics of the political system in BiH are its asymmetry, polycentrism and ethnification.

Asymmetry of the political system is discriminatory by itself, as citizens do not enjoy the same status, rights and responsibilities in different parts of the country. For example, citizens in the territory of Republika Srpska exercise most of their rights at the municipal level while citizens in the Federation of BiH do so at the cantonal level (as the authority of municipalities is reduced) to meet those rights stipulated by the cantonal constitutions. Therefore, each canton has its own constitution, parliament, government, ministries, financial institutions, and police etc. The cantons are indeed 'small states'. They are centres of political power and political decision making in the Federation of BiH. The two-level system in Republika Srpska (municipality–entity) and the three-level system in the Federation of BiH (municipality–canton–entity) puts citizens into different positions inevitably resulting in discrimination.

Polycentricism of the system creates discrimination from within, placing citizens into different positions (particularly in the cantons). Considering all their characteristics, the cantons are states; as such they can function almost autonomously. This implies an open space for discrimination, where, due to such structural disorder, there are no horizontal inter-cantonal relations. The legislation of one canton is not necessarily compatible with the legislation of another and as a consequence, the possibilities for discrimination multiply.

Most likely, ethnification is the strongest producer of discrimination: all elements of the system are exclusively based on the ethnic matrix and on the assumption that territories with ethnically homogenous populations exist – which is not the case in BiH and leads to the exclusion of all those who do not match these categories. This phenomenon and its consequences can be illustrated by numerous examples, which will be presented in the chapter. Ethnification of the system is installed by the BiH Constitution in such a way that the whole system – from the state level institutions, entities, cantons and municipalities to the District of Brčko – are set up with ethnic belonging as the main precondition not only for their functioning but also for enjoying human rights.

In this way the elements of the system function on almost ethnically clean territories (the last local elections showed that in BiH there are almost no municipalities inhabited by more than 10% of so-called *other nations*).[1] This situation is a consequence of the war and, in fact, one of its key objectives was fully implemented in practice: creation of ethnically clear territories. The last 25 years have seen three large ethnic migrations. The first process started at the very beginning of the war (1991 and 1992) when people migrated to various Western countries and – to a lesser extent –to the neighbouring countries of Croatia and Serbia. The second took place in the period immediately after the war (1996–2000). Finally, the third had an 'internal' character since many Bosniaks, Serbs and Croats moved within the territory of BiH, migrating to the territories inhabited by majority of 'his/her own (ethnic) kind'. It is impossible to gather precise data either on this third migration or on 'return'. Most of those internally displaced took their identity documents and registered in their pre-war home towns, but without intending to physically return. They did not settle in their pre-war settlements because of lack of employment, and safety issues. In other words, the return of refugees and displaced people has been minor. This was confirmed by the first, preliminary results of the population census in BiH in 2013: ethnic communities are territorially and ethnically homogenised. This produces autarchy and autism in segments of social environment, while such environment reproduces autarchic and autistic social consciousness.

Structural disorder is evident in all spheres of life in BiH: including in the economy, social relations, in political decision-making, education, science and technology and development strategies. A crucial problem is that the normative sphere – encompassing the legal dimension (constitution, laws, bylaws etc.) – that regulates the social relations has been developed without the participation of any local institution. Under normal conditions this sphere should have been determined on the one hand by the social reality and on the other by general

1 The last local elections in BiH were held on 12 October 2014.

social and political interests in a long-term process. However, in the case of BiH, the normative sphere was imposed from the outside, and was shaped by the ethnical matrix.

The Constitution of BiH, with the amendments to the entity constitutions, does not even determine what type of state Bosnia and Herzegovina is. It treats its inhabitants, not like citizens or human beings, but exclusively as Serbs, Croats, Bosniaks and so-called 'others'. Based on these postulations, the Constitution of BiH also installs the political system institutions. Social, collective and individual freedoms and human rights are legally acknowledged by integrating the most important international conventions and declarations into the Constitution. The Constitution is discriminatory in all of its articles. Generally, the consequences are well known: the individual declaring her/himself as Serb, Croat or Bosniak and not wanting to be 'other' is deprived of almost all rights. S/he cannot be elected, cannot participate in social life, and cannot perform senior functions in the economic sector as it is still under strong party control. Furthermore: Serbs living in the Federation of BiH are deprived of their right to vote for the representative of their ethnic group standing for the BiH Presidency. Their passive right is also deprived, as they cannot be elected to that position. A Serb member of the Presidency can only be elected from the territory of Republika Srpska. The situation is identical for Bosniaks and Croats living in Republika Srpska (Article IV of the BiH Constitution). The discrimination is even more evident with regard to the group of so called 'others': they have absolutely no rights. The entire parliamentary system is based on discrimination, as Box 1 illustrates.

Examples of discrimination

The Parliamentary Assembly of BiH is composed by the House of Representatives and the House of Peoples. Both demonstrate discrimination as a result of the division of seats available. The system of election of the members of the House of Representatives stipulates that two-thirds out of total of 42 delegates must be elected from the territory of the Federation of BiH and one-third from the territory of Republika Srpska. Discrimination is further evident even in the House of Peoples (total of 15 delegates) as five Bosniaks and five Croats are appointed from the territory of the Federation of BiH and five Serbs are appointed from Republika Srpska (Articles IV and V of the BiH Constitution).

As far as the BiH Presidency is concerned, the Constitution entails some provisions that look like mockery. For example, only nine votes of the House of Peoples' delegates are required to remove a member of the Presidency from office. There is an annex to this provision: the House of Peoples has 15 delegates, thus the simple majority would consist of eight votes. However, as each of the constituent peoples has five representatives in the House of

Peoples, the Constitution requires a majority of votes *from each ethnic delegation*: nine in total.

There is a similar situation in the House of Representatives in the BiH Parliamentary Assembly, which is supposed to be the house of citizens. A simple majority is not sufficient to adopt a law, a majority of delegates from each of the entities must support it. This means that a majority of delegates from the specific territories is required. This implies that the House of Representatives is not a real house of citizens, but rather another House of Peoples.

This shows that the highest legislative institutions in BiH are based on the logic of tribalism. If another very complicated mechanism of so-called *protection of vital national interests* is added, we are getting closer to acknowledging that the normative sphere is one of the key generators of discrimination in BiH.

In other words, all institutions in BiH are essentially houses of peoples: including the three-member Presidency, the Council of Ministers, and the Parliamentary Assembly of BiH. In such a legal framework, human rights are reduced to the level of collective rights, while individual rights are discredited. Almost all legislation on the lower levels is formulated similarly as well as the Election Law. In addition, another paradox exists as some parts of the BiH Constitution are not harmonized with the entity constitutions. These constitutions were amended several times upon request from the entity elites or by instructions from the international institutions, but have never been harmonised with the BiH Constitution. All this further complicated the already complex organisation of the state administrations in BiH (Bieber, 2009). We can conclude that the Dayton Peace Accords – which represent the BiH Constitution – ended the war and brought peace to BiH, but at the same time also fixed the results that have been achieved by war. In other words, the Dayton Agreement has verified the domination of the ethnic matrix and has fostered the ethnic divide. As such, it cannot be a basis for harmonisation of social relations within BiH.

3. Reforms of the political system and changes in the normative sphere – a precondition for reconciliation

Reforms of the political system are a must in order to pave the way for a process of reconciliation within BiH. However, to overcome the ethnic matrix and discrimination, constructions resulting from the normative sphere must be put on a different basis. The constitutional reform proposal prepared by the Expert Group established by The Citizens' Forum Tuzla (Forum građana Tuzle, 2012) addresses this problem, outlining the central points around which the basis for reform should be built: the principles of freedom, equity and equality on individual and collective levels. On the individual level, a citizen should be granted the status of the constituent subject in the constitutional organisation of BiH. This includes the right to freedom of opinion, freedom of expression, freedom of receiving and transferring information and ideas without interference from the government, freedom of assembly and association, free elections, freedom of creation, and equality before the law. Another important principle is respect and guarantee of human rights. Human rights – so far – have been reduced to ethnic rights.

Authority should be shaped in such a way that it guarantees freedom, equality and equity on both individual and collective levels. Legislative institutions should essentially be organised into two chambers (houses). This would contribute to better forms of communication between the political representatives and the citizens. The current system of cantons should also be reviewed since it is based on ethnic principles only and is therefore a subject of polycentrism.

With regard to the issue of freedom, constitutional changes have to answer two questions: (1) Who votes? and (2) Who is getting elected? In the current system, citizens are not elected, but ethnic groups are and those who vote are also not considered as citizens but rather as members of the ethnic groups. In order to expand the space for freedom, exclusivity of tri-partite ethnic functioning of the institutions should be eliminated. Additionally, with regard to freedom, there is a need to define a referendum as an important form of decision-making on key issues.

It is necessary to eliminate the discriminatory elements related to active and passive rights to vote, and to overcome the ethnification of the executive power, judiciary and public administration. As a similar logic prevails in the sphere of the economy, labour markets and education, these must also be changed. There is an urgent need to define a unified economic space in BiH. The economy as well as the education system should be independent from politics and the influence of political parties. Additionally, if we want a modern constitutional framework, then separation of the church from the state needs to be secured. This should be promulgated not only in the constitutions, but in all the relevant laws.

The biggest challenge for BiH today is the creation of a functioning state. The Dayton Peace Accords were primarily focused on establishing peace; they were not aimed at establishing a coherent organisation of the state. First of all, the state identity of BiH needs to be defined. Is it a republic? How is it organised (as federal, confederal or some other system)? Of course, there are even more questions: Whose state is BiH? Is it a state of the ethnic groups (e.g. Serbs, Croats, Bosniaks) or is it the state of all citizens who inhabit the territory?

4. Ethnicity and nationality as synonyms: forming identities through construction of the 'self' and the 'others'

In an analytical sense, it is important to emphasise the difference between ethnicity and nationality. An 'ethnic group' covers people who share cultural traditions (in its broadest sense) and a feeling of community within a specific group, existing as a subgroup within the broader society. By this definition, Bosniaks, Serbs and Croats in BiH are ethnic groups. In comparison to ethnicity, a nation is a wider term referring to a state. But in our political practice and social awareness, ethnicity and nationality are almost perceived as being the same, so the ethnic identification can be a synonym to nationality. The political solution to the constituency of three ethnic groups in BiH and to their constituent – *state-forming* – character ties ethnicity to the state, its institutions or certain parts of its territory. This causes differentiation between the constituent and non-constituent groups, leading to discrimination where the first literally excludes the second. In addition, the constituent ethnic groups are in continuous political struggle for more representation of the constituency in the institutions of the system and in the specific territory, which may contribute to increase inter-ethnic distances.

This problem has been confirmed by sociological and socio-psychological research in BiH. Puhalo (2003) has analysed the attitudes and relations among the population of the Republika Srpska, the Federation of BiH and the ethnic groups living in former Yugoslavia. The study showed that people in the Federation of BiH reject Roma first, followed by Albanians, Macedonians and Serbs. Those living in Republika Srpska are the least favourable to Bosniaks and Roma, followed by Croats, Macedonians and Slovenians. Montenegrins are least rejected by the population of Republika Srpska. Research conducted by Opačić et al. (2005) in BiH, Serbia and Croatia also identified huge ethnic distances among the populations in BiH, Croatia and Serbia: 15% of the Serbs do not want to see Albanians even as tourists in their country, 12% of the Croats feel the same not only for Albanians, but also for Serbs. The Croats' issues with Roma are slightly smaller than with Albanians and Serbs. For 10% of the Bosniaks, the Serbs are not welcome as tourists, while 11% do not want a Serb living in the same town. Serbs are not welcome as neighbours for 15% of the Bosniaks. The percentage of Bosniaks who are against any friendship with a Serb is even higher (22%). Serbs think similarly of Bosniaks and Croats.

Another study has analysed the attitudes of secondary school students in Banja Luka and Sarajevo (Turjačanin, 2004). The objective was to determine to what extent the youth accept the ethnic groups they live with and how they treat foreigners. Both Banja Luka and Sarajevo students have smaller ethnic distances with Italians and Germans in comparison to the ethnic groups living in BiH. The research shows that ethnic distances are still so strong in BiH that we can speak of it as a deeply divided society. Numerous factors (historical, ideological, political, and psychological factors) have contributed to this situation. The entire history of BiH showed divisions and was marked by many stereotypes, due to different religious orientations, in medieval times, under Turkish rule and during the Austro-Hungarian Empire. Even during Tito's communist regime in Yugoslavia, when people had lived together, the question was often raised whether such co-existence was a political illusion. One of the key concerns today is the fact that the normative sphere legalised ethnification, thus giving it full legitimacy. This fosters ethnic distances and consequently discrimination. Therefore, the question of what kind of state BiH will be and how it should be organised is a key priority in the current situation:

> With no intention of minimising the significance of the Dayton Peace Accords as it had stopped bloodshed in BiH, it should be emphasised it had not completely and clearly defined internal organisation of BiH. This is why it sometimes seems as an 'asymmetric confederation', a 'union of two independent political entities', a 'segmented state', a 'weak confederation', an 'incomplete federation' etc – not established in a way that other European countries had been (. . .).
>
> (Mujagić, 2010, p. 50)

One of the most important indicators for discrimination is the issue of so-called 'mixed marriages':

> 'Mixed marriages' have often been marked as marriages of those who betrayed 'their' nation or as institutions of heretics who, including their children, do not know what is their religion, to which ethnic group they belong to.[2] These testimonies could simply be described as a collection of examples of brutal and heartless discrimination, humiliation and social exclusion of all those living of being born in a 'mixed marriage.'
>
> (Perišić, 2012, p. 11)

The reasons for this include a variety of (ideological, political and even medical) causes, showing that entire social relationships have been refracted through the marginalised population of 'mixed marriages'. In such concurrence, even the issues that should be deeply humane turn into their opposite, as the example in Box 2 illustrates.

This story raises important questions: Isn't this tragedy and aren't all our numerous tragedies, anything else but a consequence of construction? Isn't the set of attitudes towards 'mixed marriages' also a construction? All this implies that the ethno-nationalisms existing in our region is construction. However, the problem is that such constructions not only determine all the attitudes and decisions of the current political elites in BiH, but also social as well as individual awareness. We have to find a way to gradually replace these forms of construction by a series of acts and actions that can substantially question, transform and break down its hermetic walls. The last seems particularly important since ethnic enclosure is the appearance of the autistic logics of construction. The construction is self-sufficient and communicates only with its own internal content. The prejudices and stereotypes that stem from these constructions contribute to foster the 'ideology

2 For further research on this issue see Semprini (1999), Vukšić (2007), and Puhalo (2009).

A true love story

During the years of war, in one of our cities a great love story happened. Two young people sincerely and deeply loved each other. He was a Muslim (as it was called at that time), and she was an Orthodox Serb. They got married and he changed his religion, converted and became an Orthodox or, as it is usually (incorrectly) equalised, he became a Serb. They lived happily, but as life is mysterious and unpredictable, soon he fell in love with another girl who was a Muslim. The couple got divorced and he married the new girlfriend. One day they started a bitter fight and he, becoming infuriated, killed his new wife. Consequently, he was given a long prison sentence. According to the records from the court hearings the key motive for the murder was that she had hurt his Serb national feelings during a fight.

This event occurred during the war in BiH, in 1993, in the town of Bijeljina.

of blood and soil', and various forms of racism which is the inhumane face of discrimination.

In BiH today, nationalism is a common state of social awareness. Society has become an amorphous mass without differentiated social groups. The middle-class has been destroyed, and urbicide – the inversion of rural and urban – performed. The only social differentiation in existence is a small group of enormously rich people and a vast majority of enormously poor people. In addition to this, politics has moved far away from its origins – it does not care for the 'polis', but has been constantly reduced to a brutal power struggle in which the parties involved show a lack of ideas, programmes and vision. On top of this, corruption and crime are an integral part of our reality.

This reality continuously produces turbulences and profiles the state at the subjective level which becomes empowered and multiplies structural disorders in the social reality. Studying in-depth the complex inter-relations of these two spheres seems important and deserves continuous research. This requires interdisciplinary approaches, involving political science, sociological and psychological approaches as well as cultural and anthropological studies.

As has been outlined above with reference to empiric studies, there are huge ethnic distances in BiH. In some segments, they are even more developed than they were during the war, but they appear in a refined form today. Such distances necessarily destroy the social tissue. Everything becomes problematic including the question of identity. Generally, two main theses exist in BiH in order to explain identities: the first states that a Bosnian-Herzegovinian identity exists. The other argues that three different and separate ethnic identities (Bosniak, Serb and Croat) prevail. However, both of these identities are constructed, and therefore artificial.

A Bosnian-Herzegovinian identity has not yet been profiled in awareness and reality. The three individual identities thesis does not respect one key fact: centuries of cohabitation of ethnic communities in this region has produced ethnic identities that are not pure. These identities connect and even permeate. This has also been confirmed by socio-psychological research.

According to Turjačanin and Čekrlij (2006) it turns out that European identity dominates, ethnic identity is ranked second and the national identity third. At first glance, this seemed surprising, but these researchers warned that the strong favouring of European identity is nothing more than an artificial substitute for a non-existent national identity, which could also be considered as an unconscious psychological reaction against the background of people's experience that their entire life in BiH is reduced to their ethnic identity.

5. Bosnia-Herzegovina as an unfinished state: the need for democratic transformation

Today, 20 years after the Dayton Peace Accords, BiH remains an unfinished state. Different constructions exist in different social sectors, particularly in the subjective sphere. This means that the country is still in a 'pre-political' state. The past two decades have been marked by two phases of this pre-political state. The first phase, lasting for almost ten years, was one of specific ideological differentiation. There had been more than 100 political parties registered. There had been only two-and-a-half ideologies: (1) nationalism; (2) a Balkan form of social democracy; and (3) a form of ideology that was represented by former communists (Živanović, 1997; 2000). Among these, the nationalistic ideology was dominant. However, after a certain degree of political transformation we entered the next phase of the pre-political state. The influence of the ethnic matrix, legalised and legitimised through the normative sphere, erased ideological differences. Each political party is now a subject of ethno-national politics, not because it wants to be, but because otherwise it cannot exist. In other words: nowadays in BiH political parties can only be recognised and differentiated according to their ethnic affiliations, based on whether they are Bosniak, Serb or Croat political parties. Their official titles are of formal character only. The parliamentary clubs of delegates at all levels function the same way, as clubs of Bosniak, Serb and Croat delegates.

The political sphere in BiH offers numerous examples for the fixation of this matrix. The category of 'protection of vital national interest' has been introduced by the constitutional system and further developed as a guiding principle of policy making. This has at least three far-reaching consequences: First, national political parties are almost automatically favoured as authentic protectors of vital national interests. Second, this means that only these parties are supposed to win the elections for this interest to be protected. Indirectly, these parties are protected by the constitutions and the Election Law itself. Third, this forces other political parties – even those of social-democratic orientation or any other profile – to implement or promote the same ideas as the ethno-national parties. This results in absolute ideological levelling. In such circumstances, there is no choice as only one ideology exists on the political stage.

This levelling significantly narrows the political sphere. It also extracts the centres of decision-making out of the institutions to the political party leadership. These narrow groups of party leaders make key decisions instead of the parliaments and the institutions of the political system. Consequently, these institutions become just a transmitter to formally confirm something that has already been decided.

The characteristics of societies based on autarchy and discrimination have been widely investigated. However, there is something that has not so often been the focus of analysis: The phenomenon of increasing distance of the political elites from their party members and from the citizens. That is a political autism which is an important characteristic of power. Psychiatry teaches us that autism is a severe and incurable disorder. Some of its general characteristics are: (a) extreme withdrawal from communication with the environment and reduction of almost all social contact; (b) speech difficulties and difficulties in its use; (c) repetitive behaviour (repetition of rituals and speech); (d) being fascinated with round objects and those rotating; and (e) an awareness of the environment, but rejection to speak about it (Živanović, 2008). All of these characteristics can as well be observed in our political practice: separation from life and people, political speech with no messages, endless repetition of the same, and fascination with rotations of political mandates.

It is not possible to enter into deeper analysis of this problem here, but it should be emphasised that political autism is a fruitful ground for discrimination and production of other social deformations. One of these is the phenomenon of an 'irresponsible society'. Our society functions as an 'irresponsible society' as there is no institutionalised responsibility, neither in laws nor in practice. We should try to understand this phenomenon. There is an installed inversion of responsibility in our society meaning that those who are elected are not accountable to those who voted for them, but rather to their party leaders, and to some extent to the institutions of the international community in BiH. This process is established on two levels: formal (legal regulations) and informal. The second level is, of course, a far more serious problem. Instead of political practice having extravert character, it is predominantly introverted.

This is why major social problems stay unresolved while new challenges emerge, and social processes are becoming more and more conflicting. It seems that the politicians do not take notice of these developments. Their position can be identified with conformism that aims at maintaining the status quo. Any change of the current situation would significantly question or put at risk numerous benefits that the conformity offers. These are not primarily material benefits. The intellectuals' conformism – for instance – is often expressed as a need to be as close as possible to the groups in power, to circumnavigate safely all social turbulences and to fully 'embed' into the status quo.

We can say that political conformism co-exists with political autism. This naturally leads to the lack of authority of our political institutions and politicians themselves. More precisely, it is about the dislocation of authority, because as soon as they passed their responsibility to someone else they gave up their authority, too. Inversion of responsibility is not the only cause for autism, there is another factor that contributes to this: the fact that a significant number of elected representatives have been personally compromised, either as fellow travellers or key players in the world of crime and corruption. All this contributes to a situation where voters' distrust against elected politicians is constantly increasing and where great part of citizens feel excluded from politics. This exclusion finds its expression in a variety of forms, such as: election abstinence, self-isolation, and social passiveness. This demonstrates that the subjective sphere also contains elements of construction.

6. International contributions to construction: lacking a strategy for overcoming the Dayton structure

Looking back at the 20 years that have passed since the Dayton Peace Accords were signed we should add some comments on the approaches of the international community to BiH. Two phases can be identified: the first phase was marked by a very active engagement of international organisations, and the second phase can be described as a so-called 'mediation phase'. Looking back to these experiences and balancing the international engagement one can conclude that the Dayton Peace Accords stopped the war in BiH, but the practice of the international community in the past 20 years also showed numerous shortcomings. We can only stress the most significant ones here.

The key problem is that the international community does not have any strategy for long-term engagement either in BiH or in the region. Lacking such a strategy, the international institutions perform on a level of daily politics. They are similar to our local political parties. Both are without any vision. Therefore, the institutions of the international community often act reactively, sanctioning but not resolving the problems. In addition, the official local partners of the international community are those who are most responsible for the war and destruction of the region: the ethno-national political elites. It is a well-known rule: those who created the war can hardly build the peace. In the past few years, in the phase when the international community took over a role as a facilitator in BiH, new questions of responsibility emerged. Both on a declaratory level and in political reality, the problem of ruling the country was handed over to the local authorities. However, previously we could see that the local authorities functioned in a conformist way. The result is a kind of 'irresponsible protectorate'. Of course, such a situation opens the field for numerous deformities including the construction of discrimination.

Finally, there is one crucial question that needs to be answered and relates to the future: how can we start a process of deconstructing discrimination and its underlying factors? I suppose the answer to this question is the necessity for the population in BiH to dismantle the existing domination of ethnic matrix. I already indicated that changes in the normative sphere are crucial. The Constitution of

BiH needs to be deconstructed to set up a type of state that is not solely based on tribal structures. This also means that we will need a more normative definition of the elements of civil society. Some of the important issues in this regard are: individual human rights and equality and equity of citizens before the law. The issue of collective human rights is also important, but exclusiveness of these rights needs to be eliminated, since the ethno-national should not exclude the civil and *vice versa*. There is another important premise: legal presumptions for the status of individuals, human rights and freedom rights should be ensured and harmonised on the whole territory of Bosnia and Herzegovina. Furthermore we need a unified economic space in our small state. Generally, we need a fundamental political and economic reform and a long-term effort for deconstruction of the current political system. Resolving the problem of the state structure is a priority. In my opinion it is even more important than the economy – as the economy cannot develop in a positive way without a functioning state and reliable legal framework. That framework is necessary for the affirmation of the idea of a state of social justice. Defining the system of responsibility is crucial for all of these dimensions.

7. Conclusion: we need renaissance instead of reforms

As outlined above, we need a fundamental change both in the political and normative sphere. To be realistic, changes in the normative sphere will be slow, as there is no political will for any essential change. The current forms of organisation of the society and the state in BiH fully serves the needs of the ethno-national oligarchy but not the needs of the majority of the BiH citizens, as we could witness for the last two decades. A political slogan that was popular in the beginning of the 1990s in BiH and all over the Balkans said: *Our goal is to reach our past!* Unfortunately it turned out that this was not only a slogan, but a morbid project that was successfully implemented. Physically we live in the first decades of the third millennium but essentially we exist in an ancient history. This is why de-ethnification of the society in BiH is a key element and a precondition to deconstruction of discrimination. De-ethnification represents a process that needs to entail social reality and social awareness. Experts state it is necessary to implement reforms in all sectors of life: economic reforms, reforms of the political system, education, science, culture, reforms of the system of values etc. Personally, I do not like the word *reform*. As I am aware, this word means *repeated form, the same form*. I prefer the word renaissance.

We really need renaissance. I emphasise this above all because of the human factor. The current average state of social awareness in BiH is total resignation and hopelessness. People need their hope back. This is a real need. There are many diagnoses about what happened here during the last two decades. There are many proposals for what to do and what changes we need. But it seems that we can hardly find the answer to the question: who can be the drivers of social change? Which social power can lead the project of renaissance and deconstruction?

The question who can be agents of change in BiH is very important. The problem is that it is really hard to find an answer. Social cohesion and trust have been completely destroyed in this country. Furthermore many groups of the Bosnian-Herzegovinian society are excluded from both political power and social influence. Young people are excluded from the labour force and they have been leaving the country. Bosnian-Herzegovinian society is getting older and older, and the total number of citizens is rapidly decreasing. The older population is also excluded from the labour sphere while intellectuals are largely the poltroons and conformists. They behave in such a way to be close enough to the ruling – above all political – elites. The academic community and the universities are very conservative and as a rule are under formal or informal political-party influence. I have often said that we live in a society whose most progressive segment are retired people. This is not a joke, this is our reality.

The urgent need for a renaissance has also been confirmed by the results of the general elections that were held in BiH on October 12, 2014. As many analysts had expected, the ethno-nationalistic parties were the winners of these elections, namely, the Party of Democratic Action (Bosniak Party), the Croat Democratic Union (Croat Party) and two blocks of the Serb parties: one gathered around the Alliance of Independent Social Democrats and the other led by the Serb Democratic Party. It should be clarified that the Alliance of Independent Social Democrats has not been a social democratic party, but rather the Serb ethno-nationalistic party, often expressing radical views. The losers in these elections are the citizens of BiH, whose lives are reduced to an ethnic matrix. This is too tight a framework for meeting the challenges the country faces at present and in the future. These elections also showed that the internal divisions in BiH will continue. The winners favour preservation of the status quo, meaning that none of the crucial social and political problems (re-organisation of the state, creation of a unified economic space, incentives for economic growth and employment) will be resolved in the future. All of these problems must be addressed to open the European pathway and to develop some positive visions of progress for the citizens of BiH. The elections showed that the country returned to the status-quo and a very similar political situation that we had already experienced in the 1990s. Therefore the twentieth anniversary of the Dayton Peace Accord will not offer much cause for celebration; rather it will be an occasion that urges us to search for opportunities to build a better life and a common future in this region.

It is necessary to change the difficult situation in BiH in order to open a process of deconstruction of discrimination. First of all we need a reform of the constitutional and legal system that has installed the existing state structures. This means that all elements of discrimination and tribalism have to be removed from all constitutions and laws. Furthermore there is an urgent need to start economic reform in order to overcome the period of recession in the next five years. These have to be combined with an effective anti-corruption strategy. Political decision-making processes need to be brought into the institutions of the system. Finally, judicial reform will be a key precondition for eliminating discrimination. In order to proceed in all these dimensions, a strong civil society will be needed, as well as reform of the education system that meets European standards and contributes to the elimination of discrimination. This is a necessary precondition for any process of reconciliation in this country.

References

Bieber, F. (2009). *Granice stvaranja države: da li je Briselu dovoljan Dejton?* Sarajevo: Friedrich Ebert Stiftung.

Ćurak, N. (2002). *Geopolitika kao sudbina: slučaj Bosna i Hercegovina: postmodernistički ogled o perifernoj zemlji.* Sarajevo: Fakultet političkih nauka.

Hadžikadunić, E. (2005). *Od Dejtona do Brisela.* Sarajevo: ACIPS.

Mujagić, N. (2010). *Tihi govor Bosne.* Sarajevo: Heinrich Böll Stiftung.

Mujkić, A. (2007). *Mi, građani Evropolisa.* Sarajevo: Šahinpašić.

Mujkić, A. (2010). *Pravda i etnonacionalizam.* Sarajevo: Centar za ljudska prava Univerziteta u Sarajevu.

Opačić, G. et al. (2005). *Etnička distanca i etnički stereotipi kao faktor odluke o povratku, Život u posleratnim zajednicama.* Belgrade: IAN.

Perišić, N. (2012). *Mješoviti brakovi u Bosni i Hercegovini: od poželjnog do prezrenog, mješoviti brak kao kulturna i politička kategorija u Savremenoj BiH.* Sarajevo: Friedrich Ebert Stiftung.

Petritsch, W. (2002). *Bosna i Hercegovina od Daytona do Evrope.* Sarajevo: Svjetlost.

Puhalo, S. (2003). *Etnička distanca stanovnika Republike Srpske i Federacije BiH prema narodima bivše SFRJ.* Banja Luka: Friedrich Ebert Stiftung.

Puhalo, S. (2009). *Etnička distanca i (auto)stereotipi građana Bosne i Hercegovine.* Sarajevo: Friedrich Ebert Stiftung.

Projekt (2012). *Ustavne promjene u Bosni i Hercegovini – civilna inicijativa.* Tuzla: Forum građana.

Šarčević E. (1997). *Ustav i politika: kritika etničkih ustava i postrepubličkih ustavatvorstava u Bosni i Hercegovini.* Sarajevo: UKBI.

Semprini, A. (1999). *Multikulturalizam.* Belgrade: Clio.

Turjačanin, V. (2004). 'Etnički stereotipi mladih bošnjačke i srpske nacionalnosti u Bosni i Hercegovini'. *Psihologija,* Vol. 37 (3), 357–374.

Turjačanin, V. & Čekrlija, Đ. (eds.) (2006). *Etnički, državni i evropski identitet.* Banja Luka: Friedrich Ebert Stiftung.

Vukšić, T. (2007). *Mješovite ženidbe u katoličanstvu, pravoslavlju i islamu (Dvoje njih bit će jedno tijelo).* Sarajevo: Caritas.

Živanović, M. (1997). *Stakleno oko.* Sarajevo: Bosanska knjiga.

Živanović, M. (2000). *Acta politika Serbica.* Banja Luka: Media Centar Prelom.

Živanović, M. (2008). *Ribe ne plaču: prilog fenomenologiji autizma.* Banja Luka: Littera.

Chapter 10

Economic development and perspectives for reconciliation

William Bartlett

1. Introduction

This chapter outlines the effect of the economic crisis on the economies of Bosnia-Herzegovina (BiH), Croatia and Serbia, and addresses its effects on post-war reconciliation. It also considers the role of economic elites in mobilising political support along ethnic lines, and the way in which they respond to the need for structural reform proposed by the European Union and by the need to create more competitive and open economies. The economic crisis has led to a reduction in international trade, foreign investment, remittance flows and a fall in credit for businesses and households. As a consequence, all three countries have experienced a 'double dip' recession, which has led to a sharp increase in unemployment with adverse consequences for living standards. Youth unemployment in BiH is even higher than in crisis-hit Greece. In addition, when Croatia joined the EU in July 2013, new barriers were created to trade with BiH and Serbia, as Croatia left the CEFTA free-trade area.

All this has created an adverse environment for social and political reconciliation between the former warring parties in the region. This is reflected in political developments in BiH, with a deepening rift between the two 'entities' that divide BiH on ethnic lines. The popular resentment against the ruling nationalist parties came to a head in February 2014 with four days of rioting that began in Tuzla and rapidly spread to other towns and cities. Although protests were fuelled by resentment against a corrupt political class, it is significant that with a few exceptions they did not really cross the ethnic divide and produce a popular movement based on reconciliation.[1] Tensions have also increased between Serbia and Croatia with the dispute over the use of Cyrillic lettering in the war-scarred city of Vukovar in Eastern Slavonia (see Radosavljević, 2013).

The chapter discusses the connections between economic conditions and the processes of reconciliation in and between the three countries and concludes that,

1 Protests that were held in 2013 concerning delays in issuing identification numbers for new-born babies had crossed ethnic divisions, but this was not a major aspect of the wider and more violent protests of 2014 (see Arnautović, 2013).

although there is no automatic linkage, the combination of economic crisis and resistance to pro-market reforms by the ruling elites has created an environment in which the seeds of reconciliation have fallen mainly on stony ground.

2. The economic crisis

In the early to mid 2000s, the Western Balkan countries experienced a period of rapid economic growth. Between 2002 and 2008, the average rate of growth of GDP was 5.6 per cent per annum in BiH, 4.4 per cent per annum in Croatia and 4.9 per cent per annum in Serbia (see Figure 1). The economic crisis in the global economy that began in 2008 and the subsequent Eurozone crisis brought this period of growth to an abrupt end (Bartlett & Prica, 2013). GDP growth in BiH averaged -0.2 per cent from 2009–2013, while in Serbia economic growth averaged precisely zero over this period. Croatia fared even worse, with a long-lasting recession marked by a decline in GDP of 2.5 per cent per annum.

The reasons for this dramatic reversal of fortunes can be found in the structural relationship of these countries to the EU. Each country is highly 'euroised', meaning that many business and household loans are denominated in euros or linked to the value of the euro. This in turn means that policy makers are reluctant to devalue the currency to gain a competitive advantage as such a move would cause widespread bankruptcies with businesses and households unable to pay their debts. The currency fix to the euro has been institutionalised in BiH through the adoption of a 'currency board', but the other two countries are effectively in

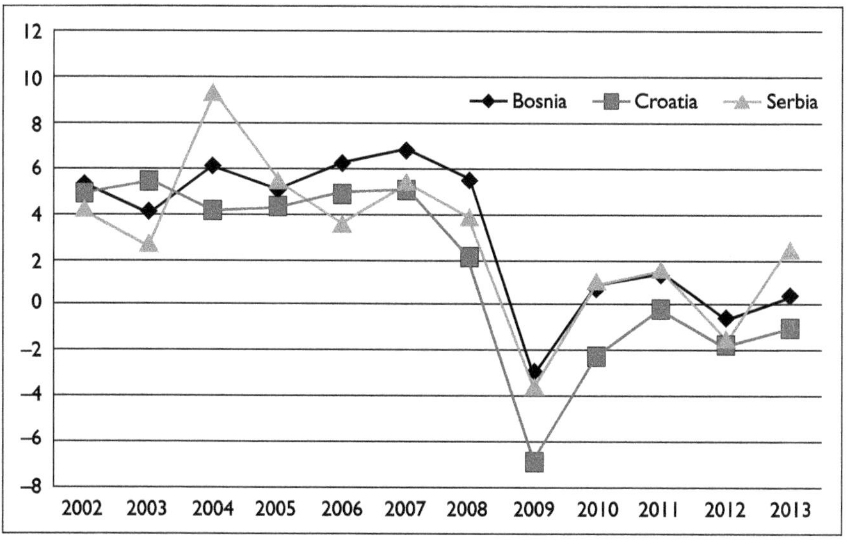

Figure 1 GDP growth (annual %)

Source: World Bank World Development Indicators online database.

the same position despite having nominally flexible exchange rates. Croatia has made a fixed exchange rate a central pillar of her macroeconomic policy for many years, and while Serbia has had a somewhat more flexible approach she has adopted a more-or-less fixed peg to the euro. All this means that exchange rate depreciation is unavailable as a method to improve competitiveness in relation to the EU, the largest trading partner of each country. The stagnation of the Eurozone economy has therefore had a depressing effect on demand for exports from the three countries over the last five years, while the short-lived periods of recovery from the crisis have been weak and patchy.

The economic crisis has been reflected in stagnant or falling living standards as measured by the level of GDP per capita, which even in current terms (i.e. not accounting for inflation) have fallen in Croatia from a peak of US$15,700 (€10,700) in 2008 to US$13,500 (€10,100) in 2013.[2] In BiH and Serbia living standards have stagnated at the equivalent of around US$6,000 (€4,100) per capita since 2008.[3]

In addition to faltering demand for the countries' exports, other drivers of economic growth have also gone into reverse. As a consequence of the global economic crisis and the near collapse of the global financial system in 2008, the inflows of foreign investment to the region began to fall sharply, and have continued to fall since then with only a slight pick-up in Serbia in 2011. In 2007, FDI inflows had reached a level of more than 8 per cent of GDP per annum, and as high as 12 per cent in BiH.[4] From 2002–2008 the average FDI inflow to the three countries taken together was 6.7 per cent of GDP, while from 2009–2013 the average annual FDI inflow to all three countries was reduced to just 2.9 per cent. FDI inflows are often considered to be a strong driver of economic growth, and the collapse of inward FDI after 2008 has therefore been a further cause of the worsening growth performance over the last five years.

Alongside the reduction in inflows of foreign capital, domestic investment has also fallen dramatically since 2008 as demand for the output of domestic businesses fell (see Figure 2). The fall in investment (gross fixed capital formation) by the private sector began earliest and was most noticeable in BiH, from a peak of 25 per cent of GDP in 2007 to a trough of just 10 per cent of GDP in 2010. The reduction in domestic investment began a little later in Croatia and Serbia, peaking in 2008, but declining to low levels in each country by 2011.

A noticeable consequence of the continuing recessionary conditions in the three countries has been an increase in the share of 'non-performing' loans as a proportion of total loans made by the banking sector. These reflect the situation of businesses and households that are no longer able to repay their loans and are

2 The euro values for GDP per capita are taken from Bulletin No. 205, Croatian National Bank, July 2014.

3 World Bank World Development Indicators online data. Retrieved from http://data.worldbank.org/data-catalog/world-development-indicators.

4 Ibid.

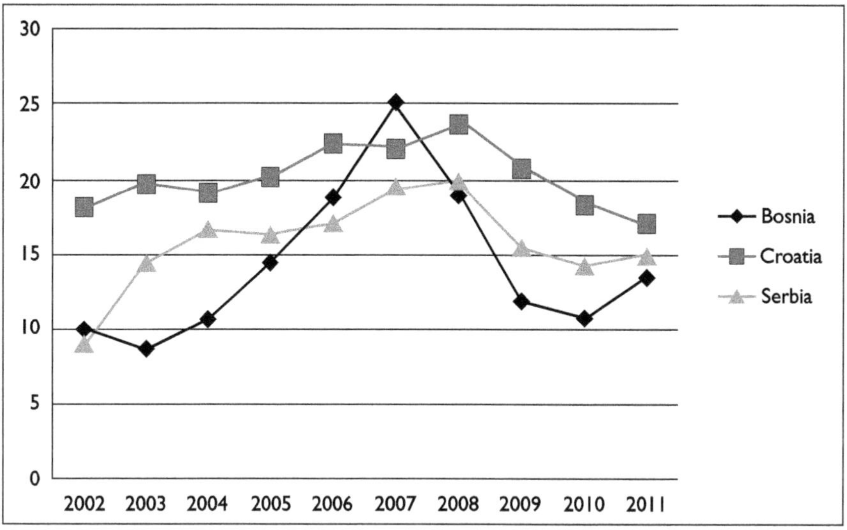

Figure 2 Gross investment, private sector (% of GDP)

Source: World Bank World Development Indicators online database. The data refer to gross fixed capital formation.

in effect bankrupt, or nearly bankrupt, although the bank will often continue to roll over the loan amount in order to avoid default on the loan.[5] The share of non-performing loans increased most dramatically in Serbia, doubling from 10 per cent in 2008 to 20 per cent in 2013.[6] The situation has been only slightly better in BiH and in Croatia where the share of non-performing loans increased from about 5 to 15 per cent over the same period. The continuous rise in the share of non-performing loans highlights the persistence of the recessionary conditions and the depth of the problem facing policy makers in the three countries.

In addition to the purely economic effects of the recession we should also consider the policy response, which has only added to the deflationary effects of the crisis. All three countries have introduced austerity policies. These were first introduced in BiH in 2012 in return for a bailout from the IMF. Austerity policies were next introduced in Croatia, following her accession to the EU in July 2013. Under the provisions of the EU's 'Excessive Deficit Procedure', Croatia was

5 Businesses have not only been unable to pay off bank loans but also workers' wages and social contributions. In Croatia, the Finance Minister announced in April 2014 that employers had failed to pay mandatory health and pension contributions for more than 200,000 workers. In Serbia, 70,000 workers had not received wages for six months or more (Radosavljević & Vasović, 2014).

6 Ibid.

obliged to make radical structural reforms and cuts in public expenditure. Serbia managed to evade austerity for longer, but the dramatically deteriorating economic situation eventually required the imposition of such measures in autumn 2014. Let us consider the policy response in each of the three countries in a little more detail.

In BiH, a €405 million stand-by arrangement was concluded with the IMF in September 2012 to counteract the continuing effects of the economic crisis. The associated economic adjustment programme envisaged a budget deficit of 4.5 per cent of GDP in 2010. This was to be achieved through cuts in public sector wages, pension reforms, and reforms of rights-based benefits and transfers awarded to war veterans and their families. The austerity programme reduced the general government budget deficit to 2.5 per cent of GDP in 2012 and 2.2 per cent of GDP in 2013. It involved cuts in the public sector wage bill, achieved by prohibiting the hiring of new employees in the institutions of BiH and entity government administrations, and by continuing with harsh cuts in social spending.

In 2013, Croatia's public debt amounted to 67 per cent of GDP, exceeding the 60 per cent target set by the EU's new Treaty on Stability, Coordination and Governance (the revamped Stability and Growth Pact) by a significant margin. The public deficit stood at 6 per cent of GDP, far from the balanced budget required by the new Treaty. In response to these breaches of EU norms, in January 2014 the European Council opened an Excessive Deficit Procedure (EDP) for Croatia. Under the EDP, the EU required Croatia to correct the deficit by 2016, setting a target for the deficit to be reduced to 4.6 per cent of GDP for 2014, 3.5 per cent in 2015 and 2.7 per cent in 2016. Croatia was required to introduce structural reforms to make the labour market more flexible and to improve the quality of public administration. However, by August 2014 it looked as though the targets for deficit reduction would not be reached. The credit rating agency Fitch forecast a 4.5 per cent budget deficit for 2014, and downgraded the country's credit rating to 'BB', well into junk status.

In Serbia, in August 2014, the newly appointed finance minister, Dušan Vujović, announced stricter control over public spending, a reduction in the informal economy and improved tax collection, and the introduction of structural reforms. Pensions were to be reduced by 10 per cent across the board. The aim of the reform was to reduce the public sector deficit from 7 per cent in 2013 to just 2 per cent by 2017. A new privatisation law was announced with the aim to sell of the remaining loss-making public companies. In a major reform the issuance of construction permits was eased through a new law which should reduce the time taken to issue construction permits from 260 days to just 28 days, making it easier to start up a new business, or expand an existing one. The Serbian Government announced that it would seek the support of the IMF with the intention to negotiate a three-year Stand-by Arrangement, which would no doubt enforce a similar austerity programme that has been applied in BiH.

In summary, the three countries have each experienced a severe economic recession over the last five years, with at best limited and hesitant periods of recovery. Their economies have been weakened by poor international competitiveness, faltering exports, chronic balance of payment deficits and a sharp fall in inflows of foreign investments. This is an inconspicuous environment for reconciliation between formerly conflicting nations and groups. The problem is most evident in BiH with the continual political standoff between the entity of Republika Srpska and the Federation, but also affects relations between the three countries at a wider level. However, despite the economic difficulties, recent years have also seen attempts to forge economic cooperation between the three countries. Building on a set of bilateral free trade agreements facilitated by the former Stability Pact for South East Europe, the three countries entered into a more wide-ranging regional free trade agreement known as 'CEFTA 2006' (Bartlett, 2008). This agreement promoted a growth of trade and cross-border investment between the three countries that has transformed their economic relations. It began a process of economic integration based on the restoration of previously existing economic links as well as the establishment of entirely new ones that have underpinned gradually improving political relations and have supported attempts at social and cultural reconciliation (Judah, 2009). The next section therefore turns to the issue of trade relations, beginning with an analysis of the broad trade developments of the three countries in recent years, and then focusing on the impact of regional free trade on bilateral trade flows between the three countries.

3. Trade, EU accession and reconciliation

Apart from brief episodes such as in the early-mid 2000s, economic growth in the three countries has been held back by low international competitiveness and a consequent balance of payments constraint that comes into play whenever economic growth is sustained for any significant period of time. Growth has been associated with increases in imports that have not been balanced by equivalent increases in exports, making the economies dependent on external sources of financing to sustain growth spurts. As the economic crisis took hold, growth collapsed and along with that imports fell. This led to an improvement in the balance of trade in goods and services. By 2020 external trade in goods and services in Croatia was broadly balanced, while the deficit persisted in BiH and Serbia, albeit at a lower level in relation to GDP than it had been in 2008. Croatia has been less affected by the balance of payments constraint than the other two countries due to her high level of 'invisible' earnings from the tourism industry.

An important way in which the trade gap has been covered in the Western Balkan economies has been through the inflow of remittances from country nationals employed abroad. Such migrant remittances have been especially important for BiH and Serbia, although less so for Croatia which has been able to partially cover the trade gap through earnings from the tourism sector. In 2007, remittance flows accounted for 17.6 per cent of GDP in BiH and 7.9 per cent of

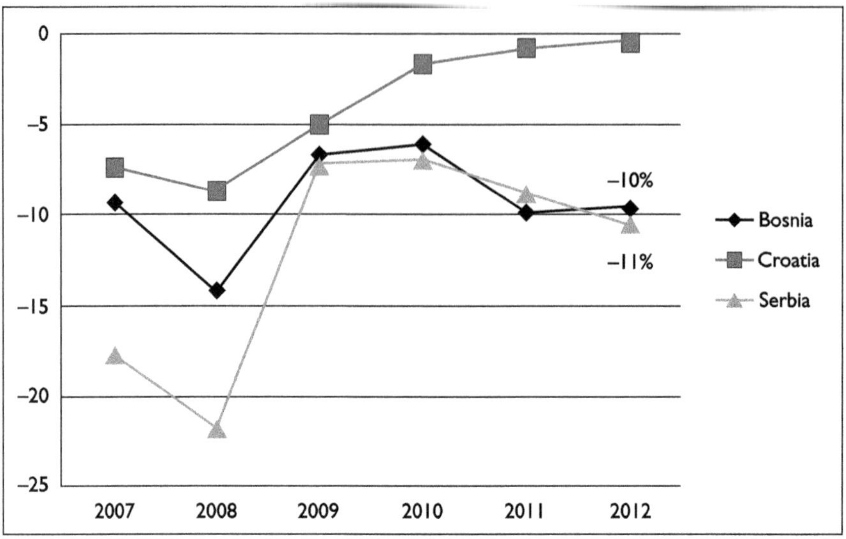

Figure 3 Current account balance (% of GDP)

Source: World Bank World Development Indicators online database.

GDP in Serbia.[7] As a consequence of the economic crisis in the countries where the migrants worked, many migrants suffered unemployment or a significant reduction in earnings. Remittances to BiH fell by almost seven percentage points to 10.9 per cent by 2012. Serbia was less affected, with only a small reduction in remittances over the same period, while the relatively low level of remittances to Croatia actually increased a little. The reduction in remittances to BiH made it more difficult to cover the balance of trade deficit and to a widening of the overall current account deficit.

In the early to mid 2000s, the current account balance of payments deficits increased as a direct result of rapid economic growth (see Figure 3). By 2008, the balance of payments deficit reached over 20 per cent of GDP in Serbia, 15 per cent of GDP in BiH and almost 10 per cent of GDP in Croatia. In part these deficits were financed by inflows of foreign investment, and international aid, but also by international borrowing with a consequent increase in international debt requiring increasing levels of debt service payments. With the onset of the economic crisis, inflows of foreign direct investment dried up making it more difficult to cover the deficits. Fortunately at the same time imports of goods and

7 World Bank World Development Indicators online data. Retrieved from http://data.worldbank.org/data-catalog/world-development-indicators.

services fell, which reduced the current account deficits that needed to be covered. In Croatia, which benefited from earnings from the tourism industry, the current account deficit was entirely eliminated by 2013, while in the other two countries the deficit was initially sharply reduced in 2010 and 2011 but then showed a tendency to increase again in the following two years, reaching 10 per cent of GDP in both countries by 2012.

As a result of continuing balance of payments deficits, the international indebtedness of the three countries has continued to increase during the period of the economic crisis. By 2013, Croatia's gross external debt stood at €45 billion, equivalent to a dangerously high 105 per cent of GDP (Croatian National Bank, 2014). External debt service accounted for 38 per cent of total exports of goods and services, meaning that more than one third of Croatia's export earnings go simply to pay for the international debt that she has incurred. By early 2014, the external debt of Serbia had reached €25.5 billion, equivalent to 65 per cent of GDP (National Bank of Serbia, 2014). In BiH the external debt was lower than in the other two countries at 54 per cent of GDP in 2013 (IMF, 2014), with debt service amounting to just 17 per cent of GDP. BiH's external debt has been kept to a relatively low level due to the austerity policies introduced under the IMF Stand-by Arrangement that had been agreed at the start of the crisis, as explained above.

3.1. Trade relations between the three countries

It is often thought that trade relations can provide a solid ground for improved social, cultural and political relations between countries. This is one of the main reasons for the foundation of the EU, or European Economic Community as it was originally called. The Stability Pact for South East Europe put a lot of effort into promoting trade between the countries of the former Yugoslavia as a means to promote post-war reconsolidation. This work has been continued under the responsibility of the successor organisation, the Regional Cooperation Council, based in Sarajevo.

Since 2007, all three countries have been members of the CEFTA 2006 free trade agreement that eliminated most tariff barriers to trade between them. The Agreement was signed in December 2006 between Albania, BiH, Croatia, Macedonia, Moldova, Montenegro, Serbia and the United Nations Interim Administration Mission in Kosovo. Croatia ratified the agreement in August 2007, Serbia in October and BiH in November of the same year. The aims of the free trade agreement were to expand trade in goods and services, eliminate barriers to trade, foster investment, provide protection of intellectual property rights, and harmonise provisions on modern trade policy issues such as competition rules and state aid. The agreement also included procedures for dispute settlement and facilitated the gradual establishment of measures for the diagonal cumulation of origin between the EU and the Western Balkan countries. Significant non-tariff barriers still exist, especially in the field of services (Handjiski & Šeštović, 2011).

For example, trade in the construction sector suffers from limitations on acceptance of foreign licenses, while restrictive regulations and state-owned monopolies limit trade in the transport sector. The legal sector is the most closed to trade, as service provision is limited to country nationals.

Despite its defects and the continuing presence of non-tariff barriers to trade, most studies of the impact of the CEFTA 2006 free trade agreement conclude that it has had a noticeable effect in boosting trade in the region. Total exports between CEFTA countries as a whole increased from €2.9 billion in 2006 to €5.5 billion in 2012.[8] The share of intra-CEFTA exports in total CEFTA exports increased from 15.2 per cent in 2006 to 20.5 per cent in 2012 (although this was down from a pre-crisis peak in 2008 of 24.6 per cent).[9] An analysis carried out by Petreski (2011) using a 'gravity' model of trade relations showed that CEFTA 2006 had a positive effect on trade in the South East Europe region as a whole up to 2009. He suggested that this might have reflected a return to more normal patterns of trade following the lowering of trade flows in the region that had taken place in the 1990s due to the effect of war and the break up of the former Yugoslavia.

The CEFTA 2006 agreement should have been especially important for BiH as Croatia and Serbia are among her major trading partners, alongside Germany and Italy. However, membership of CEFTA 2006 actually exposed Bosnian farmers to strong competition from imports from neighbouring countries including Croatia and Serbia, where farmers receive greater state support. Intra-CEFTA exports from BiH to Croatia decreased from 16 per cent of total exports to just 12 per cent between 2006 and 2012 (data are not available from BiH's export share to Serbia). Overall, BiH has had a negative trade balance with both Croatia and Serbia, suggesting that the agreement was beneficial for Croatia and Serbia, but possibly less beneficial for BiH.

Both Serbia and Croatia seem to have benefitted from CEFTA 2006. Taking the former country first, Serbia increased her trade with BiH, from a share of 4.8 per cent of total exports in 2006 to 12.8 per cent in 2012. This positive effect is substantiated by a study focusing on the effect of the agreement on Serbia by Bjelić and Mitrović (2012) who estimated that the membership increased Serbia's trade by 29 per cent above the levels that would have been achieved in its absence. Croatia also benefitted from CEFTA membership. The share of her total export trade that went to BiH increased from 12.6 per cent to 13.2 per cent between 2006 and 2012, while the share of her exports going to Serbia increased from 0.3 per cent to 4.5 per cent over the same period. However there are no detailed gravity models of Croatia's intra-CEFTA trade that would substantiate this from

8 Calculated from IMF Direction of Trade Statistics database, converted to euros using mid-year exchange rates.

9 Calculated from Eurostat data on candidate countries and potential candidates: international trade [cpc_etmain] and [ext-lt-intercc] for total CEFTA trade with the rest of the world, and IMF DOTS for total intra-CEFTA trade revalued to euros.

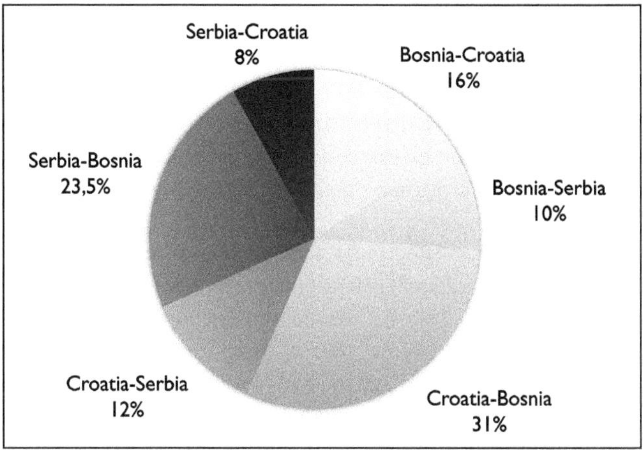

Figure 4 Shares of goods exports between BiH, Croatia and Serbia, 2013

Source: UN Comtrade, DESA/UNSD, http://comtrade.un.org.

the point of view of what might have been expected to result in the absence of the CEFTA 2006 agreement.

We can also consider the shares of trade between the three trading partners from the perspective of their bilateral exports as a share of total trilateral trade between them (scc Figure 4). By 2013, the main trade flows between the three countries were exports from Croatia and Serbia to BiH. These exports have respectively accounted for 31 per cent and 23 per cent of all trilateral trade flows, and together accounted for more than half of all trade between the three countries. On the other hand, BiH's exports to Croatia accounted for just 16 per cent of trilateral trade, and her exports to Serbia for just 10 per cent. Trade flows between Croatia and Serbia have been relatively low, accounting for just 20 per cent of trilateral exports. If we consider just bilateral flows, it is apparent that Croatia and Serbia both have trade surpluses with BiH. The trade between Croatia and Serbia is more balanced with a small trade surplus in favour of Croatia.

How can we explain these patterns? The main reason seems to be the close trade connections between Croatia and the Cantons in BiH predominantly inhabited by Bosnian Croats and the trade between the Republika Srpska and Serbia (Bartlett, 2008). Thus, trade flows are not necessarily an indicator of reconciliation between ethnic groups but may also be interpreted as reflecting the particular ethnic divisions within BiH and economic relations within ethnic groups across borders. From this perspective, the increased trade connections that have been encouraged by the CEFTA 2006 free trade agreement have not promoted regional cooperation between different ethnic groups. Nor has it provided as strong a basis for political, social and cultural reconciliation as the proponents of free trade may have wished for.

3.2. *Croatia's EU accession*

The accession of Croatia to the EU in July 2013 and her consequent departure from CEFTA 2006 created substantial difficulties for trade between BiH and Croatia and between Serbia and Croatia. Whereas previously these trade flows had been free of tariffs, the exports from BiH to Croatia and from Serbia to Croatia now faced the EU common external tariff. Equivalently, Croatia's exports to the two other countries now faced new tariff barriers where previously there had been none.

In view of the potential adverse effects of Croatia's accession, and additionally due to the unwillingness of Republika Srpska to negotiate any agreements at state level, BiH refused to adapt the Interim Agreement of the Stabilisation and Association Agreement (IA/SAA) to take into account the new bilateral trade relations with Croatia. The European Commission argued that neither BiH nor Serbia would be disadvantaged by such an adaptation, as the trade concessions applicable to these countries with the EU of 27 Member States would have been adjusted in order to reflect the new situation of an enlarged EU-28. To the evident frustration of the EU[10] the trade part of the SAA/IA had still not been adapted following Croatia's accession to the EU.[11]

Despite the European Commission's protestations that BiH and Serbia would not suffer from Croatia's accession, trade flows were adversely affected. In the first four months of 2014, exports from BiH to Croatia were down by 25 per cent compared to the same period in the previous year. BiH compensated for this to some extent by a 10 per cent increase in exports to other CEFTA members, but the overall effect was negative.

4. Social developments and reconciliation

The period of economic growth in the early to mid 2000s had brought about a steady fall in the unemployment rate in Croatia. In Serbia, unemployment began to fall from about 2006, as before then the privatisation programme initiated in 2000 had led to a loss of jobs in formerly socially owned enterprises. In BiH the picture was more mixed. Although unemployment fell during the period 2004–2005 and 2006–2008, there was overall little change in the unemployment rate in 2008 compared to the position in 2002. Thus, considering the effect on unemployment, economic growth yielded substantial benefits in Croatia, modest benefits in Serbia and hardly any benefits in BiH. Since the onset of the crisis, the unemployment rate has steadily increased in all three countries, and by 2012 had reached 28 per cent in BiH, 20 per cent in Serbia and 16 per cent in Croatia.

10 European Commission, 2013a.
11 European Commission, 2013b, p. 4.

As in many European countries, youth unemployment has been a particularly severe problem. It has increased to extremely high levels in BiH, reaching 59 per cent in 2013.[12] The youth unemployment rate was only a little lower at 51 per cent in Croatia[13] and 50 per cent in Serbia.[14] These high levels of youth unemployment have led to strident calls for labour market reforms. These have been designed to reduce the protection for employees, in order to convince employers that they can safely take on new workers without having to enter into any sort of long-term commitment. Labour market reforms of this type have recently been introduced in Serbia. In Croatia, Laszlo Anders, EU Commissioner for Employment and Social Affairs, has called for implementation of a second phase of labour law reform, 'to make the labour market more flexible and prevent further labour-market segmentation' (Andor, 2014). It remains to be seen what their effects will be.

High and increasing unemployment has led, not surprisingly, to increased rates of poverty and inequality. In 2011, the poverty rate (i.e. the percentage of the population living below the national poverty line) was 18 per cent in BiH, 20.5 per cent in Croatia and 24.6 per cent in Serbia.[15] These data on relative poverty understate the real level of disadvantage experienced by the poorest members of the populations, as they do not take into account the absolute levels of material deprivation. Recently, the EU has developed a new indicator of the proportion of people at risk of poverty or social exclusion, which takes into account the absolute as well as the relative level of poverty. According to this measure, the proportion of the Croatian population at risk of poverty or social exclusion in 2012 was 32.3 per cent, much higher than the average of 24.8 per cent in the EU-27 as a whole. Estimates of the proportion at risk of poverty or social exclusion in BiH reach as high as 58.6 per cent (Bartlett, 2013). No data for this measure are available for Serbia. These very high rates of poverty and social exclusion give rise to social tensions that may inhibit reconciliation between communities and nations.

In addition to the high level of absolute and relative poverty and social exclusion, we can also note the high levels of income inequality in the three countries. Income inequality is generally less than inequalities in wealth as highlighted by the recent publication by the French economist Thomas Picketty (2013). However, there is little reliable evidence available to measure inequalities in wealth for the countries under investigation, so I consider here only inequalities in income. Figure 5 shows that the top 10 per cent of income earners receive 27 per cent of the total incomes in BiH and Croatia and 24 per cent of the total income in Serbia. In contrast, the bottom 10 per cent receives just three per cent of the total income in BiH and

12 Agency for Statistics of BiH, 2014.
13 Eurostat online data variable [lfsq_urgan]. Retrieved from http://appsso.eurostat.ec.europa.eu/nui/show.do?dataset=lfsq_urgan&lang=en.
14 Statistical Office of the Republic of Serbia 2014.
15 World Development Indicators Database, World Bank online data. Retrieved from http://data.worldbank.org/data-catalog/world-development-indicators.

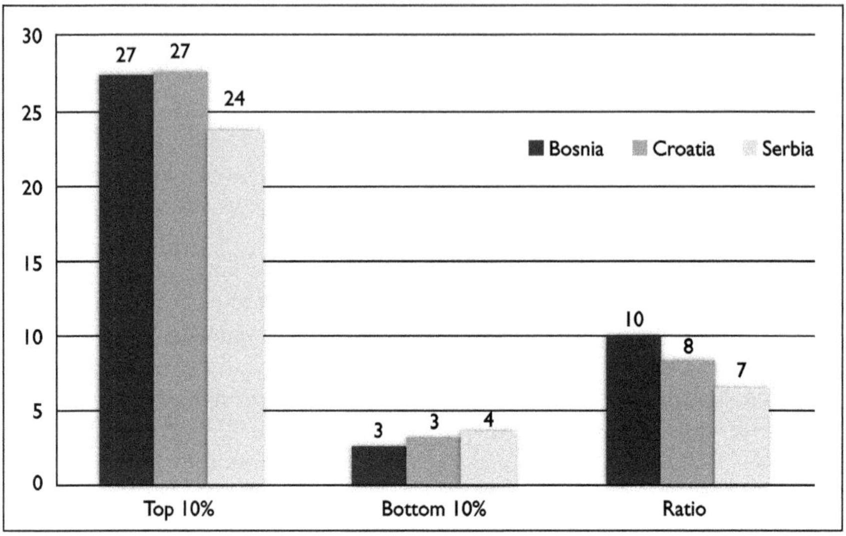

Figure 5 Income shares of top 10 per cent, bottom 10 per cent and ratio

Source: World Bank World Development Indicators online database.

Croatia, and four per cent of the total income in Serbia. The ratio between the income shares of the top 10 per cent and the bottom 10 per cent reached a factor of ten in BiH, eight in Croatia and seven in Serbia. These data imply a very high level of income inequality in the three countries, which is all the more subjectively felt by the non-elite, considering that as recently as 25 years ago in the former Yugoslavia inequality of incomes was extremely low (Flakierski, 1989).[16]

The high levels of inequality that are observed in the three countries suggest that economic elites have succeeded in capturing a significant part of the economic surplus generated by the productive sector of the economy. In the former Yugoslavia, elites had used ethnic mobilisation to preserve their favoured positions and to counter democratisation and competitive market principles of equal opportunities for all (Gagnon, 2004). Given the continuity of elite strategies since the time of the break-up of Yugoslavia, it is not surprising that ethnic mobilisation still forms a strong element of the political culture in the three countries and a significant obstacle to reconciliation between nations and communities. The formation of the current elites in the three countries has been based upon the particular strategies of privatisation of the socially owned enterprise sector that were adopted.

16 See Hoffman et al., 2012, for some evidence that wage inequality has been increasing over time in Croatia. Wage inequality among men in Serbia apparently fell between 2001 and 2005, partly due to the existence of a relatively high minimum wage level at the time (see Kecmanović, 2012).

In Croatia, the privatisation process began in the early 1990s. The largest and most profitable companies were transferred to a new elite of privileged owners with party connections: 'a narrow elite made up of those who had the capital to buy the most attractive parts of the socially owned assets' (Čučković, 1995, p. 87). Other beneficiaries included managers of socially owned firms who obtained loans from the banks using the future value of the companies' own shares as collateral (Krištofić, 1999). Managers with connections to the ruling party, government officials and politicians found it easier to get loans of this type (Bićanić, 1993). Often, state-controlled banks gave loans to managers to buy out their companies without proper guarantees that the loans would ever be repaid (Čengić, 1996). Many companies that were not sold remained as nationalised or partly nationalised companies under the ownership of the Croatian Privatisation Fund. Other sections of the population that were less favourably placed, such as public sector workers and farmers without privileged access to privatised resources, were effectively losers from the privatisation process. Overall, a determinedly national and clientelistic form of capitalism appears to have become entrenched in Croatia (Cvijanović & Redžepagić, 2011).

In BiH, privatisation began after the end of the war in the late 1990s based upon voucher privatisation, and unlike the privatisation process in Croatia employees were not offered discounts on the purchase of shares in their enterprises. Vouchers could be used to buy shares in enterprises, apartments or could be invested in Privatisation Investment Funds, although the use of vouchers to purchase shares in small companies was limited to 65 per cent of the value of shares, while the remaining 35 per cent of the value had to be paid for with cash. This effectively excluded poor people from the proceedings and many individuals sold their vouchers on the open market to raise much needed cash. This enabled the Bosnian 'tycoons' to accumulate vouchers at knockdown prices. In the fractured Bosnian state this phenomenon inevitably took on an ethnic dimension, with vouchers being accumulated in the hands of tycoons based in the different ethnic communities. In RS the state gained a stake in the enterprises through the 30 per cent of the shares that had been transferred to state funds. In FBiH company managers gained a strong influence in many of the privatised enterprises.

A privatisation law was adopted in Serbia in August 1991. The main new shareholders were managers who bought shares at heavily discounted prices, while 'employees were unable to participate in the process because of their total pauperization' (Lazić & Sekelj, 1997). Following many reversals and false starts, a more serious privatisation process began after the democratic opposition came to power in 2000. A new privatisation law enabled the direct sale of socially owned and state owned enterprises. Between 2001 and 2003 about 1,000 mostly medium-sized enterprises were sold in auctions, and 25 large enterprises sold by international tenders. By 2005 some 1,631 enterprises had been privatised. Following the assignation of Serbian Prime Minister Djindjić in 2004, the pace of privatisation slowed down. The second wave of privatisation appears to have been manipulated by the Serbian tycoons who had gained the strongest positions during the privatisation processes in the 1990s. An attempt of PM Djindjic to impose an 'extra profits' tax was rejected by the Serbian Parliament. There remains a 'widespread suspicion that there is a strong bond between wealthy businessmen and the political leadership which fosters corruption and shapes legislation' (Vujačić & Petrović-Vujačić, 2011).

The difficulty with this model of privatisation based upon sale of enterprises to new tycoons and incumbent managers has been that the productivity of the productive sector of the economy has suffered, leading to the problems of low competitiveness analysed previously in this chapter. Unlike in the Central European countries where a 'comprador elite' managed to attract large inflows of foreign investment (Drahokoupil, 2008), the main forms of foreign investment that entered the three countries and the rest of former Yugoslavia have been in the financial sector, and the resulting take-over of the banks by foreign owned banks from Italy, Austria, Greece and Germany has led to the rapid 'financialisation' of the economies. This has contributed to a further widening of income inequalities as it has enabled the wealthiest members of society to borrow money that has been used to acquire rent-yielding assets while the poorer members of society have been burdened with high-interest loans taken out for consumption purposes (Bateman, Sinković & Škare, 2012). Not surprisingly, these borrowers often find it difficulty to repay as evidenced by the sharp increase in the share of non-performing loans. Financialisation has therefore further contributed to the entrenchment of existing elites, to the widening of income inequality and hence placed obstacles in the way of reconciliation and the deepening of regional cooperation.

Possibly, if the 'comprador' elite had been more influential in these three countries and the influx of productive foreign direct investment in the manufacturing sector consequently larger, the political pressure from interest groups in favour of greater regional cooperation and reconciliation might have been stronger. As it turned out, each country (and entity in the BiH case) continues to be governed by elites that adhere to national development strategies that are best served by continuing to pursue essentially ethnic concepts of the nation state.

Even though Croatia has entered the EU, and Serbia is an EU candidate, the countries still experience difficulties in attracting foreign investment. Their institutional and regulatory arrangements remain unattractive to foreign investors and geared more towards the preservation of the interests of domestic business owners (the 'tycoons') who often have a near-monopoly position on some important protected domestic markets. The existence of barriers to the entry of new businesses into these cosy markets is evidenced in the World Bank 'Doing Business' survey which ranks countries according to their 'ease of doing business'. Out of 189 countries around the world, BiH is ranked as 131, Croatia, 89 and Serbia, 93.

5. Conclusions

This chapter has shown that each of the three countries has experienced a dramatic reversal of economic fortunes over the last six years as a consequence of the global economic crisis and the subsequent crisis of the Eurozone. These external shocks have had substantially adverse impacts on trade, foreign direct investment and remittances, and have led to a collapse in business investment and a dramatic increase in unemployment and poverty. In a context of excessive income inequality between a small elite and the great majority of the people, this turnaround in economic fortunes has provided an unfavourable context for post-war reconciliation.

The chapter has further argued that domestic economic policies throughout the period of transition have exacerbated the difficulties in overcoming the ethnic tensions inspired by war and conflict. Indeed, as has been eloquently argued by others, the ethnic conflicts were arguably stirred up in the first place by the regional elites in the former Yugoslav republics who were unwilling to renounce their privileged positions in favour of a transition to a liberal democratic competitive market model of capitalism. Instead, the economic and political model that was followed in the three countries, influenced also by the circumstances of war and conflict, have led to an illiberal transformation in which the dominant elites sought to preserve their privileged positions through privatisation processes that largely transferred social property to the same narrow elite.

The new elites, often former managers or politically connected business people in the three countries, have been mainly domestically orientated, and have lacked the comprador character of elite formations in central Europe that organised the large-scale inflow of foreign direct investment into the productive sectors of those economies. This domestically oriented economic model remains largely in place today, and underlies the poor export performance of the three economies, which are weighed down by uncompetitive and quasi-monopolistic structures that inhibit the entry of new businesses and are rather unfriendly to foreign investors. The relatively small inflow of foreign direct investment has mainly entered the financial sector, contributing to a rapid process of 'financialisation', which has mainly benefited the existing elites and led many households and small businesses into debt during the recession, resulting in a rapid rise in non-performing loans and increasing numbers of businesses being unable to pay their employees' wages or social contributions.

In each of the three countries, national elites continue to mobilise politics along ethnic lines in order to maintain their privileged positions, most notably in the entities of BiH, but also in Croatia and Serbia despite some high level gestures towards political reconciliation. While there is no automatic and linear relationship between the business cycle and the motivations for and movement towards reconciliation, it seems likely that such a depressed economic environment would be unfavourable to reconciliation. When we also consider that the narrow elite that dominates the three countries has used ethnic mobilisation in the past to secure their positions, it seems likely that similar behaviour can be expected today, and that genuine structural reforms that would move the economies to a more competitive model of development will be resisted under the banner of national self-interest and ethnic mobilisation.

The way forward to break this unfavourable cycle might be a more rapid progress to EU accession to integrate the economies of BiH and Serbia more closely into that of Croatia and the rest of Europe, and to open both the elites and the rest of the populations to a more international competitive and open perspective on economic, social and political opportunities. This may also be the way to eventual reconciliation between the people of the region. However, the smooth progress of EU integration of BiH and Serbia and the resolution of the continuing economic crisis in Croatia is not a foregone conclusion, as the sections of the elites that are in favour of liberal reforms are relatively weak. Other international actors including Russia, China and United Arab Emirates provide alternative visions of economic governance that may seem more attractive to those sections of the elites that are in favour of avoiding reform and of the continued entrenchment of existing privileges. Which way the countries move in the future will be critical for progress in normalising their relations and processes of reconciliation, both within themselves and among each other.

The international community and especially the EU could assist the process of reconciliation by providing a more attractive perspective of future integration. This is especially important at the moment, as the counter-attractions of new international actors seem to be on the rise. The process of integration should be speeded up, a process not helped by the recent announcement that the role of the EU's Commissioner for Enlargement is to be downgraded to that of Commissioner for Neighbourhood Policy and Enlargement Negotiations. The prospects for admittance of new EU member states now seem many years away. In the meantime, however, there is much the EU can do to encourage the pro-reform forces in BiH and Serbia. It would be especially important to encourage a progressive perspective among young people by stepping up support for their intra-European mobility (including to and from Croatia) through study programmes and involvement in international events. Improving their employability through more inclusive and better resourced vocational education linked to on-the-job training should also be a key priority. The EU has much to offer young people in its newest member state and in the aspiring candidates and potential candidate countries. It should take its foot off the break and demonstrate that reconciliation is not simply a Balkan issue but should tie all European countries together in a time of profound uncertainty and change.

References

Agency for Statistics of Bosnia-Herzegovina (2014). Labour Force Survey, Sarajevo. Retrieved from www.bhas.ba/saopstenja/LFS%202014%20Preliminarni%20bos.pdf.

Andor, L. (2014). *Opportunities and challenges in the Croatian labour market.* Speech to Croatian Chamber of Commerce, Brussels, July. Retrieved from http://europa.eu/rapid/press-release_SPEECH-14-542_en.htm.

Arnautović, M. (2013). Bosnian 'baby-lution' gains force as protesters unite across ethnic lines. *Radio Free Europe & Radio Liberty*, June 12. Retrieved from www.rferl.org/content/bosnia-baby-lution-jmb-iinfants-documentation/25014979.html.

Bartlett, W. (2008). 'Regional integration and free-trade agreements in the Balkans: opportunities, obstacles and policy issues'. *Economic Change and Restructuring*, 42, 25–46.
Bartlett, W. (2013). *Gap Analysis in the Area of Social Protection and Inclusion Policies in Bosnia-Herzegovina*. Sarajevo: UNICEF.
Bartlett, W. & Prica, I. (2013). 'The deepening crisis in the European super-periphery'. *Journal of Balkan and Near Eastern Studies*, 15(4), 367–382.
Bateman, M., Sinković, D. & Škare, M. (2012). 'The contribution of the microfinance model to Bosnia's post-war reconstruction and development: how to destroy an economy and society without really trying'. *ÖFSE Working Paper 36*, Vienna: Österreichische Forschungsstiftung für Internationale Entwicklung.
Bićanić, I. (1993). 'Privatization in Croatia'. *East European Politics and Societies* 7(3), 422–439.
Bjelić, P. & Mitrović, R. D. (2012). 'The effects of competing trade regimes on bilateral trade flows: case of Serbia'. *Proceedings of Rijeka Faculty of Economics*, 30(2), 267–294.
Čengić, D. (1996). 'Privatization and management buy-out: The example of Croatia'. *Communist Economies and Economic Transformation*, 8(4), 549–563.
Croatian National Bank (2014). Bulletin No. 205. Zagreb, July.
Čučković, N. (1995). 'The privatisation process and its consequences for the distribution of welfare: the case of Croatia'. *Moct-Most* 5, 75–90.
Cvijanović, V. & Redžepagić, D. (2011). 'From political capitalism to clientelistic capitalism: the case of Croatia'. *Proceedings of Rijeka Faculty of Economics: Journal of Economics and Business*, 29(2), 355–372.
Drahokoupil, J. (2008). 'The rise of the comprador service sector: the politics of state transformation in Central and Eastern Europe'. *Polish Sociological Review*, 2(162), 175–189.
European Commission (2013a). *Statement on the negotiations with Bosnia-Herzegovina on the bilateral trade regime after the accession of Croatia to the EU* [MEMO-12-736_EN, 1]. Brussels. Retrieved from http://europa.eu/rapid/press-release_MEMO-13-736_en.htm.
European Commission (2013b). Progress Report on Bosnia-Herzegovina. Brussels.
Flakierski, H. (1989). *The Economic System and Income Distribution in Yugoslavia*. New York: M. E. Sharpe Inc.
Gagnon, V. P. (2004). *The Myth of Ethnic War: Serbia and Croatia in the 1990s*. Ithaca, NY: Cornell University Press.
Handjiski, B. & Šestović, L. (2011). *Barriers to Trade in Services in the CEFTA Region*. Washington DC: World Bank.
Hoffman, S., Bićanić, I. & Vukoja, O. (2012). 'Wage inequality and the labour market impact of economic transformation: Croatia, 1970–2008'. *Economic Systems*, 36(2), 206–217.
IMF (2014). Stand-by Arrangement with Bosnia-Herzegovina. Washington DC, February.
Judah, T. (2009). 'Yugoslavia is dead: long live the Yugosphere'. *LSEE Paper No. 1*, London: LSE.
Kecmanović, M. (2012). 'Men's wage inequality in Serbia's transition'. *Economic Systems*, 36(1), 65–86.
Krištofić, B. (1999). 'Who is running Croatian enterprises?' *Post-Communist Economics*, 11(4), 503–517.
National Bank of Serbia (2014). *Analysis of the Republic of Serbia's Debt*. Belgrade, March.
Petreski, M. (2011). No country was ever ruined by trade: South East European trade analysis [Working Paper]. Retrieved from. www.freit.org/WorkingPapers/Papers/TradePolicyRegional/FREIT371.pdf.

Radosavljević (2013). Thousands of Vukovar Croats rally against Serb Cyrillic signs. *Reuters*, February 2. Retrieved from http://uk.reuters.com/article/2013/02/02/uk-croatia-protest-idUKBRE91109E20130202.

Radosavljević & Vasović (2014). All work and no pay for thousands in the Balkans. *Reuters, July 10*. Retrieved from www.reuters.com/article/2014/07/10/us-balkans-salaries-specialreport-idUSKBN0FF0UB20140710.

Statistical Office of the Republic of Serbia (2014). Labour Force Survey, Statistical Release No. 172, 28/07/2014. Retrieved from http://pod2.stat.gov.rs/ObjavljenePublikacije/G2014/pdfE/G20141217.pdf.

Vujačić, I. & Petrović-Vujačić, J. (2011). 'Privatization in Serbia – results and institutional failures'. *Economic Annals*, LVI(191), 89–105.

All links mentioned in this chapter were accessed on April 15, 2015.

Conclusion

Chapter 11

Dealing with past violence as a long-term challenge – lessons from the Balkans

Martina Fischer

1. Lessons regarding the importance and limits of legal accountability mechanisms

Transitional justice processes started quite early in the Western Balkans compared with many other war-torn societies, due to the establishment of the International Criminal Tribunal for the former Yugoslavia (ICTY), which was created by the United Nations in 1993 in response to the ongoing war in Bosnia-Herzegovina (BiH). The ICTY has taken the lead in prosecuting war crimes and crimes against humanity committed in the Western Balkans during the 1990s. In all, the Tribunal has indicted 161 persons for serious violations of international humanitarian law. At the time of writing, proceedings have concluded for 147, 80 have been sentenced, and proceedings for 14 accused are still ongoing.[1]

At a time when local institutions were unwilling or unable to investigate war-related crimes to an adequate extent, the ICTY has made an important contribution to establishing legal accountability and fact finding. At the same time, the legitimacy of the International Tribunal has always been controversial in the region itself, as opinion polls and scholarly analyses have shown (see Subotić, 2009; Subotić, 2011; Mertus, 2007, and the chapters by Banjeglav and Hoffmann in this volume).

The legitimacy of the International Tribunal was particularly questioned by relevant political leaders for more than a decade. Although the governments of Bosnia-Herzegovina, Croatia and the Federal Republic of Yugoslavia[2] committed to peaceful settlement of conflicts and cooperation on issues related to transitional justice by signing the Dayton Peace Accords (DPA) in 1995, it took more than a decade for all of these states to fully cooperate with the Hague Tribunal (in particular the governments of Croatia and Serbia proved less than cooperative in the post-war era), and it took nearly two decades until all war criminal suspects were delivered to The Hague.

1 See www.icty.org/sections/TheCases/KeyFiguresoftheCases#, accessed 14 April 2015.
2 At that time consisting of Serbia and Montenegro.

It has been argued that the ICTY has countered the trend towards silencing or denying atrocities (Orentlicher, 2008; Orentlicher, 2010) and that its decisions have enhanced public discussions on war events. Other scholars have argued that the Tribunal's sentences have also fuelled nationalistic discourses about the war (Allcock, 2009) and fostered hostility in some local communities, for instance in Bosnia-Herzegovina (Meernik, 2005). While the ICTY's contribution to accountability is widely acknowledged in the academic literature, the question of whether its work has contributed to the 'restoration of peace and reconciliation', as stated in UN Resolution 1534 and promoted by high-ranking representatives and the Tribunal's own reports,[3] is still the subject of controversy.[4]

Some communities in Serbia and in the Republika Srpska in BiH have regarded the ICTY, from the outset, as being biased (Mertus, 2007), and as a distant mechanism imposed from outside (McMahon & Forsythe, 2008). Similar reactions were reported from Croatia (see Tamara Banjeglav's contribution in this volume). A huge acceptance deficit was revealed by opinion polls (Mertus, 2007) and was due to distorted media reporting and problems of communication between the ICTY and its local publics. The lack of formal procedural law for victims and victims' organisations and the practice of plea bargaining also came in for heavy criticism and damaged the Tribunal's reputation, as outlined by Klaus Hoffmann in this volume. This prompted the ICTY to set up regional offices in Sarajevo, Belgrade and Zagreb, and to start an ambitious public relations campaign (a so-called 'outreach strategy') to maintain closer contact to the media and civil society. However, although the ICTY was created to establish individual guilt and responsibility for war-related crimes, it has been unable to communicate these guiding principles of its work in an appropriate manner to the people in the region. Instead, verdicts have all too often been perceived as sentences that aim to establish collective guilt, holding entire nations or countries responsible rather than individuals.

An important lesson from the post-war period in the Balkans is therefore that *courts need effective communication strategies from the very beginning, in order to connect with the general public and to guarantee that their principles and decisions are broadly understood.* Such strategies cannot completely eliminate but do at least reduce the risk of facts and verdicts being distorted by media and political groups that are interested in divide, and maintaining the conflict, rather than bridge building. This is also another important challenge for national transitional justice strategies and domestic courts mandated to investigate and prosecute war crimes. Creating functioning legal mechanisms for detention, prosecution and defence that guarantee a fair trial for

3 See, for instance, the joint statement of the President of the ICTY (Antonio Cassese) and the Prosecutor from November 1995, online at www.icty.org/sid/7220, and the first Annual Report, online at www.icty.org/x/file/About/Reports%20and%20Publications/AnnualReports/annual_report_1994_en.pdf (accessed 31 March 2015).

4 For an analysis of the ICTY's acceptance and impact on societies in the region, see Allcock, 2009; Arzt, 2006; Mertus, 2007; Fletcher & Weinstein, 2004; McMahon & Forsythe, 2008; Sajkas, 2007; Nettelfield, 2010.

the accused is an important challenge. At the same time, it is necessary to train judges and prosecutors in how to communicate effectively with the media and systematically involve investigative journalists and media experts right from the start.

Criticism of the work of the ICTY was also expressed by human rights activists. The local human rights community had initially both called for and welcomed the establishment of an international mechanism for war crimes prosecution. However, their criticism referred to some of the Tribunal's legal practices associated with the Anglo-American legal tradition, and in particular the practice of cross-examination, which proved to be very demanding for the witnesses (see Klaus Hoffmann's chapter in this volume). Furthermore, they pointed to deficits regarding the protection of witnesses and victims, and – more generally – also regarding the weak status of the victims, who could only be heard as witnesses. However, practitioners who voiced criticism of the ICTY also said there was no other alternative, as domestic courts were not in a position to serve accountability. They were convinced that without this international mechanism, the human rights movement in the Western Balkans would have been worse off. Some of them also argue that the ICTY had a de-escalating effect since it could approach suspects from all sides equally, irrespective of their nationality, and this was only possible because the judges and prosecutors came from countries not involved in the war (Petrović-Ziemer, 2013b, p. 50).

As the ICTY for a long period served as the only comprehensive cross-border mechanism for fact finding and prosecution of war crimes, it became an important point of reference for human rights and victims' groups and even for peace activists (Petrovic-Ziemer, 2013b, p. 50). Even critical activists agree that the International Tribunal was of great assistance in uncovering mass graves and finding missing persons. It is now widely acknowledged that the ICTY has made an important contribution to establishing facts about the massacres and atrocities, and that the database compiled in more than two decades of its existence is of indispensable value in informing future generations about the crimes committed in the 1990s.[5] It is also widely acknowledged that the ICTY, together with the OSCE and EU, has substantially contributed to the advancement of domestic institutions for war crimes prosecution and training of judiciaries, which will continue to take on a central role and responsibility with regard to fact-finding and accountability in the future as the mandate of the ICTY comes to an end and a substantial number of cases have yet to be concluded (see Klaus Hoffmann's and Martina Fischer's contributions in this volume).

Looking back on experience in the Western Balkans, another important finding *is that the work of the legal institutions responsible for war crimes prosecution* (both the

5 This was revealed by the research project 'Dealing with the Past and Peacebuilding in the Western Balkans', based on 150 interviews conducted among Transitional Justice experts in 28 municipalities in Serbia, Croatia and BiH in 2010–2012 with support from the German Foundation for Peace Research (Fischer & Petrovic-Ziemer, 2013).

ICTY and the domestic courts) is, on the one hand, very much *dependent on the cooperation with state authorities, in particular a functioning police* to provide access to archives containing information about past events and guarantee the safety of victims and witnesses. On the other hand, the effectiveness of the legal institutions also very much depends on good cooperation with civil society actors (CSOs), especially groups and individuals engaged in war crimes reporting and trial monitoring, providing psychological support for victims and witnesses, and assisting with documentation and contacts for the tracing of missing persons (Petrović-Ziemer, 2013b). Furthermore, when tracing the missing and establishing the details of war crimes and crimes against humanity, legal and fact-finding institutions are very much dependent on cooperation with local authorities and CSOs (i.e. associations of relatives of the missing), and observations of citizens.

1.1 The limitations of legal instrument and retributive approaches to justice

In sum, four major limitations of legal approaches can be outlined:

(1) The ICTY had great difficulty in apprehending several of the most notorious war crimes suspects (including Ratko Mladić and Radovan Karadžić). In the first years after the war, international forces were not equipped with a mandate to detect and arrest fugitives. Furthermore, international law does not contain any general and binding rules for this process. As a consequence, several prominent war crimes suspects indicted by the ICTY remained at large for a very long time, being celebrated as heroes by nationalist politicians in several areas.

(2) Another problem and limitation of the legal (retributive) approach is that in almost every case, only the military commanders have been brought to justice. Recent decisions by international tribunals have shown that it is almost impossible to hold political actors to account for mass crimes (as outlined by Klaus Hoffmann in this volume); uncovering politicians' active involvement in mass crimes and detecting substantive evidence of their personal guilt seem to be the most difficult tasks and challenges.

(3) Two decades after the 1990s wars, only a small number of war crimes cases have been concluded (mostly related to mass crimes), while an estimated 3,000 minor cases are pending and need to be investigated by the courts in the region (as outlined by Klaus Hoffmann in this volume). However, it is very unlikely that all of these cases can be dealt with and concluded during the lifetime of the accused and the witnesses.

(4) Unfortunately, the work of the courts has not been complemented by programmes that provide compensation for the victims. This deficit was also mentioned by the former President of the ICTY, Patrick Robinson, who in a speech before the UN Security Council in December 2009 suggested

> establishing a 'claims commission'.[6] In his address before the UN General Assembly on 9 October 2009, ICTY President Robinson concluded 'that the international community has forgotten [the victims]. Currently, there is no effective mechanism by which victims can seek compensation for their injuries, despite the fact that their right to such compensation is firmly rooted in international law'.[7] He emphasised that compensating victims of crimes in the former Yugoslavia should complement the Tribunal's efforts, as 'justice is not only about punishing perpetrators but also about restoring dignity to victims by ensuring that they have concrete means to rebuild their lives' (ibid.). He called upon the UN General Assembly and the UN Member States to support the creation of a trust fund, arguing that: 'The Tribunal cannot, through the rendering of its Judgements alone, bring peace and reconciliation to the region. Other remedies must complement the criminal trials if lasting peace is to be achieved, and one such remedy should be adequate assistance to the victims for their suffering'.[8]

The limitations of retributive justice, mentioned above, were the reason why many Transitional Justice protagonists in the Western Balkans called for additional approaches for dealing with the past. In particular, civil society actors, with support from several political leaders, are convinced that, in addition to criminal justice, other mechanisms are necessary to continue fact-finding and to address the victims' needs for acknowledgement.

The campaign for a Regional Commission for Truth-seeking and Truth-telling about War Crimes in the Former Yugoslavia (REKOM)[9] evolved as a reaction to some of the shortcomings mentioned above. It is concerned with giving a voice to the victims and aims to enhance debate on how symbolic or material compensation could be provided. The protagonists of this campaign – numerous CSOs and individuals from various ex-Yugoslav countries – have managed to set up effective networking arrangements and partnerships across different levels of action (international/regional/local, governmental/non-governmental), as outlined by Jelena Subotić and Martina Fischer in this volume.

It is important to mention that the campaign for RECOM, which evolved in the Western Balkans over the past decade, does not discuss a truth commission as an alternative but a complementary mechanism that should be an add-on to the work of the courts. However, it remains to be seen whether the idea will gain the necessary political support and generate a 'critical mass' of political institutions and societal actors in the region who push for implementation of a regional truth

6 See www.icty.org/sid/10280 (accessed 31 March 2015).
7 See www.icty.org/sid/10244 (accessed 31 March 2015.
8 See www.icty.org/sid/10850 (accessed 31 March 2015).
9 See www.zarekom.org/The-Coalition-for-RECOM.en.html (accessed 31 March 2015); for a detailed analysis of the dynamics of the REKOM process, see Petrovic-Ziemer, 2013b; Fischer, 2013a.

commission. International protagonists who decided to fund the campaign hope that this will happen, but at the same time argue that even if it does not gain the necessary support from the governments and state institutions, the campaign as such was important in raising awareness of issues related to the past (Fischer, 2013b, p. 76). However, the campaign for the establishment of a cross-border mechanism for fact-finding and documentation is historically unprecedented and therefore deserves special attention from a scholarly perspective as well.

Three more lessons can be learned from the Western Balkans with regard to the outreach and impact of legal instruments dealing with war crimes committed in the Western Balkans:

- Even if criminal justice (prosecution of war related crimes) is in place at a very early stage (as was the case in the Balkans), this does not necessarily add to a broader societal dialogue on the past that would lead to questioning of selective forms of remembrance. War crimes courts (either internationally or domestically driven) have very limited, if any, direct reconciliatory effects on war-affected societies in the short term. This does not mean that they cannot have indirect reconciliatory effects in the long term, as their data will help to inform future generations that may have a stronger desire for reconciliation, as outlined by Hazan (2007) with reference to the effects of the Nuremberg trials in Germany after the Second World War.
- Although tribunals give victims the chance to speak out, the space that courts can provide for acknowledgement of their suffering is extremely limited. In such a setting, speaking out against perpetrators can also create additional burdens and harmful situations for the victims. Courtrooms are not the places where victims can tell their story in a protected setting, and where acknowledgement or 'healing' of trauma and grievances (Hamber, 2003; Hamber, 2009) takes place. In order to minimise the negative effects for those who testify, institutions for the prosecution of war crimes need to take particular care of the victims (and witnesses), and prepare them properly so that they know what to expect during the trial, and what they can expect from the trial (establishing the facts, but no healing and no redress).
- At the same time, tribunals need to guarantee the physical safety of those who decide to testify. This can only be done in close cooperation with state authorities, based on institutional reforms that establish the rule of law and a functioning police. Programmes for the protection of victims and witnesses before, during, and after the trials are crucial for effective war crimes prosecution. At the same time, this is a highly complicated and very cost-intensive endeavour. In a setting where the violence had regional scope, and crimes have to be tried in different countries (as was the case in the Western Balkans), cross-border cooperation between courts and police is a must and a precondition for organising the necessary degree of safety. However, if such protection is not guaranteed, if victims and witnesses risk their lives and health and put their families in danger, they will shy away from testifying.

1.2 The need for victim-centred approaches and advancing gender justice

In the transitional justice debate, scholars and practitioners have step by step widened the agenda and highlighted the need for victim-centred approaches (Lekha Sriram et al., 2013, p. 4). The need for strengthening the victims' rights had already been emphasised in the UN context by Luis Joinet in his Report on the administration of justice and the question of impunity to the UN Sub-Commission in 1997, subsequently revised by Diane Orentlicher in 2005 at the request of the UN Human Rights Commission.[10] The so-called 'Joinet&Orentlicher' principles presented the main arguments against impunity and pointed to state responsibility and to the right of redress for individual victims of grave human rights violations. Experience from the Balkans has shown that dealing with the past processes have to take the victims' concerns into consideration to a far greater extent and put more emphasis on gender aspects. Several advancements in international law and legal practice have been reported in this respect. One major success is that *gender perspectives* have been given more prominence, thanks to feminist scholars and practitioners, in particular women's organisations from the ex-Yugoslav region. Rape and sexual violence have now been recognised as war crimes under international law. Furthermore, other international tribunals (i.e. the Tribunal for Lebanon) and the International Criminal Court have integrated some of the lessons learned from the problematic practices at the ICTY and upgraded victims' rights, by opening up the possibility for victims' organisations to play an active role in war crimes trials, which was not the case in the ICTY's procedures (Hoffmann, 2011, p. 85).

International actors and local CSOs alike appreciate that the ICTY has classified rape as a war crime, and that it established new standards and reformed court procedures with regard to sexual violence and gender-specific war crimes. It is reported that these norms have also informed the practice of some of the domestic war crimes chambers in the Balkans (Petrovic-Ziemer, 2013a). However, international observers see a need for the courts in the region to be much more sensitive to the special experiences of victims and witnesses of such crimes (Fischer, 2013b, p. 86). Furthermore, they need to complement the retributive practice with restorative approaches. Although NGO campaigns helped to ensure that some compensation for raped women has been fixed in legal regulations, compensation is still outstanding in many cases (ibid.). Therefore gender justice will remain a particular challenge for the implementation of transitional justice strategies at both a regional and a national level (see the chapter by Olivera Simić in this volume). In order to advance in this field, it is also necessary to overcome policies that entrench unequal treatment of civilian and military war victims.

10 The report was drafted by Joinet in 1997 at the request of the UN. Sub Committee for the Prevention of Discrimination and Protection of Minorities: see E/CN.4/Sub.2/1997/20/Rev/1. For the update by Orentlicher see E/CN.4/2005/102/Add.1.

We can summarise the lessons regarding the legal instruments applied in transitional justice processes in the Balkans as follows.

The transitional justice strategies developed so far in the countries that form the 'Dayton triangle' still very much rely on retributive justice (investigation of war crimes and punishment of the perpetrators) as the main instrument for dealing with the past. None of the countries has developed a holistic approach that goes beyond war crimes prosecution and is based on a broader understanding of justice aimed at transforming negative social relationships into positive relationships. Punishing war criminals and establishing the facts about war-related crimes are necessary but legal approaches alone cannot pave the way to healing and coming to terms with the legacies of the past. Advancements will also largely depend on the political will for innovative, restorative approaches. Gestures of recognition and healing processes are still outstanding in the region. Material compensation for victims remains a largely unaddressed challenge; the same applies to symbolic forms of reparation. In the region of the former Yugoslavia, many places where war-related crimes and atrocities took place are still unmarked. More comprehensive concepts and approaches to justice and initiatives for truth recovery (narrative, dialogical, and societal forms) are needed to make more progress in terms of healing, trust and relationship-building.

2. Truth recovery as a long-term endeavour: the need to accept diverse interpretations of the past

Transitional justice experts have argued that processes of dealing with the past should address different dimensions of truth recovery (Boraine, 2006): forensic truth (evidence and facts about human rights violations and missing persons); narrative truth (story-telling by victims and perpetrators and communicating personal truths to a wider public); dialogical truth (by interaction, discussion and debate on past events); and healing/restorative truth (documentation of facts and memorisation to give dignity to the victims and survivors). But it would be too much to expect that all of these challenges could be addressed at the same time, and immediately after war.

As experience in the Western Balkans shows, establishing forensic truth takes decades in war-affected areas. Twenty years after the end of the war, families are still searching for missing relatives. In BiH in particular, tracing and identification of victims from the war is still an important issue frequently reported in the news, especially from spring until late autumn, when much of the exhumation work is done. It was only in 2013 that one of the largest mass graves was discovered in this country. In such a context, given that factual truth has not fully been established, it is hard to believe that a shared truth – in the sense of a common interpretation of the past – can be achieved among those who were involved on different sides in the war. Even if so-called 'undeniable facts' are uncovered by the courts and various fact-finding commissions, the interpretation of such facts may still be seen as controversial in a war-torn society for decades to come. The question is whether a 'common memory' (Boraine, 2006)[11] of past events can be achieved at a later stage. From the Balkans, we can learn that societies that have gone through large-scale ethnopolitical violence have to accept that many different interpretations of the past exist (as Jelena Subotić has outlined in this volume) and that this situation can last for more than one or two decades, maybe even for more than one generation.

Transitional justice experts and conflict transformation theorists have argued that there is a need to take into account that contrasting interpretations of history are likely to be expressed in war-torn societies. Memory politics (e.g. commemoration efforts or initiatives for schoolbook revision)[12] thus face the question: which particular version should be taken as the 'official' truth? And another question arises: does the search for a generally agreed and acceptable version of history actually lead to reconciliation? Several authors have expressed doubt (Brounéus, 2008; Gibson, 2006) or see no evidence to either confirm or deny this relationship (Alidu et al., 2009). Sceptical scholars argue that selective forms of remembrance cannot be challenged by a simple call for a 'shared truth' as long as many different and competing truths exist. In certain contexts and stages it may be more important to encourage people and convince them that they should accept the existence of contrasting narratives and to enhance understanding of the other's views. However, certain questions remain unanswered, namely how far such insight can go, whether it can run alongside acceptance of facts, and create a deeper understanding ('empathy') of the suffering of the 'others', and to what extent attempts to confront people with different truths may be an excessive demand.

The most drastic examples of how competing views of history impact on a war-torn society are discussed by Briony Jones and Jelena Subotić in this volume. The fact that, two decades after the war, the school system in some provinces of BiH continues to educate children separately is alarming, perhaps indicating that there are grounds for pessimism about the prospects of reconciliation. Many would argue that there is a risk that such schools perpetuate ethnopolitical divides. However, this example shows the complexity of the problems related to identity constructs and the ongoing fears faced by multi-ethnic societies after experiencing large-scale violence. One important lesson from the Balkans is that in a setting where the question of who was victim and who was perpetrator is so heavily contested, and where identities of defence (Bašić, 2004; Bougarel, 2007; Kuljič, 2010), and strong notions of victimhood (Enns, 2004; 2012; Franović, 2008; Nikolić-Ristanović, 2000; Jalušić, 2004) continue to dominate the public and

11 Alex Boraine (a former member of the South African TRC and founder of the International Center for Transitional Justice) is convinced that divided societies need to achieve 'at least a measure of reconciliation' by creating a 'common memory that can be acknowledged by those who created and implemented an unjust system, those who fought against it, and the many more who were in the middle and claimed not to know what was happening in their country' (Boraine, 2006, p. 22).

12 See Dimou, 2009; see also, as an example, the history textbooks and publications provided by the Joint History Project at the Center for Democracy and Reconciliation in Southeast Europe www.cdsee.org/jhp/download_eng.html (accessed August 24, 2015).

political discourse, establishing a 'shared truth' (as a consensus on a set of undeniable facts) can only be a long-term endeavour and must be left to the next generations.

3. Reconciliation as a long-term project for generations

Scholars and practitioners alike agree that reconciliation must be seen as a long-term process (rather than a state or outcome) that takes generations rather than decades. This does not mean that reconciliation initiatives cannot start as early as possible. Even during and immediately after the end of the 1990s wars in the Balkans, civil society actors, including several women's organisations, launched initiatives for bridge-building across the divides (Large, 1997) which were important steps in maintaining social bonds on which civil society actors could build in the following post-war period. However, on the political level of reconciliation, progress has been extremely slow so far and seems to marked by some recent backlashes.

Indeed, several chapters in this volume show that today, 20 years after the end of the wars of the 1990s, important obstacles to reconciliation continue to exist in the Balkans, stemming from psychological and historical reasons (see the chapters by Jelena Subotić and Vesna Nikolić-Ristanović & Sanja Ćopić in this volume), and in some cases perpetuated by the legal and political system and identity constructs (see the chapter by Miodrag Živanović). Furthermore, economic relations have just reflected the current divisions and not been able to change the overall picture; after all, the desolate economic situation worsens the prospects for reconciliation (see Will Bartlett's chapter in this volume).

However, when discussing the prospects for reconciliation, it is important to follow a pragmatic understanding that does not overload people in war-affected societies with excessively ambitious expectations. A research project 'Dealing with the Past and Peacebuilding in the Western Balkans',[13] conducted at the Berghof Foundation, revealed that transitional justice protagonists in the region are ambivalent towards this term, which was mainly introduced by international actors in their discourses (Fischer & Petrović-Ziemer, 2013). Some of the local practitioners we interviewed were reluctant to use the term and explained that they preferred to use 'relationship-building', 'bridge-building', 'trust-building' or 'co-existence' in their daily work in local communities or cross-border encounters. But several local practitioners also adopted the concept of reconciliation, arguing that the societies in the region somehow need to come to terms with their past and 'reconcile', as achieving 'co-existence' alone would not be sufficient. Those who used the term 'reconciliation' explained that reconciliation is needed both within the societies of the three countries and among the different societies across the borders. However, they use the term in a fairly pragmatic sense. We met very few

13 The field research was conducted from 2010–2012 in BiH, Croatia and Serbia; for details see fn 5.

activists who would support a moral notion that links forgiveness to the concept of reconciliation (as suggested by the Christian understanding).

As outlined in the previous sections, to be effective, transitional justice processes need support from both state administrations and civil society actors. The same applies to the long-term process of reconciliation. The need for the orchestration of 'top-down' and 'bottom-up' processes has been emphasised in the academic literature on peacebuilding and conflict transformation. Bloomfield argues that structural (top-down) and cultural (bottom-up) forms of reconciliation have to be seen as complementary and mutually supportive (Bloomfield, 1997; 2006). Many authors are convinced that civil society actors have a crucial role to play in this context (Assefa, 2005; Kritz, 2009; Kriesberg, 2007a; 2007b; Lederach, 1997; Simić & Volčić, 2013; Fischer, 2007).

Developments in the Western Balkans have shown that civil society is a highly complex and ambivalent system with both constructive and destructive potential. Fixing or reducing the concept to 'NGOs' or explaining it solely in terms of a normative connotation would fail. While initiatives by peace activists, women's groups and the human rights community have garnered much attention, the potential of victims' association and war veterans' unions in the field of transitional justice and reconciliation (see Martina Fischer's contribution in this volume) is still largely under-researched. At present, most of the literature regards them primarily as a 'security problem' that has to be managed (McEvoy, 2012). Several authors have suggested widening the analytical view (Dudouet, 2009; Ricigliano, 2005; Conciliation Resources, 2009) and emphasise the need for a sound analysis of the multiple identities that former combatants develop in war-to-peace transition, in order to better understand their action and impact on peace processes. It would be important to invest more capacities in exploring the potential of veterans (and veterans' associations) instead of seeing them primarily as spoilers or problematic actors in conflict transformation and reconciliation.

Initiatives for political reconciliation and symbolic reparations have been rare so far in the Balkans. Public apologies have been made by several high-ranking politicians but with very limited reconciliatory effects as, more often than not, there was an absence of reciprocity (see the chapters by Nikolić-Ristanović & Ćopić and by Fischer in this volume), which is considered to be an indispensable precondition for achieving reconciliation, according to conflict transformation theory. Kriesberg (2007, p. 254) is convinced that reconciliation can only take place if it entails significant complementary reciprocation. If members of one side assert truths that are ignored or denigrated by the other, their assertion is hardly a mark of reconciliation, as the truths need to be shared or at least acknowledged to indicate some degree of reconciliation on that dimension. Expressions of regret or apology and acts of contrition must be recognised and, in a sense, accepted by the other side if reconciliation is to progress. Similarly, terms that only one side deems just and the other regards as unjust do not indicate a significant level of reconciliation on that dimension. Given that relevant issues of transitional justice (acknowledgement, symbolic and material compensation) are still outstanding in the Balkans, and political leaders' willingness to engage in bridge-building has not substantially increased in the past two decades, one might argue that the prospects for political reconciliation are very poor. The question whether gestures of apology are seen as legitimate also depends on the question whether the personality who apologies is seen as sincere and credible. Acts of apology by persons who where formerly actively involved in the war and supporting its underlying nationalist purposes are much harder to accept than gestures by politicians who have been opposing the war. This became obvious in the commemorations of the mass killings in Srebrenica in July 2015. The Prime Minister of Serbia, Aleksandar Vucic who was among the prominent international visitors of Srebrenica was physically attacked during the event that took place at the cemetery of Potocari. He had condemned the mass killings of 1995 as a "monstruos crime" but avoided to call them genocide. Participants of the funeral reminded of previous speeches held by Vucic in the early 1990s, carrying posters with a quote that is still well remembered by many Bosniaks: "For each Serb killed we will kill 100 Muslims".

An ongoing problem is that gestures of apology still tend to be driven by international requirements and expectations rather than being an expression of a broader political will to transform conflicts and relationships. Another problem stems from the fear that symbolic reparations such as apologies might lead to political demands for material reparations. Finally, the variety of notions of victimhood that are widespread both in the political discourse and among societies in the region, affecting the macro and the micro level (structures and institutions, individual and collective identity), form one of the main obstacles to reconciliation.

Finally, the study of developments in the Western Balkans shows that 20 years after Dayton, complex processes of victimisation (Enns, 2007; Enns, 2012; Kiza, 2006; Nikolić-Ristanović, 2000; Nikolić-Ristanović, 2008) continue to dominate the public discourse. Notions of victimhood and patterns of legitimising one's own involvement in war as an unavoidable act of defence are combined with selective cultures of remembrance. Historic myth (Popovic, 2003), political mythmaking related to unification strategies in the newly established post-Yugoslav states, and discourses of victimhood are widespread in all societies in the region (as outlined by Jelena Subotić, Dinka Čorkalo and Dean Ajduković in this volume). Political and media debates on the question of who is the bigger, biggest or sole victim still arouse strong emotions, and only very brave politicians have the courage to call a crime a crime and take political responsibility for crimes committed in the name of their nation. More research needs to be focused on the *analysis of war-related identities*, how they develop over time, and which factors contribute to their transformation. In societies affected by ethnopolitical violence, memories are often selective. Cultures of remembrance established in education, memorials and museums as well as official transitional justice policies mirror this problem. Olivera Simić's contribution in this volume gives an illustrative example of this, by describing the lack of empathy and acknowledgement as far as Serb women from BiH who were raped during the war are considered. Victims' hierarchies and new injustice are likely in such a setting. Furthermore, a danger is that both individual and collective identities remain locked in notions of victimhood, basing their identities mainly on the notion of being a victim, and losing connection with the dynamics of present and future generations.

In situations where political actors still largely shy away from serious attempts at reconciliation, initiatives by civil society actors (peace groups, human rights organisations, women's and youth groups, victims' and veterans' movements) can still create important impetus and help to establish the basis for bridge-building and restoring trust and relationships. Several dialogue fora and oral history projects (Gojković et al., 2003; 2004; 2005; Rill & Franović, 2005) have been set up, involving people from across the borders and from divided local communities. Furthermore, several efforts have been undertaken in the field of education (as outlined by Briony Jones and Jelena Subotić in this volume). The production of alternative textbooks can offer a more nuanced view of history and support the creation of empathy towards different interpretations of past events (Dimou, 2009; Koulouri, 2001; Koulouri, 2002; Šebek, 2014). The problem is that the excellent textbook material produced is still not used very much, or its use is not permitted, in official curricula; it therefore cannot have a major impact on the reality in the classrooms or influence broader social reality. Nevertheless, more of these materials are needed.

The arts, in particular film, theatre, music and literature, also have enormous importance in raising awareness of the past and in healing because they are not only about rational facts and figures; they also appeal to people's emotions (Fischer, 2013; Fischer, 2015). International support for the Sarajevo Film Festival, for example, not only has a cultural but also a political dimension, as film production can help to widen perspectives and facilitate reflection on war-related events. Initiatives such as the multi-religious choir "Pontanima", created by the Franziscan priest Ivo Markovic in Sarajevo after the war, have also given important incentives to create space for creative cooperation accross the ethno-nationalist lines. The question of whether artistic initiatives can have an impact on societal debates very much depends on the more general political conditions. In a context in which politicians are willing to launch official gestures for reconciliation and dealing with the past becomes an element of formal education, cultural events can form an additional approach for addressing painful elements of the past in a way that addresses people's emotions, thus influencing individual and collective perceptions.

4. International support for local and home-grown initiatives

The picture painted by the authors in this volume regarding the prospects of reconciliation in the region is not very promising and more initiatives for bridge-building and trust-building within and among the societies that have been at war with each other will be needed. At the same time, we see that various initiatives have already been taken in the past two decades (mostly based on international support), several of which are ongoing, although bottom-up and top-down activities do not yet converge in a synergetic way. Initiatives both at the society and the political level have not yet been combined in a way which can be described as 'critical yeast' (Lederach, 2005)[14] in terms of providing the basis for a broader process of reconciliation. However, as outlined in this section, such a process will take more than two decades and may need to involve the next and future generations. International support will, at least to a certain degree, still be needed to support progress in this area as well.

An important lesson from the Balkans is that *international actors who decide to support processes of reconciliation and base their peace building programmes on this concept should be aware that very different understandings of reconciliation exist in diverse religious and cultural traditions*. 'Western' understandings of the concept are often framed along the (Christian) notion of 'mercy' and 'forgiveness'. Organisations that use reconciliation as a key term for their activities in post-war settings should be aware that many individuals and groups may have good reasons to reject such an normative approach, and argue that it is solely up to the victims to decide whether they want to forgive or not, and it is not up to outside experts to introduce such an idea. Others may have good reasons to decide that they would not wish to reconcile at all (see Hamber & Kelly, 2004; 2005; Hamber & Wilson, 2002). International actors should therefore follow a pragmatic approach that is free from the notion of forgiveness. Reconciliation, instead, needs to be framed as a process that aims to establish trust and relationships; in other words, a minimum of 'working relations' among previously hostile individuals and groups (Bloomfield, 2008).[15]

The most important contribution that international actors can make to establish more favourite conditions for a process of reconciliation is creating more promising economic prospects and providing incentives for stronger economic relations and integration among the countries previously at war with each other. One way to support this is by accelerating the process of EU integration. Economic development, which must offer young people prospects for the future, is an important

14 While in social sciences, the concept of 'critical mass' has been used to explore how social ideas come to be accepted by society and impact on reality so that social change can be achieved, Lederach (2005) argues that processes of social change do not only depend on a critical number of people who become engaged. According to Lederach, there is a need to explore how small changes lead to exponentially larger changes. Focusing on the quantity of people involved is not enough, so we also have to look at the quality of change and which kind of spaces are needed to sustain change. Involving a small number of people at the right places, drawing on the relevant resources, spaces, networks, and personal connections, is more important than numbers. According to Lederach, the missing ingredient is not the critical mass but the 'critical yeast' (ibid., p. 91).

15 Bloomfield (2003, p. 12) sees reconciliation as an 'over-arching process which includes the search for truth, justice, and forgiveness, healing . . . through which a society moves from a divided past to a shared future', a process of looking at the past in a way that allows people to see it in terms of 'shared suffering and collective responsibility', which may help to restore confidence. He promotes a rather pragmatic understanding and argues that reconciliation is needed 'to underpin democracy by developing the working relationships necessary for its successful implementation' (ibid., p. 11). Bloomfield later specified that reconciliation is a process of 'gradually (re)building relationships between communities alienated by sustained and widespread violence, so that they can over time negotiate the realities and compromises of a new, shared and socio-political reality', a process within which justice, healing, truth-telling and reparations are the component parts (Bloomfield, 2008, p. 265).

precondition for reconciliation, as outlined by Will Bartlett in this volume.[16] It remains to be seen whether the Brdo-Brijuni Process established as a series of annual meetings of the political leaders in the Western Balkans[17] will have an impact at this level. Economic development as such will probably not be an automatic guarantee of trust- and relationship-building but any situation that gives people hope of a better life and recognises the potential of the future generations makes reconciliation more likely to happen.

An important finding from the Western Balkans' experience is that an international long-term commitment is needed to ensure that engagement does not stop once a region is considered 'stabilised'. Post-war regeneration takes time, and in societies or countries emerging from large-scale ethnopolitical violence the transition from a negative to a positive peace (Clark, 2009) takes more than one or two decades. It is obvious that reconciliation can only be enhanced by the war-affected people, political leaders and civil society actors in the region. At the same time, international support for such a long-term process can be helpful, provided that external actors respect local ownership and the dynamics of the process and refrain from imposing blueprints or models of how and when societies have to deal with the past. What works in one setting does not necessarily work in another. Templates should be avoided, since what is helpful in one context may be irrelevant or harmful in another. Researchers unanimously agree that the process of facing the past cannot simply be transferred from one historical or regional situation to another. It must be developed out of each specific context and in accordance with given cultures and societal dynamics. Nevertheless, looking at experiences from different cases and regions can provide important insights, help to systematise complex demands, and prevent peace builders from rushing into action (or actionism) that is based on impatience, unrealistic or overly ambitious expectations.

References

Alidu, S. et al. (2009). '"Truths" and "Re-imaging" in the Reconciliation Process'. *Peace Review*, 21, 2, 136–143.

Assefa, H. (2005). 'Reconciliation. Challenges, Responses and the Role of Civil Society'. In P. van Tongeren et al. (Eds.), *People Building Peace 2. Successful Stories of Civil Society* (pp. 637–645). London: Lynne Rienner.

16 See also Bartlett & Prica, 2012; Gamberale, 2008.

17 The Brdo-Brijuni Process was initiated by the political leaders of Slovenia and Croatia in 2010. It continued in 2013 and 2014 as a process for regional cooperation between the countries in the Western Balkans and particularly the successor states to the former Yugoslavia, aimed at improving mutual understanding and mutual support in preparing to meet the requirements of the EU accession process. The latest meeting was held in Dubrovnik on 15 July 2014, focusing on political relations in the region, continuation of the European Union enlargement policy, key infrastructural projects and energy policy. Germany's Chancellor Angela Merkel participated as a guest. See http://europeanwesternbalkans.com/2014/07/15/annual-meeting-of-the-brdo-brijuni-process-in-dubrovnik-on-15-july-2014/ (accessed 28 March 2015).

Barsalou, J. (2005). *Trauma and Transitional Justice in Divided Societies.* USIP Special Report 135. Washington: United States Institute of Peace.

Bartlett, W. & Prica, I. (2012). *The Variable Impact of the Global Economic Crisis in South East Europe.* London: London School of Economics and Political Science.

Bašić, N. (2004). *Krieg als Abenteuer. Feindbilder und Gewalt aus der Perspektive ex-jugoslawischer Soldaten 1991–1995.* Gießen: Psychosozial-Verlag.

Bloomfield, D. (2008). 'Reconciliation'. In V. Rittberger & M. Fischer (Eds.), *Strategies for Peace. Contributions of International Organisations, States, and Non-State Actors* (pp. 261–269). Opladen-Farmington Hills: Barbara Budrich.

Bloomfield, D. (2006). *On Good Terms. Clarifying Reconciliation.* Berghof Report No. 14. Berlin: Berghof Research Center.

Bloomfield, D. (2003). 'Reconciliation: An Introduction'. In D. Bloomfield et al. (Eds.), *Reconciliation after Violent Conflict. A Handbook* (pp. 10–18). Stockholm: International IDEA Handbook Series.

Boraine, A. (2006). 'Transitional Justice – A Holistic Interpretation'. *Journal of International Affairs*, 60, 1, 17–27.

Bougarel, X. (2007). 'Death and the Nationalist: Martyrdom, War Memory and Veteran Identity among Bosnian Muslims'. In X. Bougarel et al. (Eds.), *The New Bosnian Mosaic. Identities, Memories and Moral Claims in a Post-War Society* (pp. 167–192). Aldershot: Ashgate.

Brounëus, K. (2008). 'Truth-Telling as Talking Cure? Insecurity and Retraumatization in the Rwandan Gacaca Courts'. *Security Dialogue*, 39, 1, 55–76.

Clark, N. (2010). 'Education in Bosnia-Hercegovina: The Case for Root-and-Branch Reform'. *Journal of Human Rights*, 9, 344–362.

Clark, N. (2009). 'From Negative to Positive Peace: The Case of Bosnia-Hercegovina'. *Journal of Human Rights*, 8, 360–384.

Conciliation Resources (2009). *Choosing to Engage: Armed Groups and Peace Processes.* Accord Policy Brief 2009.

Dimou, A. (2009). *Transition and the Politics of History Education in Southeast Europe.* Göttingen: V&R, unipress.

Dudouet, V. (2009). *From War to Politics: Resistance/Liberation Movements in Transition.* Berghof Report No. 17, Berlin: Berghof Conflict Research.

Đurić-Kuzmanović, T. et al. (2008). 'Gendered War, Gendered Peace. Violent Conflicts in the Balkans and their Consequences'. In D. Pankhurst (Ed.), *Gendered Peace. Women's Struggles for Post-War Justice and Reconciliation* (pp. 265–291). New York, London: Routledge.

Enns, D. (2012). *The Violence of Victimhood.* University Park: Penn State University Press.

Enns, D. (2007). *Identity and Victimhood: Questions for Conflict Management Practice.* Berghof Occasional Paper No. 28. Berlin: Berghof Research Center.

Fischer, M. (2015). 'Eine neue Herausforderung – Kultur in der Konflikttransformation und Friedenskonsolidierung'. In K. J. Maaß (Ed.), *Kultur und Außenpolitik. Handbuch für Wissenschaft und Praxis* (pp.169–189). 3rd revised and extended edition. Baden-Baden: Nomos-Verlag.

Fischer, M. (2013). 'Gegen Trauma und Tabu'. In *EUNIC-Jahrbuch 2012/2013, Kulturreport, Vol. 5* (pp. 77–85). Brussels: EUNIC, Institut für Auslandsbeziehungen.

Fischer, M. (2013a). 'Summary Analysis'. In M. Fischer & Lj. Petrović-Ziemer (Eds.), *Dealing with the Past in the Western Balkans. Initiatives for Peacebuilding and Transitional Justice in Bosnia-Herzegovina, Serbia and Croatia.* Berghof Report 18 (pp. 131–157). Berlin: Berghof Foundation.

Fischer, M. (2013b). 'Analysis of Interviews with International Actors'. In M. Fischer & Lj. Petrović-Ziemer (Eds.), *Dealing with the Past in the Western Balkans. Initiatives for Peacebuilding and Transitional Justice in Bosnia-Herzegovina, Serbia and Croatia.* Berghof Report 18 (pp. 71–87). Berlin: Berghof Foundation.

Fischer, M. (Ed.) (2007). *Peacebuilding and Civil Society in Bosnia-Herzegovina. Ten Years After Dayton.* 2nd edn. Münster: Lit-Verlag.

Fischer, M. & Petrović-Ziemer, Lj. (Eds.) (2013). *Dealing with the Past in the Western Balkans. Initiatives for Peacebuilding and Transitional Justice in Bosnia-Herzegovina, Serbia and Croatia.* Berghof Report 18. Berlin: Berghof Foundation.

Franović, I. (2008). *Peacebuilding and Dealing with the Past in the Context of Ethnonationalism. The Case of Bosnia and Herzegovina, Croatia and Serbia.* Berghof Occasional Paper 29. Berlin: Berghof Research Center.

Gamberale, V. (2008). 'The Role of Economic Development in Reconciliation: An Experience from Bosnia and Herzegovina'. In P. Rothfield et al. (Eds.), *Pathways to Reconciliation. Between Theory and Practice* (pp. 149–158). Aldershot: Ashgate Publishing Company.

Gibson, J. L. (2006). *Overcoming Apartheid: Can Truth Reconcile a Divided Nation?* New York: Russell Sage Foundation Publications.

Gojković, D. et al. (Eds.) (2005). *Ne bilo ga nikada i nigdje* [May it never and nowhere happen again], Belgrade: Dokumentacioni Centar Ratovi 1991–99.

Gojković, D. et al. (Eds.) (2004). *Ljudi u ratu – Sudbine civila* [People in War – The Destiny of Civilians], Belgrade: Dokumentacioni Centar Ratovi 1991–99.

Gojković, D. et al. (Eds.) (2003). *Ljudi u ratu – Ratovanja I* [People in War – Warfares I], Belgrade: Dokumentacioni Centar Ratovi 1991–99.

Hamber, B. (2009). *Transforming Societies after Political Violence: Truth, Reconciliation, and Mental Health.* New York: Springer.

Hamber, B. (2003). 'Healing'. In D. Bloomfield et al. (Eds.), *Reconciliation after Violent Conflict. A Handbook* (pp. 77–96). Stockholm: International IDEA Handbook Series.

Hamber, B. & Kelly, G. (2005). 'The Challenge of Reconciliation in Post-Conflict Societies. Definitions, Problems and Proposals'. In I. O'Flynn & D. Russel (Eds.), *Power Sharing. New Challenges for Divided Societies* (pp. 188–203). London: Pluto Press.

Hamber, B. & Kelly, G. (2004). *A Working Definition of Reconciliation.* Belfast: Democratic Dialogue.

Hamber, B. &. Wilson, R. A. (2002). 'Symbolic Closure through Memory, Reparation and Revenge in Post-Conflict Societies'. *Journal of Human Rights*, Vol. 1, No. 1/2002, 35–53.

Hazan, P. (2007). 'Das neue Mantra der Gerechtigkeit. Vom beschränkten Erfolg international verordneter Vergangenheitsbewältigung'. *Der Überblick*, 43, 1–2, 10–22.

Hazan, P. (2006). 'Measuring the Impact of Punishment and Forgiveness. A Framework for Evaluating Transitional Justice'. *International Review of the Red Cross*, 88, 861, 19–47.

Hoffmann, K. (2011). 'Internationale Strafgerichte und Tribunale und ihre (potenzielle) Rolle im Versöhnungsprozess'. In S. Buckley-Zistel & T. Kater (Eds.), *Nach Krieg, Gewalt und Repression. Der schwierige Umgang mit Vergangenheit* (pp. 81–90). Baden-Baden: Nomos.

Jalušić, V. (2004). 'Gender and Victimization of the Nation as Pre- and Post-War Identity Discourse'. In R. Seifert (Ed.), *Gender, Identität und kriegerischer Konflikt. Das Beispiel des ehemaligen Jugoslawien* (pp. 40–67). Reihe Soziologie, Forschung und Wissenschaft 9. Münster: Lit-Verlag.

Kiza, E. et al. (2006). *Victims of War: An Empirical Study on War-Victimization and Victims' Attitudes towards Addressing Atrocities.* Hamburg: Hamburger Institut für Sozialforschung.

Koulouri, C. (Ed.) (2002). *Clio in the Balkans. The Politics of History Education.* Thessaloniki: Center for Democracy and Reconciliation in Southeast Europe.
Koulouri, C. (Ed.) (2001). *Teaching the History of Southeastern Europe.* Thessaloniki: Center for Democracy and Reconciliation in Southeast Europe.
Kriesberg, L. (2007a). 'External Contributions to Post-Mass-Crime Rehabilitation'. In B. Pouligny et al. (Eds.), *After Mass Crime. Rebuilding States and Communities* (pp. 243–271). New York: United Nations University.
Kriesberg, L. (2007b). 'In Theory – Long Peace or Long War. A Conflict Resolution Perspective'. *Negotiation Journal*, 23, 2, 97–119.
Kritz, N. J. (2009). 'Policy Implications of Empirical Research on Transitional Justice'. In H. van der Merwe et al. (Eds.), *Assessing the Impact of Transitional Justice. Challenges for Empirical Research* (pp. 13–22). Washington DC: US Institute of Peace Press.
Kuljić, T. (2010). *Umkämpfte Vergangenheiten: Die Kultur der Erinnerung im postjugoslawischen Raum.* Bonn: Bundeszentrale für politische Bildung.
Large, J. (1997). *The War Next Door. A Study of Second-Track Intervention during the War in Ex-Yugoslavia.* Lansdown, Gloucestershire: Hawthorn-Press.
Lederach, J. P. (2005). *The Moral Imagination: The Art and Soul of Building Peace.* Oxford, MA: Oxford University Press.
Lederach, J. P. (1997). *Building Peace. Sustainable Reconciliation in Divided Societies.* Washington DC: United States Institute of Peace Press.
Lekha Sriram, C. et al. (Eds.) (2013). *Transitional Justice and Peacebuilding on the Ground. Victims and Ex-Combatants.* London: Routledge.
McEvoy, K. (2012). 'Agents of Change – Ex-Prisoners, Ex-Combatants and Conflict Transformation in Northern Ireland'. In V. Dudouet, H. J. Giessmann & K. Planta (Eds.), *Post-War Security Transitions. Participatory Peacebuilding after Asymmetric Conflicts* (pp. 105–122). London: Routledge.
Meernik, J. (2005). 'Justice and Peace? How the International Criminal Tribunal Affects Societal Peace in Bosnia'. *Journal of Peace Research*, 42, 3, 271–289.
Mertus, J. (2007). 'Findings from Focus Group Research on Public Perceptions of the ICTY'. *Südosteuropa*, 55, 1, 107–117.
Mertus, J. (2004) *Women's Participation in the International Criminal Tribunal for the Former Yugoslavia (ICTY). Transitional Justice for Bosnia and Herzegovina.* Cambridge, MA: Women Waging Peace Policy Commission.
Nikolić-Ristanović, V. (2000). *Women, Violence and War. Wartime Victimization of Refugees in the Balkans.* NY: Central University Press.
Petrović-Ziemer, Lj. (2013). 'Analysis of Interviews with Civil Society Actors'. In M. Fischer & Lj. Petrović-Ziemer (Eds.), *Dealing with the Past in the Western Balkans. Initiatives for Peacebuilding and Transitional Justice in Bosnia-Herzegovina, Serbia and Croatia* (pp. 45–70). Berghof Report 18. Berlin: Berghof Foundation.
Popović, T. (2003). *Die Mythologisierung des Alltags. Kollektive Erinnerungen, Geschichtsbilder und Vergangenheitskultur in Serbien und Montenegro seit Mitte der 90er Jahre.* 1st edn Zürich: Pano.
Ricigliano, R. (Ed.) (2005). *Choosing to Engage: Armed Groups and Peace Processes.* Accord Issue 16. London: Conciliation Resources.
Rill, H. & Franović, I. (2005). *Ne moze meni biti dobro ako je mom susjedu lose* [I Cannot Feel Well if My Neighbour Does Not]. Belgrade: Centre for Nonviolent Action.
Šebek, N. (2014). 'The Development of Teaching Materials to Further Peace'. In B. Gruber (Ed.), *The Yugoslav Example. Violence, War and Difficult Ways Towards Peace* (pp. 169–188). Münster, New York: Waxmann-Verlag.
Simić, O. & Volčič, Z. (Eds.) (2013). *Transitional Justice and Civil Society in the Balkans.* New York: Springer.

Index

For Product Safety Concerns and Information please contact our EU representative GPSR@taylorandfrancis.com
Taylor & Francis Verlag GmbH, Kaufingerstraße 24, 80331 München, Germany

www.ingramcontent.com/pod-product-compliance
Ingram Content Group UK Ltd.
Pitfield, Milton Keynes, MK11 3LW, UK
UKHW020014200926
475702UK00014B/1882
9781138084384